Future Publishing Ltd, 30 Monmouth Street,
Bath BA1 2BW
Tel: 01225 442244 Fax: 01225 732275
Email: windowsmagazine@futurenet.com
Web: www.facebook.com/windowsmag

EDITORIAL
Editor Nicholas Odantzis

ART
Art editor Matt Orton

CONTRIBUTORS
Editorial Alex Cox, Dan Grabham, Matthew Hanson
Production Katharine Davies

SENIOR MANAGEMENT
Publisher Ian Robson
Group publishing director Nial Ferguson
Group art director Steve Gotobed
Creative director Bob Abbott
Editorial director Jim Douglas

ADVERTISING
Advertising director james.ranson@futurenet.com
Advertising sales manager ashley.snell@futurenet.com
Senior advertising manager charlie.said@futurenet.com
Senior sales executive michael.carrington@futurenet.com
Senior sales executive sally.mclachlan@futurenet.com
Account manager tamzyn.young@futurenet.com

CIRCULATION AND MARKETING
Marketing manager ben.tatlow@futurenet.com
Trade marketing manager colin.hornby@futurenet.com

PRINT PRODUCTION
Production controller roberta.lealand@futurenet.com
Logistics manager mark.constance@futurenet.com
Ad production coordinator nola.cokely@futurenet.com

INTERNATIONAL LICENSING
Licensing & syndication director regina.erak@futurenet.com

Printed in the UK by William Gibbons and Sons Ltd
on behalf of Future Publishing.
Distributed in the UK by Seymour Distribution Ltd,
2 East Poultry Avenue, London EC1A 9PT. Tel: 0207 429 4000

Future produces high-quality multimedia products which reach our audiences online, on mobile and in print. Future attracts over 50 millions consumers to its brands every month across five core sectors: Technology, Entertainment, Music, Creative and Sports & Auto. We export and license our publications.

Future plc is a public company quoted on the London Stock Exchange (symbol: FUTR).
www.futureplc.com

Chief executive Mark Wood
Non-executive chairman Peter Allen
Chief financial officer Graham Harding
Tel +44 (0)207 042 4000 (London)
Tel +44 (0)1225 442 244 (Bath)

© Future Publishing Limited 2013. All rights reserved. No part of this magazine may be used or reproduced without the written permission of the publisher. Future Publishing Limited (company number 2008885) is registered in England and Wales. The registered office of Future Publishing Limited is at Beauford Court, 30 Monmouth Street, Bath BA1 2BW. All information contained in this magazine is for information only and is, as far as we are aware, correct at the time of going to press. Future cannot accept any responsibility for errors or inaccuracies in such information. You are advised to contact manufacturers and retailers directly with regard to the price of products/services referred to in this magazine. If you submit unsolicited material to us, you automatically grant Future a licence to publish your submission in whole or in part in all editions of the magazine, including licensed editions worldwide and in any physical or digital format worldwide. Any material you submit is sent at your risk and, although every care is taken, neither Future nor its employees, agents or subcontractors shall be liable for loss or damage.

We are committed to only using magazine paper which is derived from well managed, certified forestry and chlorine-free manufacture. Future Publishing and its paper suppliers have been independently certified in accordance with the rules of the FSC (Forest Stewardship Council).

Welcome

Several months have passed since the launch of Windows 8, and by now many of you will have, at the very least, sampled the new operating system, if not gone straight out and bought a brand new PC and got stuck into it immediately. Others may be hanging on, waiting for the right moment, until Windows 8 finally sways them or their current PC packs in. But whatever stage you're at in the Windows lifecycle, *Windows 8: Expert Tips and Tricks* is a great way to enhance your experience of the new operating system.

If you're at the very beginning of the learning curve, you can find out exactly what you need to do to get off the ground instantly, while those who have been using it for some time now – and even those who consider themselves experts already – will benefit from all the great tips and tricks included within, which show you how to extract the maximum potential from your Windows 8 PC. With every turn of a page, you're guaranteed to discover something new and amazing that you didn't know before, and we reckon you'll be glad that you found out.

Nick

Nicholas Odantzis
Editor

Chapter 1

Contents

HANDY GUIDE Learn the Windows 8 touch gestures

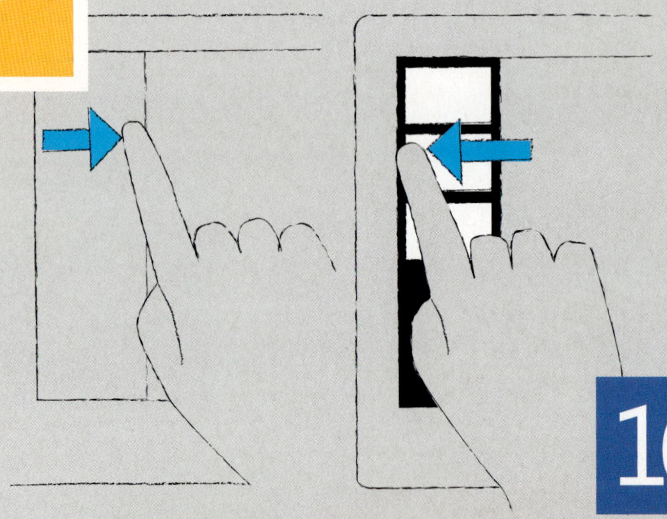

16

HOT STUFF! Turn your desktop into a masterpiece with these tips

35

 ### Learning the basics

 ### How to customise

 ### Explore features

 ### Under the hood

08 Get used to the Start screen
10 Conquer the Lock screen
12 First steps with Windows 8
16 Gestures explained
18 Windows 8 for beginners
24 Ultimate shortcuts

30 Customise Windows 8
32 Mastering the desktop
35 Make Windows look amazing
40 Streamline your Start screen
42 Create amazing-looking tiles
44 Get Win 7's Start menu back
46 Use dual monitors

50 Windows 8 apps
52 Exploring Explorer
54 Easy Transfer
56 The touch keyboard
58 Search in Windows 8
60 Master Jump Lists
64 Explore the Action Center
66 Essential apps

70 Explore under the hood
72 Mastering the ribbon
74 Bypass the Start screen
76 Solve problems
78 Start afresh
82 Speed up with ReadyBoost
84 Storage Spaces
86 Increase battery life
90 Install Windows 8
92 Use Windows 8 File History

Chapter 2

100 TAKE CONTROL Make anything open with the application of your choosing

LOCK IT DOWN Create a crack-proof PC

130

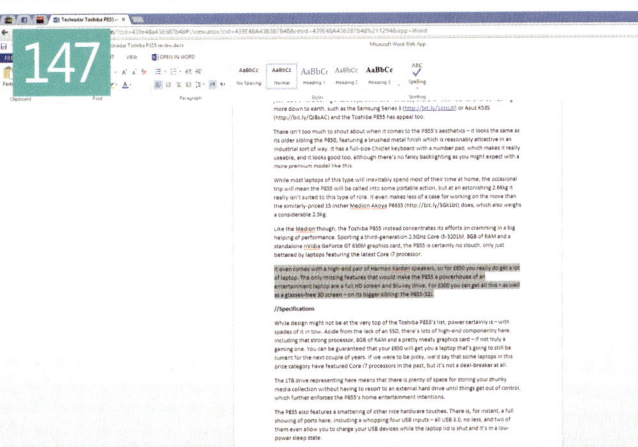

147

FREE OFFICE SUITE! Don't pay for it – get it for nowt

118

IT'S GOOD TO TALK Keep in touch with everyone you know

154

MASTER THE CLOUD Top tips for storing your files online

 Upgrading Windows 8

 Security and safety

 Get creative

 Enhanced social life

96 Get more from Windows 8
98 Improving your audio
100 Set default programs
101 Speed up your startup
102 Internet Explorer 10
106 Stay entertained
108 Find your way with Maps
110 Buy amazing apps
112 Schedule maintenance tasks
114 Synchronise settings
116 Set up a HomeGroup
118 10 tips for using SkyDrive

124 Stay safe with Windows 8
126 Improving internet security
128 Look after your kids
130 Uncrackable passwords

136 Do more with Windows 8
138 Getting more creative
140 Be more productive
142 Try the Photo app
146 Make a note of anything!
147 Get Microsoft Office for free!

150 Get more from social networks
152 Improving social horizons
154 Keep in contact with People
158 Do more with Mail
160 Social networking

Learning the basics

TRY THIS!
Play around with gestures
16

Everything you need to know to help you get up and running

Section 1

8	Get used to the Start screen
10	Conquer the Lock screen
12	First steps with Windows 8
16	Gestures explained
18	Windows 8 for beginners
24	Ultimate shortcuts

DO THIS NOW...

Get used to the Start screen

Master the new Windows 8-style interface today

A life of tiles

Windows 8's new interface is a lot less scary than it sounds – it's designed to be really user-friendly, with bright tiles and touch-friendly apps (that also work with a mouse). The Windows 8-style interface sits on top of the desktop – rather than replacing it – and is a new way to interact with Windows. On a tablet, swipe left or right to scroll the screen, and tap any tile to launch its app. If using a mouse, you can spin the mouse wheel to scroll back and forth. Then there's keyboard navigation – press [Home] or [End] to jump from one end of your Start screen to the other, or use the cursor keys to select a tile, tapping [Enter] to select that app.

Pin to Start

Press the [Windows] key to return to the Start screen. Any app is pinned (attached) automatically to your Start screen; right-click (or swipe down on) apps you don't need and select 'Unpin' to remove them. And you can drag and drop tiles around to organise them. If there's an app you use all the time, you don't have to find it via the search system. Finding apps with a keyboard is also simple – just start typing the app's name. To pin Control Panel to Start, for instance, type 'Control'. Right-click the Control Panel tile on the Apps Search screen, and click 'Pin to Start'. On a touchscreen, press and hold the icon, then flick down and select 'Pin to Start'.

GET USED TO THE START SCREEN

Make groups from your apps
To see a list of all your apps, hold down the [Windows] key and [Q]. You can right-click or swipe up from the bottom to see the App bar, too; then select 'All apps'. Browse to find what you need and click an app to launch it. By default, Start screen apps are displayed in what seems like a random fashion, but it's easy to sort them into groups. Drag a few apps together in a column (to start a new group, drag a tile into the gap between existing groups). Zoom out (by pinching or clicking the minus icon in the bottom-right) and you can now re-order these groups.

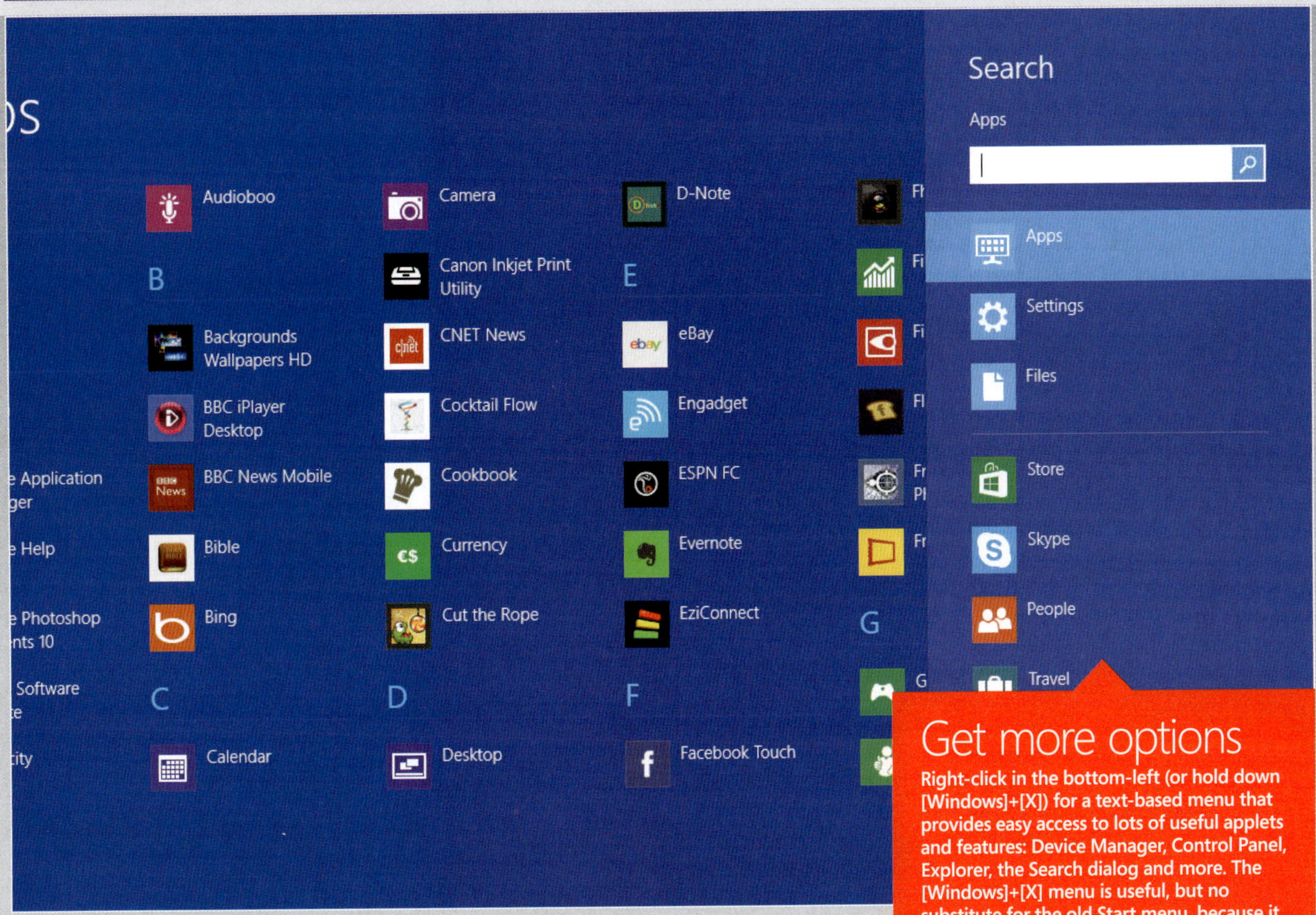

Get more options
Right-click in the bottom-left (or hold down [Windows]+[X]) for a text-based menu that provides easy access to lots of useful applets and features: Device Manager, Control Panel, Explorer, the Search dialog and more. The [Windows]+[X] menu is useful, but no substitute for the old Start menu, because it doesn't provide access to applications. To find this, press [Windows]+[Q], or either right-click an empty part of the Start screen or swipe your finger up from the bottom of the screen, and select 'All Apps' to reveal a scrolling list of all your installed applications. Browse the various tiles to find what you need and click the relevant app to launch it.

25 TOP TIPS TO...

Conquer the Lock screen

The Lock screen is the first thing you see, and it should be the first thing you make your own

1 The Lock screen looks pretty but you can switch the picture. Press [Windows]+[I], click 'Change PC Settings', and open the Personalisation menu – the first things you see are your options for replacement images.

2 You don't have to stick with the classy images Microsoft has provided. You can slap a picture of your baby, cat or favourite pot plant on the Lock screen instead – just click the 'Browse' button and choose the image you want to use.

3 At the bottom of the Lock screen you'll see a few quick updates about happenings on your PC. You can see more, though. At the bottom of the Personalise screen, you'll see options that enable you to change the specific icons that get displayed.

4 Certain apps – Calendar and Weather, by default – can show you more information on the Lock screen. Just make sure the app you're interested in is highlighted at the very bottom of the Personalise page of Control Panel.

5 You can take the Lock screen further with third-party apps. Search the Windows Store for Incredilock; it's free, offers hugely customisable wallpapers, and can add things such as to-do lists to your Lock screen.

6 Open up the Start screen control panel ([Ctrl]+[I], then 'Change PC Settings') and go to the 'Users' tab. Here you can change your login password. Note that changing this also changes it for other machines or services (such as Outlook mail) your account is linked to.

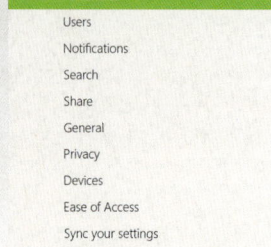

Configure what you see on the Lock screen by tweaking the apps on the Personalise panel

CONQUER THE LOCK SCREEN

Chameleon is full of beautiful photography, perfect for making your Lock screen look amazing

7 We've got more about it on page 128, but you should try the picture password function on the 'Users' tab of 'Change PC Settings'. It's the most fun way to log in to your PC, and it's pretty secure, too. Just try not to leave tell-tale smears on your touchscreen…

8 Want to bring the Lock screen up in a flash if, for instance, you're stepping away from your PC for a while? Easy – either click your profile picture at the top-right corner of the Start screen and click 'Lock', or just press [Windows]+[L] at the same time.

9 You can customise your Lock screen colours separately from your Start screen colours. Open the desktop, hit [Windows]+[R], type 'regedit', and go through HKEY_LOCAL_MACHINE, SOFTWARE, Microsoft, Windows, CurrentVersion, Explorer and then Accent. Right-click 'Accent', create a new Dword, and call it DefaultColorSet. Now edit this, switch the base to decimal and set this to be a number between 0 and 24.

10 Fancy ditching the Lock screen altogether? Hit [Windows]+[R], type 'gpedit.msc', go to 'Computer Configuration > Administrative Templates > Control Panel > Personalisation', and change 'Do not display the lock screen' to enabled.

11 Why not add some pep to your Lock screen by automatically changing its image? Search the Windows Store for Chameleon. It takes a number of pictures from cool sources such as National Geographic and Bing, and automatically pastes a new one on the Lock screen at a set interval.

12 Another option for shuffling your Lock screens is Lockerz – you can give it a selection of your local pictures or even hook it up to your SkyDrive account for a truly personal random experience.

13 Many apps can add information to your Lock screen beyond those installed by default. Hunt through the Windows Store and you should be able to find plenty of apps that you can configure to display at lock; things such as Twitter clients, third-party weather apps, and more.

14 Enough about the Lock screen, apart from to tell you that there are loads of ways to get past it to the login screen: click it, drag it up, spin your mousewheel, or hit [Space] to progress.

15 You see your account picture on your login screen. Or you might not. If you've not set one up, you just see a silhouette. Use the 'Users' menu in 'Change PC Settings' to add a picture of yourself – this follows you anywhere you use your Microsoft login.

16 The login screen has a neat feature for visually impaired users in the bottom-left, so you can turn on narration, the magnifier and more before you log in. Press [Tab] then [Enter] if you want to get there without clicking.

17 You can also use the accessibility dialog to turn on the on-screen keyboard. Useful on touchscreens and for those who can't use a keyboard.

18 Log out! Shut down! Do it all without logging in. There's an icon at the bottom-right of the login screen that does the business; access it by tapping [Tab], [Tab], then [Enter], then selecting the function you want with the arrow keys.

19 Once logged in, you might want to try getting around the Start screen using nothing but your keyboard. Use the arrow keys to flick between icons, and [Enter] to run your selection.

20 Jump through the Start screen by using [Page Up] and [Page Down] to hop to either end, or use [Tab] to jump up to your profile picture.

Quick tips

21 Use the mouse wheel to scroll through your Start screen, particularly if you have a lot of items on there. It is the quickest way to see everything.

22 You don't actually need to see everything, though; start typing the name of the app you're looking for and it appears on the right.

23 Don't forget the 'All apps' menu, which shows everything, not just those apps you've got pinned to your Start screen. Right-click on the Start screen and choose its icon, bottom-right.

24 Right-click any of the apps in the 'All apps' screen and select 'Pin to Start' to make them visible on the Start menu.

25 Many different people can use the same machine. If you've set up more than one in the 'Users' tab of the 'Change PC Settings' screen, just click your profile picture to switch accounts.

Learn how to...

Take your first steps

If you're new to Microsoft's latest operating system, you may be wondering how to get started, so begin your Windows 8 journey here

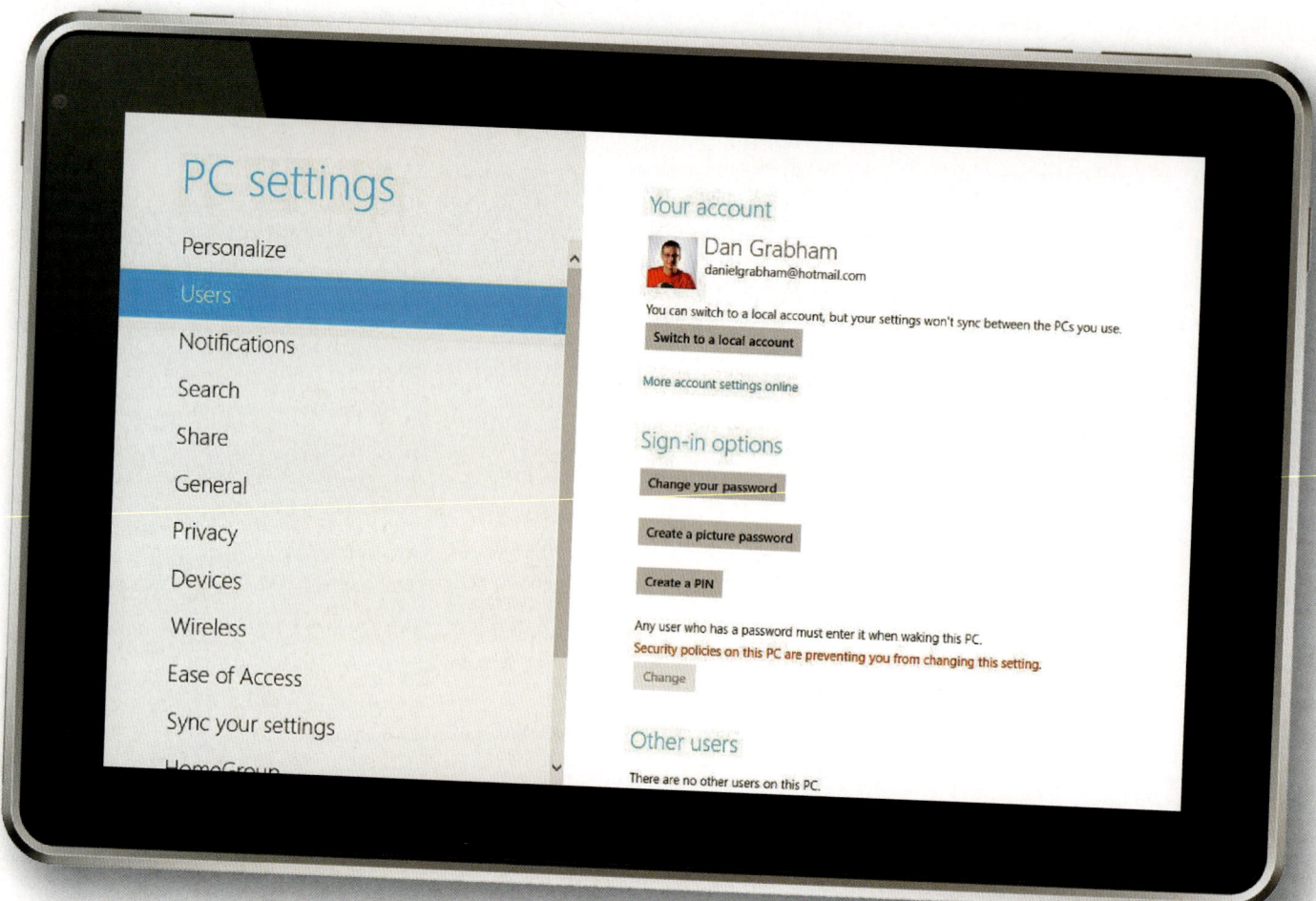

1 Add user accounts
It's easy and transferable

Making separate user accounts for different people is a simple process and is perfect for families who share and enjoy multiple devices. You can either add a user account from the desktop Control Panel (as you would in previous versions of Windows), or choose 'Settings' from the Charm bar, then choose 'Change PC settings' and select 'Users'. You can log in with any user account – even while somebody else is logged in to the same device. You need to log in with a Microsoft account, which can be created in a few easy steps. If you previously had a Hotmail or Windows Live account, or used Windows Live Messenger or Outlook.com, you can use this account without creating a new one, and you can take some settings with you, whichever computer you log in to.

TAKE YOUR FIRST STEPS

2 Set up your email
Your inbox upgrade

Windows 8 includes Mail – a simple but effective email client that delivers messages from a variety of sources to a single inbox. You can set up your email using various accounts, including Google and Microsoft (Hotmail or Outlook.com). If you have an Exchange account for work, you can set that up, too, provided your company has enabled external email access. The Mail app strips out all the extraneous email functions that you don't really need, helping you focus on your messages, folders and different accounts. You can read, reply and attach files with minimum fuss. Highlighted emails are displayed in full on the right. Emails from people you follow on social networks display their Facebook or Twitter avatar – useful for sorting out emails from your friends.

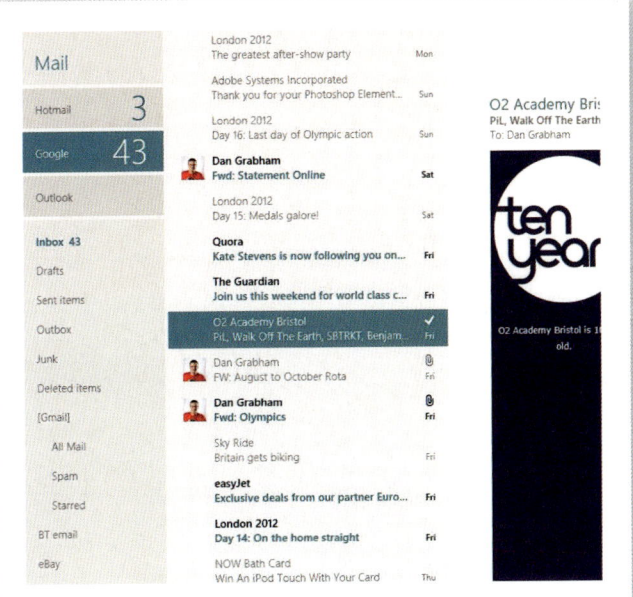

Top Tips!

Sign out
Should you wish to sign out or lock your computer, simply click your account picture in the top-right of the Start screen to do so.

Start typing
Want to find an app to launch in the Start screen? Then just begin typing its name – all possible matches soon appear so you can easily choose the app you want.

3 Add new apps
See what's in Store

Windows 8 brings you a completely new way to install software – the Windows Store. You can search the Store from the Charm bar to find the app you want. It features thousands of tools specially designed for Windows 8, ranging from big names such as Sky News, Wikipedia and AccuWeather to small, independently developed but useful apps such as Tweetro for Twitter or Quick Note for, well, taking quick notes. The Spotlight feature shows you the best new Windows 8 apps and there are lists of the top free and top paid-for apps, too. All apps carry a user rating, enabling you to make a more informed choice, and All Star apps are those that people have rated most highly. More apps are appearing all the time, so visit the Windows Store today.

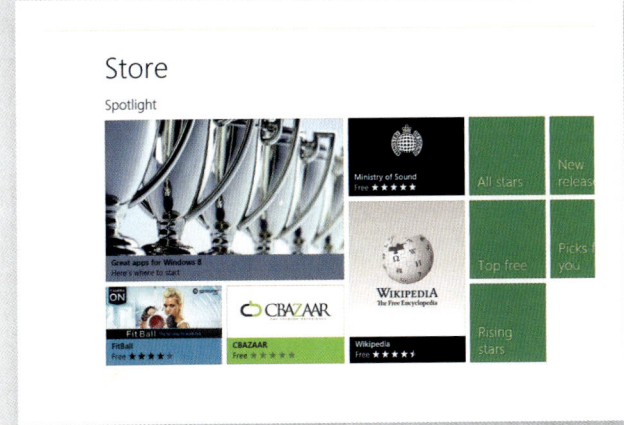

> "Emails display your contacts' Facebook or Twitter avatars"

4 A more beautiful web
It's faster too

Windows 8 includes a completely new web browser – Internet Explorer 10. It's been built to be fast and fluid, and works perfectly with Windows 8. There's a desktop version, but the browser works flawlessly within Windows 8 UI as well. It's brilliant for touchscreens, too. Swipe up to view your tabs, or down to view the address bar and Favorites. You can pin favourite websites to your Start screen. As with everything in Windows 8, you can use the Charm bar to search for what you need, change Internet Explorer settings, or share sites with friends – just swipe and tap. Internet Explorer 10 also includes SmartScreen and Tracking Protection for greater control over your personal information.

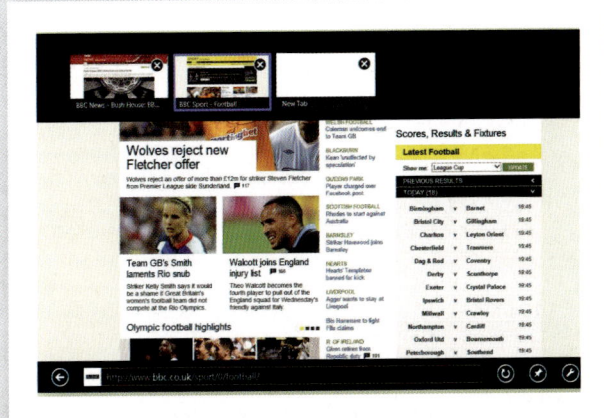

5 Switch your apps
It's quick and easy
Windows 8 makes it simple to switch between apps. While the traditional keyboard shortcuts still work – [Alt] + [Tab] or [Windows] + [Tab] – touchscreens give you a whole new way of moving between programs. Just flick in from the left and you can rapidly move between open applications, or switch to the desktop view. Each app appears as an image of the screen itself – just stop flicking to settle on the screen you want to see. If you don't have a touchscreen, simply place your pointer in the bottom-left to see the Start screen icon and move your mouse straight up. Previews of all the open apps appear and you can select the one you need. In the desktop, app switching works just as before and you can move between open desktop apps using the Taskbar.

6 Snap windows and multi-task
Work in two apps at the same time
Unlike the iPad, Windows 8 enables you to snap windows side-by-side, so you can effortlessly work on two things at the same time. Just drag any app from the top and have it snap to the left or the right quarter of the screen, so you can browse the internet while keeping tabs on your inbox, or work on a Microsoft Word document while keeping up with all the latest news. What's more, it doesn't matter whether you're using one of the sleek new Modern UI apps from the Start menu, or a classic application from the desktop from a previous version of Windows – Snap just works. It's designed to make working in multiple apps easier than ever.

7 Personalise your Live tiles
Start by adding a colour scheme
The Start menu is made up of square or rectangular icons called tiles. Each one represents a different app on your system, but these aren't just icons – some are Live tiles. This means the Mail icon can display your latest messages and you can see the next appointment in your Calendar, to name but two examples. You can move these around by clicking and holding on a tile, before dragging them to where you want them. Windows 8 is designed to be a colourful and beautiful experience, and it's easy to make it your own. To give the Start screen a colour scheme of your choosing, go to 'Settings', click or tap 'Personalization' and choose 'Start screen'.

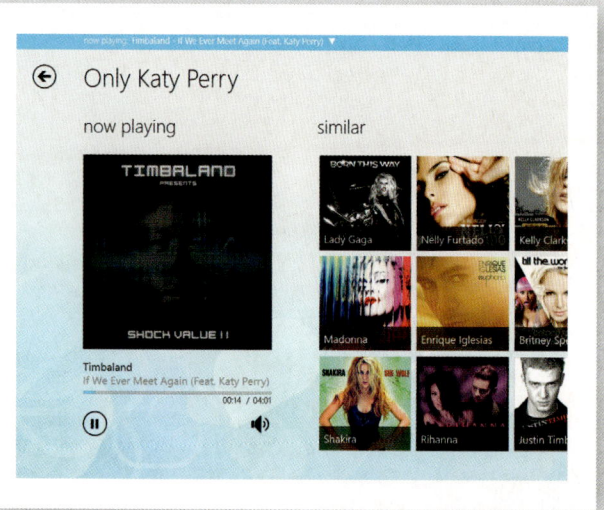

TAKE YOUR FIRST STEPS

8 Share and share alike
Bring people together

Sharing is a big part of Windows 8 and being able to show your friends, family and colleagues things that you've discovered with your computer is integral to your experience. All operating systems enable you to browse hotels online, and many have apps that enable you to find reviews and deals, but only Windows 8 has a built-in sharing tool that enables you to send what you've found to your contacts and social networks quickly and easily. You can do this via the Charm bar, which is accessed from the right-hand side of the screen. Hit 'Sharing' and a number of options appear. It's the same for any app in Windows, so there are no hidden options and no confusion – just a single way to share your discoveries with those who matter.

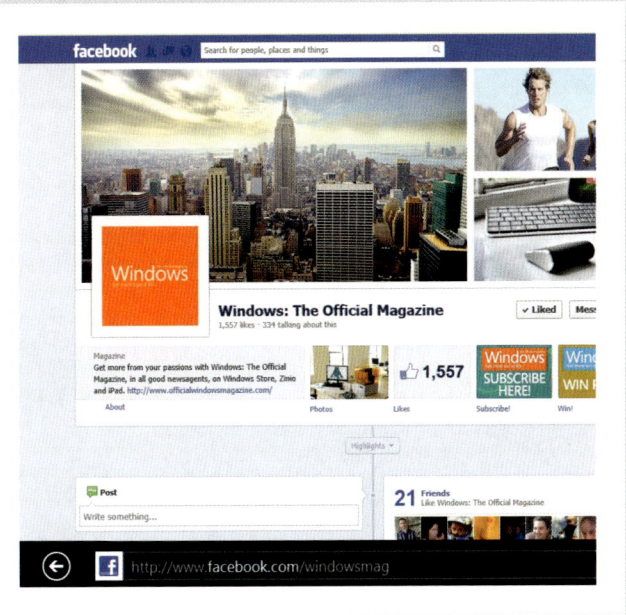

Top Tip!

Right-click for options
If you're looking for more options from your apps, just right-click. A context menu appears, enabling you to tweak settings.

Personal pin-ups
You can pin your friends and family to the Start screen, which means it's easier to stay in touch with the people who matter most to you.

> "Your Start screen will really come to life with Live tiles"

9 Get pinning
Windows 8 is a pinboard for your life

Unlike other operating systems, the Start screen isn't just for apps. You can add anything to the homepage, from your favourite websites to contacts from the People app, and even books from the Kindle Store, so you can have the things you love right at your fingertips.

10 Find anything
Advanced searching

Windows 8 is built to enable you to find what you want from a single location, and that's done via the Search charm. The Charm bar is accessed from the right-hand edge and enables you to search Windows and apps alike. Instead of searching your email, the internet, Facebook and Twitter separately, one search term rules them all, putting information at your fingertips. If you're using a Windows 8 laptop, searching is even quicker. Just start typing anywhere and the Search charm fires into life immediately, enabling you to find whatever you need (see page 58 for more details). It's a new way of working, but one that makes using your Windows computer so much easier – therefore next time you need to find that email or file, just search instead.

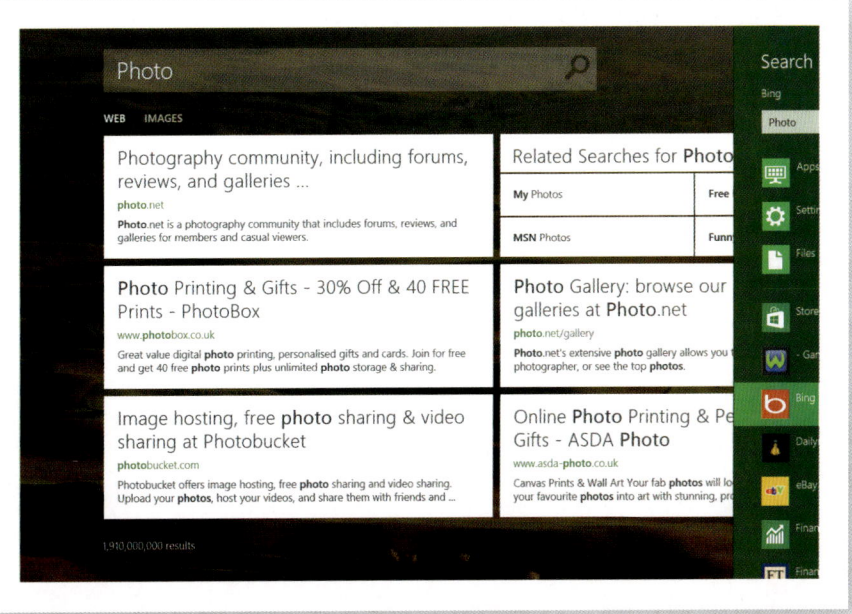

Learn how to...

Use touchscreen gestures

Using a touchscreen is incredibly intuitive but if you're used to controlling your PC with a keyboard and mouse, you'll find this guide really handy

Select or perform an action

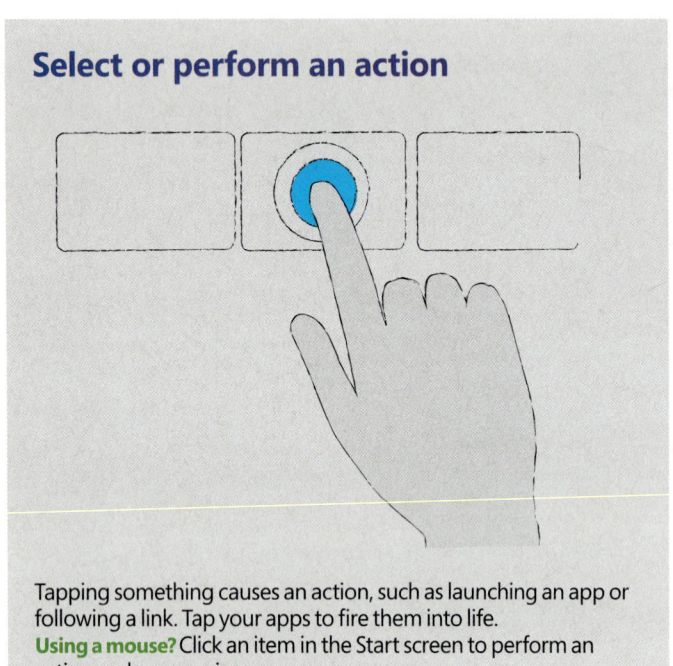

Tapping something causes an action, such as launching an app or following a link. Tap your apps to fire them into life.
Using a mouse? Click an item in the Start screen to perform an action such as opening an app.

App-specific commands

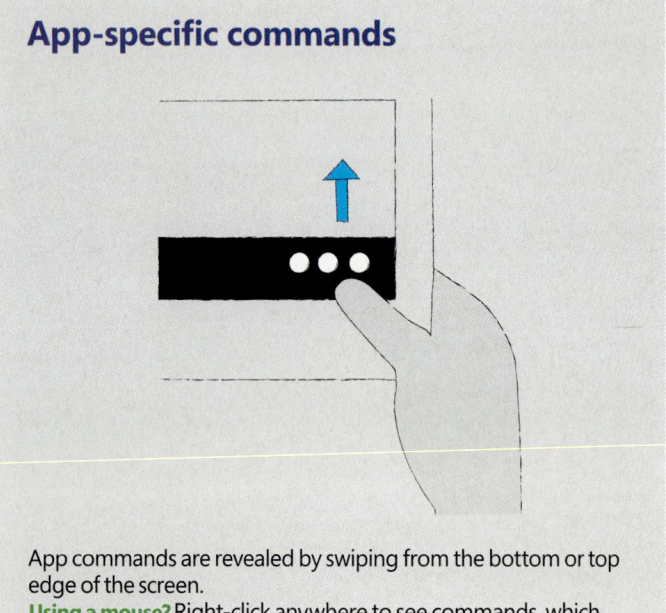

App commands are revealed by swiping from the bottom or top edge of the screen.
Using a mouse? Right-click anywhere to see commands, which depend on the specific app.

Get more options

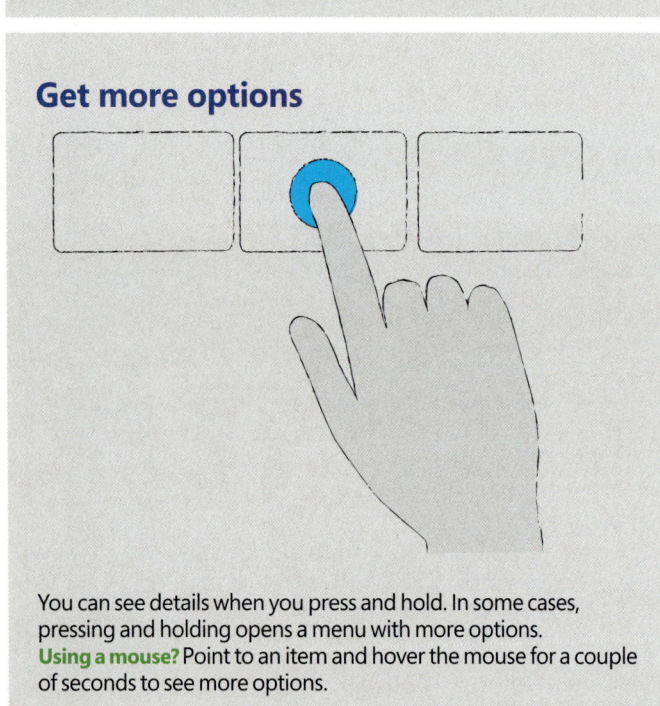

You can see details when you press and hold. In some cases, pressing and holding opens a menu with more options.
Using a mouse? Point to an item and hover the mouse for a couple of seconds to see more options.

Drag and move items

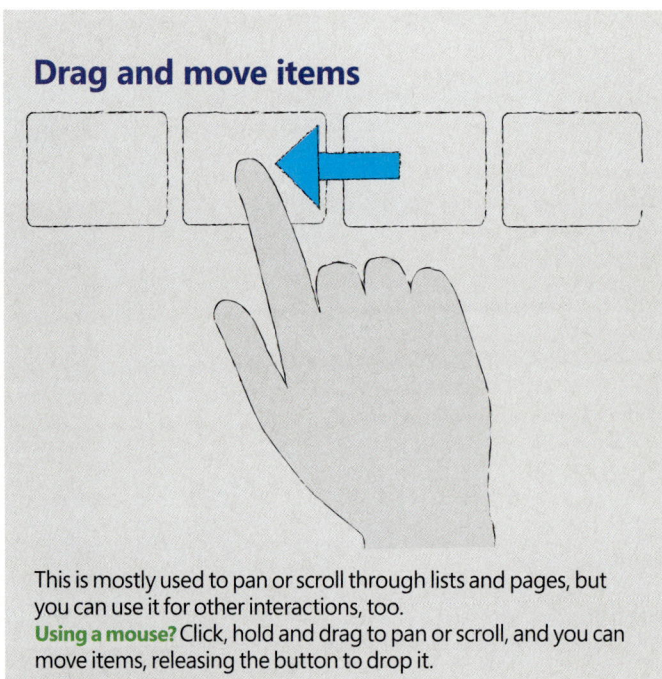

This is mostly used to pan or scroll through lists and pages, but you can use it for other interactions, too.
Using a mouse? Click, hold and drag to pan or scroll, and you can move items, releasing the button to drop it.

USE TOUCHSCREEN GESTURES

Find recently used apps

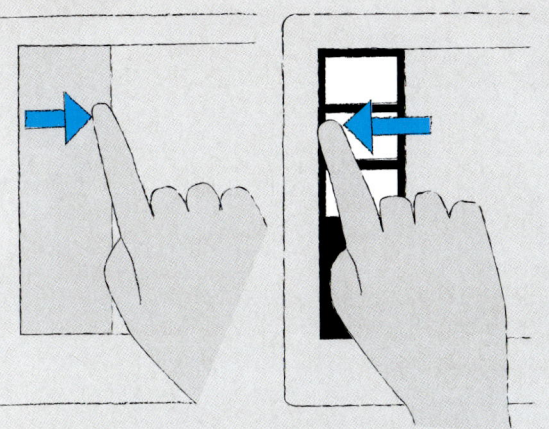

Swiping in and back out on the left brings up the most recently used apps, and you can select an app from that list.
Using a mouse? Place the mouse in the top left and slide down the left side of the screen to see recently used apps.

Close an application

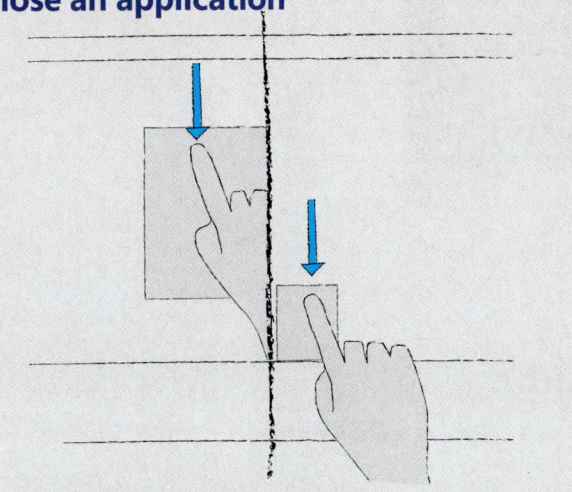

Unused apps don't affect your performance, but if you want to close one anyway, just drag the app to the bottom of the screen.
Using a mouse? Click the top of the app and then drag it to the bottom of the screen.

Zoom in and out

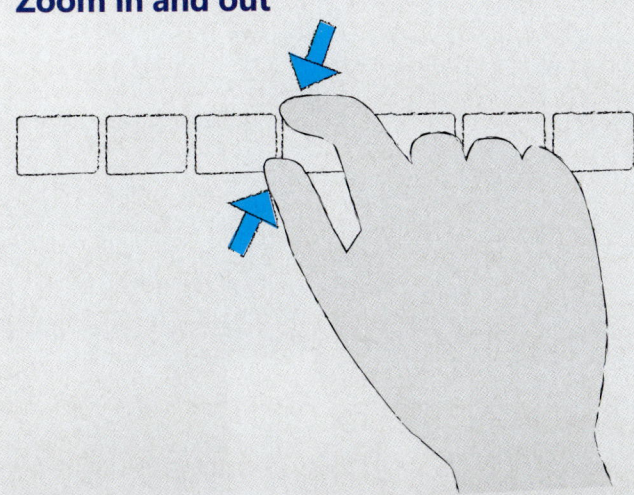

You can start zooming by pinching or stretching two fingers on the screen to enlarge or reduce the size.
Using a mouse? Hold down the [Ctrl] key while using the mouse wheel. Alternatively, click the minus symbol in the bottom-right.

Settings commands and search

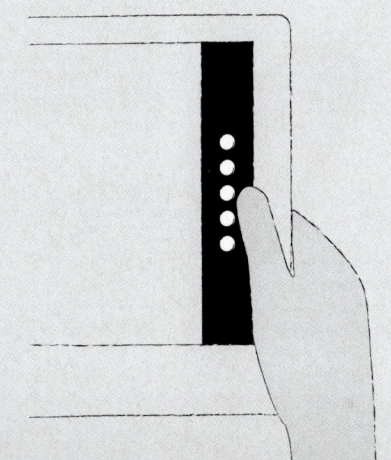

Swipe from the right side to reveal the Charms, with system commands such as search, settings and sharing options.
Using a mouse? Place the mouse in the upper or lower right corner of the screen and move your mouse up the right edge.

Turn and pivot items

Hold two or more fingers on an object and rotate. You can turn the whole screen 90° when you rotate your device.
Using a mouse? Support for rotating an object depends on the specific app.

Switch between apps

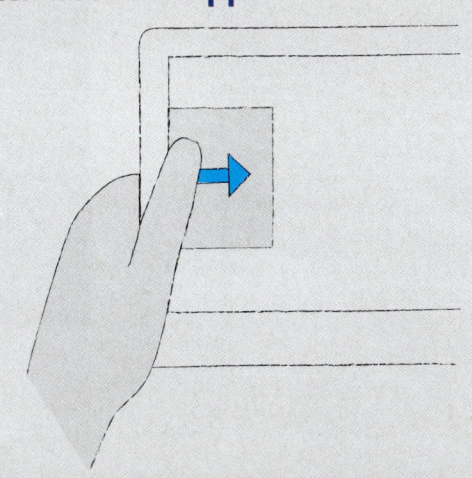

Swiping from the left reveals thumbnails of your open apps so you can switch to them quickly.
Using a mouse? Place the mouse pointer in the upper-left and click to cycle through apps.

WINDOWS 8 FOR BEGINNERS

NEW USERS GUIDE

Windows 8 for absolute beginners

Never touched a PC before? Intimidated by Windows 8? Just take a few tentative steps and you'll be away in no time

Are you completely new to Windows? That's OK. We all were once upon a time, even the grizzled Windows veterans who put together this guide. We can remember our first tentative steps with a mouse and keyboard, so we'll assume nothing. While some people might take its features for granted, we're not going to assume that you're confident with Windows, or that you've even seen it before. We're going back to basics. We'll take you through Windows in terms that even a complete computer newcomer can understand; once you've made your way through this guide, we think you'll know enough to embark upon a further journey of exploration, perhaps through the rest of the guides in this packed title.

We're also aware that Windows 8 isn't exactly the most friendly-looking operating system for veterans of older versions of Windows. We're here to prove your initial suspicions wrong. It's certainly different, but it's not nearly as intimidating or alien as it might initially look. We'll plough through its key features, and you'll know your way around the new operating system in minutes. The point is that Windows 8 is still Windows at its core; it's close to what you know from before, you just have to relearn a few things.

Before we start, let's go over a couple of conventions. We're going to write as though you're using a mouse or laptop trackpad, and a keyboard. When we say click, we're referring to tapping the left mouse button once; we refer to the right button specifically when you need it. There is, however, every chance that you'll be trying Windows 8 on a touchscreen device, such as a tablet, where you might not have access to a physical mouse or keyboard. In this case, tap the screen once to perform the equivalent of a left click, and tap and hold in one spot for a while to perform the equivalent of a right click – you'll see a translucent square box emanating from the point at which you've tapped.

Many of the actions we describe can be performed using touchscreen gestures – special finger movements – and you can find out more about these on page 16. We'll stick to mouse and keyboard in this guide to avoid confusion. So let's wade in!

Windows 8: Expert Tips and Tricks

Chapter 1 | 19

The lock screen doesn't do much, but it's handy to see a few stats before you begin

Let's start at the very beginning, before we even start up the computer. A PC that is not currently running can be in one of three states: completely off, where there's no power being consumed; in hibernation, which also doesn't consume power but still remembers your last state; and sleep, which consumes a small trickle of power, but starts Windows very quickly. Whichever state your computer is in, you should be able to wake it up by pressing the power button – if it's only asleep, a tap on the keyboard is enough.

When you've started your computer, you're first shown the Lock screen. This screen shows a pretty picture in the background, the clock, and a few icons representing statistics, such as your device's battery life (if it has a battery). It's just a useful way to see these things at a glance; it doesn't have much of a purpose other than that. Press [Space], click the mouse, or roll your mouse's scroll wheel to continue.

Next you see the login screen. Windows should ask for a password here. Because many different people can use a single computer, each person is given an account ensuring that their files and documents are protected from other users. If you don't see your account here – if, for example, it's asking for a password for your partner – click the left-pointing arrow to go to the Users screen, where you can select the correct account by clicking it. Pop your password in the appropriate box (you can click the small eye icon on the right of the password box to reveal it, if you want to see what you're typing), and press [Enter] to log in.

Start it up

Next we come to the colourful, boxy Start screen. Each box represents a different app that you could potentially run on your PC. Users of previous versions of Windows will be familiar with the Start menu, and this is essentially the same thing, only turned up a notch. Take a look; applications such as News or Photos may be animated, showing you the latest headlines or your favourite snaps. These are Live tiles, which make the Start screen extra-useful; they don't slow your computer down, they just give you a little extra.

Try running an app now, by clicking on the News icon. It opens up into a large pretty picture, and a completely full-screen experience, which might be different from what Windows veterans are used to. Use the scroll wheel to slide left and right, click on a story that interests you to see more, then click the left-pointing arrow at the top-left of the story to go back to the main

Try these apps first...

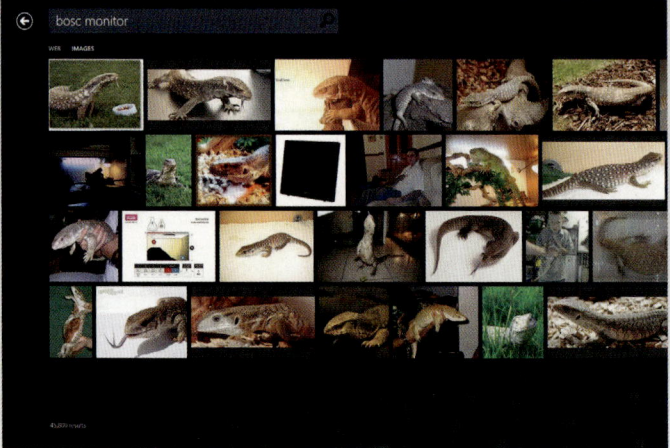

1 Calendar
Using the Calendar, you can really start to get organised, and leave yourself little reminders on the Lock screen, too. Right-click and you see options that enable you to switch between day, week and month views, and double-click a day or a time to add a new event. Make sure you click the icon in the shape of a disk, next to the 'x' icon, to save any events you make.

2 Bing
Bing is by far the prettiest way to search the internet, and its app makes it even prettier. Just click in the search box at the top, type what you're looking for, and press [Enter]. Your search results are presented in that familiar Start screen style; use your mouse wheel to scroll through, click any results you're interested in, and you're sent straight to Internet Explorer.

WINDOWS 8 FOR BEGINNERS

Hot corners...

Change app
Hover your mouse here, and you see an image of the last app you were using. Click to switch to it, and to cycle through all recent programs.

Charm bar
Hold your mouse in the top/bottom-right and the Charm bar pops up. Move your mouse over it to see your options, and to display the clock.

Link to Start
Hover to see a quick link to the Start screen. You can click this or move your mouse upwards to see a clickable list of recently used apps.

More options
Right-click anywhere in the Start screen environment and you get a menu with extra features, such as a hidden back button for an app.

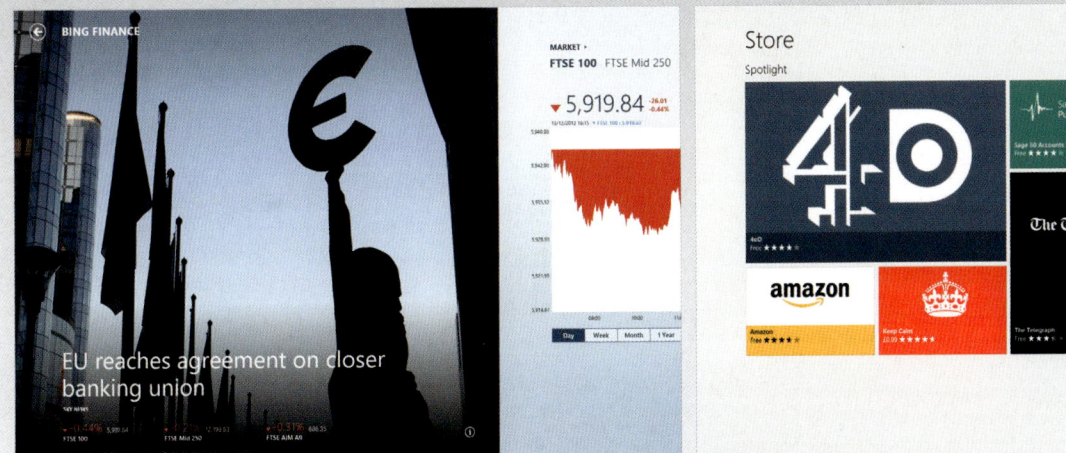

3 Finance
Run Finance to see, yes, the latest financial news presented in an easy-to-understand format. Scroll through it with your mouse wheel to see the latest stock market graphs, and a list of watched stocks. Try clicking the plus button next to your watched stocks to add another to the list. Just type in the name of the company or its stock market symbol and click 'Add'.

4 Store
The Windows Store is where you take Windows 8 further, adding brand new apps, many of which are completely free. If there's something you're interested in, just type in any word (you don't have to click anything) and press [Enter] to search the store for it. Click an app you're interested in, then click 'Install' to add it to your Start screen. It's so easy!

The Start screen is very important – it's where you start your apps, and where you start your Windows journey

view. If you right-click now, you'll see a menu slide down from the top of the screen, which enables you to alter crucial options about the app.

Congratulations – you have just about mastered everything there is to learn about navigating through the Windows 8 Modern interface, apart from one thing: whenever you're ready to go back to the Start screen, just press the [Windows] key on your keyboard. Remember these steps and you'll have no problem using any app you choose.

Check the desktop
Windows veterans might be a little uncomfortable at this point, because the Start screen is very different from the way older versions of Windows worked. But don't fear – look for the Desktop box on the Start screen, click it, and you're taken to the familiar

> "Windows 8 is divided – it has its Start environment and its desktop"

Windows environment that you've come to love.

We should explain – Windows 8 is a little divided, because it has its Start environment, which we just explored, and its desktop environment. Each runs different programs, although you'll find, as you use Windows for a while, that you can launch desktop-based software from your Start screen, too. You should see a yellow folder icon at the bottom of the desktop; click on this, and you launch Windows Explorer, the program that enables you to see and manipulate the files on your computer. We're not going to get too concerned with its ins and outs here – you can find out more about Explorer on page 52 – but it's a good chance to show you a little about how programs work on the desktop.

Move your mouse over the corner of the Explorer window, or one of its

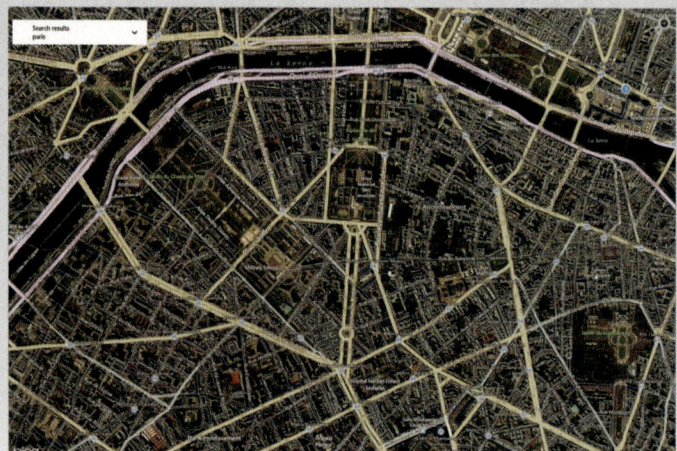

1 Start to search
You could poke around Windows 8 looking for what you want all day, particularly if you've got a lot of different apps installed. But we don't recommend it. If you know what you're looking for – photographs, internet, music, whatever – it's much quicker to just go to the Start screen and start typing a word related to whatever it is you're looking for.

2 Open an app
Whatever you type appears in a box on the right of the screen, and the apps that Windows thinks are related appear in the large area on the right. You only need to click on one of these to start it up. Try typing 'maps' and running the app to bring up Bing Maps. Some apps don't automatically search when you start typing, so press [Windows]+[Q] to bring up the sidebar.

WINDOWS 8 FOR BEGINNERS

edges, and the cursor changes into a pair of arrows pointing in opposite directions. Click and hold the left button, and you can resize the window; release the button when you're done. Now look to the top-right of the window. The line minimises the window, meaning it stays running but shrinks into its icon at the bottom of the screen. Click the icon and it should pop back up. The square maximises the window, so it fills the whole screen. Click it again, and it should return to its original size and position. The X, in the red box, means close. Click it and whatever program you're running should quit.

Obviously there is a lot more to learn about the desktop, but a grasp of these few points should get you comfortable with starting, manipulating and closing any desktop programs you might run later on. You get back to the Start screen the same way as you did when running full-screen apps – just press the [Windows] key.

Shut down
One final trick: shutting down your PC. Most PCs enter sleep mode if you tap the power button; although it drains a little power, this is a preferable state for your PC because you can get back up and running seconds after powering it back on. You can also restart or power off your PC. Press [Windows]+[I] at the same time and the Settings panel slides out; click the power buttons and select the option you want.

Your next steps

Once you've grasped the very basics, we recommend wading in, having a fiddle, and seeing what you can do with Windows 8. There's nothing explicitly scary about it. Take the skills you've learned here and explore. Run some more programs – check out Bing Travel, or the Sports app – and get on the internet with Internet Explorer, too.

If you're a Windows veteran, install some programs, and check out the Start screen; they appear just as though you had installed them to the Start menu of old. Get used to using the [Windows] key to get back to the Start menu, and [Windows]+[D] to bring up the desktop in a flash, if that's where you feel most comfortable.

Most of all, whoever you are, have fun. There's loads you can do with Windows 8, and it's hugely expandable, thanks to the thousands upon thousands of apps that make up the Windows Store. Change it, tweak it, make it your own, but most of all enjoy it. It's your OS.

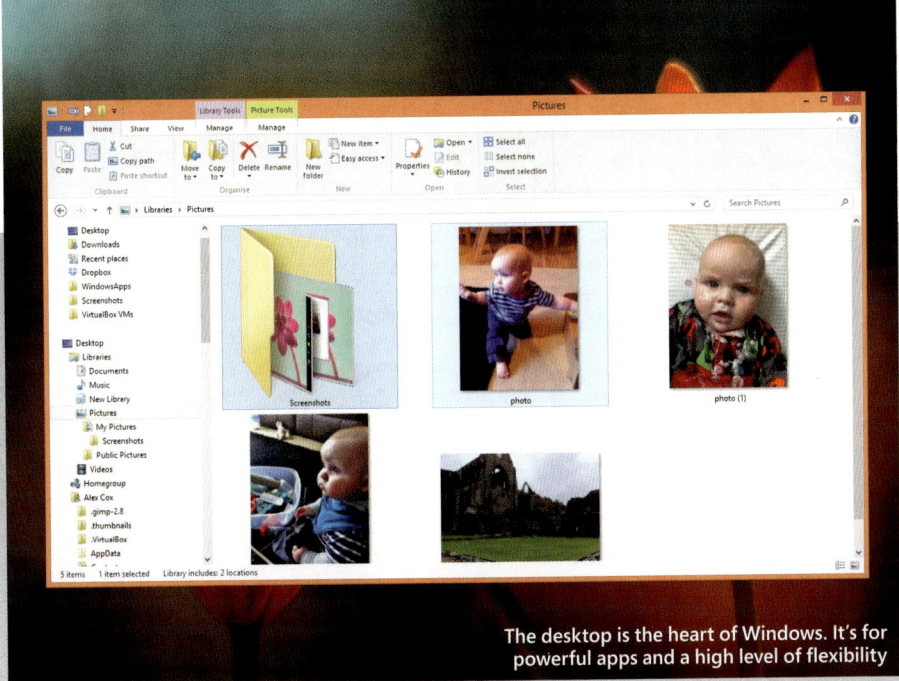

The desktop is the heart of Windows. It's for powerful apps and a high level of flexibility

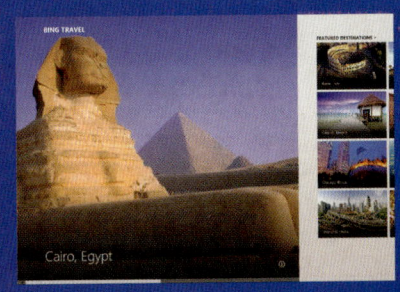

See the world with the Travel app. It's one of the many possibilities Windows 8 offers

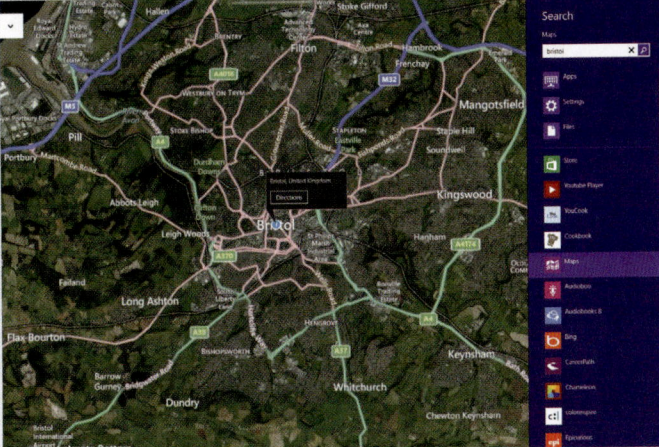

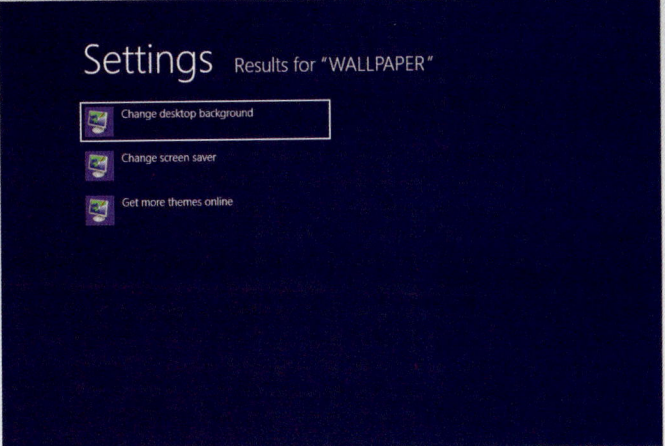

3 Search inside
Now you can search deeper, and find things within an app in the same way. If you've run Maps, this means you can hunt for a location just by typing it in – press [Enter], and Maps should zoom straight to your destination. Very handy. You can also use a postcode here, and see more results by clicking the box that appears at the top-left corner of the screen.

4 Find more
Go back to the Start screen and type in 'wallpaper'. Although no apps match your search on a clean Windows 8 system, you should see that 'Settings' has a number next to it in the box on the right. Click this and you're shown Windows 8's appropriate settings screens – 'Change desktop background' enables you to customise your desktop to your liking.

TIPS AND TRICKS

The ultimate Windows 8 shortcuts

Make life a lot easier – and save a bunch of time too – with this collection of 40 great shortcuts for Windows 8

1 Quick search
Just type
This should be the very first shortcut that you learn, simply because it's the one that you're going to use most in Windows 8. When you're in the Start menu (the one with the tiles), just start typing to instantly reveal the search function and find what you need in Windows 8.

2 Alternative search
[Windows key]+[Q]
If you're not in the Start menu (you might have a program open, for instance), simply typing doesn't allow you to quickly search for stuff. Instead, you need to use this keyboard combination, which instantly reveals the search function, so you don't have to open the Charms bar to find it. Then, as before, simply start typing to find what you're after.

3 Switch windows
[Windows key]+[Tab]
Hold down [Windows key] and press [Tab] to open the Modern Taskbar and scroll through your last used apps. If you have multiple apps open, you can keep pressing [Tab] to cycle through them all – just release [Windows key] when you land on the app that you want to open. Here's another handy thing to remember: the Start screen is always open at the bottom of the Modern Taskbar, so you can always get back to it in a jiffy.

4 Charms bar
[Windows key]+[C]
This is the bar that gives you access to most of the major functions in Windows 8 – use it whenever you're not sure about what you need!

5 Lock it
[Windows key]+[L]
Going away from your computer for a while and don't want any unscrupulous types – OK, just your kids then – getting on to it? All you have to do is use this shortcut combination and it instantly takes you to the Lock screen, meaning you need to enter a password to get back on.

6 Zoom, zoom
[Windows key]+[+] or [-]
Use these shortcuts to quickly zoom in and out of whatever you're looking at on screen using the magnifier tool. This is particularly handy when you find yourself looking at a piece of text or an image that is just a little too small for the eye to comprehend.

7 Switch apps
[Windows key]+[J]
When you've got two windows snapped side by side (either to the left or right side of the screen), you can use this shortcut to swap between the two. It might not seem as though anything has happened, so if you start doing something, such as using the scroll wheel, you'll notice the focus has in fact changed.

8 Bigger or smaller
[Ctrl]+mouse wheel up/down
While the magnifier tool can make things on your screen appear bigger, by using this shortcut, you can physically change the size of elements on your screen, such as a bunch of photographs within a folder or applications pinned to your Start screen or desktop.

ULTIMATE SHORTCUTS

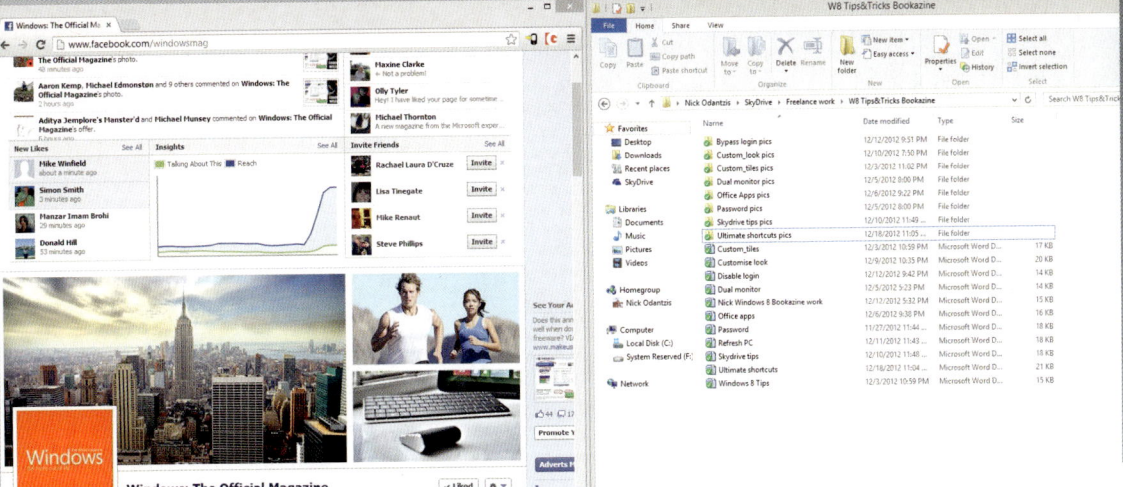

Snap windows to the sides of the screen for extra productivity!

9 Lock orientation
[Windows key]+[O]
If you've got a tablet, this trick is right up your street – it stops the screen from switching between portrait and landscape view when you rotate it. Alternatively, if you've been figuring out how to turn auto-orientation back on, this is also for you!

10 Change language and layout
[Windows key]+[Space]
This is really convenient for those who like to switch between the languages they use and the type of keyboard layout they use.

11 Launch Explorer
[Windows key]+[E]
To quickly get to the files and folders on your hard drive (in desktop mode), use this shortcut and it launches Windows Explorer.

12 Launch anything
[Windows key]+[R]
Great for old-school types, this combination enables you to launch the famous Run command and therefore launch any file, program and much more, just as long as you know the correct name to enter.

13 Last app
[Windows key]
You've probably done this one a few times by accident already while experimenting with Windows 8, but now you can find out what it actually does. By tapping [Windows key] once, you go back to the Start screen if you have an app open. If you're on the Start screen already, you simply switch back to the last app you used.

14 Peekaboo
[Windows key]+[,]
No matter what you currently have opened on your desktop, you can always keep an eye on what's happening behind the scenes using the Peek option in Windows 8. Just hold the comma key to get a longer look at what's going on.

15 Switch screens
[Windows key]+ [PgUp] or [PgDn]
Here's a great shortcut tip if you have a dual monitor setup on your desktop. By using the [PgUp] key, you can quickly move what you're working on to the left monitor and by using [PgDn], you can move it across to the right monitor.

16 Screen grab
[Windows key]+[PrtScn]
People have been capturing screenshots of their computer escapades for years, but Windows 8 has changed the whole routine and – thankfully – made it even easier to do. By using this shortcut, not only is a screenshot of what's on your screen captured, but it's also saved automatically into your 'Pictures > Screenshots' folder, so you can easily find it later.

17 Quick menu
[Windows key]+[Z]
When you're using a new-style app from the Start screen (such as Mail or People), you can quickly bring up the menu relating to that particular app by using this shortcut.

18 Second screen
[Windows key]+[P]
If you'd like to hook up a second display and spread your productivity load across two screens, you can quickly switch to a second screen or projector. If you keep tapping [P], you can also cycle through the second screen settings, so you can choose to extend your display, duplicate it, or even use just your second screen (which is really handy if you want to watch a movie from a laptop on a big screen, for instance, without the laptop screen being on as well).

19 Essential features
[Windows key]+[X]
It doesn't matter where you currently are in Windows 8, remember this essential shortcut – it opens a whole world of handy features once activated, such as Power Options and the Task Manager.

20 Back and forth
[Windows key]+[D]
This shortcut is incredibly simple but it's one of those things that you'll wonder how you ever managed without it before. When you're in desktop mode, it quickly minimises all your open windows and takes you to the desktop, and when you use the shortcut again, it displays the open windows once more.

Quickly zoom in and out of things with a simple shortcut

Chapter 1 | 25

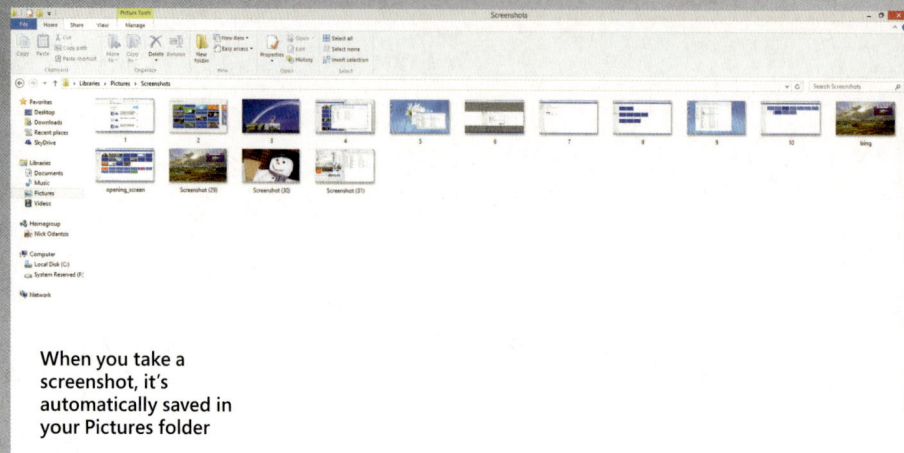

When you take a screenshot, it's automatically saved in your Pictures folder

21 Handy snap
[Windows key]+[Shift]+[.]
If you like keeping an eye on a variety of open apps while working on other things, this is essential. By using it you can quickly snap an app to the left side of the screen (and right, when you use it again) – perfect for programs such as Messenger or Mail, when you want to know what's going on at a glance at all times, but you don't want to lose the focus of your most important tasks.

22 Switch everything
[Alt]+[Tab]
Although [Windows key]+[Tab] is great for switching between open apps, this goes one step further and enables you to cycle through any kind of app or window on your desktop that is open. The beauty of it is that you can pause and preview an open app or window by simply cycling to the one you want to view and keeping [Alt] held down.

23 Select them all
[Ctrl]+[A]
When you're in a folder of files – such as photos, music, anything really – you can quickly select them all at once, which is handy if you need to move them all at the same time.

24 Get rid of it
[Shift]+[Del]
When you delete something on your hard drive, it goes to your Recycle Bin so you can keep or permanently delete it at a later date. To save time, you can permanently delete things using this shortcut – use it with care, though!

25 Close it
[Alt]+[F4]
One of the most frequently used shortcuts – it's essential if you like to close things quickly. It can be used for quickly shutting down apps (in Start and desktop mode), windows, or even closing Windows 8 itself, which is handy when you want to shut down your PC without wasting time.

26 Taskbar preview
[Windows key]+[T]
To get a thumbnail preview of what's happening in all your open windows in desktop mode, use this and keep pressing [T] to cycle through them all.

27 New folder
[Ctrl]+[Shift]+ [N]
This is a great one if you are constantly creating new folders in Windows Explorer to put your files in. It automatically adds a folder ready for you to rename.

28 Browse in private
[Ctrl]+[Shift]+[P]
Doing a bit of internet surfing that you'd prefer to keep private? Well, in that case, you need to quickly switch to the private browsing mode, so nobody can find out what you're up to. Of course, this only works in Internet Explorer on the desktop.

29 Snap desktop windows
[Windows key]+[arrow]
Using a combination of the arrow keys, you can take full control of the windows in desktop mode. You can snap them left or right (using the left or right arrow key) for when you want to work on multiple things at once, or you can make them full-screen once more by using the up arrow key.

30 Get help!
[F1]
Don't feel all alone when you've got a problem. No matter where you are in Windows 8, you can find help by simply pressing this key and looking for the solution to your problem in the help facility. ■

Shortie cuts

31 Copy an item
[Ctrl]+[C]

32 Paste an item
[Ctrl]+[V]

33 Undo an action
[Ctrl]+[Z]

34 Share charm
[Windows key]+[H]

35 Zoom the Start screen
[Ctrl]+[Plus] or [Minus]

36 Search files
[Windows key]+[F]

37 Open Settings
[Windows key]+[I]

38 Open Devices
[Windows key]+[K]

39 New tab
[Ctrl]+[T]

40 Refresh the screen
[F5]

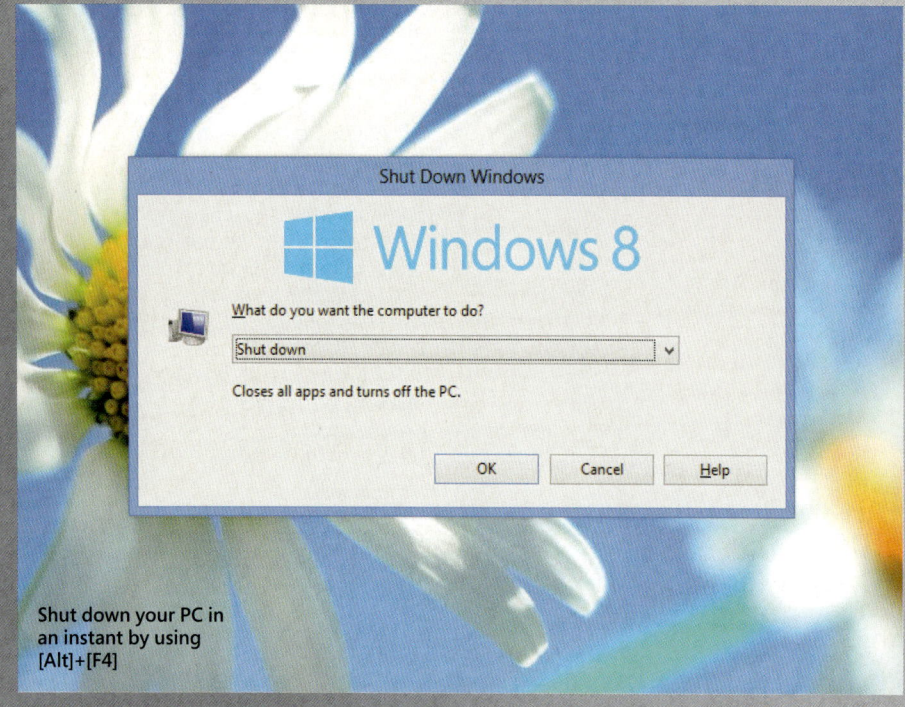

Shut down your PC in an instant by using [Alt]+[F4]

How to customise

TRY THIS!
Customise your tiles
42

Get your new operating system working the way you want

Section 2

30	Customise Windows 8
32	Mastering the desktop
35	Make Windows look amazing
40	Streamline your Start screen
42	Create amazing-looking tiles
44	Get Win 7's Start menu back
46	Use dual monitors

DO THIS NOW...

Customise Windows 8

Making Windows 8 your own is easier than you'd think

Get a fresh new Lock screen

If you'd like to change your Lock screen image, press [Win]+[I], or click/tap the Settings charm and go to 'Change PC settings'. Choose 'Personalise'. You'll then see that you can change your Lock screen image. Choose from one of the default options by clicking one of the pictures shown, or click 'Browse' to look through more images on your PC. You can also define which apps can display their status on the Lock screen from here, although the app must specifically support this before it's accessible from your Personalise settings.

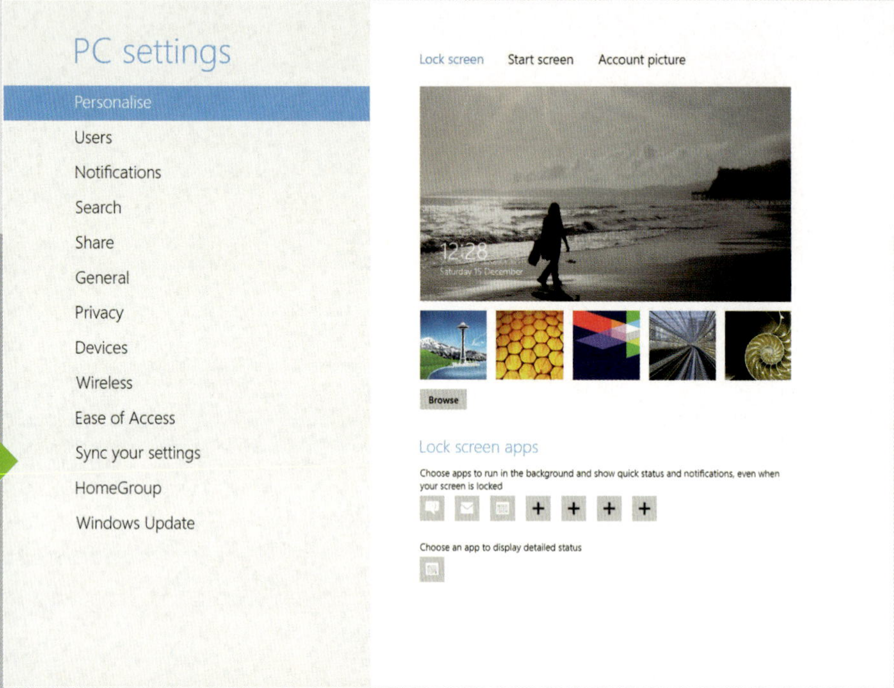

Make a picture password

One of the cleverest options in Windows 8 is to create a picture password, where you choose an image, then draw on it with taps, lines and circles – only someone who can reproduce this pattern can log on. It works better with a touchscreen, but you can try it with a mouse. Select [Win]+[I] (or go to the Settings charm), then go to 'More PC Settings'. From the menu options, select 'Users > Create a Picture Password'. It won't be to everyone's taste, but it is a great new way to log on to your Windows 8 PC (turn to page 128 for a complete guide).

CUSTOMISE WINDOWS 8

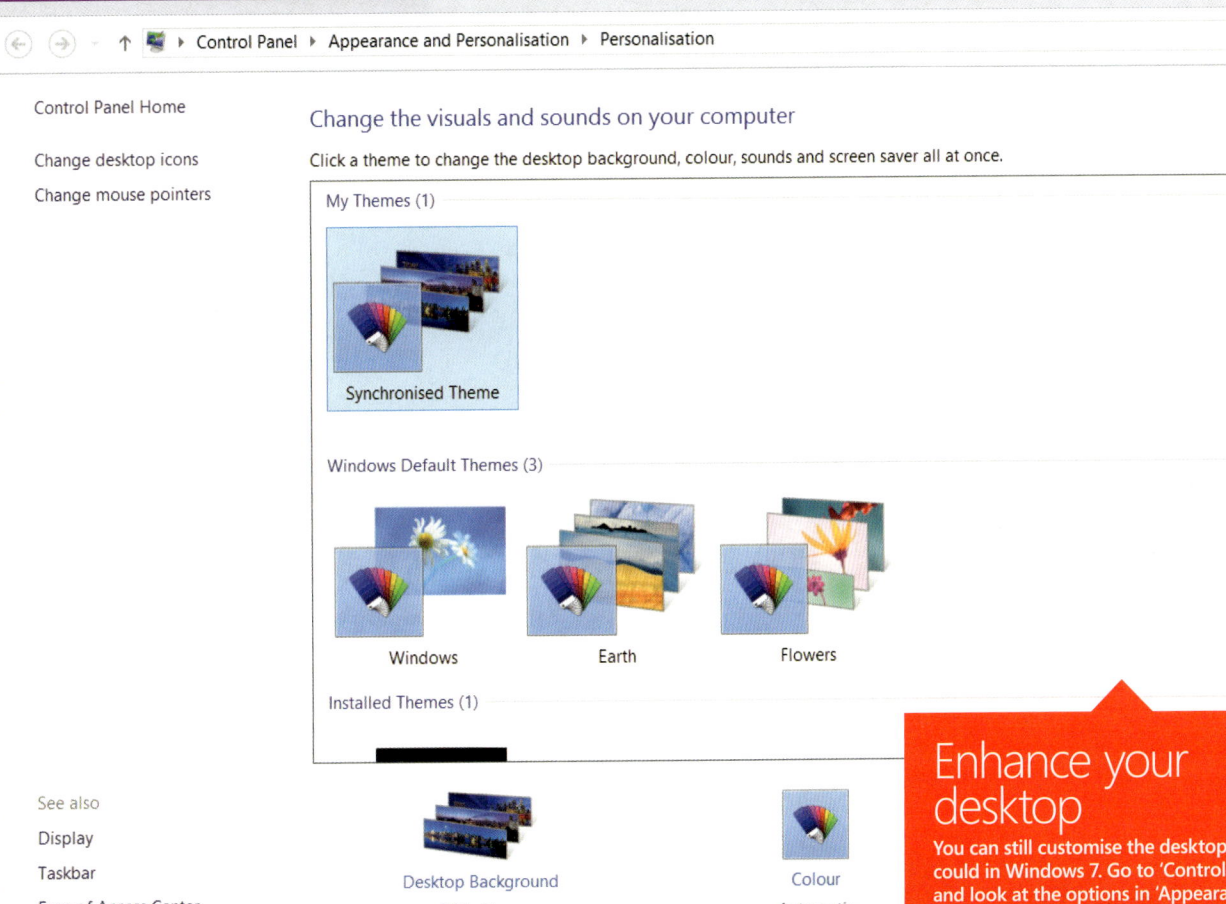

Personalise your Start screen

'PC settings > Personalise' is also the way to change the look and colour of your Start screen; just select Start screen from the options at the top. From here, you can choose one of the many colour themes available – move the slider to the theme you want – while you can also choose a pattern, too. The main picture previews what your Start screen will look like with the changes. The Personalise area is also where you can change your account picture to be whatever you want – it doesn't have to be a boring headshot if you don't want it to be!

Enhance your desktop

You can still customise the desktop as you could in Windows 7. Go to 'Control Panel' and look at the options in 'Appearance and Personalisation', or right-click on the desktop background and select 'Personalise'. Here you can change the theme, modify your desktop background, opt for different colours or sounds and, of course, choose that all-important screensaver from the options available. Should you wish, you can click the 'Get more themes online' button to search for more desktop backgrounds – we downloaded a nice cityscape from there.

Windows 8: Expert Tips and Tricks

25 TOP TIPS FOR...
Mastering the desktop

The Windows desktop has been around for 18 years, but if it's new to you, here's how to get to grips with it

1 Right-click the Taskbar (the area at the bottom of the desktop, with your running programs on it) and untick 'Lock the Taskbar' to open it up for further experimentation.

2 Once you've unlocked the Taskbar, you can make it bigger to give yourself more space for icons. Just hover your mouse over the top edge until it turns into an arrow cursor, then click and drag to expand or contract the size of the Taskbar.

3 If the Taskbar is unlocked, click an empty bit of it, then hold and drag it to the screen edge you want it to sit on. If it's locked, use the Taskbar Properties menu to select its location.

4 Go back to the Taskbar Properties menu. The 'Use Taskbar icons' checkbox enables you to choose how big app icons appear on your desktop.

5 Use the 'Taskbar buttons' menu in Taskbar Properties to choose how icons on your Taskbar are displayed; if you've used Windows XP, try 'Combine when Taskbar is full' for a familiar view.

6 Clicking the up arrow icon on the left of the notification area displays anything that's hidden. You can then click 'Customize' to show and hide more notifications and running programs.

7 Set windows to cascade, and they're arranged on top of each other, with space to click each one and switch between them. Right-click the Taskbar and choose 'Cascade windows'.

Use the 'Show windows stacked' option to quickly rearrange your desktop and see all your open windows

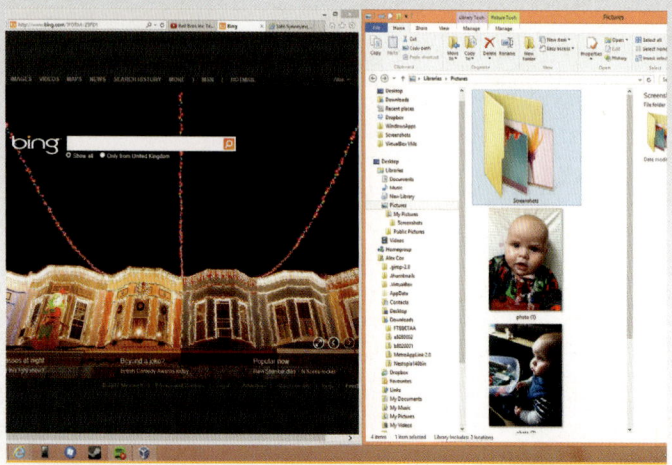

32 | Chapter 1   Windows 8: Expert Tips and Tricks

MASTERING THE DESKTOP

8 Stacking and side-by-side are useful options for window arrangement – right-click the Taskbar and select the appropriate option. You can also drag your windows to each side of the screen to snap them in place.

9 Did you know you can launch a new window of any running program by holding [Shift] and clicking its icon on the Taskbar? Well, you can.

10 Right-click the Taskbar and select 'Properties'. There's an option there to 'Auto-hide the Taskbar' – this means you can make the Taskbar roll up out of the way until you move your mouse to the edge of the screen it's sitting on.

11 Need to get your hands on the touch keyboard, the Internet Explorer address bar, and more? Right-click the Taskbar and add the appropriate toolbar from, yes, the Toolbars menu.

12 Right-click the Taskbar, highlight 'Toolbars' and select 'New Toolbar'. Choose a folder on your computer and you get a new icon on the Taskbar that links you straight to its contents.

13 Right-click the Taskbar and open the Properties menu. Check the box next to the sentence that begins 'Use Peek...', click 'Apply', and from now on you get a quick glance at the contents of your desktop when you hover your mouse in the bottom-right corner.

14 Task Manager is a super-useful program that enables you to keep tabs on exactly what's going on with your PC. There are two quick ways to access it: press [Ctrl]+[Shift]+[Esc] together; or right-click the Taskbar and choose the appropriate option. While it's open, you see a new icon in your notification area that gives you an at-a-glance view of your device's performance.

15 The desktop tends to be a dumping ground for files – files you're just temporarily storing, files you want to access quickly, files you've just downloaded – which means it can quickly get cluttered. Right-click the desktop and select 'View > Small Icons' to shrink them down a bit, enabling you to fit more on.

You can change the way icons are displayed on your taskbar quickly and easily for a truly custom experience

16 The standard grid for icons keeps everything neat and tidy, but you might want to arrange your icons with more precision. Right-click the desktop, select 'View' and uncheck 'Align icons to grid', then you can click and drag to drop them wherever you like.

17 Don't want icon-arranging precision? Would you prefer Windows 8 to do the job for you? Fine! Checking the option that says 'Auto Arrange Icons' under the Desktop View menu forces your icons to a grid. You can still drag them around to rearrange their order, but they automatically snap into place, going from top-left to bottom-right.

18 Right-click the desktop, go to the 'View' menu, and uncheck the option that says 'Show Desktop Icons'. All the icons on your desktop disappear, leaving your unsullied desktop wallpaper. Don't panic, though; your files and folders still exist. They're just hidden. Open an Explorer window and visit the Desktop folder from there, and you'll see all your hidden files.

19 Check out the menu that appears if you right-click the desktop and hover over 'Sort by' – it automatically swishes your icons around based on whatever option you choose. This isn't a permanent change, but bear in mind that it does mess up any nifty arrangements you've made previously.

20 Your desktop is essentially just a folder, and as such you can treat it the same as any other folder on your computer. That means you can create new documents, shortcuts and folders by right-clicking, hovering over 'New', and choosing the appropriate option.

Quick tips

21 Would you like more information about the time? By left-clicking on the clock on the Taskbar, you can bring up a more detailed timepiece.

22 Right-click on the clock, choose 'Adjust Date/Time', and then use the 'Additional clocks' tab to add world time to the expanded view you get.

23 If you move the mouse over to the right-hand side of your screen (or swipe in from the right) you'll be able to see the Modern UI digital clock.

24 By default, the clock is set automatically, but you can change it manually if you would prefer by right-clicking, selecting 'Adjust Date/Time', and clicking the appropriate button.

25 You can change the source clock that sets your time for you in 'Adjust Date/Time'; use the 'Internet Time' tab, and click the button there.

SERIOUS ABOUT HARDWARE?

CPU SUPERTEST — TOP 10 CHIPS RATED
CAN PILEDRIVER BEAT INTEL'S CORE i5?

PERFORMANCE GEAR & GAMING
PCFormat

ISSUE 275/FEBRUARY 2013

Sapphire Edge VS8 Mini PC

INTEL vs AMD
MICRO MACHINES

¤ Intel's Next Unit of Computing
¤ Sapphire's Edge VS8
¤ More than just media boxes?

"MORE POWER THAN YOU'LL EVER NEED!"
AMD's Radeon HD 7990 lands

NOW ON GOOGLE PLAY
Download the day they go onsale in the UK!

NO.1 FOR REVIEWS
VIEWSONIC VX2370
CRUCIAL TACTICAL LP
SAMSUNG 5-SERIES
LOGITECH G710+
ZOTAC A75-ITX

SPECIAL REPORT
PC GAMES FOR 2013
Revealed: the games to watch out for

BUILD IT! YOUR OWN MINECRAFT SERVER
Create block building heaven

BUILD IT! AN INCREDIBLE LOW-POWER GAMING RIG
Throw out the hungriest components

Intel NUC DC3217BY

PERFORMANCE ADVICE
FOR SERIOUS GAMERS
ON SALE EVERY MONTH

MAKE WINDOWS LOOK AMAZING

Learn how to…
Make Windows look amazing!

Windows 8 is ready for you to put your personal touch on it – let's make it look beautiful!

Windows 8 is undoubtedly the best-looking version of the operating system that's ever been made, but that said, it's still set to look as plain as possible out of the box, and it doesn't yet have your personal touch added to it. However, it's easy enough to customise the way Windows 8 looks, whether you prefer to use just the Start screen or you like to delve into the familiar scenario of the desktop – with a few clicks of the mouse or taps of the touchscreen, you can alter the way things are displayed to your liking, making it look exactly the way you want. We're going to show you how to go through the basics of customising the operating system's looks, and once you've done that, you can really get stuck in and start improving things you didn't even know existed.

Colour
The Start screen comes in 25 colours. Go to 'Charms > PC settings > Personalize > Start screen' to choose a different one.

Image
The default Start screen background is a solid colour – in the Personalize menu you can select a more extravagant background style.

Accessibility
To make it easier to read, go to 'Charms > PC settings – Ease of access' and toggle 'High contrast' or 'Make everything on screen bigger'.

Change the Lock screen

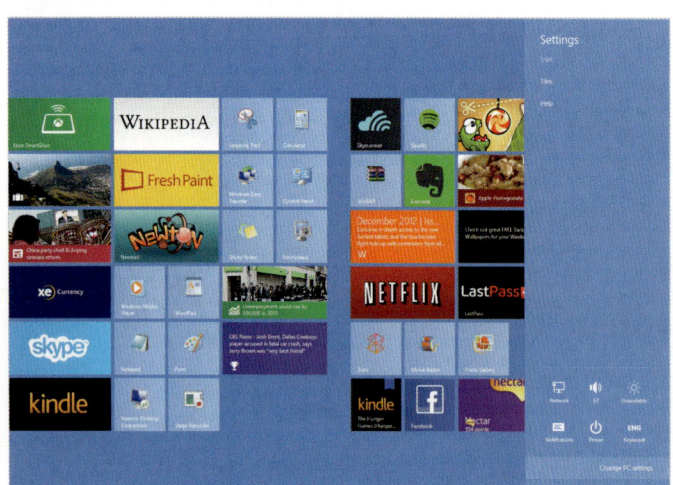

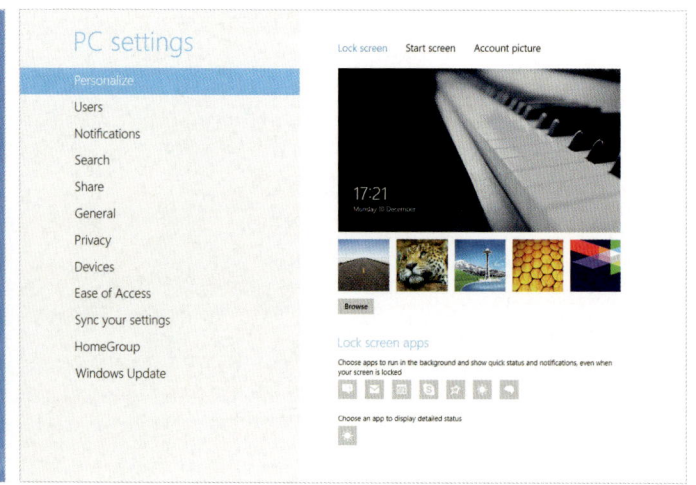

1 Unlock its potential
The Lock screen is what you see when your PC first starts up, before you enter the Start screen. It shows an image across the entire screen, and there's a variety of notifications, such as the time and whether you have any new messages. To customise it, open the Charms bar, select 'Settings' and then hit 'Change PC settings'.

2 Good image
When you open PC settings, you land on the right area of the menu to modify the Lock screen. You'll see the image that's currently selected for the Lock screen – select a new one from below and you see a preview of it above. Or get a custom image by clicking 'Browse' and selecting one from your PC. Make sure it's high resolution.

MAKE WINDOWS LOOK AMAZING

Account pic
To change your pic, go to 'Charms > PC settings > Personalise > Account picture' and hit 'Browse' to use one from your PC.

Jargon buster!

Charms
Move your mouse to the right-hand side of the screen or swipe in using your finger and you'll see the Windows 8 Charms – you can use these to perform key tasks such as Search and Share.

Windows Store
The new online store from Microsoft, offering a multitude of apps that enable you to add extra functionality to your Windows 8 device. Many of these apps are free to download.

Organise apps
You can rearrange the way apps appear, dragging and dropping to move them, and can group them so they're easy to find at a glance.

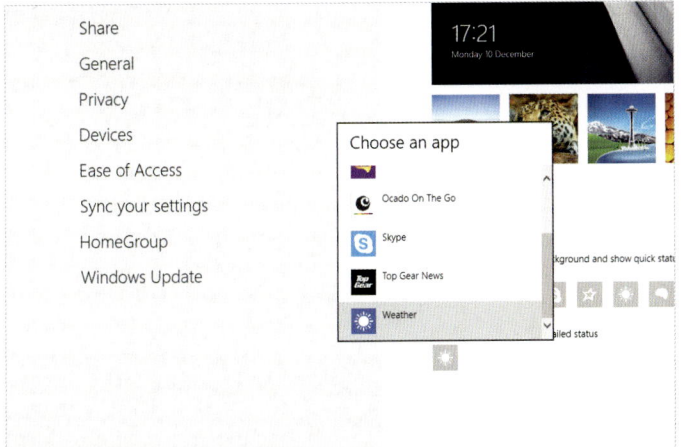

3 Change notifications
You can change the notifications that appear on the Lock screen by changing which apps are enabled. Below where it says 'Lock screen apps', click on one of the app icons to change what is displayed, or choose to display nothing. Below this you can choose to display a single app in greater detail, so click it and select one.

4 Grab an app
An easier way to change your Lock screen is to get an app from the **Windows Store**. Open the Windows Store and search for 'Lock screen' apps. We went for Background Wallpapers HD, which offers hundreds of stunning free wallpapers, which you can preview and set as your Lock screen by right-clicking or swiping down.

Windows 8: Expert Tips and Tricks | Chapter 1 | 37

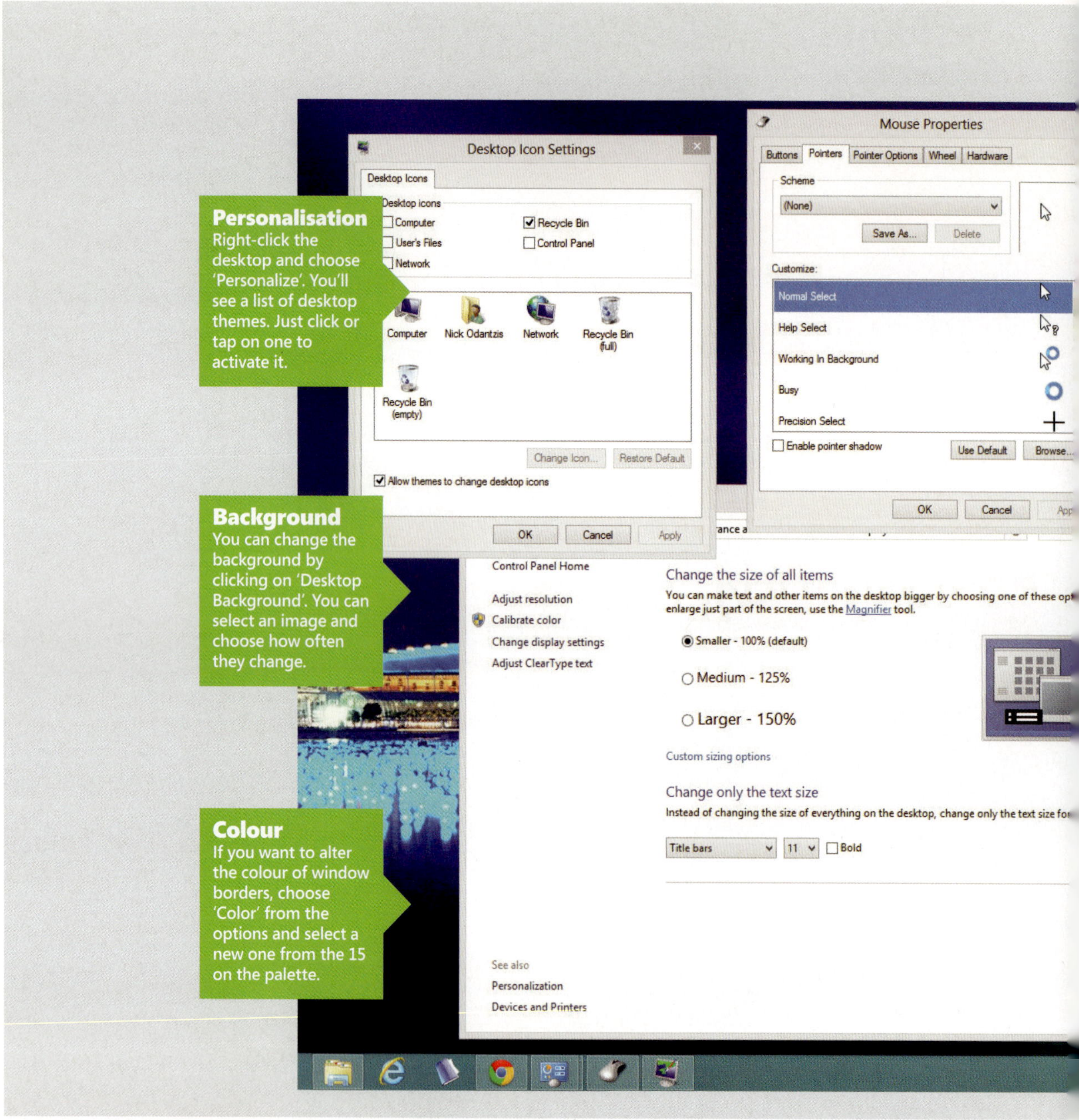

Personalisation
Right-click the desktop and choose 'Personalize'. You'll see a list of desktop themes. Just click or tap on one to activate it.

Background
You can change the background by clicking on 'Desktop Background'. You can select an image and choose how often they change.

Colour
If you want to alter the colour of window borders, choose 'Color' from the options and select a new one from the 15 on the palette.

Four steps to desktop heaven

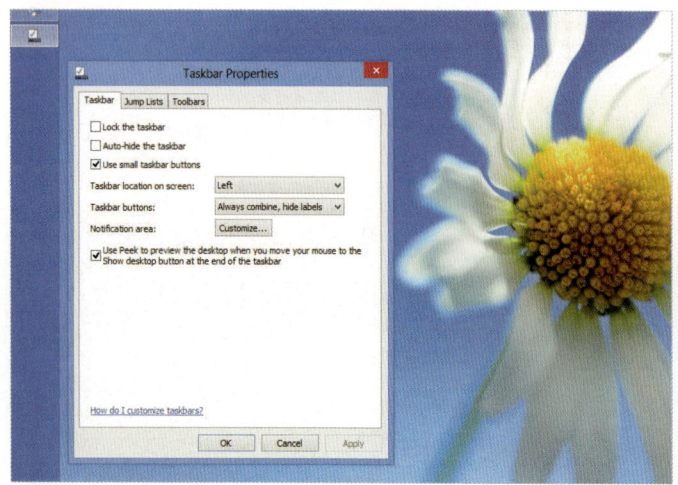

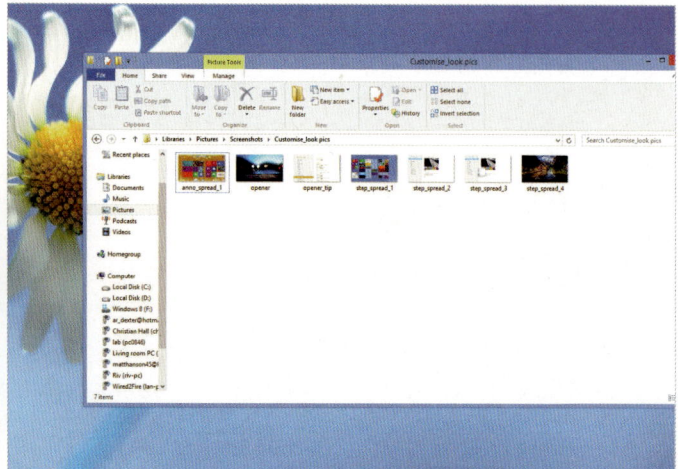

1 New Taskbar
The Taskbar at the bottom of the screen contains applications and notifications, making it easy to access things in an instant. However, you can customise it to suit your needs. Right-click the Taskbar and select 'Properties'. You can change its location, make it bigger, or hide it until you point your mouse cursor over it.

2 Icon size
If you have a lot of icons on your desktop background, or even if there are only a few, you might be interested to know that you can instantly change the size of them depending on your tastes. Hold down [Ctrl] on the keyboard and use the scroll wheel on your mouse to increase or decrease the size. You might like the results…

MAKE WINDOWS LOOK AMAZING

Size matters
Hit 'Display' and you can change the size of everything you see – perfect if you're using a high-res display and find things a little small.

Jargon buster!

High-res
High-resolution – an image that is sharply defined and highly detailed, due to being composed of a higher number of pixels than normal.

Icons
The small pictures that appear on your desktop to represent folders and shortcuts. They're made from specialised .ico files, that contain a number of versions of the image at different resolutions.

Icons
You can also change desktop icons. Go to 'Change desktop icons', select one and choose 'Change icon'. This opens up a list of new icons to use.

Mouse
There's an option to change the type of mouse pointer. Go to 'Change mouse pointers' and under the 'Pointers' tab, select a new scheme.

More themes
You can find a whole plethora of amazing themes provided by Microsoft online. Below 'My themes', click or tap on 'Get more themes online'.

3 Dock it
Interested in modifying your desktop so it looks and acts a bit more like a certain fruity-sounding alternative to Windows? Well, you can install your own customised Mac-alike application dock by downloading ObjectDock from www.stardock.com. It's free and you can add your own programs and folders for easy access in one place.

4 Go further
If you want to push the boundaries of customisation, many people turn to the excellent application Rainmeter. You can create a unique desktop to the point that you might not even recognise Windows, but the great thing is that you get total control over what you see. Download it for free from www.rainmeter.net.

Learn how to...

Streamline your Start screen

The introduction of the Start screen is one of Windows 8's biggest changes. Make sure you learn how to get it to work exactly the way you want it to with this handy guide

WORKS WITH
Windows 8
Windows 8 Pro
Windows RT

Out of all the innovations that Microsoft brought to Windows 8, the most revolutionary – and also the most divisive – was the Start screen. Replacing the Start menu of past versions of Windows, this new screen is our entry point to Windows 8, giving us access to our favourite apps, settings and programs. This means that if you want to really get the most out of Windows 8, you're going to want to get your Start screen organised so that it's quick and easy to use. As with a lot of Windows 8, there are some obvious tools to help you get started, but there are also some hidden gems that can really help you get your Start screen in order, so it works just the way you want.

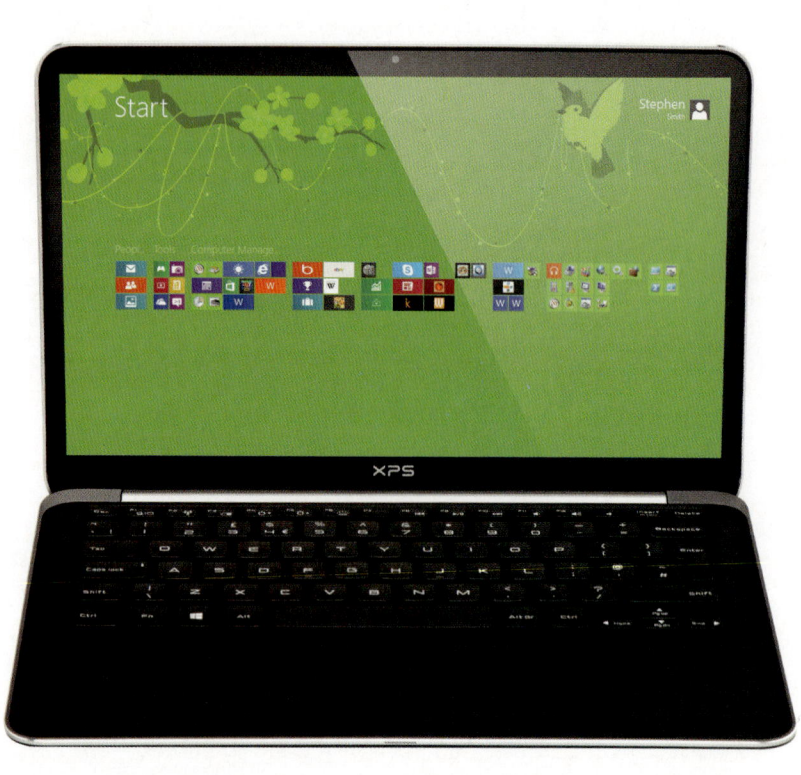

Sorting your Start screen

1 Moving your tiles
Your Start screen is made up of **Live tiles** that represent your apps and programs. When you install something, its tile appears on your Start screen, but that doesn't mean it has to stay where it's put. Press and hold your finger (or mouse) over the tile you want to move, then drag it where you want it to go.

2 Removing tiles
You may find your Start screen filling up with tiles for all the apps and programs you install. This can make it look cluttered, so if you want to remove tiles from your Start screen, without uninstalling an app, either touch the app's tile and drag it to the bottom of the screen, or right-click the tile and select 'Unpin from Start'.

STREAMLINE YOUR START SCREEN

3 Resize your tiles
Some tiles are square; others are rectangular. If you want to change the size of the tile, press it, then drag to the bottom of the screen, or right-click it, and select 'Smaller' or 'Larger'. Not all app tiles can be resized, but most of them can be tweaked in this way.

4 Uninstall apps
If you want to remove the app or program from your computer completely, press the tile and drag it to the bottom of the screen, or right-click it and select 'Uninstall'. If you bought the app, you can re-download it from the Windows Store without paying for it again.

5 Get a better view
You can zoom out to view your entire Start screen. To do this on a touchscreen, place your thumb and a finger on the screen and bring them together in a pinching movement. With a mouse and keyboard, press the '-' icon at the bottom-right of the screen.

6 Group your apps
You can group apps together, so you could group People, Mail, Messaging and Calendar apps, and name them 'People'. Arrange the tiles as in Step 1, then zoom out. Press and hold your finger over the group, then release (or right-click), and select 'Name group'.

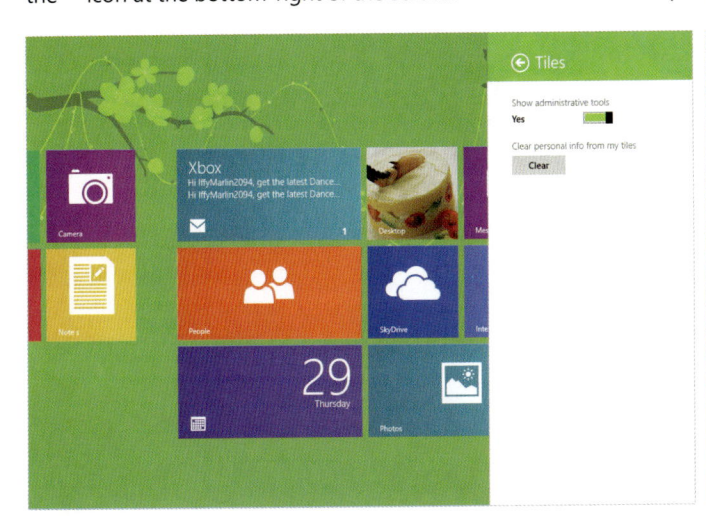

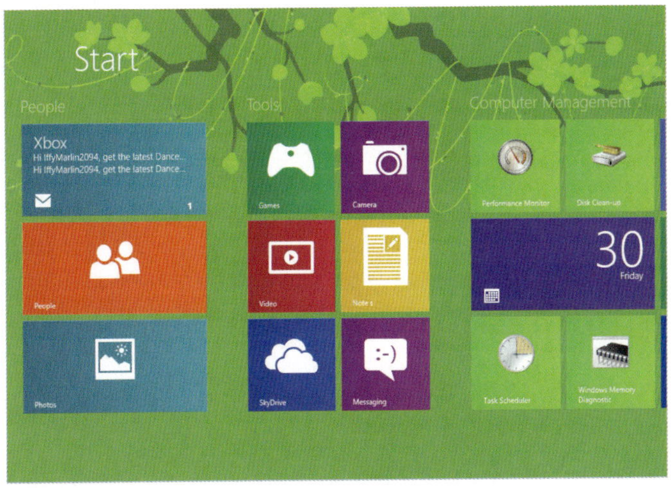

7 Add advanced tools
If you're a Windows 8 power user, you may want to have quick and easy access to some of Windows 8's more powerful tools straight from your Start screen. Bring up the Charm bar from the right-hand side of the screen, select 'Settings' then 'Tiles', and toggle 'Show Administrative Tools' to 'On'.

8 Enjoy your new Start screen
You've now learned the most important tips and tricks for organising your Start screen, and you should be seeing the benefit of a better laid-out and more intuitive screen. The work doesn't stop here, though – take time to keep your Start screen organised, especially when you install apps, and you'll be thankful you did.

Jargon buster!

Administrative Tools
These tools will be familiar to people who have used Windows in the past and are comfortable with using some of its more advanced settings. If you're not that computer savvy, you won't want to use these, but they can help you ensure that Windows 8 is running as well as it can.

Live tiles
One of the best things about Windows 8 – which actually debuted in Windows Phone 7 – is Live tiles. These tiles update themselves when the app they represent needs to tell you something – for example, if you get an email.

Windows 8: Expert Tips and Tricks | Chapter 1

Learn how to...

Create amazing-looking tiles

Some of the tiles don't look too great, so let's make them ping out!

WORKS WITH
Windows 8
Windows 8 Pro
Windows RT

One of the things that make Windows 8 stand out from all previous versions is its Start menu and the Live tiles that sit on top of it, feeding you information at regular intervals, such as your favourite photos or the latest news, without you doing anything. Many of these Live tiles look great because they're designed to, but there are lots that look quite boring, such as the ones for Microsoft Office and Spotify, or those that link to folders on your hard drive. In short, any tile that hasn't come from the Windows Store doesn't look that good. There's a way to make any tile on the Start menu look fantastic, however, using a program called Modern Tile Maker. In 15 minutes you can get programs, files, folders and even internet links looking just like the rest of your tiles.

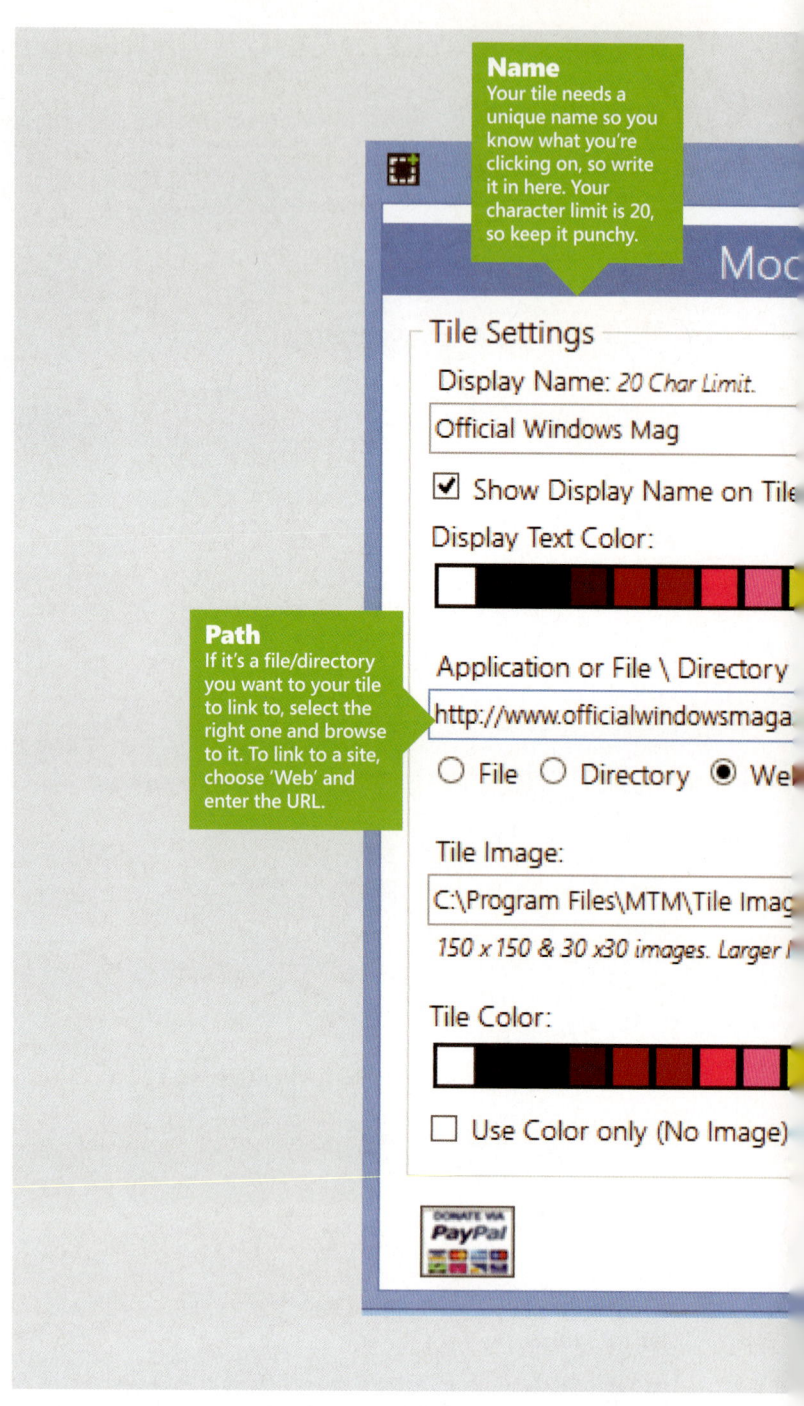

Name
Your tile needs a unique name so you know what you're clicking on, so write it in here. Your character limit is 20, so keep it punchy.

Path
If it's a file/directory you want to your tile to link to, select the right one and browse to it. To link to a site, choose 'Web' and enter the URL.

Get modern-looking tiles

1 Get the software
Download Modern Tile Maker from http://bit.ly/ZRQM7U and open the zip file. Open the MTM set-up file, choose to run it, and the set-up screen should appear. Hit 'Install' to begin installing Modern Tile Maker. You can tick the check box to add a tile for Modern Tile Maker on the Start menu if you think you will use it regularly.

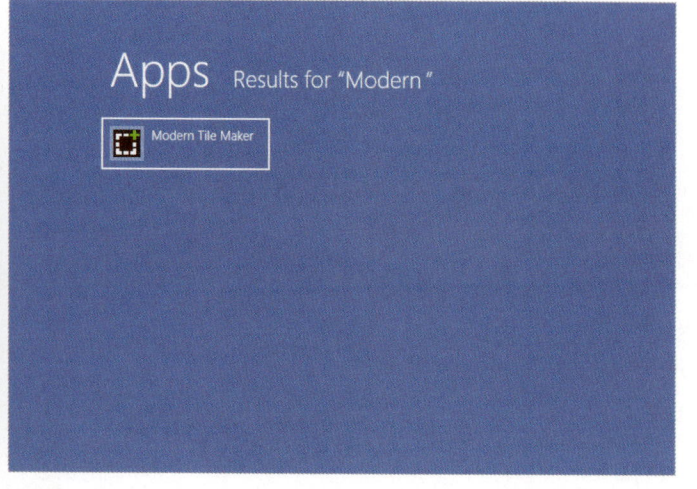

2 Find it
Modern Tile Maker doesn't automatically open, so you must find it from your list of installed programs. Open search ([Windows key] + [Q]), type in 'Modern Tile Maker' and open it when it appears. Select 'Yes' when a prompt appears. The main program window opens and you'll see a range of options for creating your custom tile.

CREATE AMAZING-LOOKING TILES

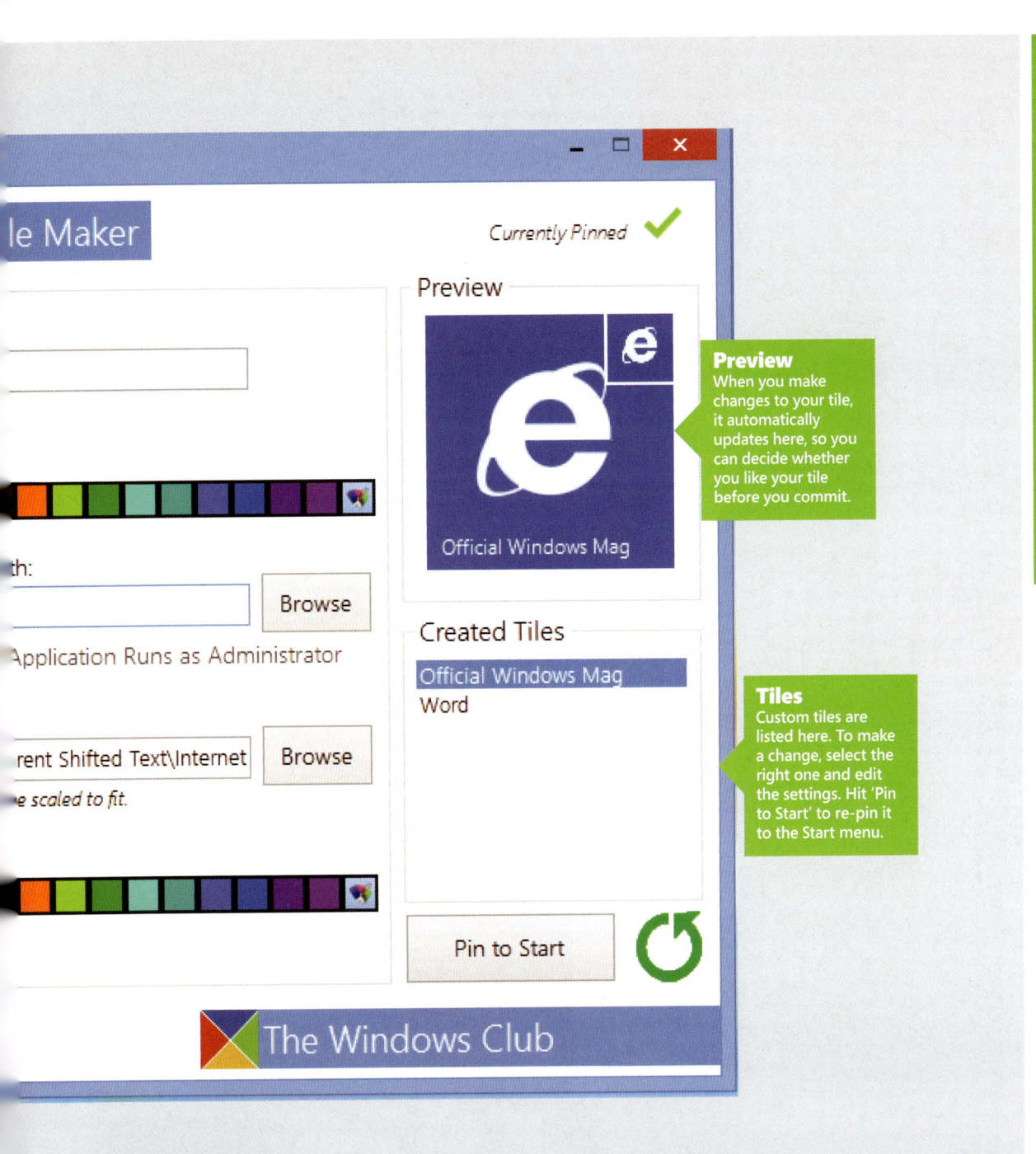

Jargon buster!

Live tiles
A type of Start screen tile that pushes updates to you regularly, to keep you abreast of all the latest happenings. These could be new photos, messages or news stories, depending on the tile itself.

Pin
A term used to explain what happens when you attach an app, folder or link to the Start screen or the old-style desktop.

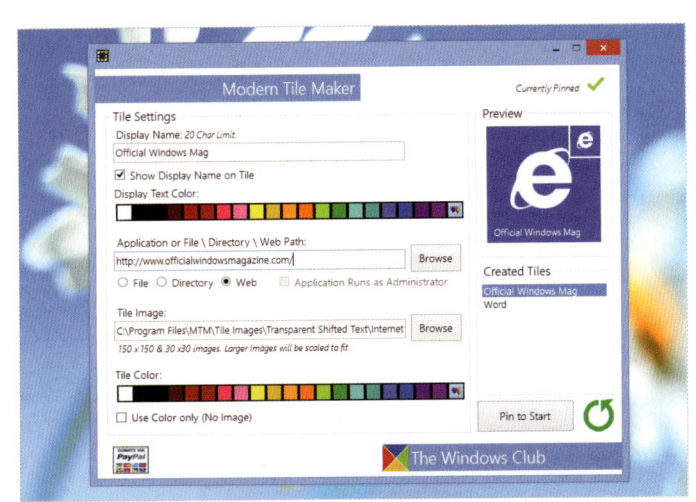

Preview
When you make changes to your tile, it automatically updates here, so you can decide whether you like your tile before you commit.

Tiles
Custom tiles are listed here. To make a change, select the right one and edit the settings. Hit 'Pin to Start' to re-pin it to the Start menu.

3 Link to it
Create a name for your tile in the 'Display Name' area and decide on the text colour. Where it says 'Application Path', choose whether you want to link to a file, directory or website. If it's a file or directory, select the appropriate checkbox and browse to its location. To create a web link, select 'Web' and type the address.

4 Choose image
Hit the 'Browse' button next to the 'Tile Image' box and find an appropriate image. If it's a web link, open one of the 'Transparent' folders and choose 'InternetExplorer'. Open it and you'll see the icon in the preview area. Change the colour of the tile, then hit '**Pin** to Start'. That's it – you can now see your new tile on the Start menu.

Learn how to...

Master the new Start screen

Everything begins at the Start...

WORKS WITH
Windows 8
Windows 8 Pro
Windows RT

Undeniably, it's the most striking change in Windows 8. When you log in to your PC, the first thing you see is the brand new Start screen, a bold, colourful, animated page of rectangles that bears a striking resemblance to the interface on Windows Phone devices. They're all based on a Microsoft design concept called the Modern UI, a layout that puts full-screen, dedicated apps at the forefront, and brings you information without having to open a thing, thanks to Live tiles. We won't pretend it's not a little intimidating at first, but once you've found your way around, it's as quick as the classic Start menu.

Move easily
Tap, hold and drag items to move them around. They group automatically – drop them to the right if you want to add a gap between groups.

Live tiles
Some tiles bring you news, pictures and more automatically. If constant updates annoy you, right-click the icon, then 'Turn live tile off'.

Customise your Start screen

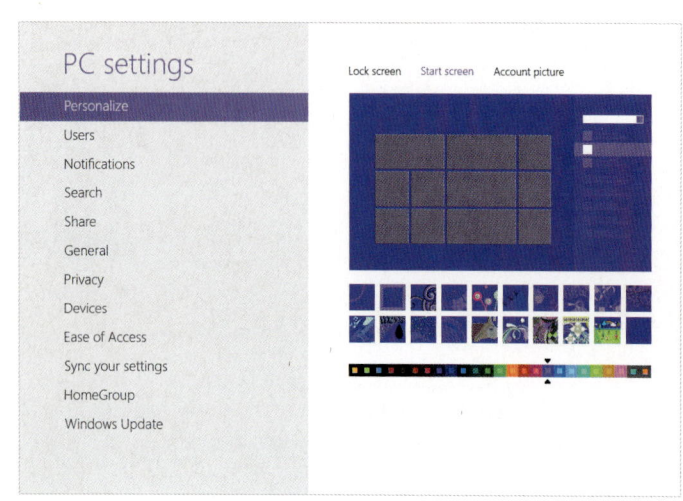

1 Tweak the colours
Although you choose your favourite colour combination when you install Windows 8, you can tweak it whenever you like. The option is a little hidden, though. You need to bring up the Charms bar, choose 'Settings', then select 'Change PC Settings'. From there select 'Personalize > Start Screen', and select a new combo.

2 A fancy background
The same screen enables you to tweak your Start screen background. Although there's no direct way of inserting your own pictures here, there's a selection of 20 artistic designs, which morph depending on the colour scheme you've chosen. If you don't want a picture, choose the bottom-right entry, which is blank.

MASTER THE NEW START SCREEN

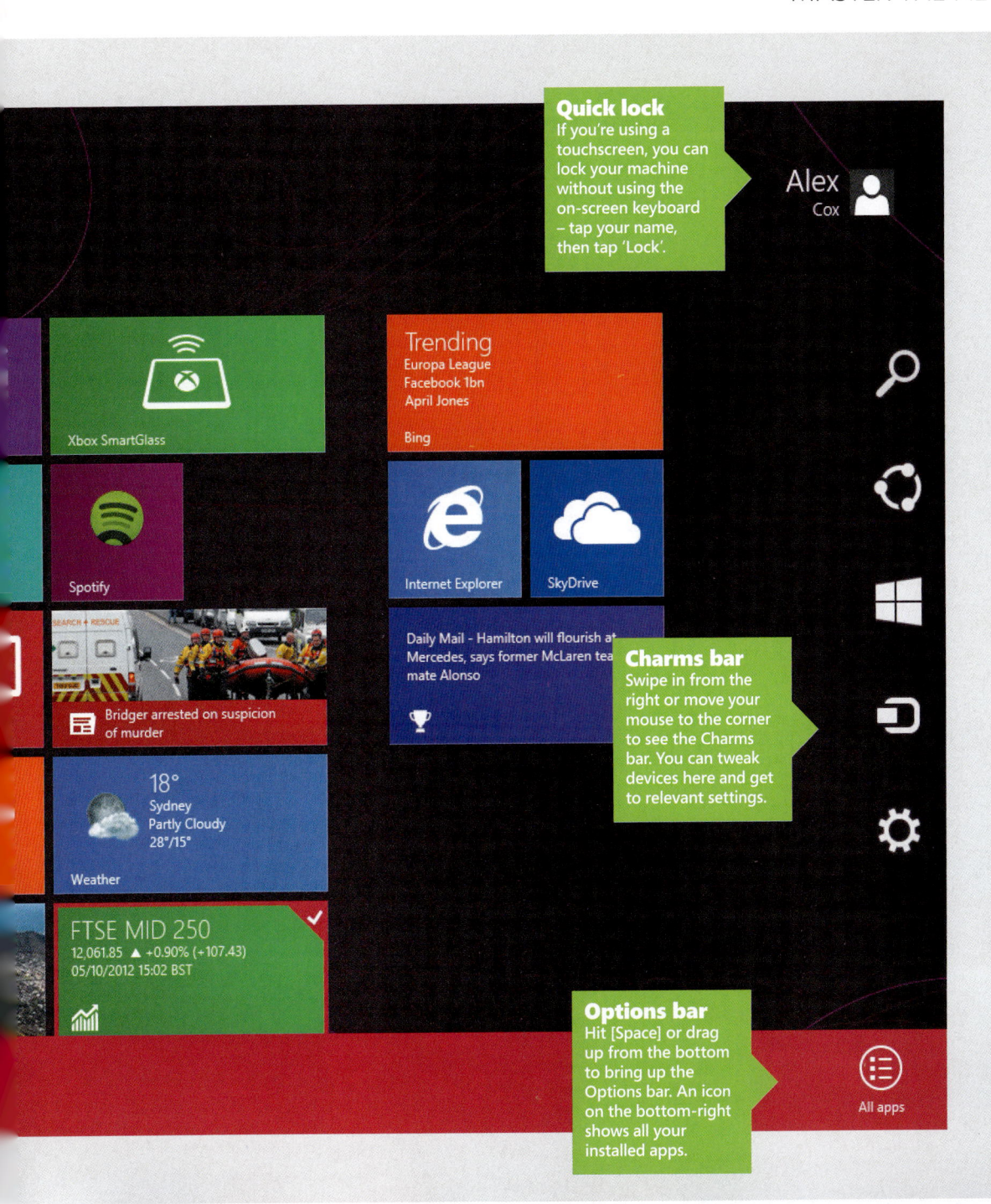

Quick lock
If you're using a touchscreen, you can lock your machine without using the on-screen keyboard – tap your name, then tap 'Lock'.

Jargon buster!

Apps
Standing for applications, apps is the popular term for small programs that you can download directly to your PC, tablet or smartphone.

Touchscreen
Technology that senses the movement and location of your fingers on a screen, and this is used to control the gadget, rather than keyboards or trackpads.

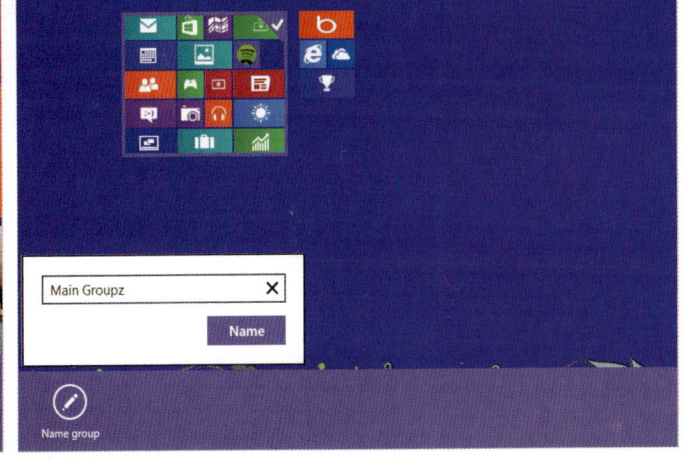

Charms bar
Swipe in from the right or move your mouse to the corner to see the Charms bar. You can tweak devices here and get to relevant settings.

Options bar
Hit [Space] or drag up from the bottom to bring up the Options bar. An icon on the bottom-right shows all your installed apps.

3 Remove items
Back at the Start screen, right-click (or tap and hold) on an item to bring up its options menu. You can uninstall apps completely from your computer, but we find the 'Unpin from Start' option a lot more useful; it clears the icon from your Start screen, but the app remains accessible from the 'All apps' screen, bottom-right.

4 Move and name groups
Use the semantic zoom button (the little minus sign) at the bottom-right to zoom out, or pinch your fingers on a touchscreen. You can drag groups of icons around to rearrange their order, or right-click (or tap and hold) to bring up the option to rename the group. This then appears on the non-zoomed version.

Windows 8: Expert Tips and Tricks   Chapter 1 | 45

Learn how to...

Get the best of both worlds

If you want to use the brand new Start menu and the old-style desktop in Windows 8, you can easily run them side by side with two monitors, giving you the ultimate computer setup

WORKS WITH
Windows 8
Windows 8 Pro
Windows RT

When you hit the 'Desktop' button on the Start screen in Windows 8, you're transported to the familiar-looking desktop you may remember from earlier versions of Windows. It's there when you want to install old-style software that still exists for Windows (instead of apps in the Windows Store) or use vintage programs such as Windows Media Center. If you use the desktop mode as much as the tiled Start screen, flicking between the two can become irritating. But if you have a spare monitor at your disposal, you have a brilliant option, which enables you to see the Start screen on one monitor and the desktop on the other, so you can quickly swap between the two and see what's happening on each at the same time. Try it for size!

Work with two monitors

1 Hook it up
First, you need to get your second screen hooked up to your Windows 8 PC. How you do this depends on the connections on your computer. Most come with a VGA or HDMI input, so you need the appropriate cable to connect PC to screen. If you can't match the connector at both ends, you can easily get an adapter to suit.

2 Simple second
Open the Charms menu on the right-hand side of the screen and choose the 'Devices' option from the list. Then select 'Second screen' and from the four options that appear thereafter, choose 'Extend' – this is the simplest way to enable you to extend your Start screen to a Start screen with desktop.

GET THE BEST OF BOTH WORLDS

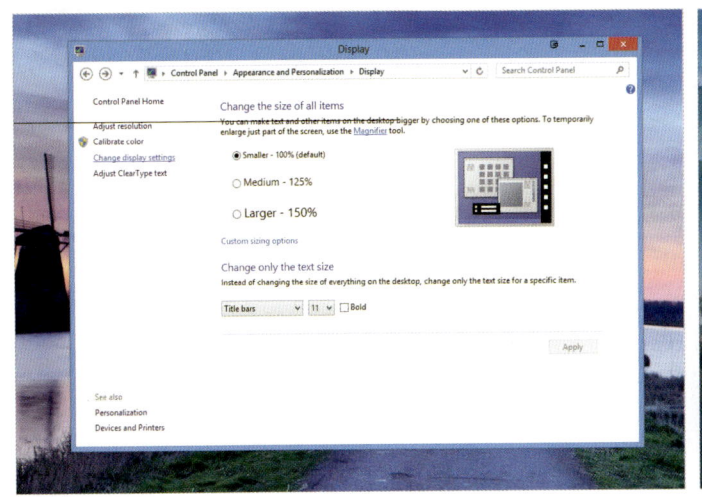

3 Advanced settings
The slightly trickier way of adding a second screen is to use the Display Settings found in the desktop mode. Go to the desktop, right-click it and select 'Personalize' from the menu that appears. Then, in the left-hand side of the screen, hit 'Display' and then select 'Change Display Settings' in the next window.

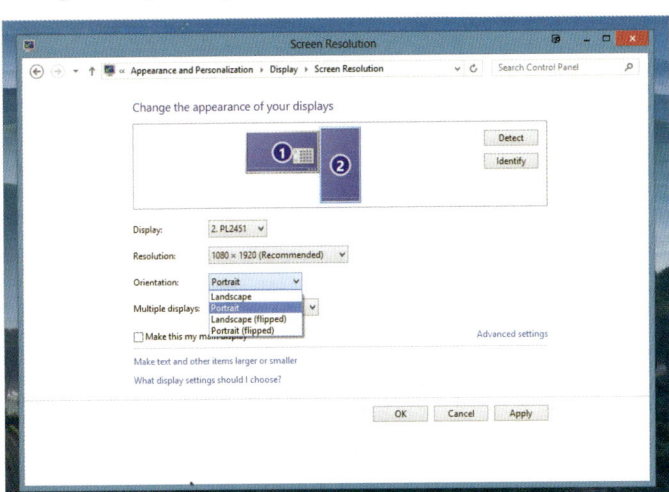

4 Keeping up appearances
Here you need to adjust settings so that they represent the physical setup on your desk. So, if you want the second screen to sit to the left of the main one, drag the number 2 screen to the left of number 1. Change the resolution to suit on your second screen (this depends on the size of screen you've connected it to) and that's it.

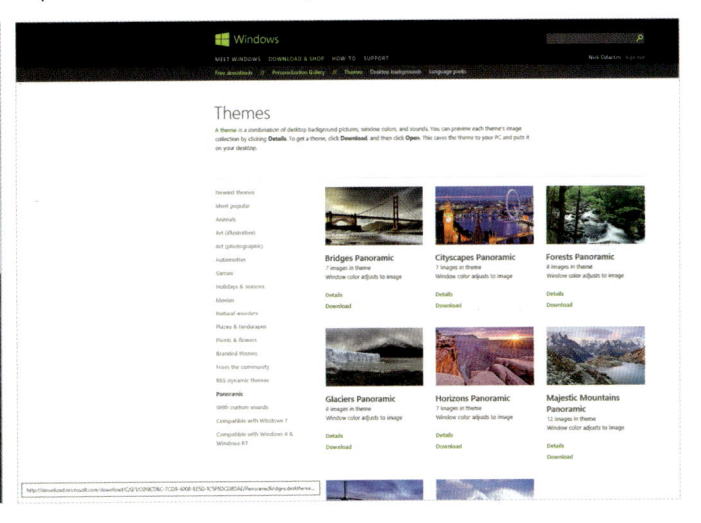

5 Changing orientation
If you have a second screen that rotates on its axis to portrait mode (great for working on documents or reading websites), select display number 2 from the drop-down menu next to 'Display', and select 'Portrait' from the drop-down menu next to 'Orientation'. Now just ensure 'Extend these displays' is selected and press 'OK'.

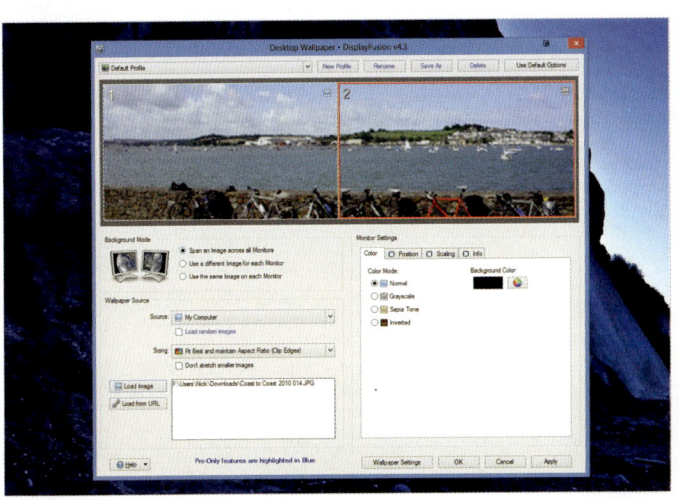

6 Stretch the image
Once your second screen is set up, make it stand out – get an amazing panoramic desktop theme from http://bit.ly/SjtC8O, enabling you to stretch one image across two screens. To activate it, download and install it, and it automatically displays. Alternatively, right-click the desktop and select 'Personalize' to change to another.

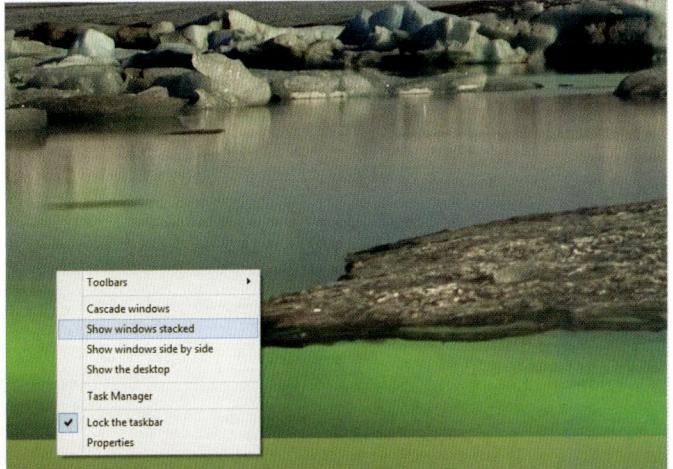

7 Get more functionality
DisplayFusion (www.displayfusion.com) is a great tool that gives you more control over your dual monitor setup. You can use it to display one of your images across the two monitors. Select 'Span an image across all monitors', then click 'Load from > My computer'. Check out http://bit.ly/XmaCtG for specially designed wallpapers.

8 Organise windows in a few clicks
Having more than one monitor means you have lots more space for extra windows, which makes it much easier to work in several programs at once. Windows can automatically arrange these windows so they are all neatly displayed over both monitors. Simply right-click the Taskbar and select 'Show windows stacked'.

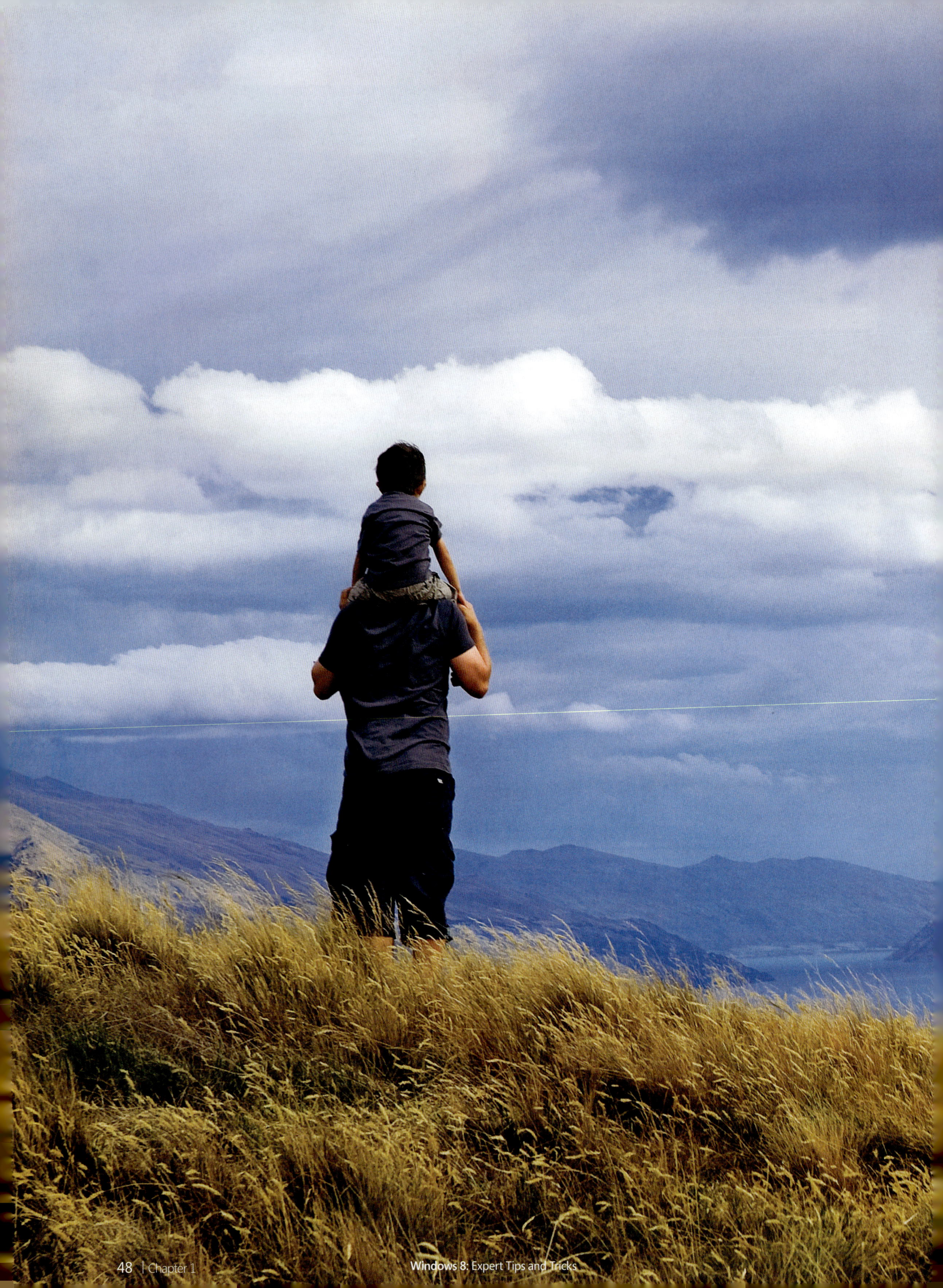

Explore features

TRY THIS!
Type with the touch keyboard
56

Discover more about how Windows 8 works

Section 3

50	Windows 8 apps
52	Exploring Explorer
54	Easy Transfer
56	The touch keyboard
58	Search in Windows 8
60	Master Jumplists
64	Explore the Action Center
66	Essential apps

DO THIS NOW...

Get more done with apps

Windows 8 apps have more features than you'd think

Use the App bar

The App bar provides extra options for Windows 8-style apps – right-click the screen or swipe up from the bottom on a touchscreen. The App bar features settings and access to extra features that aren't necessary for the main functions of the app. You can also access the App bar by pressing [Windows]+[Z] in a Windows 8-style app – it doesn't work in the desktop. Just pressing [Windows] always brings up the Start screen. If you want to cycle through apps, swipe in from the right to switch or use the top-left hot corner if you have a mouse. You can use [Alt]+[Tab] to show what's running, as you always could on any version of Windows.

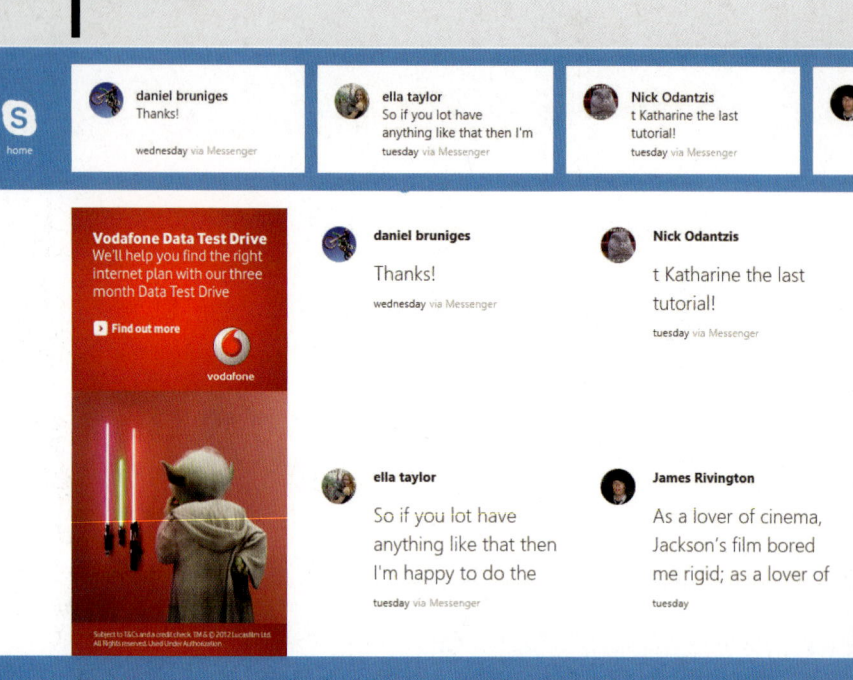

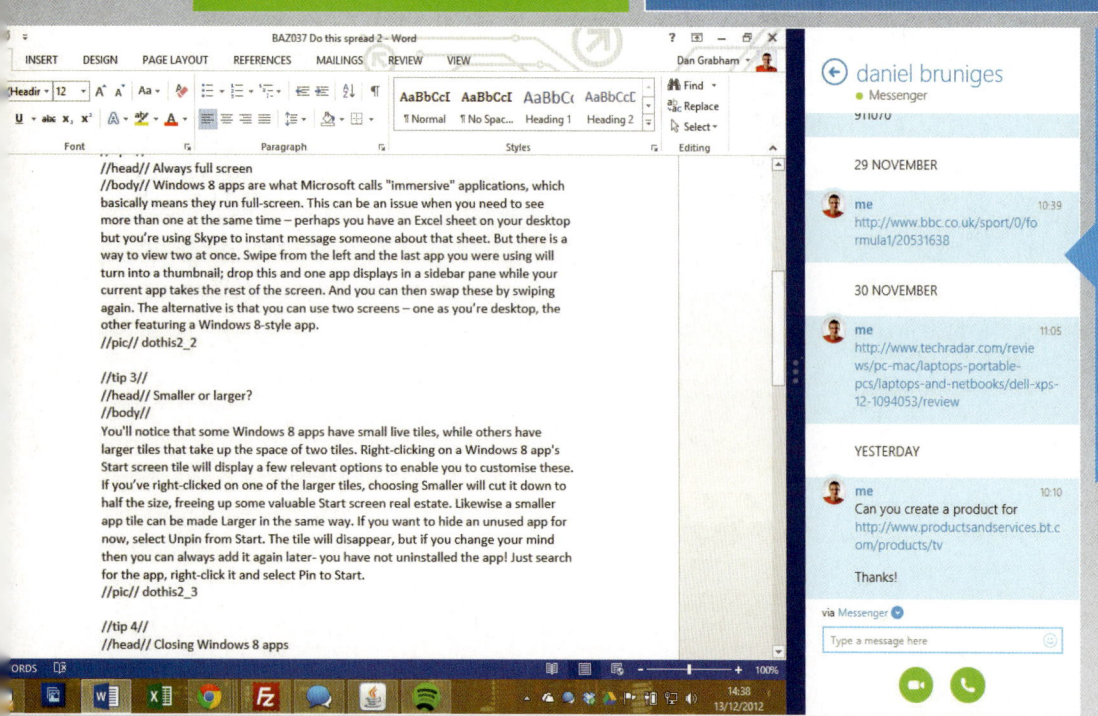

Always full screen

Windows 8 apps are what Microsoft calls immersive applications, which means they run full-screen. This can be an issue when you need to see more than one at once – perhaps you have an Excel sheet on your desktop but you're using Skype to instant message someone about that sheet. But there is a way to view two at once. Swipe from the left and the last app you were using turns into a thumbnail; drop this and one app displays in a sidebar while your current app takes the rest of the screen. Swap them by swiping again. Alternatively, you can use two screens (see page 46 to find out how to set up dual monitors).

GET MORE DONE WITH APPS

Smaller or larger?

Some Windows 8 apps have small Live tiles, while others have larger tiles that take up the space of two. Right-clicking on an app's Start screen tile displays a few options to enable you to customise these. If you've right-clicked on one of the larger tiles, choosing 'Smaller' cuts it down to half the size, freeing up some valuable Start screen space. Likewise, a smaller tile can be made larger. If you want to hide an unused app for now, select 'Unpin from Start'. The tile disappears, but if you change your mind, you can always add it again later – you have not uninstalled the app. Just search for the app, right-click it and select 'Pin to Start'.

Closing apps

Unlike desktop apps, Windows 8 apps don't have close buttons. If you want to close an app, move the cursor to the top of the screen. When it turns to the icon of a hand, hold down the left mouse button and drag it down the screen. Your app should shrink to a thumbnail, which you can drag off the screen to close it. But you shouldn't need to close apps – Windows 8 apps are suspended when you switch to something else so they're only a minimal drain on your system, and if you need the resources, they're automatically shut down – the data is saved, so when you re-launch, you can simply carry on from where you left off.

Windows 8: Expert Tips and Tricks

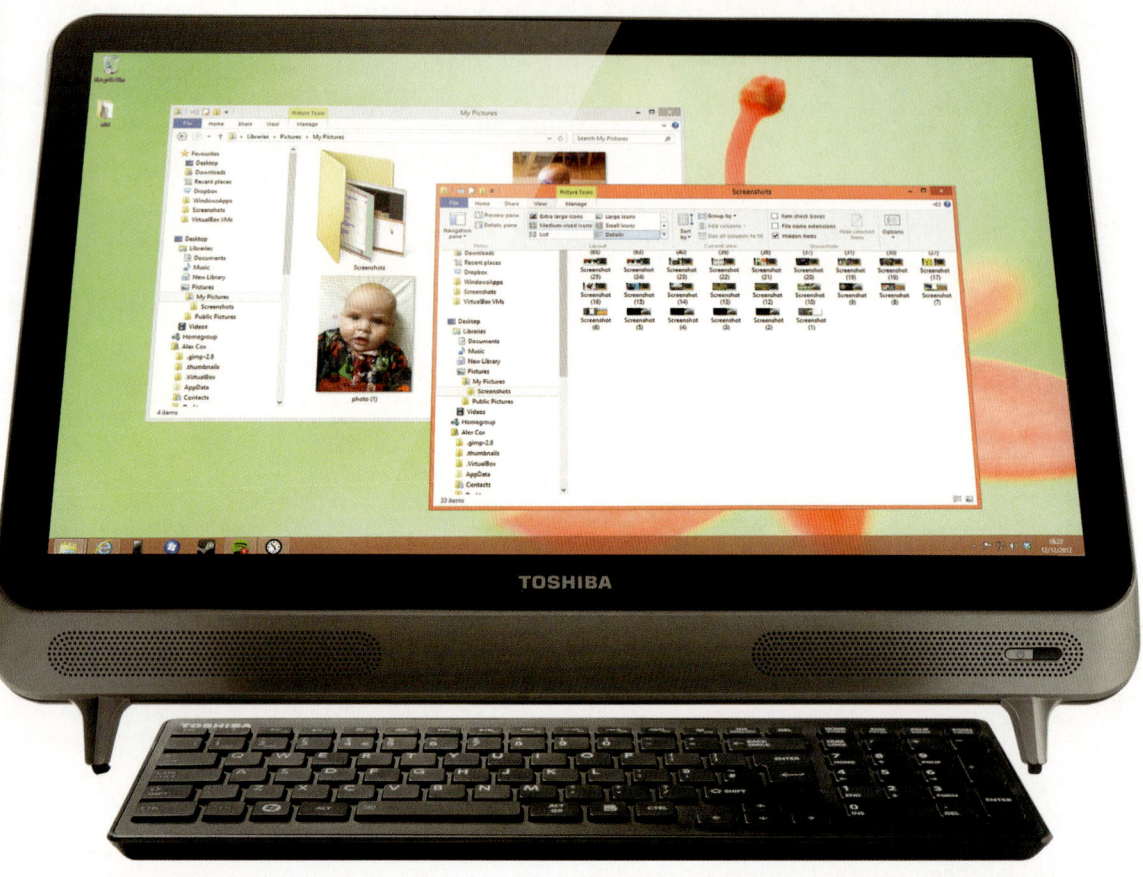

25 TOP TIPS FOR...
Exploring Explorer

Windows Explorer is one of the most crucial parts of Windows 8, but we bet there's lots you don't know about it

1 Here's something you might not know: if you're using a keyboard, you can select multiple files at once by holding [Ctrl] and clicking files you want to highlight. They don't have to be sequential, and if you make a mistake, keep holding [Ctrl] and click the incorrect file to deselect it.

2 If you're using a mouse, there's an easy way to select loads of files at once. Just click in an area of white space, hold the left mouse button down, and draw a box around the files you want to select. Combine this with [Ctrl] to select multiple bundles of files.

3 To select a number of concurrent files in a list, click the top-most item, hold [Shift], and click the item at the bottom. Again, combine this with [Ctrl] to select different bunches.

4 You can use [Shift], [Ctrl] and [Space] in conjunction with the arrow keys to select items without needing to use a mouse at all. It's fiddly, though.

5 We may be teaching our grandmothers to suck eggs here, but copy and paste are incredibly useful. Select a file, a piece of text, a picture, whatever you like, and either right-click and choose 'Copy', or press [Ctrl]+[C]. Now find a place where you want to put what you just copied, then right-click and select 'Paste', or press [Ctrl]+[V].

6 If you don't want to leave the original behind when you're pasting, just use the cut command instead. If you apply it to a file, this is the equivalent

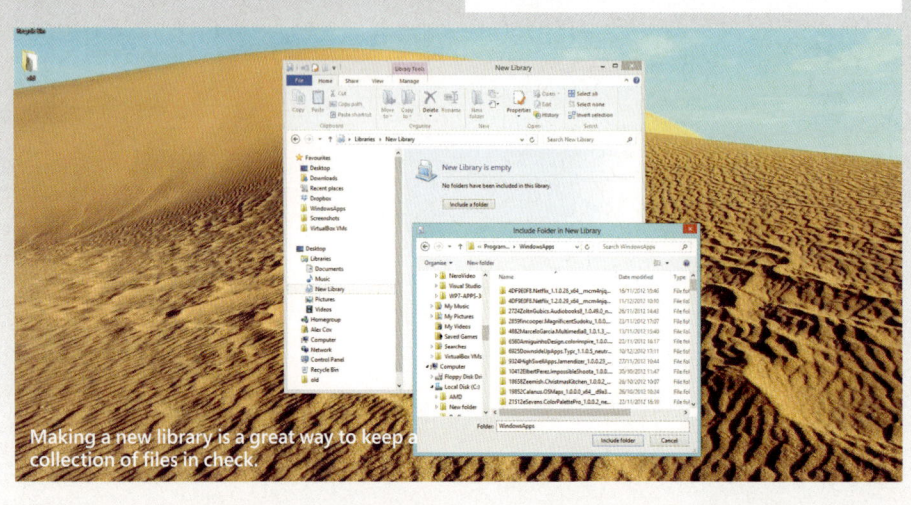

Making a new library is a great way to keep a collection of files in check.

52 | Chapter 1   Windows 8: Expert Tips and Tricks

EXPLORING EXPLORER

of moving it from one place to another. Right-click and select 'Cut', or use [Ctrl]+[X] in place of [Ctrl]+[C].

7 The undo command, [Ctrl]+[Z], is available almost everywhere. You might not see it on a right-click menu, but if you press the keys you should be able to reverse any mistake, from deleting the wrong file to typing something incorrect on the web.

8 The Send To menu (right-click an item in Explorer, then hover over 'Send To' to see it) is a quick way to sort files. You can make new compressed folders, email your item, or even send it to a location, like an external drive.

9 Want to expand the Send To menu? Hit [Windows]+[R] when you're on the desktop, type 'shell:sendto', and pop in a shortcut to whatever you like.

10 There's a quick way to make a shortcut to a file or folder if you're using a mouse. Right-click and hold the file or folder, and drag it to the location you want the shortcut made in. Now just select 'Create shortcuts here'.

11 If you followed the last tip, you'll notice you can also use the right-click and drag manoeuvre to move or copy a file. If you do it in the same folder that the file's in, you make a numbered copy; useful if you want to work on a file without damaging the original.

12 Drag any file, shortcut or folder to an empty spot on the Taskbar to pin it there; that means you can find it again in the future, run it quickly, and drag files to it to run or store them.

13 You can rename files or folders in three ways: two slow clicks on the current name makes it editable; right-click the file and choose 'rename'; or select a file and hit [F2] – handy if you have lots of files to rename.

14 Let's look at the Explorer interface specifically. By default, you have a bunch of folders listed as favourites in the left-hand navigation pane, but these might not be the folders you use frequently. Just drag any folder into this list to add them to it.

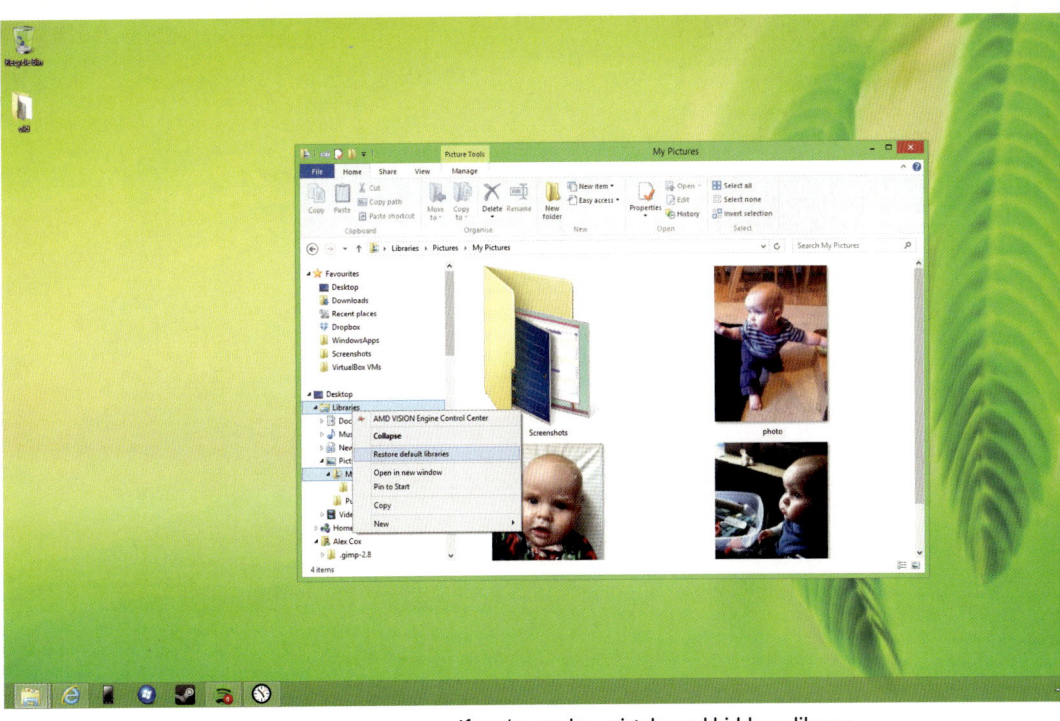

If you've made a mistake and hidden a library you regularly use, you can get it back with just two clicks

15 You'll see the libraries list on the left. You can organise documents, pictures and more here. But there's a lot more you can do with them. Let's start by hiding one of the folders from the list; click 'Libraries' to see them in the main area, right-click one, and check 'Don't show in navigation pane'.

16 If you've deleted a library from the navigation pane by accident, you can uncheck the option you used to remove it, or right-click 'Libraries' and select 'Restore default libraries'.

17 Your libraries can monitor particular folders on your PC – so if, for example, you've got a catalogue of photos, you can attach that folder to the Pictures library. Just right-click the icon for the library of your choice, click 'Properties', then click 'Add' to include the contents of a new folder.

18 You're not restricted to the libraries that come pre-installed. You can create your own to organise whatever you like; we like to use them for podcasts, for example. Right-click in empty space with the Libraries folder open, click 'New', then 'Library', and open it up to link it to a new folder.

19 The view of your new library can be tweaked based on its contents. Open the library in the main folder, click 'Manage' at the top of Explorer, then click 'Optimise library for' and select which kind of files you're storing.

20 By default, any library you create has a generic icon, but you're free to replace it. Click 'Manage/Change icon' and you're presented with a selection.

Quick tips

21 Use the small arrow icon at the top-right of the Explorer window to show or hide the ribbon, which puts useful features at your fingertips.

22 When you've got the ribbon displayed, click on any of the items in the main Explorer window. The buttons on the ribbon relating to the functions you can perform are highlighted.

23 The quick access bar is found right at the top of the Explorer window; you can use it to get the properties of the current file or make a new folder.

24 To add options to the quick access bar, just click the little arrow on its right and check those that you want to display.

25 You can move the quick access bar so that it appears below the ribbon by using the appropriate icon in its customisation menu. It's less pretty than putting it on the title bar, though. ∎

Windows 8: Expert Tips and Tricks   Chapter 1 | 53

Learn how to...

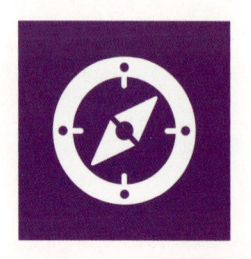

Transfer to Windows 8 with ease
Now you've taken the plunge and upgraded to Windows 8, you'll find it's simple to move files and settings from your old Windows 7 PC

WORKS WITH
Windows 8
Windows 8 Pro
Windows RT

When you buy a new computer, you might think that you are going to have to spend hours copying files across from your old machine, folder by folder, tweaking the desktop so that it looks exactly the way it used to, and adding your favourite shortcuts to the menus. However, you can do the job a whole lot faster with Windows Easy Transfer instead. It helps you to migrate all your important files and settings, such as digital photographs, contacts or favourites, from your old Windows 7 computer to a new Windows 8 one – so everything is ready to use just like before. Windows Easy Transfer is pre-installed in both Windows 7 and Windows 8, and in this tutorial we're going to show you how to use it so that your new Windows 8 machine is up and running just the way you like it in no time at all.

Move your documents

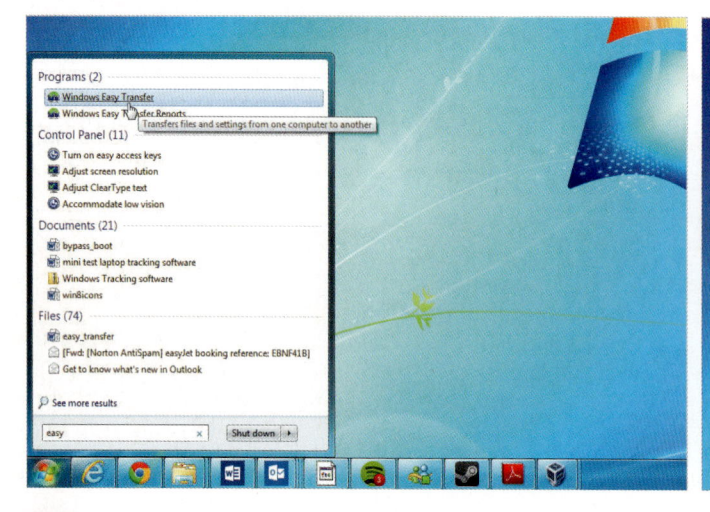

1 Start Windows Easy Transfer in Windows 7
On your old Windows 7 machine, click the 'Start' button and in the search box type 'Easy'. From the list that comes up, select 'Windows Easy Transfer'. From the screen that now opens, select 'Next' and then choose your method for transferring your files to your new computer.

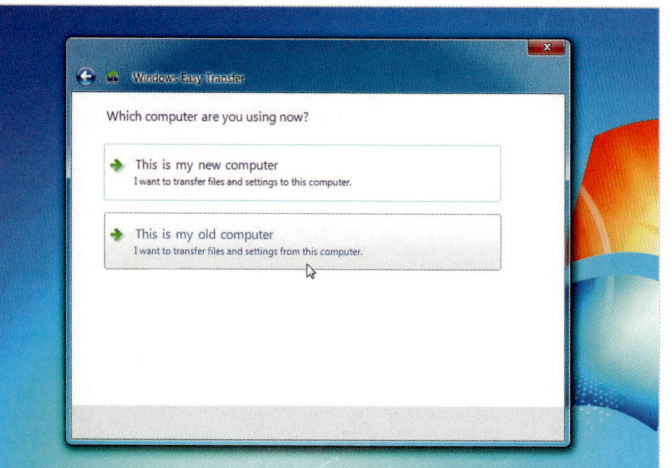

2 Find your documents
We selected 'An external hard disk or USB flash drive', as that is the most popular method of transferring files. Then select 'This is my old computer'. Windows Easy Transfer now scans your PC for your files and documents. It lets you know how much space the documents take up – so make sure your USB drive can handle it.

TRANSFER TO WINDOWS 8 WITH EASE

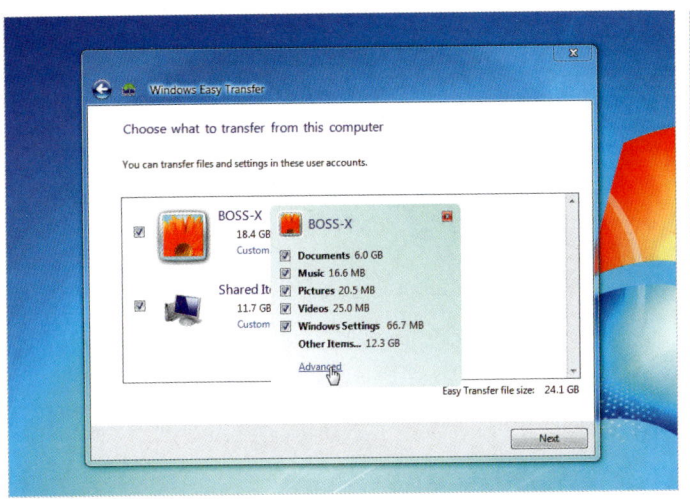

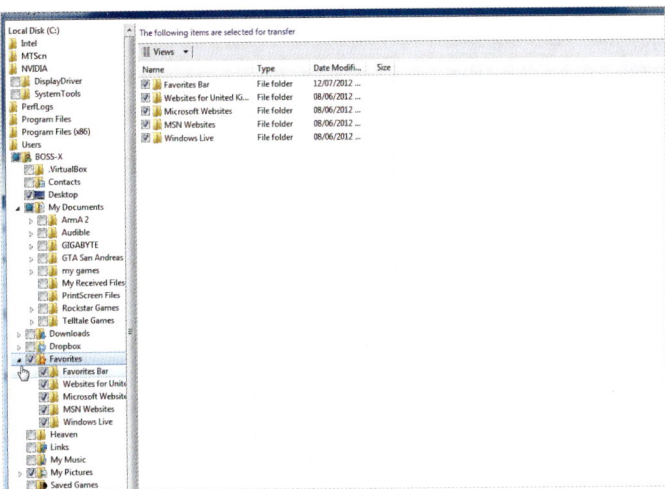

3 Select what you want to transfer over
Windows Easy Transfer is pretty good at guessing what you need to transfer over, but it might include some files you don't need, or exclude ones that you do, so click 'Customise' to quickly add or exclude files, such as 'Pictures'. You can click 'Advanced' for a selection of even more options.

4 Advanced selection of documents
From the advanced screen, you can tick or untick any folder you want to move to your new PC. This may seem overwhelming but it's a good way to make sure you transfer the essentials. Click the arrow next to any folders you include to get a list of folders and files included. Uncheck any folders you don't want. Click 'Save' to finish.

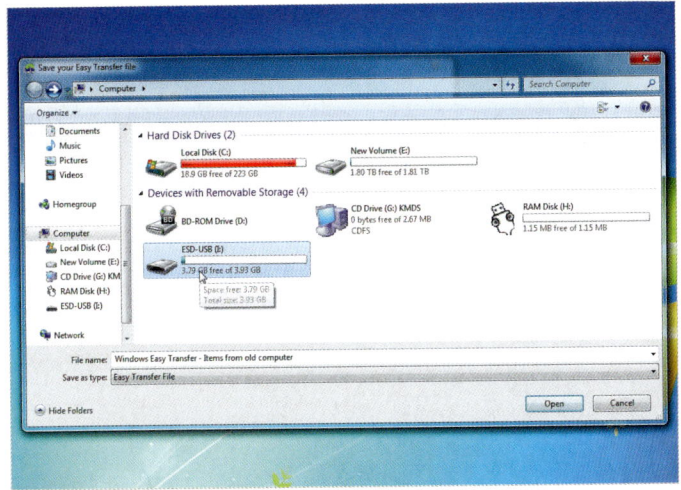

5 Save your files and settings
Click 'Next' if you want to add a password to protect your files. Click 'Save' and then select where you want to save the settings. Plug in the USB drive you want to use and select it, then press 'Save'. Windows Easy Transfer now saves your files to the location you chose. Depending on the device, it may take a few minutes.

6 Open Easy Transfer in Windows 8
On your new PC, plug in the USB drive on which you saved your files and settings in step 5, then open the Search charm in Windows 8 by hovering your mouse cursor (or touching the touchscreen) in the top right-hand side of the screen. Type 'Easy' in the search box, click 'Apps', then select 'Windows Easy Transfer'.

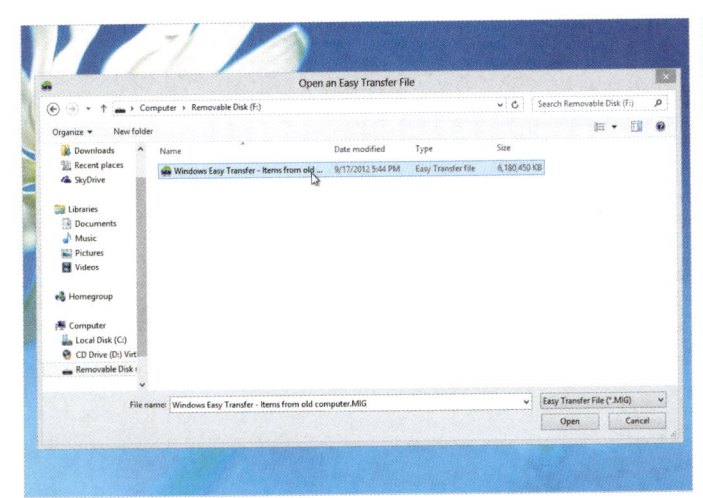

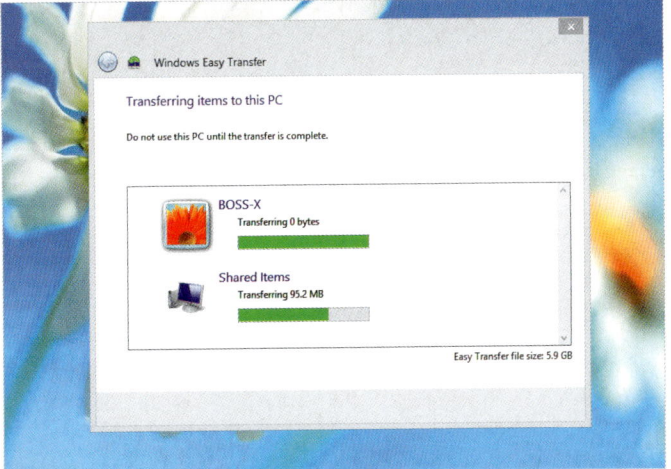

7 Transfer your files
Now follow the Windows Easy Transfer wizard as you did in Windows 7, but when it asks you which PC you are using now, select 'This is my New PC'. On the next page, select 'Yes' and then browse to the USB drive where you saved the files. Select them, then click 'Open'. Finally, click 'Transfer' to complete the process.

8 Enjoy your new PC!
There you have it, in just a few simple steps you've brought all your important files and settings with you to your new Windows 8 PC. It means you can enjoy all the new features of Windows 8 without missing all the important files and favourites. It's amazing how much time Windows Easy Transfer can save you.

Learn how to...

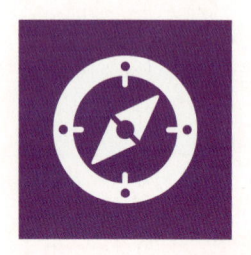

Explore the on-screen keyboard
An invaluable tool for a touchscreen

WORKS WITH
Windows 8
Windows 8 Pro
Windows RT

Windows 8 has been designed from the ground up to work brilliantly with **touchscreen** devices. One of the ways in works it so well with touchscreens is with the on-screen keyboard, which enables you to type on your screen just as easily as if you had a physical keyboard attached to your device. The large keys in particular help with fast typing, making it quick and responsive. We guide you through using the on-screen keyboard below. And even if you don't have a touchscreen display, you can still bring up the keyboard and use your mouse to type with it. It might sound a little pointless, but it's actually a very good way of securely entering sensitive passwords.

Using the keyboard

1 Keyboard options
The standard on-screen keyboard replicates a normal physical keyboard, but there are other options that you can select as well. Simply click the keyboard icon that appears on the on-screen keyboard to display more options, enabling you to choose the best one for the way you want to work.

2 Split keyboard
The first alternative keyboard layout is the split keyboard style, with the keys laid out in a more natural way, similar to ergonomic keyboards. You may find it more comfortable to use this style of keyboard, although it takes a bit of getting used to if you've been using the more traditional layout.

EXPLORE THE ON-SCREEN KEYBOARD

Jargon buster!

Stylus
A pen-like pointing device that older touchscreen gadgets required. These days you only really need your fingers.

Touchscreen
Technology that senses the movement and location of your fingers on a screen, and this is used to control the gadget, rather than keyboards or trackpads.

3 Handwriting recognition
One of the best things about tablet PCs is that with their flat designs and touchscreens, they can be great for writing on as though they were paper, using your finger or a **stylus** instead of a pen. Windows 8 comes with some powerful handwriting recognition tools – just select the option from the keyboard's menu.

4 Handwriting help
Click on the icon with the box with a question mark in it to bring up some more options if you're using the handwriting recognition part of the on-screen keyboard. Choosing an option shows a brief animation, which explains how to use the various features of the keyboard.

Windows 8: Expert Tips and Tricks   Chapter 1 | 57

Learn how to...

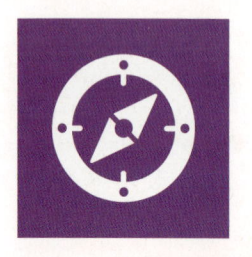

Master search in Windows 8
The search function in Windows 8 has been revolutionised, making it easier than ever to find what you're looking for

WORKS WITH
Windows 8
Windows 8 Pro
Windows RT

Windows 8 is a brand new operating system that does quite a few things differently from its predecessor, which means that being able to quickly find what you're looking for – whether that's important documents, websites, apps or settings – is of the utmost importance. Thankfully, the search function in Windows 8 has been supercharged, and it is now a central feature of the operating system. Getting to know all the tricks you can perform with the improved search function can completely transform the way you use the operating system, as well as boost your productivity.

Search better in Windows 8

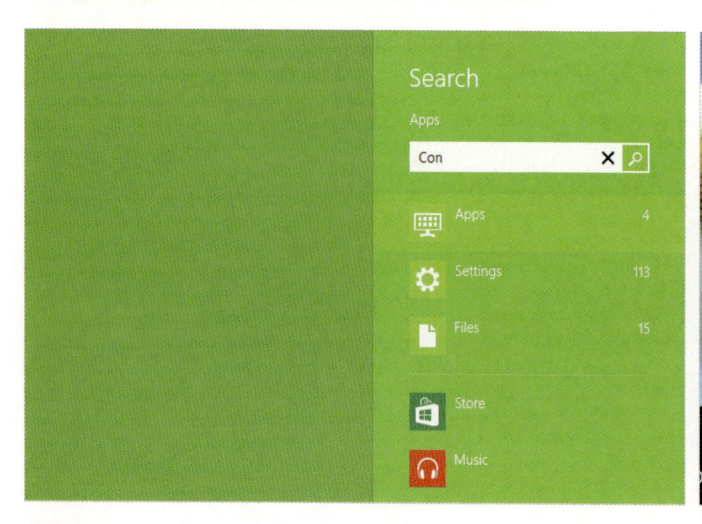

1 Search from the Start screen
In Windows Vista and Windows 7, you could press the [Windows] key to open up the Start menu and then begin typing to search your programs and documents. In Windows 8, it is exactly the same. Simply press the [Windows] key to bring up the Start screen, then just begin typing and Windows 8 starts the search.

2 Use the Search charm
Another way to quickly search from anywhere in Windows 8 is to open up the **Charm bar** of Windows 8. On a touchscreen, you can do this by quickly flicking your finger from the right-hand side of the screen, or with a mouse, simply hover the cursor to the top-right corner of the screen and select 'Search'.

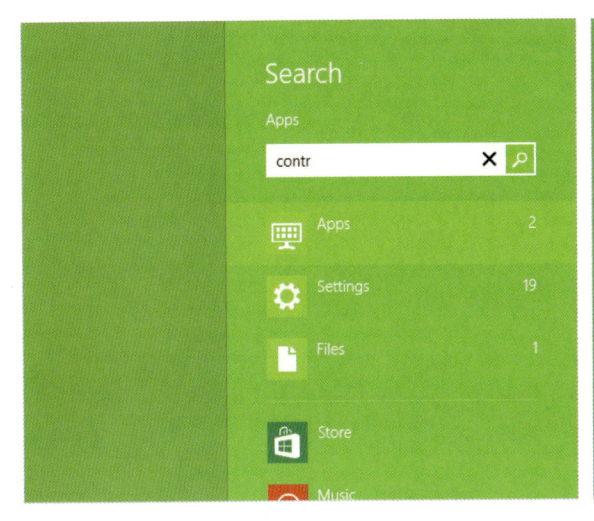

MASTER SEARCH IN WINDOWS 8

3 Begin typing
Now you'll see a text box. As you type, Windows 8 begins searching, so you don't have to wait to get results. The more you type, the narrower the search results become, but sometimes you only need to type part of the name to find what you're looking for.

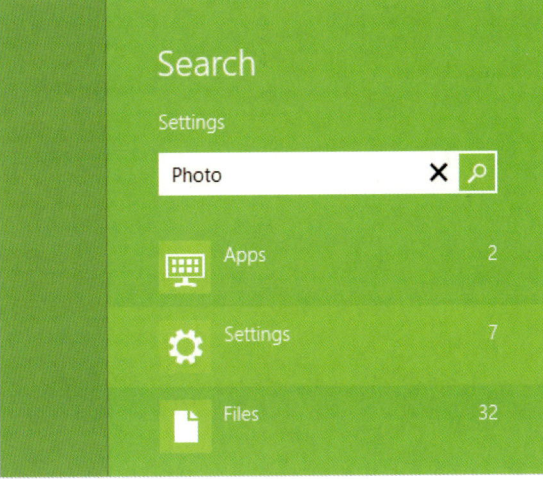

4 Choose what to search for
You'll see three categories beneath the text box: 'Apps', 'Settings' and 'Files', each with a number that indicates how many results the search has found in each category. Clicking on the name of the category displays the results. For a faster search, select the category first.

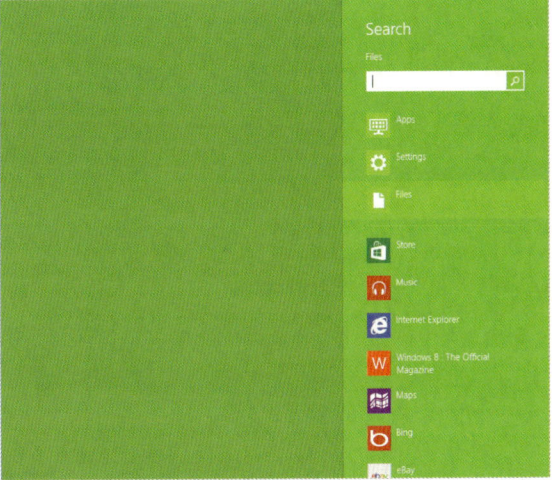

5 Search in apps
When you're searching, you'll see that under the three categories is a list of all the apps you have installed on your Windows 8 device. Clicking an app enables you to search straight from that app. For example, you could type in a postcode, then select the Maps app.

6 Search shortcuts
If using a keyboard, there's a number of shortcuts to speed up search. To search for apps, press [Windows] key and [Q]. To search for settings, tap [Windows] and [W], to search for files, press [Windows] and [F]. If you're in an app, search within it by pressing [Windows] and [Q].

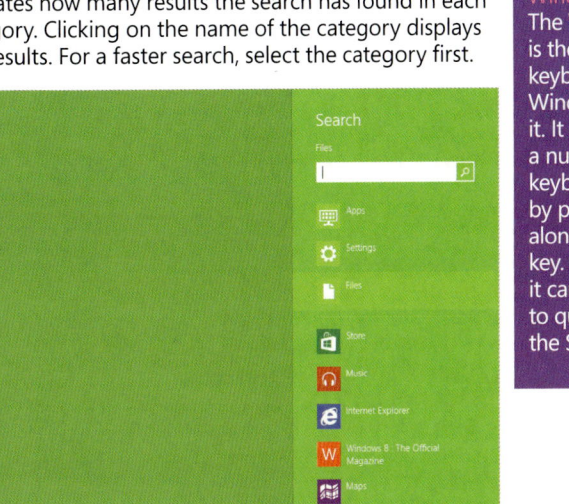

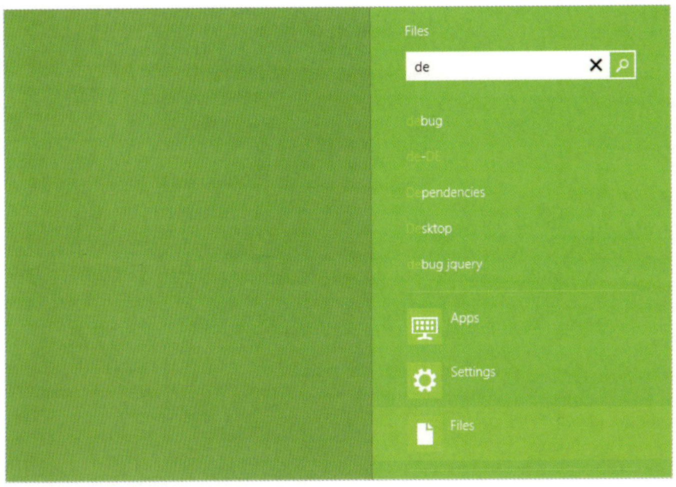

7 Search hints
When searching, Windows 8 displays hints as you type. This can be a great time-saving feature, because one of the hints may be what you were searching for. It can be especially useful when searching in apps or in the Windows Store, if you're not entirely sure about what you're looking for.

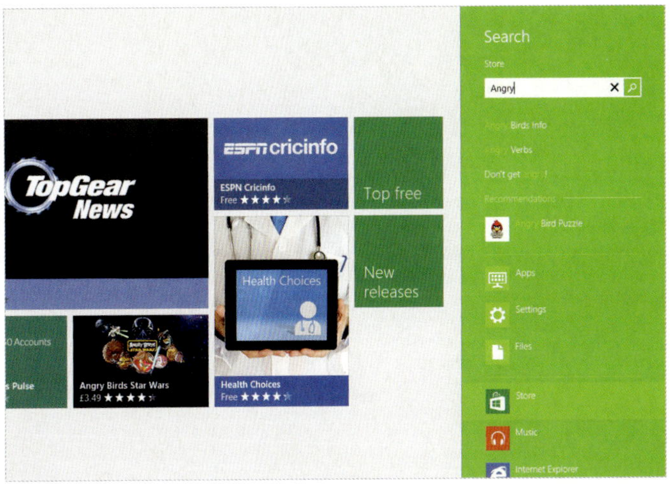

8 Make the most of search
Now you know how to get the best from the Windows 8 search function. In fact, these tips and tricks will help you in any part of Windows 8. For instance, did you know that you can begin typing in the Windows Store to start searching for apps, just as you can in the Start screen?

Jargon buster!

Charm bar
A new feature in Windows 8, which contains five charms: Search, Share, Start, Devices and Settings. You can access them at any time in Windows 8 by either swiping your finger from the right-hand edge of the screen, or by moving your mouse pointer to the top-right or bottom-right of the screen.

Windows key
The Windows key is the one on your keyboard with the Windows logo on it. It can be used in a number of useful keyboard shortcuts by pressing it alongside another key. In Windows 8, it can also be used to quickly bring up the Start screen.

Learn how to...

Master the Jump Lists

Open things easier than ever before

WORKS WITH
Windows 8
Windows 8 Pro
Windows RT

Windows 8 is packed with fantastic features, but none gives you as much control over your files as the Jump Lists. These lists provide easy access to your most common files with just a couple of mouse clicks, and spell the end of those frustrating trawls through all your different document folders, looking for a file that you use all the time. As well as being a brilliant way to save time, clever Windows users have found ways to exploit Jump Lists to make them even more useful. We've been playing around with Jumplist-Launcher, a free application which enables you to build custom lists.

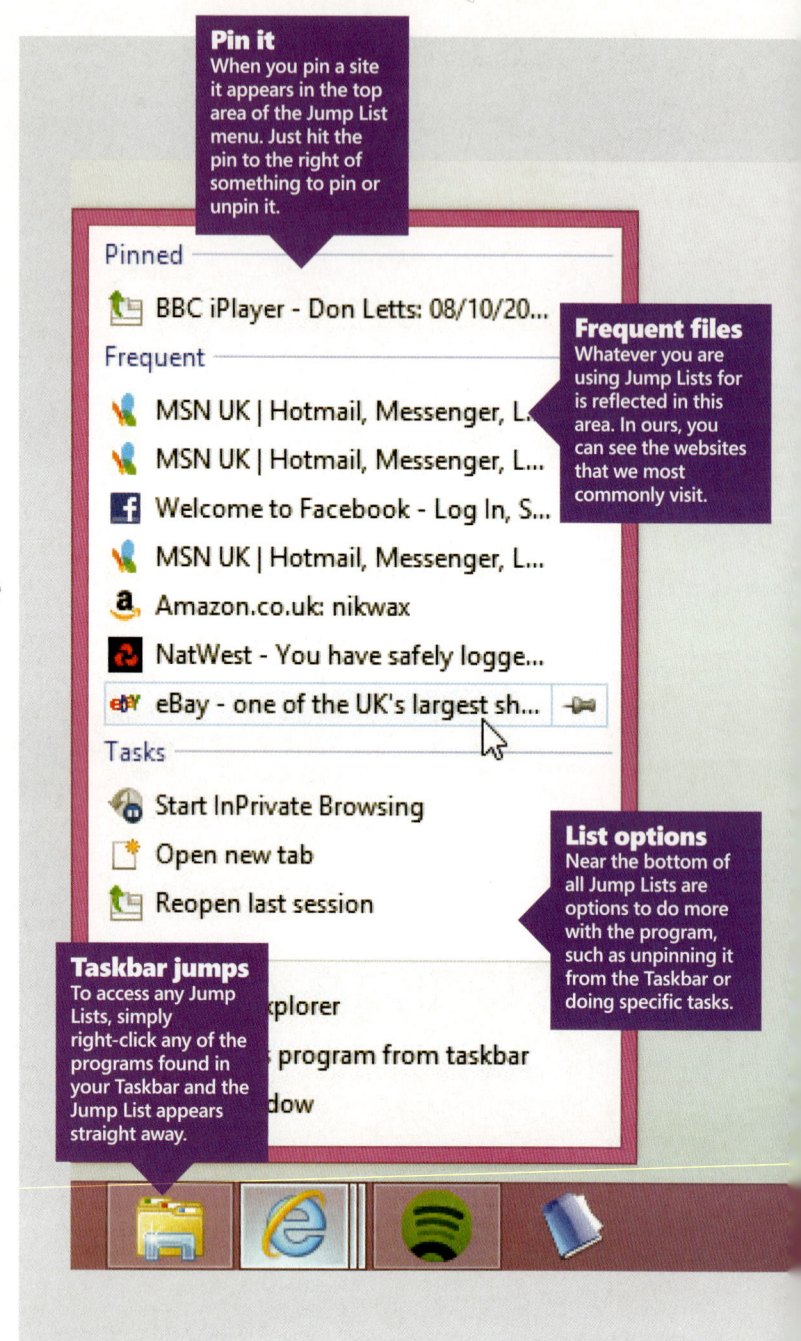

Pin it
When you pin a site it appears in the top area of the Jump List menu. Just hit the pin to the right of something to pin or unpin it.

Frequent files
Whatever you are using Jump Lists for is reflected in this area. In ours, you can see the websites that we most commonly visit.

List options
Near the bottom of all Jump Lists are options to do more with the program, such as unpinning it from the Taskbar or doing specific tasks.

Taskbar jumps
To access any Jump Lists, simply right-click any of the programs found in your Taskbar and the Jump List appears straight away.

Master Jump Lists in Windows 8

1 Pin it down
Apps found on the new Modern UI Start menu reflect the most commonly used programs in your arsenal, and it's possible to add them to your desktop Taskbar right from here. Simply click on one (or more) and right-click the bottom of the screen to activate the menu. Then, click (or tap) on the 'Pin to Taskbar' option to pin it.

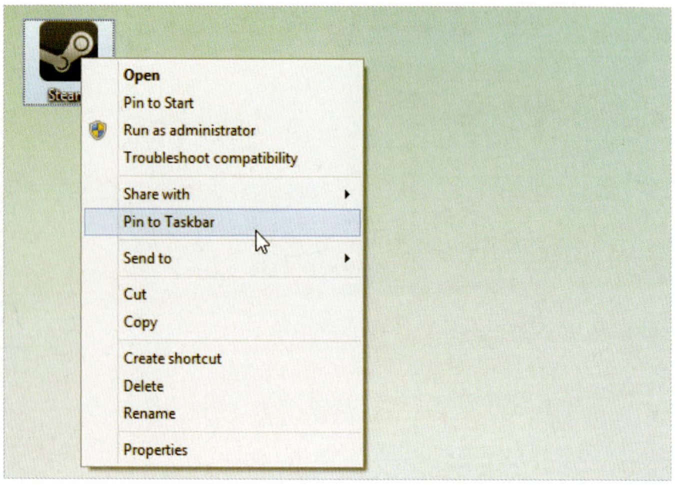

2 Tidy Taskbar
The Taskbar in Windows 8 works as a dock for all your programs, and you can launch your favourite software from there. If there's something you use a lot, pin it to the Taskbar – just right-click on the program icon on your desktop, and choose 'Pin to Taskbar' to put it in place. Add more if you like.

MASTER THE JUMP LISTS

Doing more
We're using Jump Lists in this example to help us do more with Internet Explorer. eBay was opened straight from the Jump List.

Jargon buster!

Icon
A small image or logo that you double-click to access a file, program or folder.

Jump List
A Windows 8 feature where some programs have extra right-click menus, populated by recently-used shortcuts, files, and templates.

Taskbar
The bar at the bottom of the screen, which holds open programs, windows and folders. In Windows 8 you can pin programs to the Taskbar permanently.

Unzip
To make large files smaller, you can zip them up. Do this by right-clicking the file and choosing 'Send to > Compressed folder'. This file is unreadable until it is unzipped, using the right-click menu.

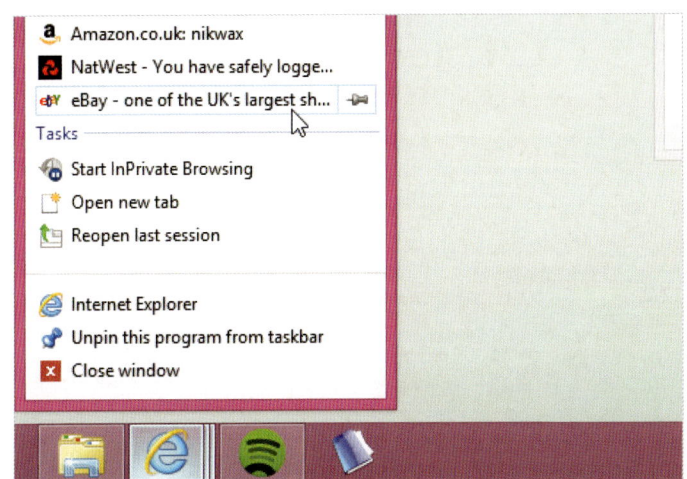

3 Right-click to find the list
Most programs, including Windows Live, Windows 8 programs such as Paint, and a selection of third-party apps, add Jump List functionality to the Taskbar. To access a program's Jump List, just right-click on its Taskbar icon – here, you can open the program or choose from recent files.

4 Save time
When you open files associated with programs on the Taskbar, they appear on the Jump List. By default, there's room for 10, and these change frequently as you open more files. If you want to ensure a file stays on the list, it's possible to fix items in place by clicking the pin icon to the right.

Windows 8: Expert Tips and Tricks · Chapter 1 | 61

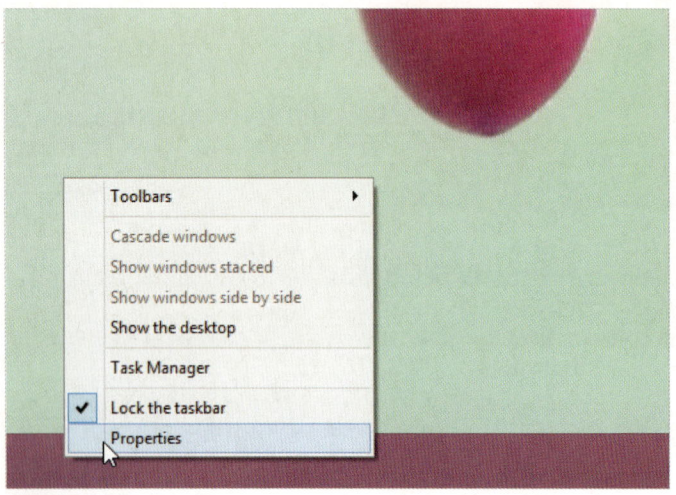

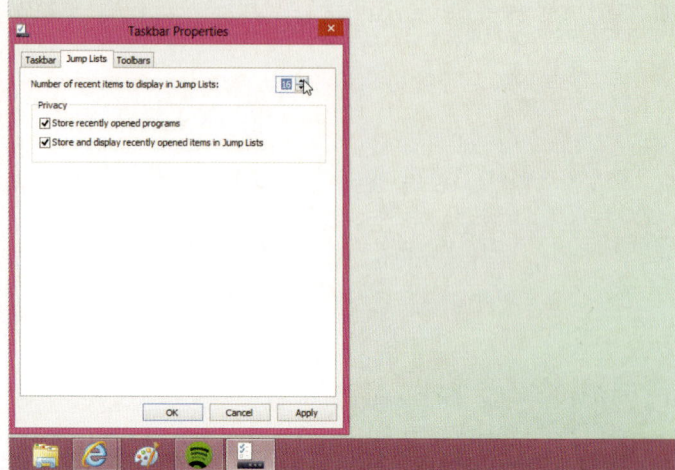

5 More for your money
Like most parts of Windows 8, the Jump List menus are fully customisable, and you can change the size of them according to your tastes using the Start menu properties. To start adjusting your Jump Lists, just right-click the Taskbar and go to 'Properties', click the 'Start menu' tab and choose 'Customize'.

6 Up the number
At the bottom of the Customize window you can increase or decrease the number of entries your Jump Lists display. The default is 10, but you can type in any number you wish, to create massive lists with access to all your files, or save on space with minimalist access as required.

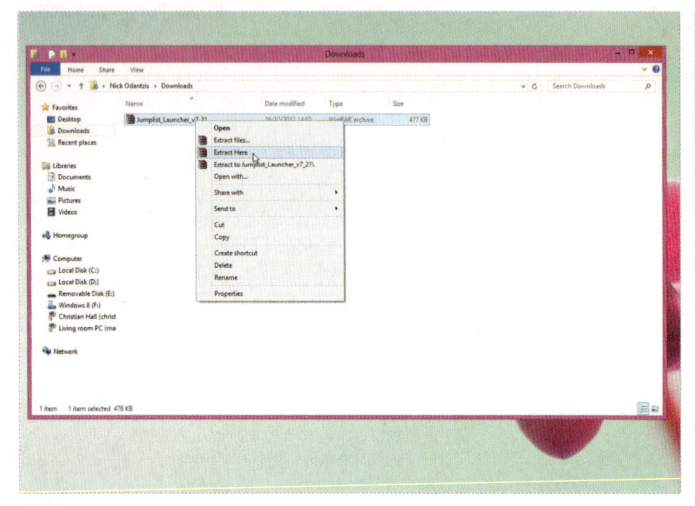

7 Set up Jump Lists
If the Jump Lists in Windows 8 help you work more effectively, try Jumplist-Launcher to build custom Jump Lists, available to download from http://en.www.ali.dj/jumplist-launcher. To open the file, you'll need WinRar which you can get from www.rarlab.com. Click 'Downloads' and pick the 32-bit or 64-bit version.

8 Customise
Once it's downloaded, unzip Jumplist Launcher, install it and as soon as it's set up and running, open it, then drag and drop files, programs or shortcuts into the main window. Once you've done this, it's easy to order your Jump Lists so they're as efficient as possible – just click the up and down arrows at the side.

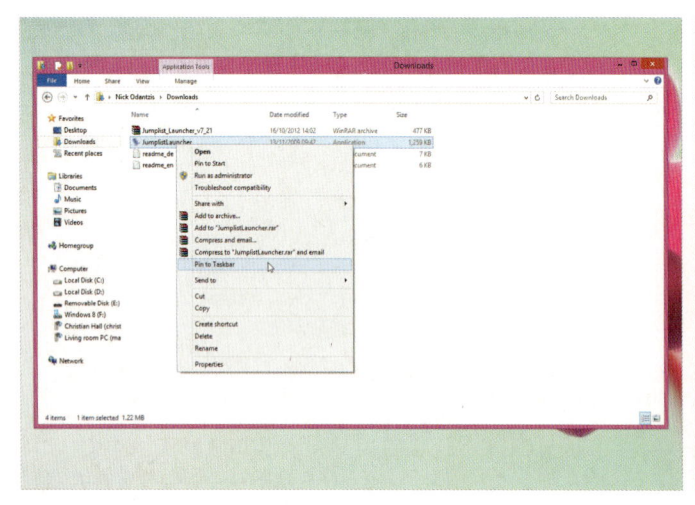

9 Ready when you are
Once you've set up Jumplist-Launcher, you'll want it to stay on the Taskbar permanently, or you will be forced to reopen the program every time you restart your computer. To do this, just right-click the Jumplist-Launcher icon and then choose 'Pin to Taskbar'. Now it is always easy to access whenever you want it.

10 Ready for launch
Now when you start your computer, you can just right-click on the Jumplist-Launcher icon on your Taskbar to bring up the customised list you created earlier. You can pin these in place by clicking the small icons to the right of the items, just as with all your other Jump List options. ■

No.1 FOR WINDOWS
Windows 7 Windows Vista Windows XP

ENJOY COMICS — THE WEB'S FUNNIEST, SENT STRAIGHT TO YOU

VIDEO CHAT — HAVE A 12-WAY CHAT AND RECORD IT, TOO

TURN BACK TIME — FIX PROBLEMS BY RESTORING YOUR PC

100% JARGON FREE!

Windows 7 Help & Advice
Plus essential tips for Windows 8, Vista & XP

REFRESH & REINSTALL
Give Windows the ultimate speed boost – in an hour!
- Revive your PC
- Remove clutter
- Repair a broken system

NEED A NEW PC?
HUGE 18-PAGE BUYER'S GUIDE
Expert reviews of the latest tablets, laptops and all-in-ones

10 ways to improve your PC's security

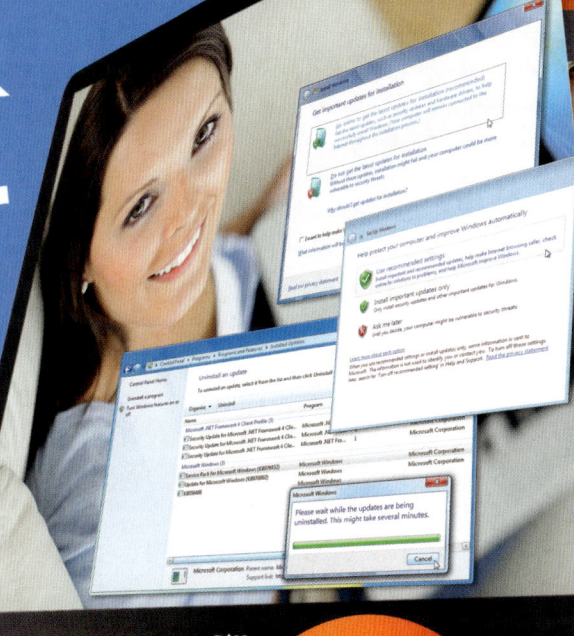

Do this today... **USE MULTIPLE MONITORS**

DO YOU NEED HELP WITH WINDOWS?
EVERY ISSUE OF WINDOWS 7 HELP & ADVICE IS PACKED WITH ESSENTIAL TIPS AND TRICKS!

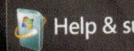

Windows tutorials | New things to do | Buying advice | Help & support | 100% jargon free

Learn how to...

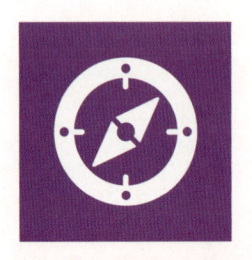

Master the Action Center

Discover all you need to know about the Action Center – it's your one-stop-shop for all system messages, warnings and updates in Windows 8

WORKS WITH
Windows 8
Windows 8 Pro
Windows RT

The Action Center was first introduced in Windows 7 and it remains an essential feature in the new operating system. It brings together all the warnings and pop-up messages you see in Windows. Action Center checks many security and maintenance-related items of your computer. When you upgrade your PC to Windows 8, Action Center tells you about the applications that you need to upgrade, for instance. When the status of something Action Center is keeping an eye on changes – perhaps your antivirus software is out of date – Action Center lets you know. You may see a pop-up appear from its Taskbar icon. Also, the status of the item within Action Center changes colour to reflect the severity of the message. Windows 8 then recommends a course of action.

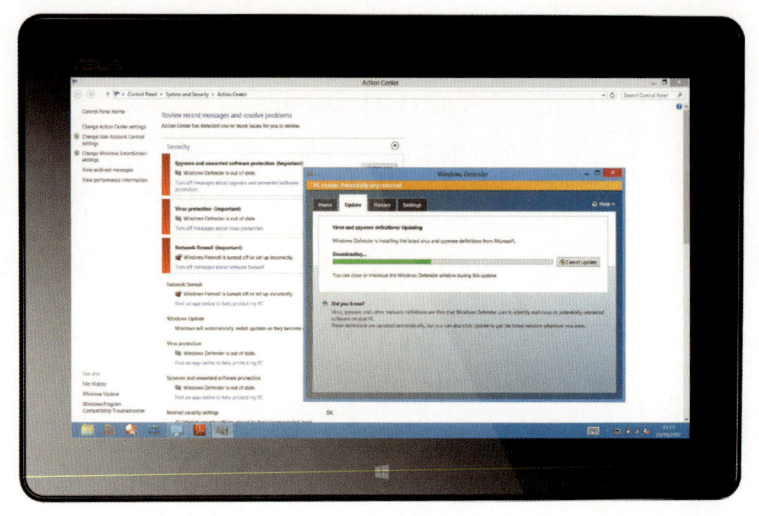

Customise the Action Center

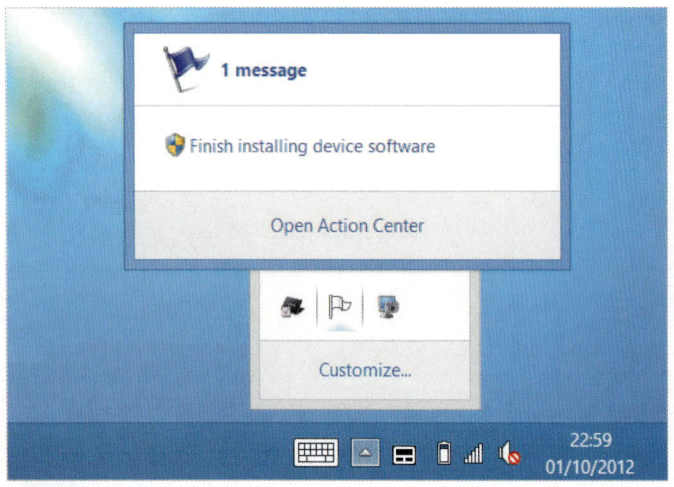

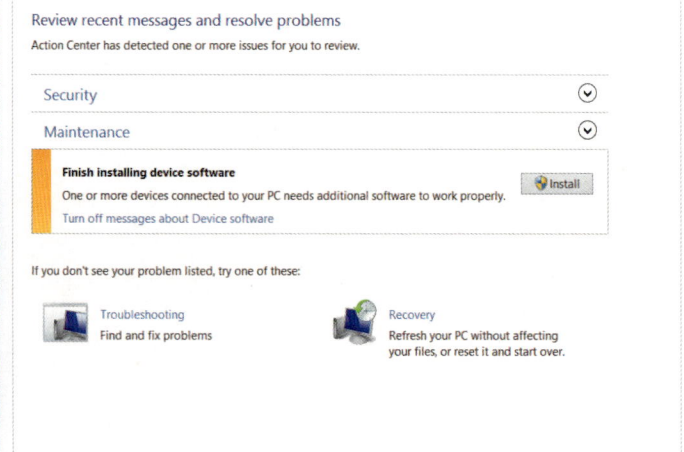

1 See the notifications
Action Center appears as a small icon in the **notification area** on your Taskbar. Right-click the icon and you'll see a pop-up telling you of outstanding issues and any other problems. As you can see, we have one issue, though you'll probably have a couple of issues, especially when you first install or use Windows 8.

2 Defending your PC
Click 'Open Action Center' on the pop-up (you can also right-click the icon or search for it in your Start menu). As you can see, there are three issues displayed on this screen – the extras are that we haven't set up **Windows Backup** yet, to save copies of our files, and **Windows Defender** hasn't been updated either.

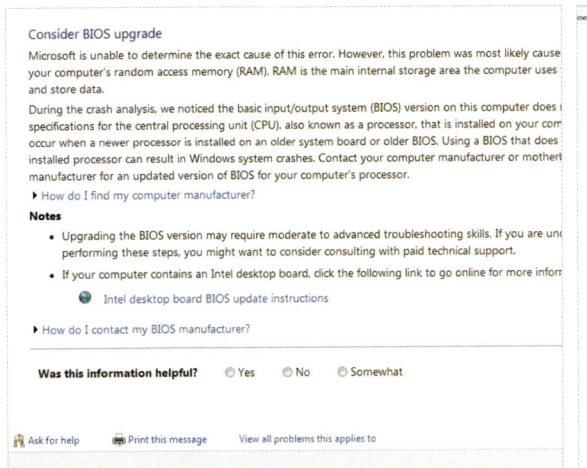

MASTER THE ACTION CENTER

> **Jargon buster!**
>
> **Notification area**
> The portion of the Taskbar that displays icons for features that are always available.
>
> **Windows Backup**
> The software within Windows 8 that enables you to schedule file backups.
>
> **Windows Defender**
> An application that helps protect your computer against pop-ups and spyware.

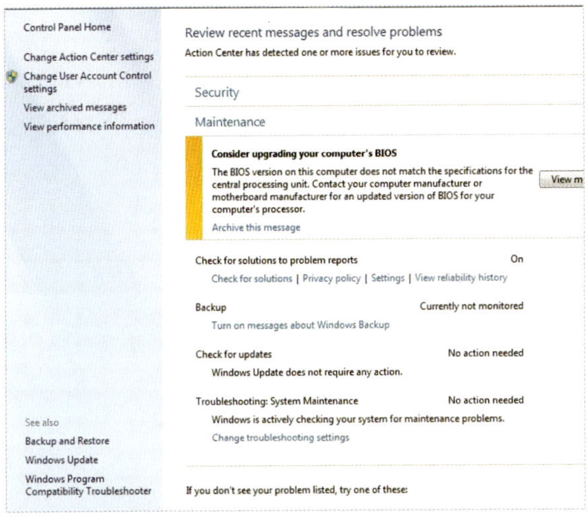

3 Perform the action
Each issue has an action to perform alongside it – we've set Windows Defender to update. This is what the screen looks like when you view message details to see extra information. The Action Center recommends the best course – here it's downloading an update.

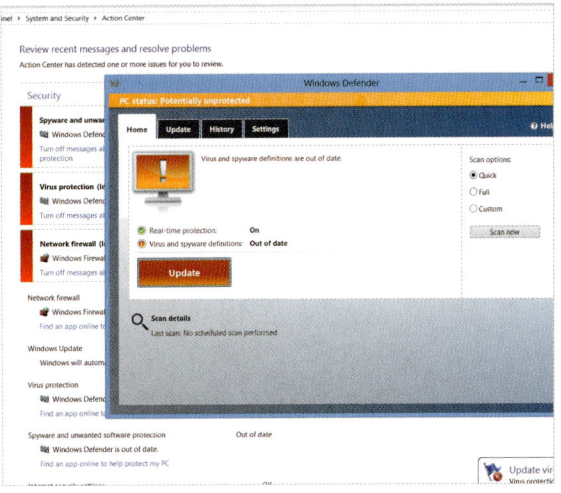

4 Sort security
One of the most important things in Windows 8 is to make sure that you are protected from any harmful viruses. Underneath Security, make sure that your firewall and protection are turned on and fully up-to-date to deal with any new threats. Take heed of the warning!

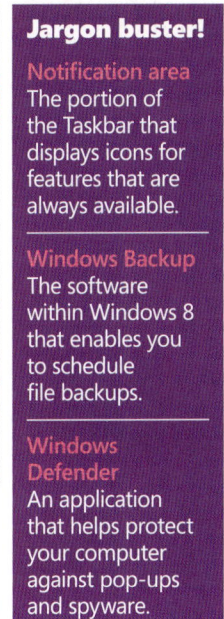

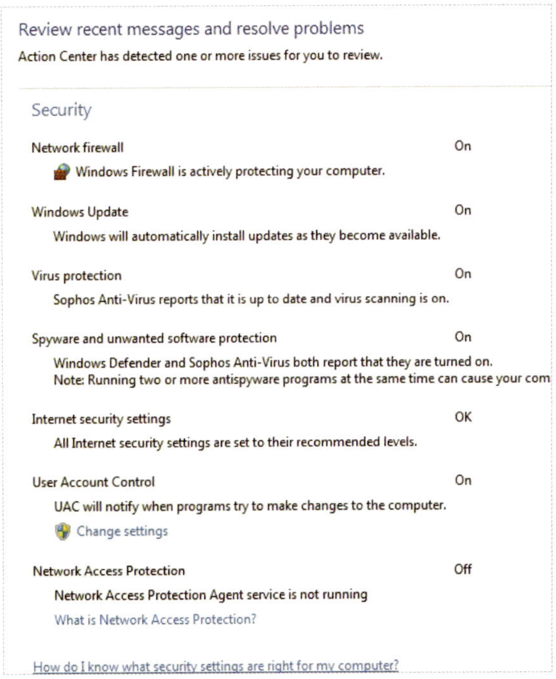

6 Get on top of security
While you're having a look around Action Center, it's definitely worth taking some time to check out the contents of the Security section. In here you'll be able to see exactly what kind of spyware and antivirus protection you currently have on your computer, and if you need to update it. Here you can see that Windows 8 is reporting that both Windows Defender and our third-party antivirus application are running smoothly.

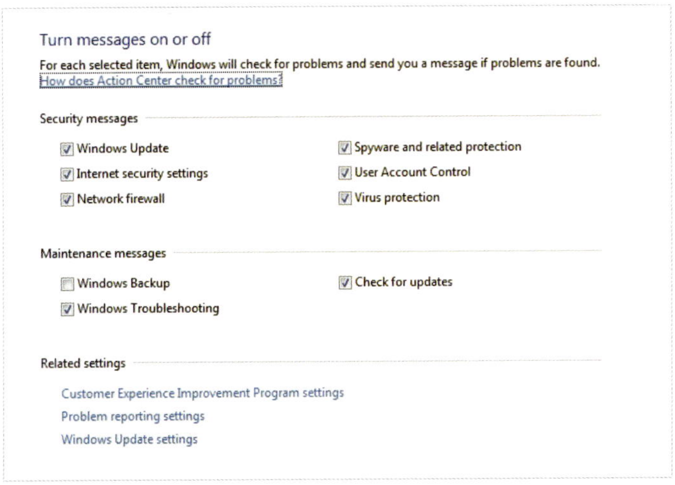

5 Expand and contract
You can display or hide extra information using the arrows on the top-right. Here you can see the activities being monitored – our system is set to 'Check for solutions to problem reports' automatically, so it looks online for solutions to any issues it encounters.

7 Change settings
From the main Action Center window, you can configure settings – click on 'Change Action Center Settings'. Here you can select the items you will get warnings about. You can also fine-tune Windows Update – the system Windows 8 uses to download updates to your computer – using the link from here.

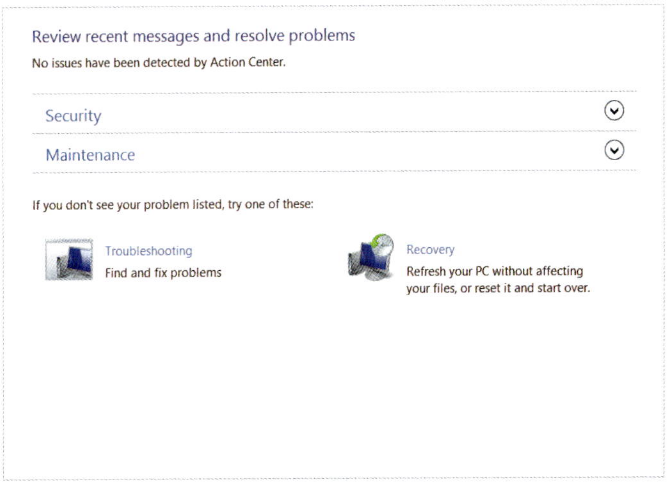

8 And that's it!
Once you've sorted out the issues shown in your Action Center, you'll have a window that looks like this – rather empty. Windows may flag up some issues from time to time, though, such as new updates for software and drivers, as well as any issues with your antivirus, backup or internet security.

Learn how to...

Install these essential free apps
The Windows Store is positively packed with apps, but if you feel spoilt for choice, here are our top recommendations to download for free

1 OneNote MX
Take notes anywhere
Everyone uses their Windows computer for surfing the internet and, more often than not, that involves planning your holidays and travels, finding new recipes and all sorts of other kinds of research. OneNote MX is an app version of the popular office tool, which enables you to create huge notebooks full of ideas and findings from the web. You can copy and paste web pages in, type notes and then share them between devices. OneNote MX isn't just limited to Windows PCs; it's available on tablets and smartphones, too, so you can have access to that bespoke recipe book or awesome travel journal wherever you are in the world. What's more, if your Windows tablet is compatible with a pen or stylus, as many are, you can write hand-drawn notes just as though it were an ordinary notepad.

2 FotoEditor
Edit and share your photos and memories
This nifty free app enables you to make quick edits to your digital photos so that they look their best when posting to social networking sites. You can add filters and crop out the bits you don't need before saving your image, ready to be shared and enjoyed by friends and family.

3 Tuba.fm
Discover music you love in Windows 8
Music and entertainment is a huge part of Windows 8, so this app for discovering new tunes that you're sure to love is essential for music fans. Tuba.fm starts you off with an artist you like, then takes you on a journey of musical discovery through similar artists.

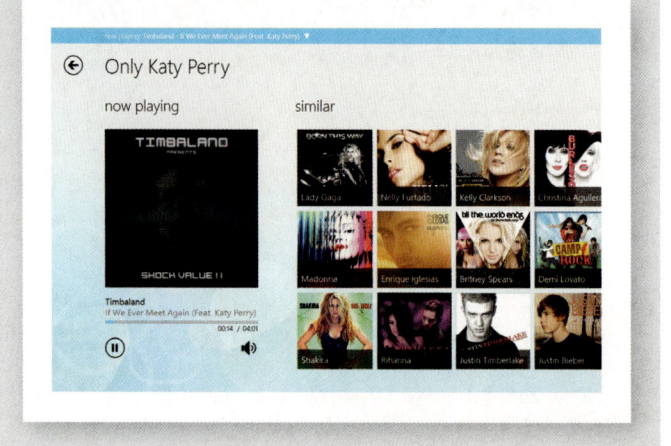

ESSENTIAL FREE APPS

Top Tip!

Get pinning
Any app can be pinned to the Start screen so it can be launched fast. Just drag it from the apps list to anywhere on the Start screen.

Switch apps fast
Cycle through apps by clicking in the top-left or sliding your finger from the left edge on touchscreen devices. [Alt] + [Tab] also cycles through apps.

4 iCookbook
Mouth-watering photography

This recipe app by Bewise is the best we have seen yet for the Modern UI style. Along with over 200,000 recipes, we're also impressed by its food photography. In fact, we're a bit too impressed with it, because it keeps making us rather hungry. Time has been taken to make sure it's easy to follow the recipes and everything is presented in a nice large font.

5 Sky News
Stylish picture-led layouts

One of the finest news apps available for the Windows 8 interface, Sky News has gone for a picture-led layout. The top stories greet you as you enter the app, and you can scroll right to see available videos and categories. UK News, World News, Business, Politics, Showbiz and Sport are the main ones, though there's another called Strange for those quirky stories you might have missed. Clicking into a story shows you the text in a nice readable font that works well whether you have a touchscreen device or are just reading on a desktop PC. You can tap or click the right or left of the screen to switch between stories, so if you're using a tablet, you can use your thumbs to tap through all the stories in the app. It's a really nice implementation for Windows 8.

6 National Rail
Never miss your train home again

This smart app not only lets you find information about your train home, but also enables you to pin your local station to the Windows 8 Start screen. It puts an end to laborious searches on the internet, instead giving you access to the information you need straight from your Windows 8 screen.

8 Daily Motion
One-stop-shop for amazing entertainment

If you think of YouTube and strip out the annoying homemade videos made by one of the internet's most vile communities, you have Daily Motion. It's a world packed with great video entertainment and this app deserves to take pride of place on your Start screen.

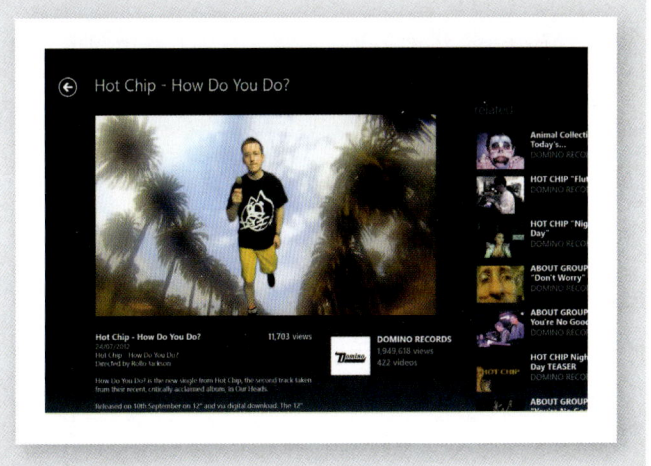

7 Kindle
Read the latest titles

You already know Amazon's Kindle devices, but did you know that the books that you've downloaded can be made available on other devices? This Windows 8 app syncs your Kindle books and you can start reading from where you left off and enjoy any custom reading settings you've set up across devices.

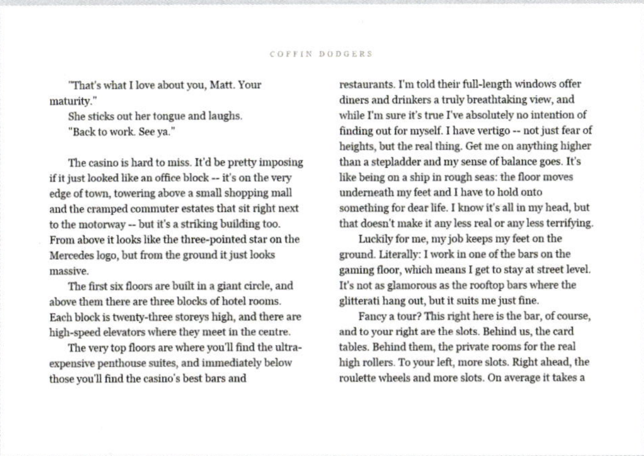

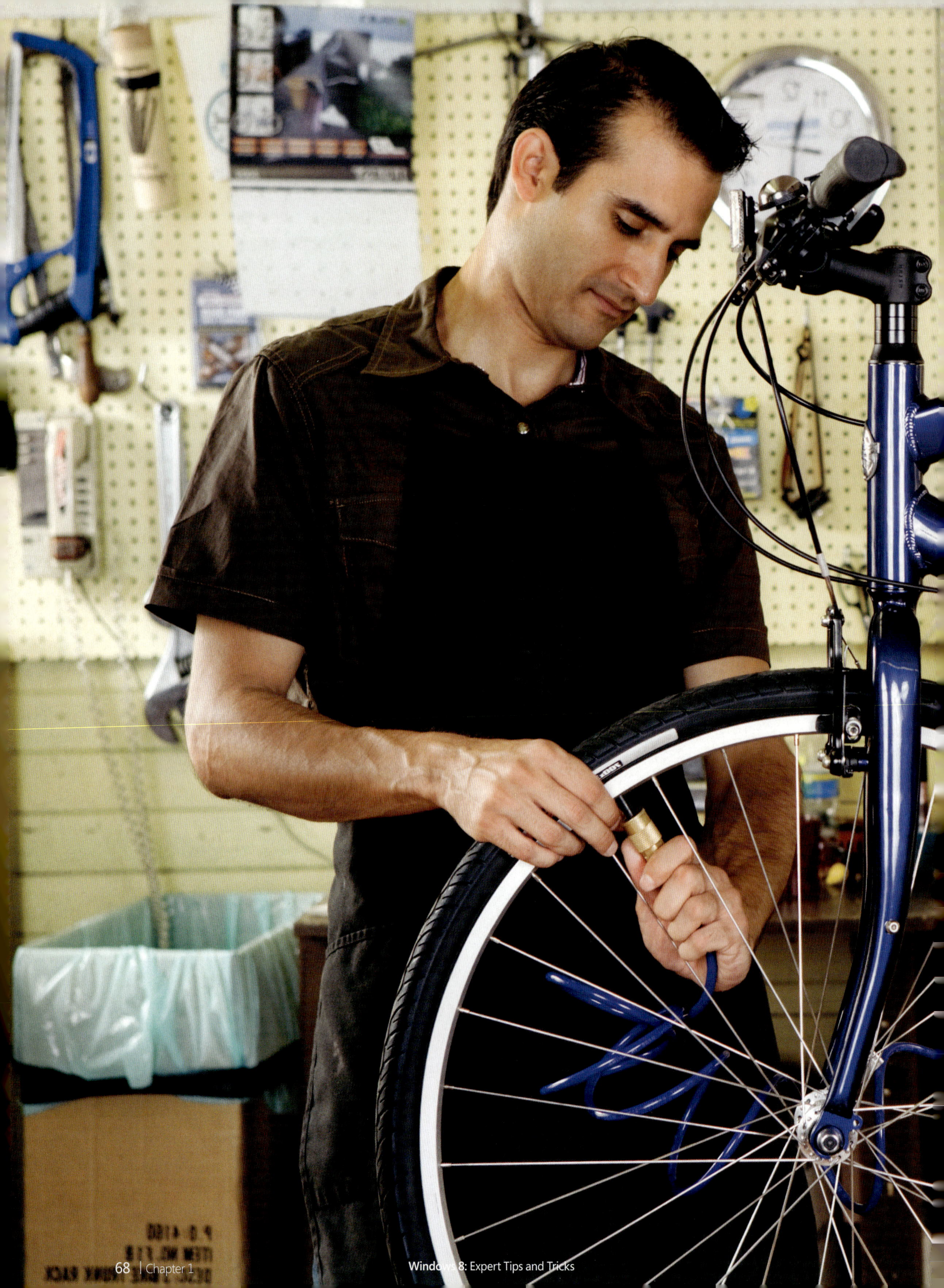

TRY THIS!
Refresh or reinstall your PC
78

Under the hood

Delve a little deeper to discover the inner-workings of your OS

Section 4

70	Explore under the hood
72	Mastering the ribbon
74	Bypass the Start screen
76	Solve problems
78	Start afresh
82	Speed up with ReadyBoost
84	Storage Spaces
86	Increase battery life
90	Install Windows 8
92	Use Windows 8 File History

DO THIS NOW...

Explore under the hood

Windows 8 has plenty of power behind the scenes

App switching

You can switch between running apps by using [Alt]+[Tab] or swiping your finger in from the left, but there's another way you can view which Windows 8-style apps are running. Holding down the [Windows] key and pressing [Tab] displays a pane on the left with your running apps. To see this with the mouse, move your cursor to the bottom or top-left corner of the screen, wait until the thumbnail appears, then drag down or up, depending on which corner you go to. You can always press [Ctrl]+[Shift]+[Esc] to see all running apps in the Task Manager, if you want extra detail about how much memory and CPU power each app is using.

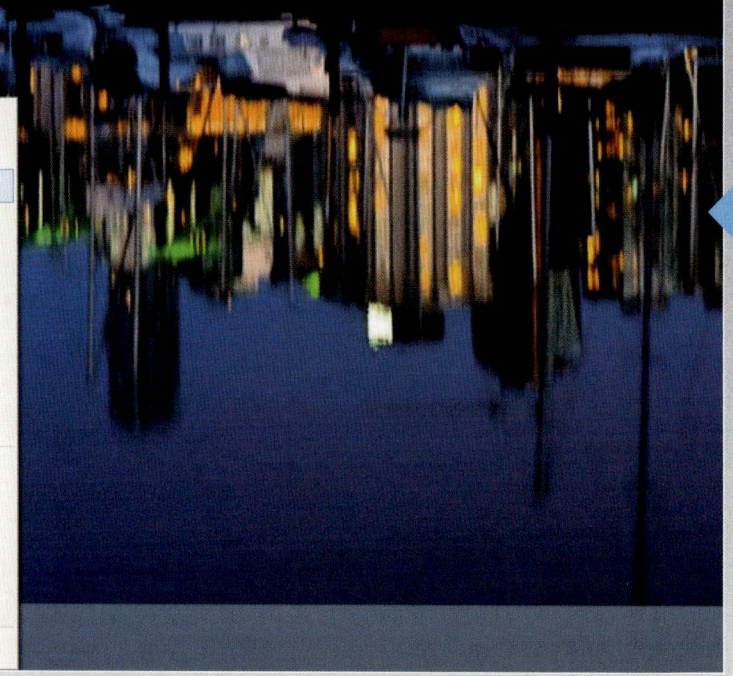

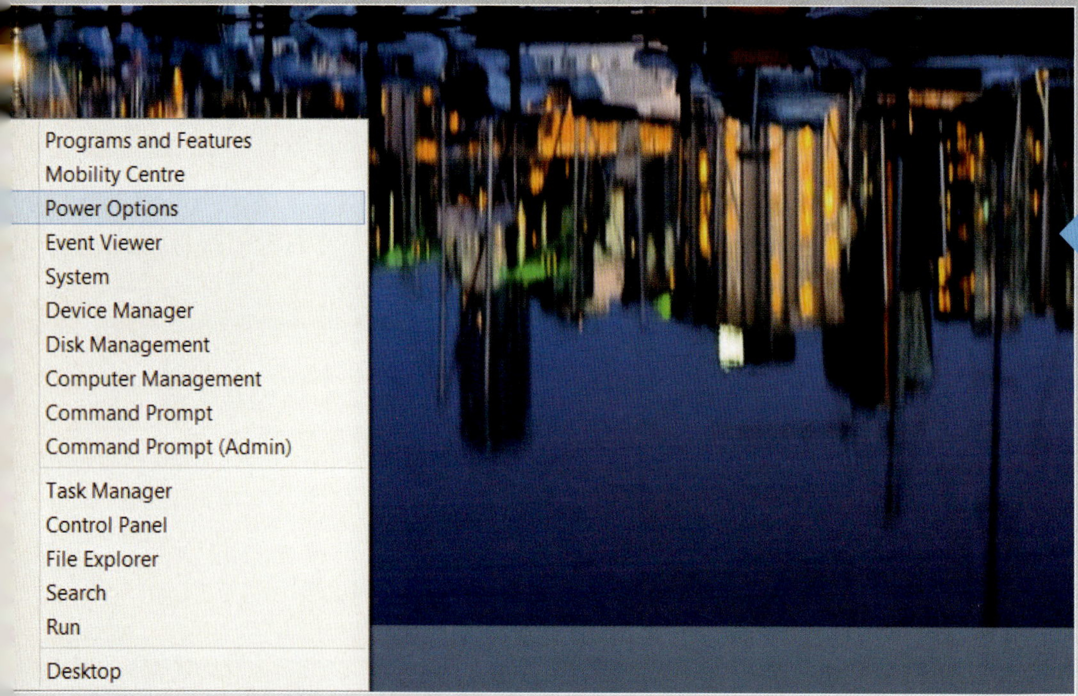

Find essential tools

The powerful new User menu is a power user replacement for the old Start menu. Move your mouse to the very bottom-left and right-click. This works in any screen, and contains quick links to all of the most important administrative functions you could possibly need when setting up or keeping your PC running smoothly. From here you can get directly to the likes of the Device Manager or Disk Management dashboard, and start tweaking things immediately. These are all the key tools you should need for the administration of your computer, but you can always choose to go to the Control Panel for extra options.

EXPLORE UNDER THE HOOD

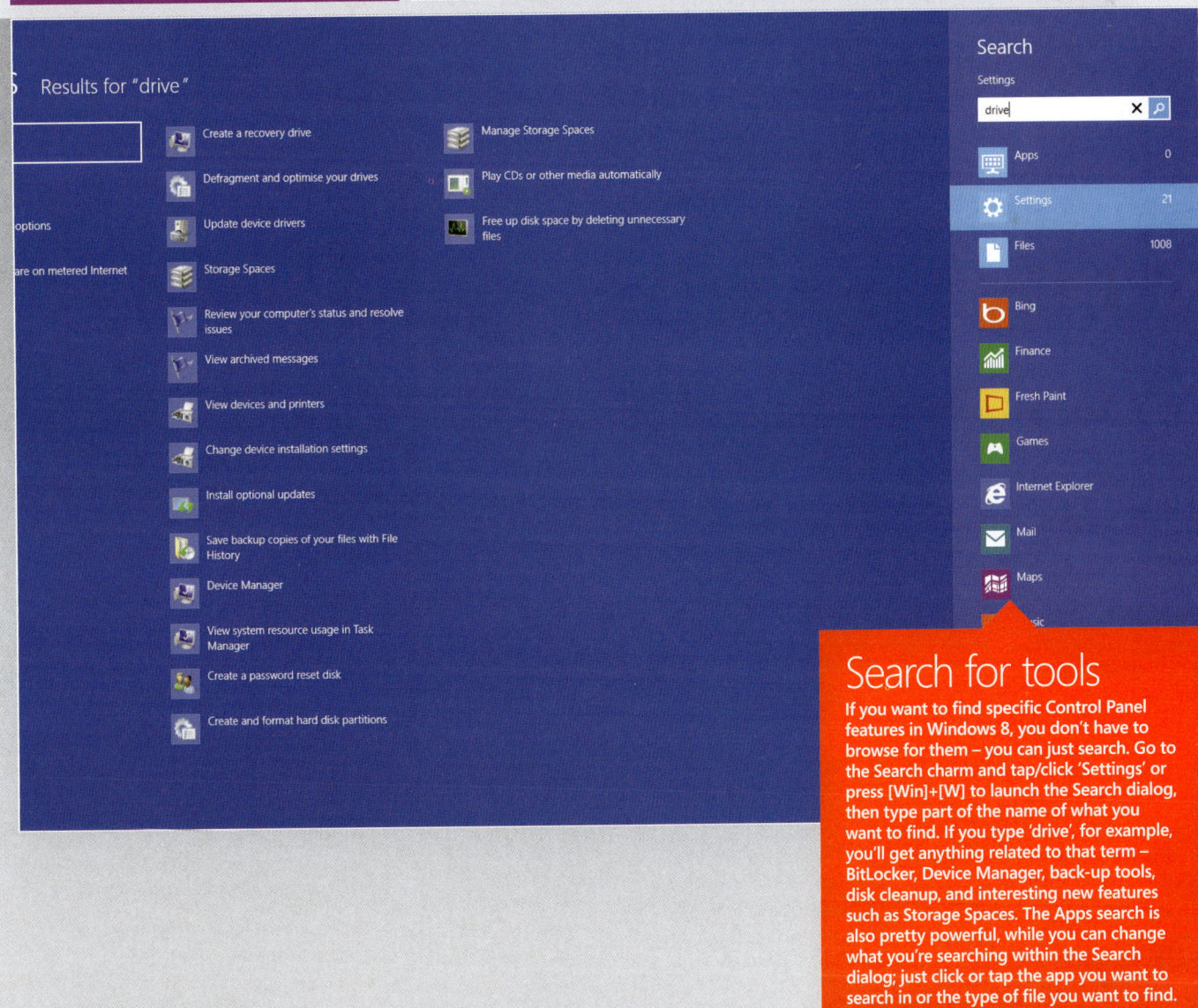

Access more tools

You can get the Windows administrative tools on to your Windows 8 Start screen via the Charm bar. Open the Charm bar from the Start screen by flicking your finger from or moving your mouse to the right-hand side, and select 'Settings' then 'Tiles'. Change 'Show administrative tools' to 'Yes', and click on an empty part of the Start screen. Scroll to the right and you'll find a host of new tiles for key applets – Performance Monitor, Event Viewer, Task Scheduler, Resource Monitor and more – ready to be accessed at a click. When these tools appear, they may be mixed in with other shortcuts, but you can move them to a single group if you like.

Search for tools

If you want to find specific Control Panel features in Windows 8, you don't have to browse for them – you can just search. Go to the Search charm and tap/click 'Settings' or press [Win]+[W] to launch the Search dialog, then type part of the name of what you want to find. If you type 'drive', for example, you'll get anything related to that term – BitLocker, Device Manager, back-up tools, disk cleanup, and interesting new features such as Storage Spaces. The Apps search is also pretty powerful, while you can change what you're searching within the Search dialog; just click or tap the app you want to search in or the type of file you want to find.

Windows 8: Expert Tips and Tricks

25 TOP TIPS FOR...
Mastering the ribbon

Become an Explorer wizard with these essential tips

1 Open an Explorer window, find and select a file, and click the 'Home' menu. By clicking the 'Copy Path' icon, you pop the file's location on your clipboard; paste it into a text document so you can find the file later on. Paste it in the address bar to go straight there.

2 Still in the ribbon's Home menu, check out the 'Easy Access' box. It gives you quick ways to pin an item or folder to your Taskbar, include a folder in a Library, or add it to your favourites.

3 The Easy Access menu also includes Map as Drive. If you're connected to a network, this enables you to choose any network folder and treat it as though it were a drive connected directly to your machine. Make sure 'Reconnect at sign in' is selected.

4 If you have a SkyDrive account, you can use the Map as Drive tool to add a direct connection to it from Explorer. Download the app from http://skydrivesimpleviewer.codeplex.com/, run it, log in, and copy your WebDAV address at the top. Then click 'Connect to a website' at the bottom of the Map as Drive tool, paste the address, and you're connected.

5 Once you've hooked up a network or SkyDrive folder, make sure you don't lose files if that resource goes offline. Just select the file you want to keep, bring up the Easy Access menu, and select 'Always available offline'.

6 The Home page of the ribbon includes a 'History' button that gives you quick access to any file's recent

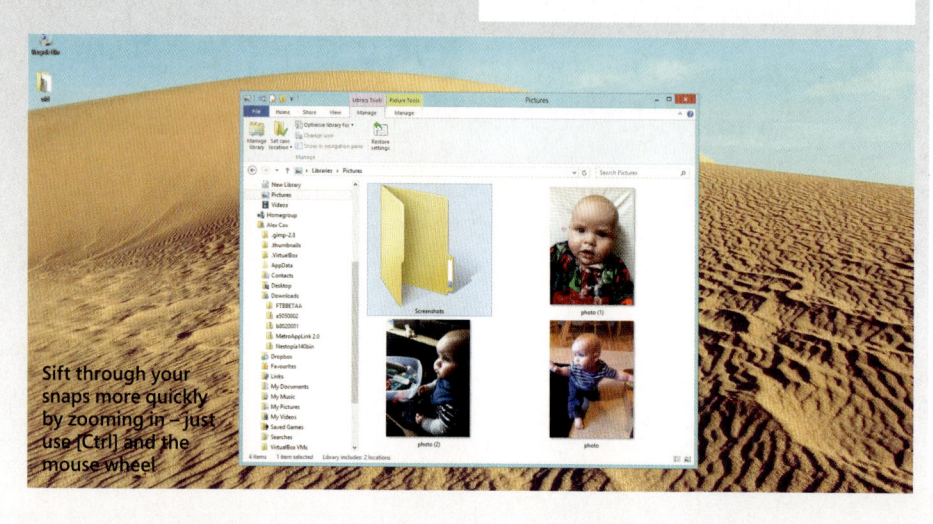

Sift through your snaps more quickly by zooming in – just use [Ctrl] and the mouse wheel

MASTERING THE RIBBON

changes. So if you've made a mistake and saved over a critical file, you can restore it to its former glory quickly.

7 Opening a picture, for example, in Explorer, throws you into the Start screen Pictures app by default. This is annoying. Luckily, you can choose to open the image in something else, such as Paint. Right-click an item and use 'Open With', or click the button on the Home page of the ribbon.

8 You can use an alternative to the Open With menu if you use a separate viewer and editor for files. Check the Home menu for the 'Edit...' button; this opens a picture in Paint, for example, even if the default viewer is Pictures.

9 The Select portion of the Home menu has one particularly useful function: 'Invert Selection'. With it you can click a file or two that you don't want to be selected from a bunch, then select the rest with a single click.

10 The 'Move to' and 'Copy to' commands on the Home menu are particularly useful because they remember the folders you've used most recently.

11 If you've got a collection of files you want to stick on a CD-R or DVD-R, the 'Burn to Disc' icon (on Explorer's Share menu) is handy. Just make sure the files fall within the capacity of the disc you're trying to burn.

12 There are two modes in which you can burn a disc. If you intend to use it on any non-Windows device (such as a DVD player), choose Mastered mode, which prevents further writing. Otherwise choose Live mode, so the disc can be written to again.

13 If you regularly use the quick access toolbar at the top of the Explorer window, you should know that you can pin any ribbon button to it. Right-click the button and select the option.

14 Check out the View menu. The most obvious option is 'Layout', which enables you to set the size of your icon, and how much info is displayed. Hover your mouse over one of the options to see a preview of how it'll look.

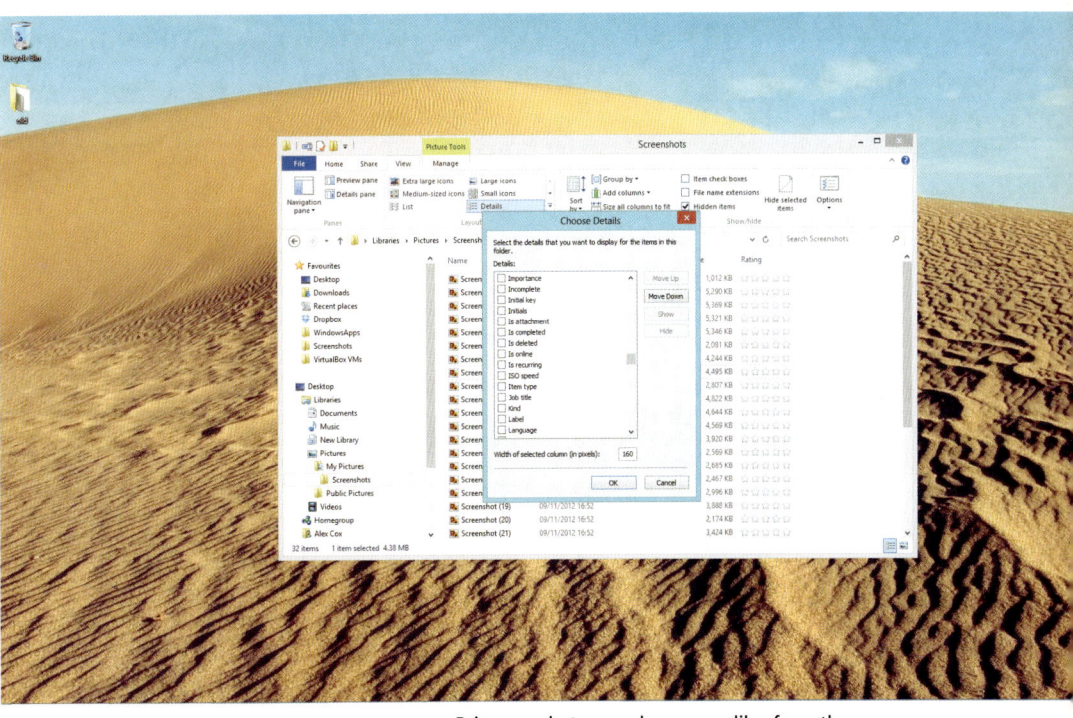

15 You can change the size of the icons in an Explorer window by holding [Ctrl] and spinning the mouse wheel. The settings apply only to the current folder, and stay the same when you return to the folder later on.

16 The Detail view is the most useful of all the icon views. You can click the headers at the top of each column to sort the files by whatever information is in that particular column – name, size, date modified, and so on. Click again to sort in the opposite order.

17 You can make some fairly significant tweaks to the Detail view. If, for example, the Size is most important, just click, hold and drag its column header to reorganise its placement in the Explorer window.

18 Drag the edges of a column in the Detail view to make it wider or narrower, or right-click any column and choose whether to size that one to fit or to do it to all of the columns.

19 You can add columns in the Detail view. Right-click any column header to see a list of potential information that could be added – much of which only applies to specific file types, such as MP3s or photos – and click 'More' to see an utterly comprehensive list.

20 You can duplicate the view you're using for all folders of the same type on your drive; click the 'Options' icon on the right of the View menu, go to the 'View' tab, then click the 'Apply to Folders' button at the top. Confirm your selection, and it's done. The 'Reset Folders' button reverses this action.

Bring up whatever columns you like, from the sublime to the utterly obscure

Quick tips

21 You don't have to use the Navigation pane, if you're comfortable without it. Just go to the 'View' tab of the ribbon, click on 'Navigation pane', and switch it off.

22 Perhaps you just want to resize the Navigation pane? Move your mouse to the edge where it meets the current folder, and the cursor turns into opposite-pointing arrows. Click, hold and drag to resize it.

23 If you want to find your current folder in the Navigation pane, just click the 'Navigation' button on the View tab, and select 'Expand to current folder'.

24 There are more panes to try. The 'Preview pane' button brings up a look at the item you've got clicked, while the 'Properties pane' shows extra information.

25 Click the 'Navigation' icon and select 'See all folders' to increase the number you can see in the left-hand pane – extra handy for moving files around. ■

Windows 8: Expert Tips and Tricks | Chapter 1 | 73

Learn how to...

Bypass Windows 8 Start Screen

If you want Windows 8 to go straight to your desktop when it starts, as in previous versions, it's easy to achieve with just a few minor tweaks

WORKS WITH
Windows 8
Windows 8 Pro
Windows RT

One of the biggest changes to Windows 8 from the previous versions of Windows is that when you start the operating system up, you are taken straight to the brand new Start screen. From here you can get quick access to all your favourite Windows 8 apps, through the attractive and informative Live tiles that keep you posted about new events in your apps. However, if you'd rather Windows 8 went straight to the desktop, where you can run more traditional Windows programs, then there is an easy solution. Best of all, this solution is just as easy to remove as it is to install, so while going straight to the desktop can help make the leap to Windows 8 more familiar when you first start using it, if you then want to fully embrace the Start screen at a later date, it's easy to do.

Load up your desktop straight away

1 Create a file
Load up Windows 8 and go to the desktop. Now open up the Documents library, then right-click and select 'New > Text Document'. This creates a new blank text document in your Documents folder. We are going to turn this simple text document into a small program.

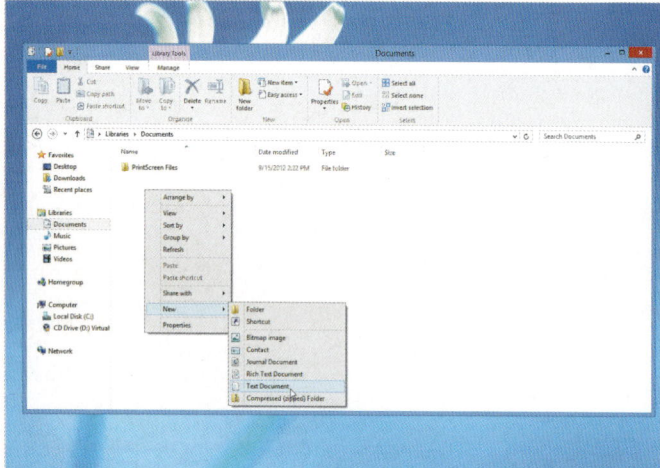

2 Enter the script
To do this, open up your new text document by double-clicking it and then enter in the following words exactly as they appear in the screenshot above:
[Shell] Command=2 IconFile=Explorer.exe,3
[Taskbar] Command=ToggleDesktop

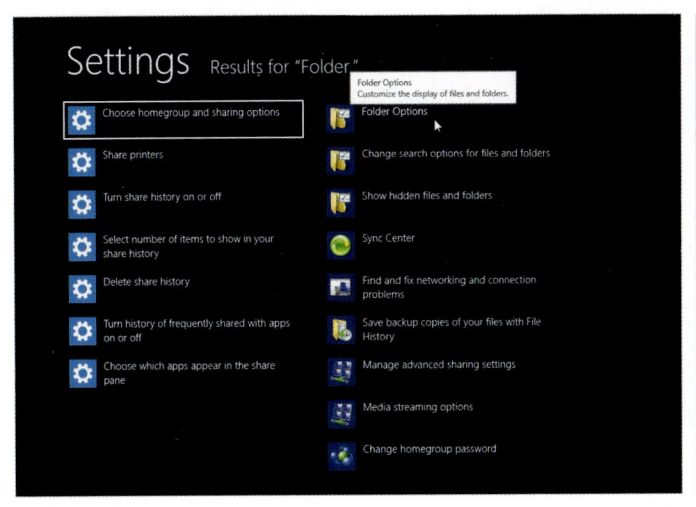

BYPASS WINDOWS 8 START SCREEN

3 Save the file
Now go to 'File > Save' to save the file, and then close the text document. Next, touch (or take your mouse cursor) to the top-right corner of the screen and select the 'Search' charm. Type 'Folder' in the text box and then, beneath it, select 'Settings'. Now click on 'Folder Options'.

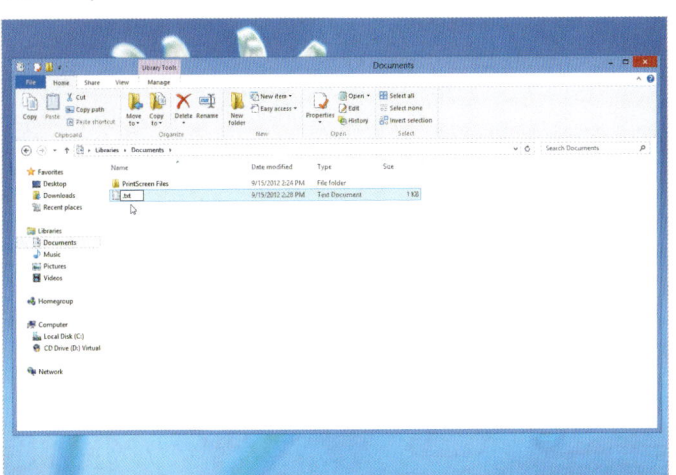

4 Change folder options
Now the 'Folder Options' window opens on your screen. Click the 'View' tab and then scroll down until you see the option that says 'Hide extensions for known file types'. Make sure there is no tick in the box next to it by clicking it, and then click 'OK'. Now you can see the relevant extensions for your files.

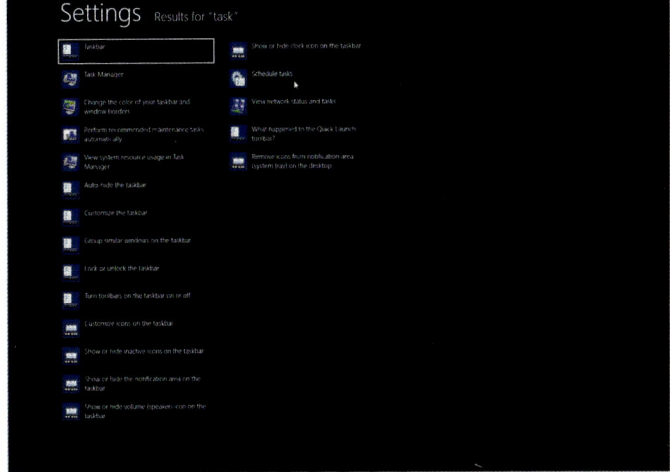

5 Change the file type of the text document
Now go back to the 'Documents' folder where the text file you created was saved. It should now be called 'New Text Document. txt'. Right-click the text document and select 'Rename'. Press [Del] on the keyboard and the name disappears, but the '.txt' bit remains. Click [Del] a couple more times to remove the '.txt'.

6 Name the file and open up Task Scheduler
Name the file 'bootdesktop.scf' (without inverted commas) and hit [Return]. You're asked to confirm the change. Click 'Yes' and the icon for the file changes. Now touch (or take your mouse cursor) to the top-right corner of the screen and select the 'Search' charm and type in 'Task', select 'Settings', then 'Schedule tasks' on the left.

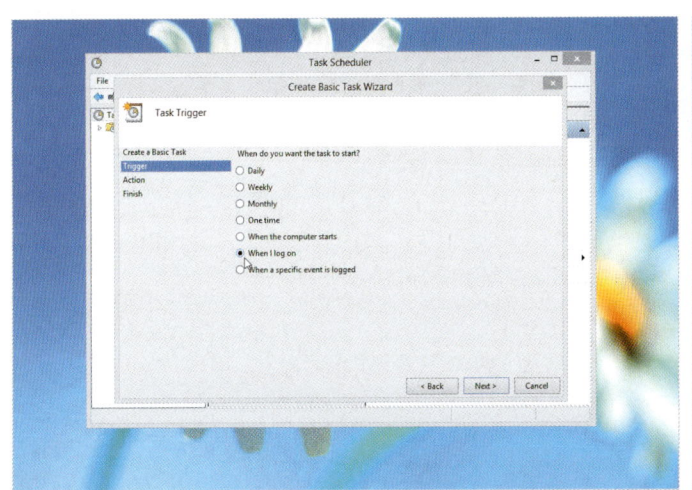

7 Create the task
In the Task Scheduler window, select 'Create Basic Task...'. Give the task a name, such as 'Desktopboot', then click 'Next'. In the next screen, select 'When I log on', then click 'Next' again. Select 'Start a program', then 'Next'. Now click 'Browse' and select 'bootdesktop. scf'. Click 'Next' again, then 'Finish'.

8 Go straight to the desktop!
Now you can restart Windows 8 and after you've logged in you get taken straight to the desktop. Later on, if you want to enable going to the Start Screen first, open up the Task Scheduler as in step 6 and select 'Task Scheduler Library'. Find the task you named 'Desktopboot', right-click it and select 'Disable'.

Learn how to...

Keep your PC in top condition
Poor PC performance is a thing of the past – with Windows 8 you can tweak all sorts of settings to get the best possible experience

Refresh your PC
Give your PC a shop-fresh feel
Windows 8 makes it easy to wipe the slate clean and return your PC to how it was when it was new (getting rid of all your data). If you don't want to be so drastic, you can refresh your PC and simply restore the operating system to full working order without affecting your files and folders. These options are available within the PC settings app (see page 78 for more).

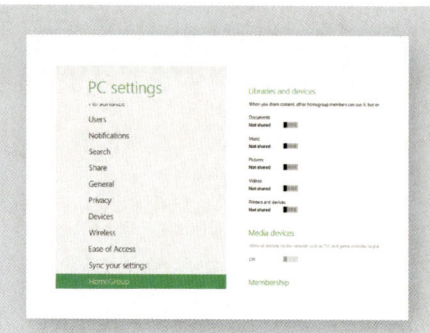

HomeGroup
Sharing made easy
Using HomeGroup, you can seamlessly connect to other Windows 7 and Windows 8 computers on your network simply by tapping in a password. Choose to share whatever types of files you want – documents, music, pictures and videos – as well as giving other PCs on your network access to a printer.

Top Tip!
Specific settings
To get to the Settings menu, just click your user picture, rather than trawling your way through the Control Panel.

Auto updates
Check that your computer has all the latest settings by using Windows Update. It should work automatically, but some updates are optional and you need to manually choose to install them.

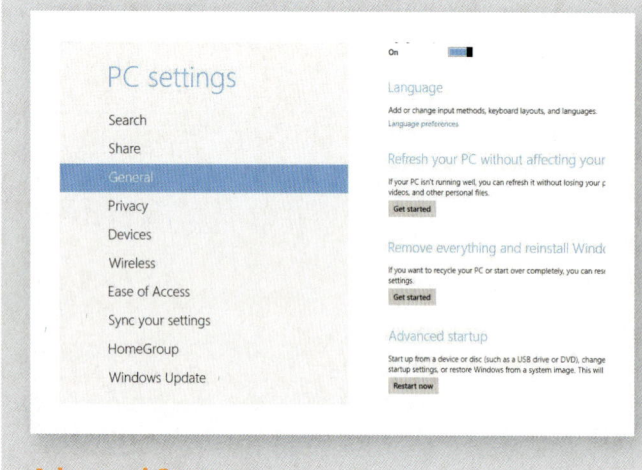

Advanced Startup
Start up from a device or disc
Advanced Startup ('PC settings > General > Advanced startup') is for when you need to do a more advanced reinstallation of the Windows operating system. This option restarts your computer so you can perform the installation. You can also change startup settings here.

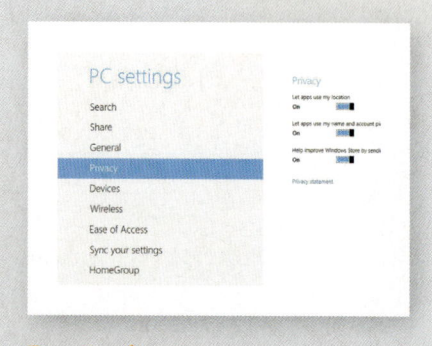

Boost privacy
Choose your options
Windows 8 features a Privacy area within the PC Settings app. From here you can determine whether Windows 8 apps are allowed to access your location, as well as whether they can access other personal details, such as your name and account picture. It's important that you keep on top of these details if you want to protect your privacy.

EVERYTHING YOU NEED TO TAKE OVER THE WEB

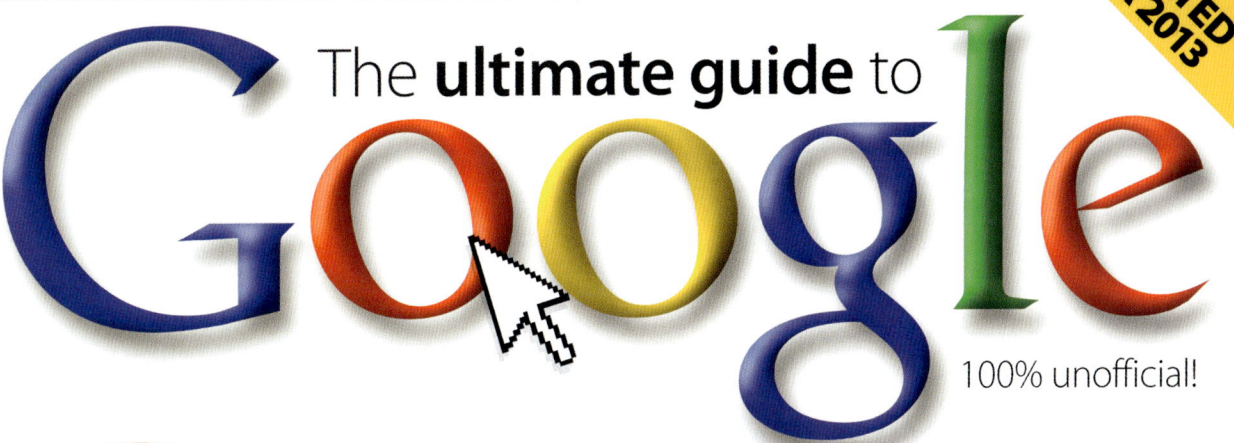

the TechPro series

The ultimate guide to Google

100% unofficial!

FULLY UPDATED FOR 2013

48 Expert tutorials and in-depth projects

For all users of PCs, Macs, iPads, tablets & smartphones

Get the best from ▶ Gmail • YouTube • Search • Google+ • Picasa • Chrome

PLUS Discover Google's Drive, Calendar, Wallet, Earth, Checkout, Analytics, Reader, Websites, Picasa Web, Finance, Docs, Blogger and much more!

OUT NOW!

Learn how to...

Start afresh!

You can get that from-the-box feeling once again by giving your Windows computer a refresh or complete reinstall – it's easy to achieve when you follow this handy step-by-step guide

WORKS WITH
Windows 8
Windows 8 Pro
Windows RT

Although Windows 8 hasn't been out for long, many of you will no doubt have started to get stuck into what the new operating system has to offer. After a while, however, through continual use, and as files accumulate, you might notice a drop in performance. The great thing about Windows 8, though, is that turning back the clock and getting your PC fresh once again is easier than ever. There are no lengthy and complicated procedures to follow – just a few button presses and away you go. Even if you've just bought a new PC, you might want to consider this procedure, because manufacturers tend to pre-install software that is not only unwanted, but can also slow it down. By doing a refresh, you can make Windows 8 totally fresh – as it should be.

Refresh and reinstall Windows 8

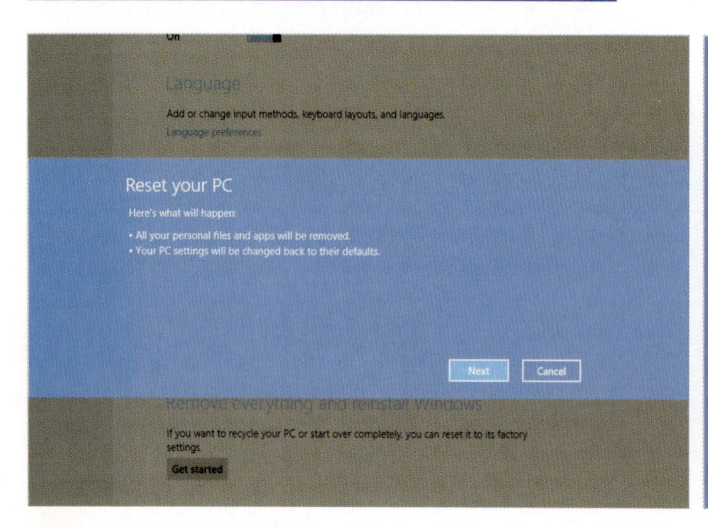

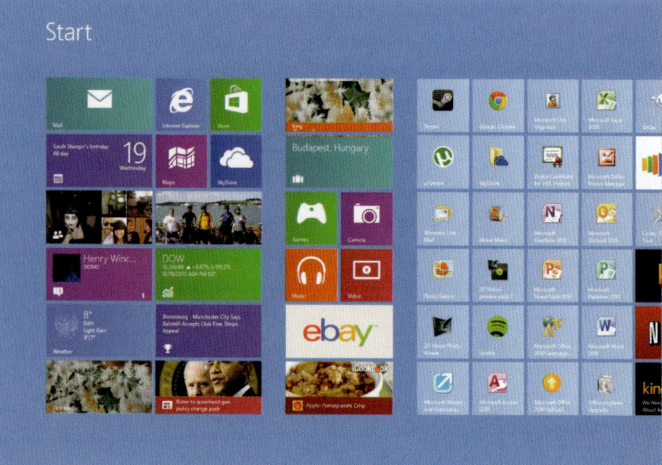

1 Refresh or reinstall
There are two ways of getting your PC back to a new state – the first is refreshing your PC, which basically rejuvenates it without deleting your apps, files and settings. The other is to reinstall Windows, which is the more extreme of the two options and causes you to lose everything, and reset it back to factory settings.

2 Choose wisely
So, you need to decide which option is for you. If you have performance problems, you should certainly try refreshing your PC. If that fails, a reset is the only answer. Go to the Charms bar, choose 'Settings > Change PC settings' and then choose the 'General' option from the menu bar.

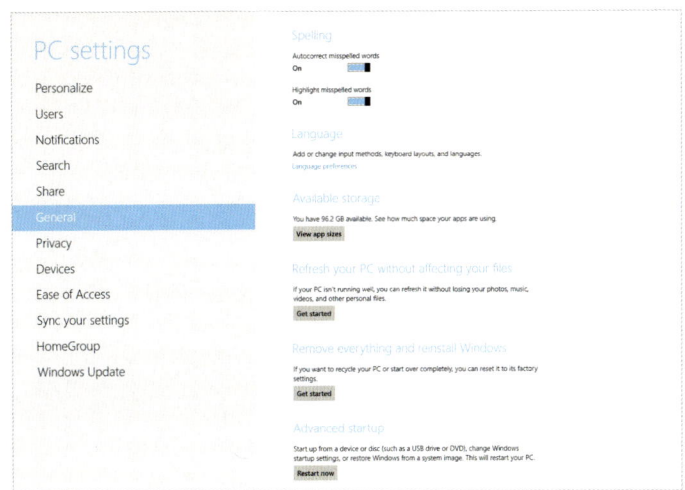

START AFRESH!

3 Refresh it
Scroll down to find both settings near the bottom. If you choose the 'light' route of a refresh, you can get that shop-fresh feeling without having to back up your files beforehand. Underneath where it says 'Refresh your PC without affecting your files', tap on 'Get started' to begin the process.

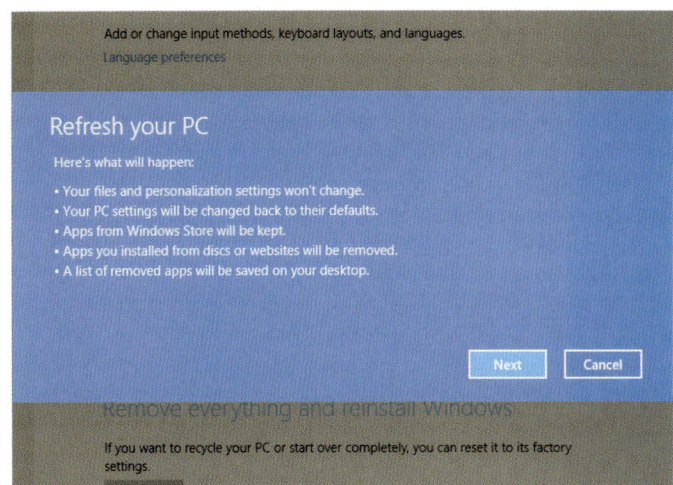

4 The process begins
You'll now see a screen that says 'Refresh your PC', giving you a brief overview of what apps, files and settings will remain after it's completed. The main thing to note is that programs on the desktop (not the Start screen) will be removed. There is a way of refreshing your PC and keeping these programs, but it's a complicated process.

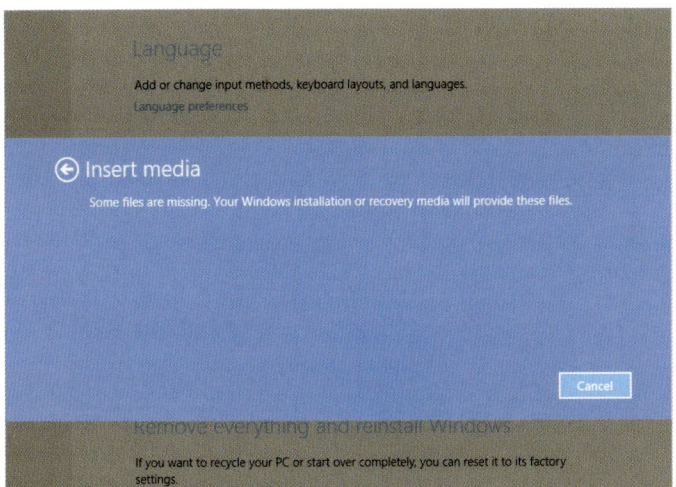

5 Preparing your PC
Hit 'Next' and Windows 8 starts preparing the refresh process. On the following screen you'll notice that the process seems to have hit a stumbling block. You need to have your Windows installation disc inserted for it to continue. Once you've done this, it tells you that your PC is ready to be refreshed, so hit the 'Refresh' button.

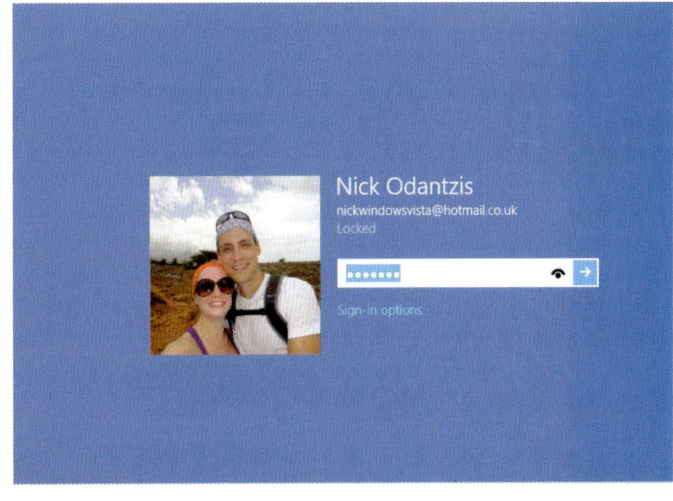

6 Start again
Refreshing your PC takes about 5 to 10 minutes, and once it's done it restarts and you're taken to the login screen. Just enter your Microsoft Account sign-in details and the Start screen appears. Go to the desktop and you'll see an icon called 'Removed Apps'. Open it and it tells you which desktop programs were removed.

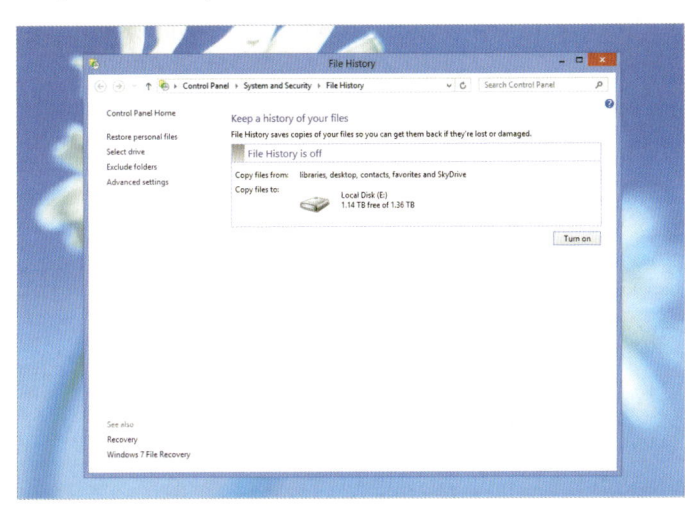

7 Go the whole hog
If you want a completely fresh start, the reinstall option is the one to go for. With this route, you lose all your files, so if you want to keep them, we suggest you first back up your files to an external drive, or alternatively you should back up your entire PC using the File History facility, which you can learn about on page 90.

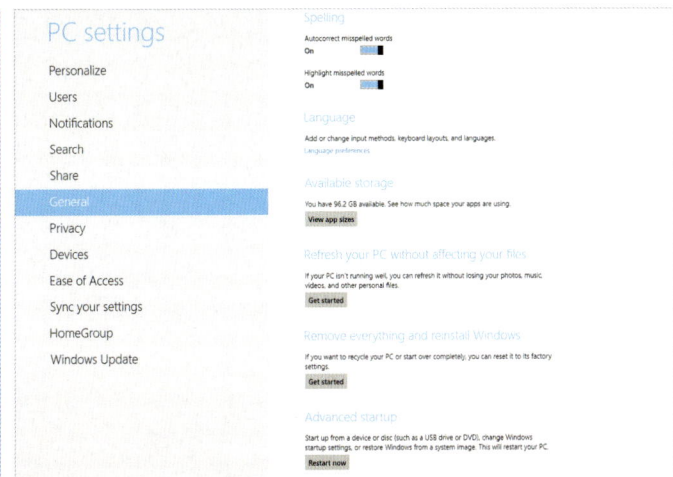

8 Start reinstalling
Now that you're ready to do the big reinstall, you need to go to the Charms bar once again, select 'Settings > Change PC settings', select 'General' from the list and scroll down until you see 'Remove everything and reinstall Windows'. Then hit the 'Get started' button to begin the reinstallation process.

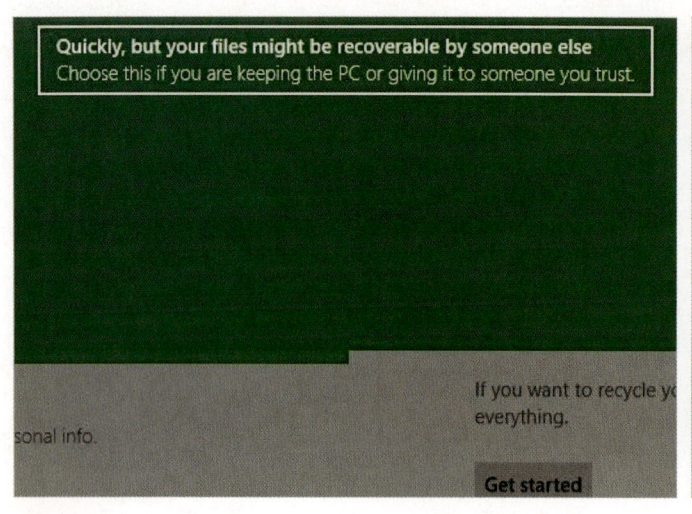

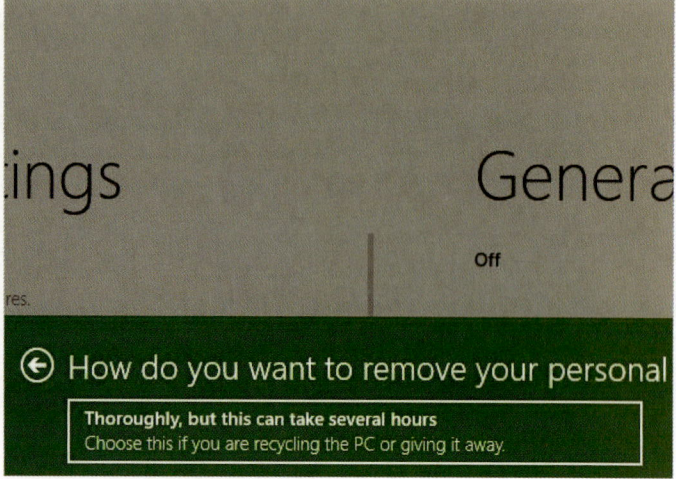

9 More options
Windows now gives you two options, depending on the type of reinstall you would like. The first one – 'Just remove my files' – is a basic option which reinstalls your PC to factory settings in the same amount of time as a refresh, but there's no guarantee all files will be completely erased. This option is fine for most people.

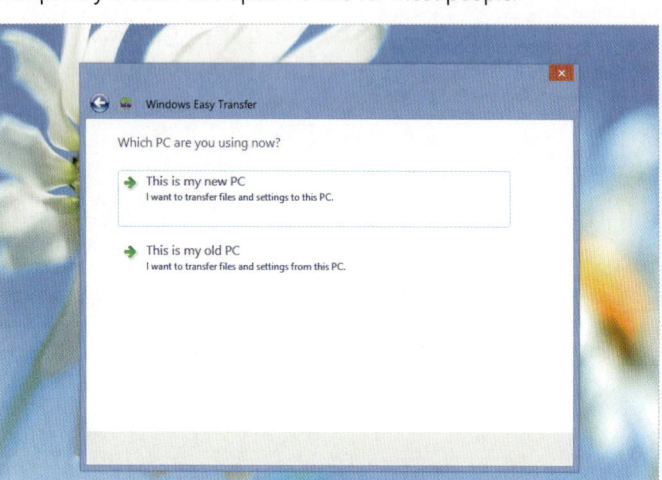

10 Remove everything
The second option – 'Fully clean the drive' – takes a lot longer to complete, but it's far more thorough and erases all your data for good. This is perfect if you store sensitive data on your hard drive and you worry about theft. So, choose the one that suits you and sit back while your Windows 8 PC is reinstalled to its original settings.

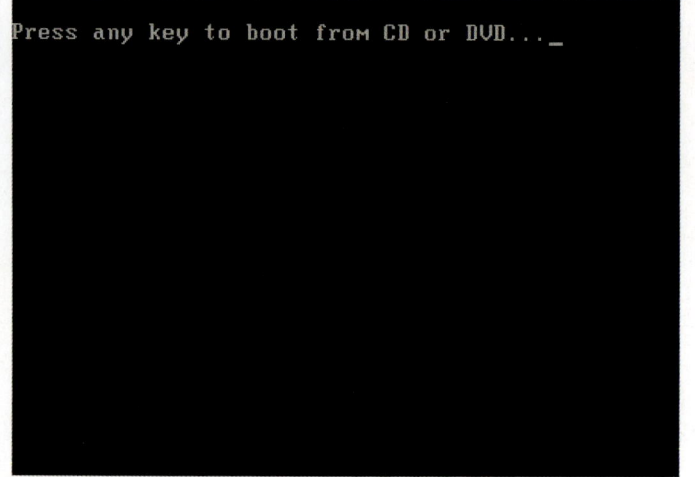

11 Restore settings
Once your PC has gone through the reinstallation, it restarts and you need to input some set-up details again. Back in Windows, your next step should be restoring your files and settings from the backup you created using File History. Or you can just transfer your backed-up files using Windows Easy Transfer (see page 54).

12 Refresh from boot
If something serious has happened to your PC, you might want to do a refresh to fix the problem. But what if you can't actually boot your PC into Windows to get to the refresh option? Well, you can insert your installation disc upon startup, and when prompted hit any key to boot from the disc drive.

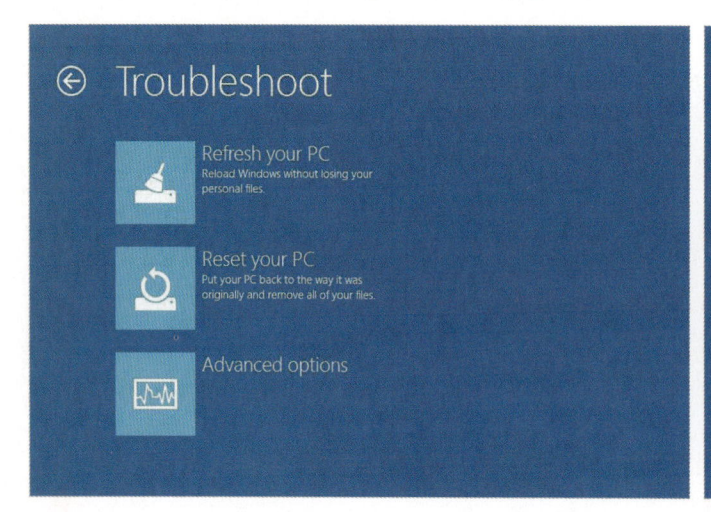

13 Don't install
Choose your language on the screen that appears, and click 'Next', but don't be tempted to hit 'Install now' on the next screen. Instead, select 'Repair your computer' from the bottom-left and hit 'Troubleshoot' on the next screen . Click or tap 'Next', choose 'Windows 8 operating system' and then choose 'Refresh' to begin.

14 That fresh feeling…
Now that you've followed this guide, you know how to refresh and reinstall your PC and, more importantly, you know which option is best suited to you. Remember, if your PC starts to slow down or if something isn't working quite right, a refresh is a great option, which will bring your PC back to life in no time at all.

YOUR ESSENTIAL GUIDE TO ALL VERSIONS OF OFFICE

2012 EDITION

YOUR ESSENTIAL GUIDE TO ALL VERSIONS OF OFFICE

Microsoft Office

- **Master the basics...**
- **Make your business shine**
- **Paid version or free?**
- And much more!

THE COMPLETE GUIDE TO
- ✓ Word
- ✓ Outlook
- ✓ Mobile Office
- ✓ OneNote
- ✓ Excel
- ✓ PowerPoint

49 TUTORIALS including Super spreadsheets, organised emails, ultimate shortcuts and more!

OUT NOW!

Learn how to...

Speed up your PC

The ReadyBoost feature in Windows 8 enables you to borrow memory from flash devices and help keep your computer running fast

WORKS WITH
Windows 8
Windows 8 Pro
Windows RT

ReadyBoost is a Windows feature – first introduced with Windows Vista, but drastically improved in Windows 7 – that enables you to borrow flash memory from USB drives, Compact Flash and SD cards to give your computer a memory boost. This feature is particularly useful when your PC is running low on memory and its performance is becoming sluggish. Usually, when your PC's memory is running low, Windows has to turn to your hard drive to store data it needs to access quickly, whereas ReadyBoost gives it the option of using external flash memory, which is a much speedier alternative. In Windows 8, ReadyBoost can now handle up to eight flash memory devices simultaneously, giving a maximum of 256GB extra memory, which can come in handy for demanding tasks such as editing photos and videos.

Start using ReadyBoost

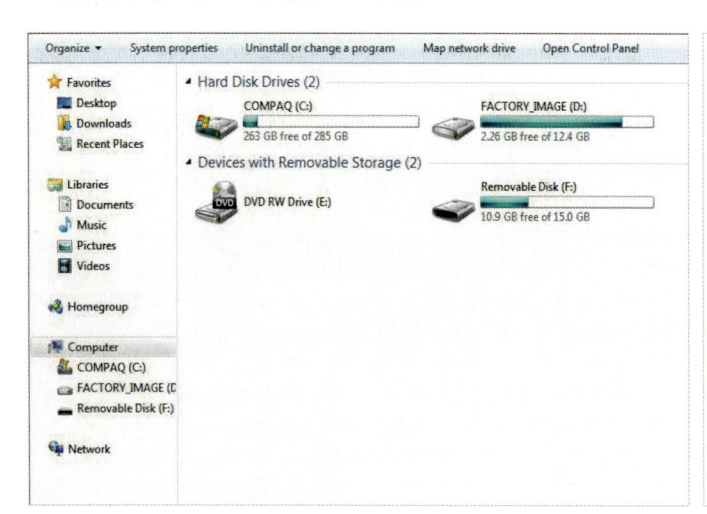

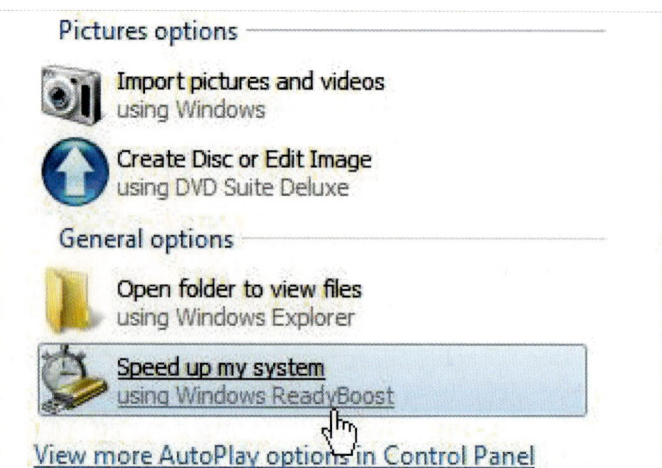

1 Add your flash memory
Windows ReadyBoost can make a real difference to your PC's performance. It works with most flash storage devices, but make sure your device has at least 1GB of free space before you begin. It's OK to use a device that has files on it, because ReadyBoost just uses the remaining space. Connect your flash device to your PC.

2 Open your options
Your computer should detect your external flash memory when you plug it in, and an AutoPlay menu should pop up. If the AutoPlay menu doesn't appear, click on 'Computer', then right-click on your flash device. Now click on 'Properties' and select the 'ReadyBoost' tab. Click 'Speed up my system'.

SPEED UP YOUR PC

Jargon buster!

RAM
Random Access Memory, which stores information on what you're doing. The more RAM, the faster it can recall your information, and the better your computer runs.

USB drive
A small, portable data storage device, which connects to your computer via the USB (Universal Serial Bus) port.

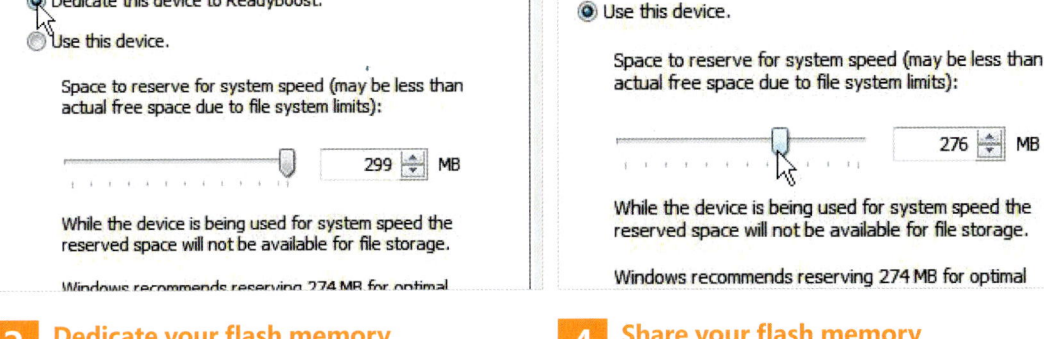

3 Dedicate your flash memory
In the AutoPlay box, click 'Speed up my system'. Then in the Properties box, click 'Dedicate this device to ReadyBoost > OK'. ReadyBoost leaves any files on your device alone, but uses all the remaining space to boost speed. You can't use this space for anything else.

4 Share your flash memory
If this doesn't suit you because you need some of your device's storage for other things, click on 'Use this device', rather than 'Dedicate this device'. You can use the slider to tell ReadyBoost how much memory it can use from your drive or card, then click 'OK'.

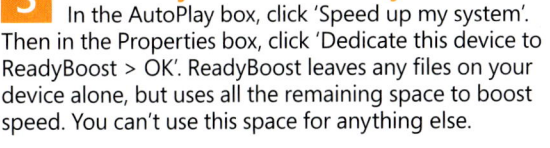

5 Check if it's working
You've turned ReadyBoost on, so continue to use your computer as before – it should be running faster. How much faster depends on the amount of flash memory you've given ReadyBoost. If it's not running as fast as you'd like, consider using additional flash devices.

6 Add more USB devices
You can use up to eight different external flash devices, thereby giving your computer up to an extra 256GB of memory. It's like adding more RAM, but without having to open up your computer and fiddle about with it. To add more devices for ReadyBoost, simply repeat the previous steps – it's as simple as that. If you decide that you need one of your devices back to use it for something else, you can turn each one off individually, too.

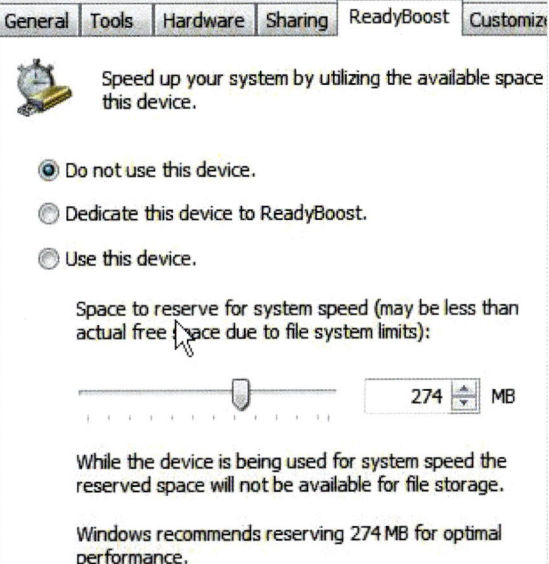

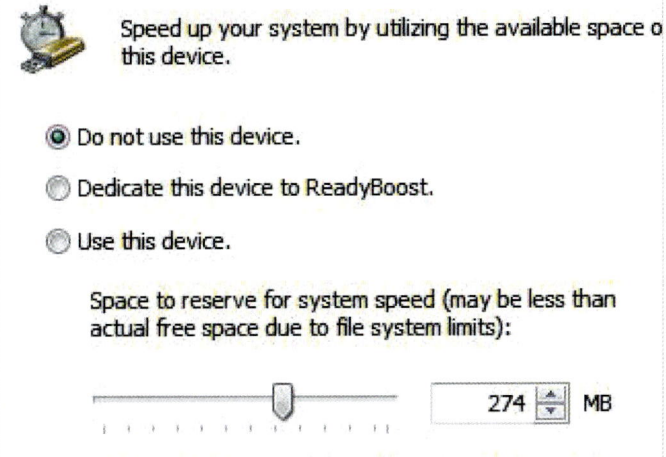

7 Turn off ReadyBoost
You can turn off ReadyBoost if you don't need the extra memory, or you want to use your external device for something else. Click on 'Computer', then right-click on your flash device and click 'Properties > ReadyBoost > Do not use this device'. ReadyBoost turns off and you can use your whole USB drive to store files.

8 Run faster
You're now making the most of the ReadyBoost features, harnessing the extra memory available in external flash devices to give your PC's memory a boost and speed up its performance. It can borrow memory from your nominated card or drive rather than your hard drive, which helps to stop it running sluggishly. ∎

Learn how to...

Maximise your drives' potential

Storage Spaces is one of Windows 8's more advanced features, and it enables you to group hard drives together to make one big drive

WORKS WITH
Windows 8
Windows 8 Pro
Windows RT

Storage Spaces is a new feature for Windows 8 that is incredibly useful – but you might not have heard of it. It's not as glamorous as the Start screen, or as life-changing as the Windows Store, but it can revolutionise the way you use your PC. Storage Spaces enables you to connect multiple storage devices, such as external hard drives, USB sticks and internal drives, and get Windows 8 to use them as one single large storage area, known as a storage pool. The advantage of this is that when you save files to this pool, data is distributed and copied over the disks. If one of the disks fails, your data isn't in danger, because it's on other drives. It's like a user-friendly alternative to complicated RAID setups. With Storage Spaces, you'll never fear losing your data again.

Use Windows 8's Storage Spaces

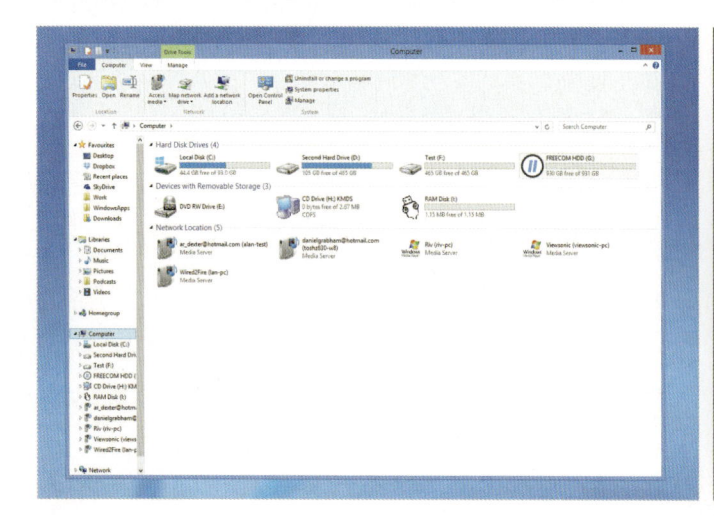

1 Make sure all your drives are attached
To begin using Storage Spaces, you first need to attach your drives. If they are internal, you need to open your computer and install them. A quicker option is to attach external drives, though for performance reasons, we recommend USB 3.0, eSata or Thunderbolt compatible drives.

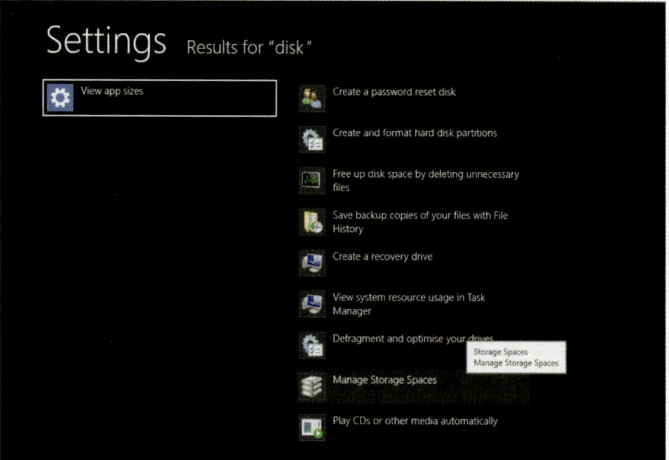

2 Open Storage Spaces
Now press the [Windows] key to bring up the Start screen, then type in 'disk'. Click 'Settings' and then click on 'Manage Storage Spaces'. From here you'll see the Storage Spaces window, and because you haven't used it before, there's just one simple option: 'Create a new pool and storage space'. Click it.

84 | Chapter 1   Windows 8: Expert Tips and Tricks

MAXIMISE YOUR DRIVES' POTENTIAL

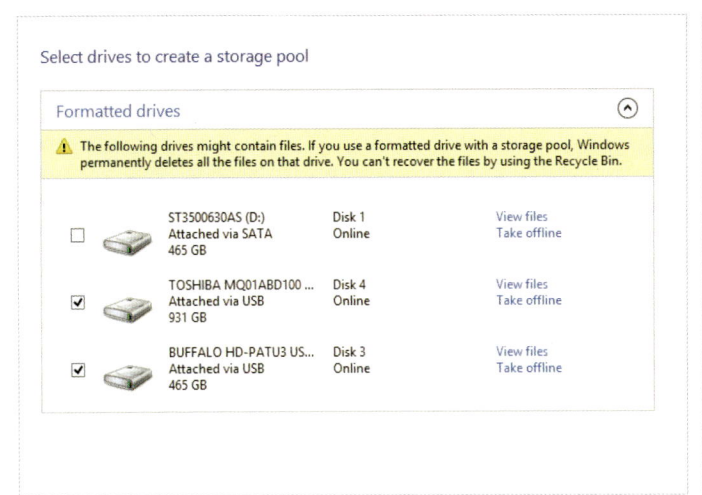

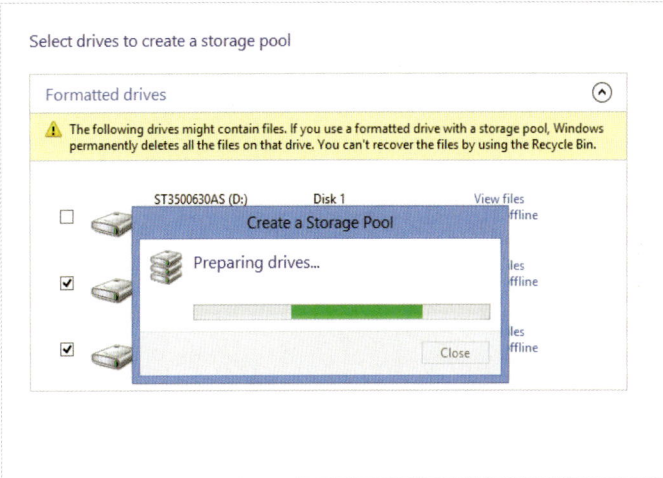

3. Select your drives
If the User Account Control asks you to confirm running Storage Spaces, select 'Yes'. In the next screen, you're shown the drives you've connected that are suitable for Storage Spaces. The hard drive with Windows 8 installed isn't shown. Any files currently on the drives are deleted, so choose carefully!

4. Check your drives and create a storage pool
To make sure there's nothing important on the drives you select, click 'View files'. Windows Explorer opens and you can check to see what files are on the drives. If there are any files you want to keep, make sure you move them to a safe location on a drive you're not going to use for Storage Spaces. When done, click 'Create pool'.

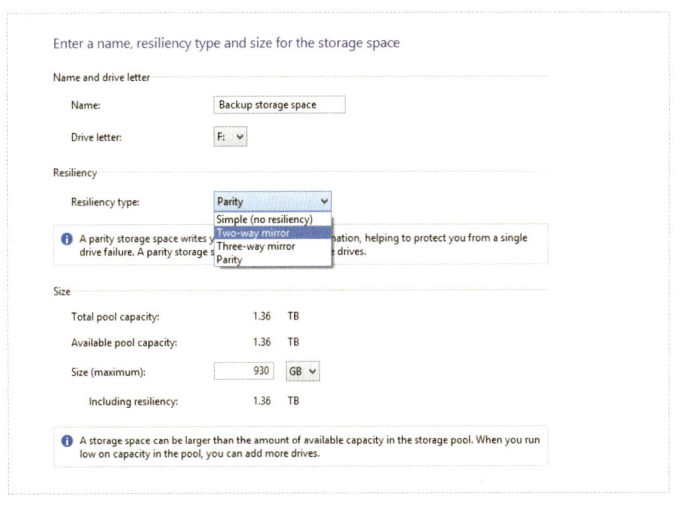

5. Configure the storage space
In the next window you get to configure the storage space. You can give it a name, assign a drive letter to it, choose its size and select the type resiliency. To begin with, give the space a name and drive letter that you'll remember. We'll then go into more detail about the resiliency.

6. Select the resiliency
Resiliency determines how Storage Spaces distributes data. 'Simple' creates a space and only one copy of your data, offering no protection. 'Two-way mirror' creates two copies, protecting data if one drive fails. 'Three-way mirror' is even better, though you need at least five drives. 'Parity' spreads data over a minimum of three drives.

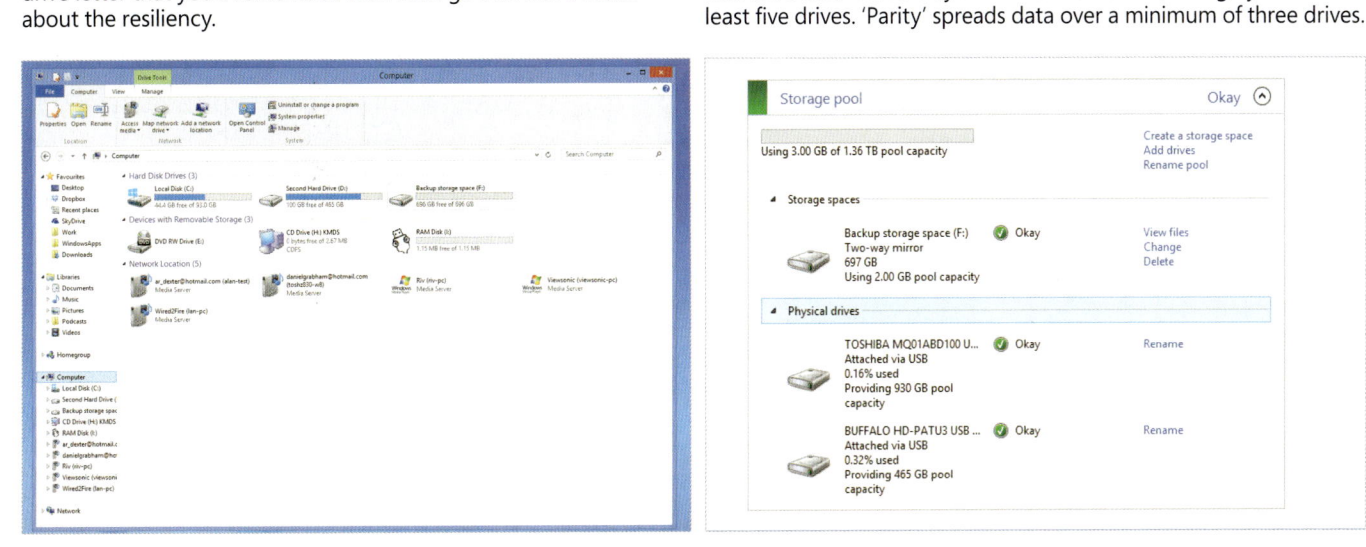

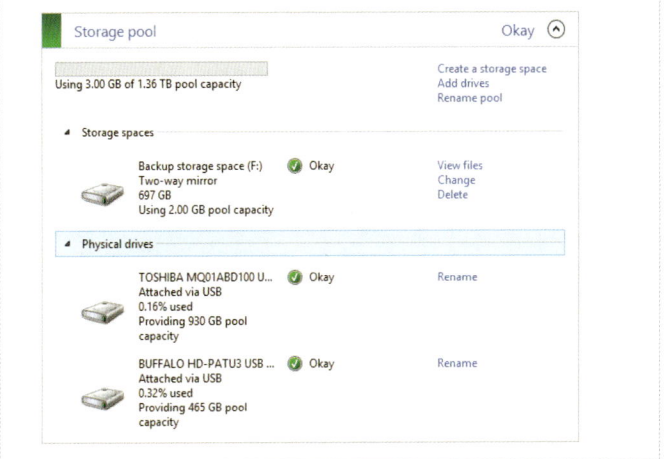

7. Explore and use your new Storage Space
When you've chosen your resiliency type, click 'Create storage space'. Once done, Windows Explorer opens the space, and it looks just like a single drive. If you navigate to 'Computer', you'll see the individual disks you selected aren't shown any more, and instead a single Storage Space is displayed.

8. Maintain your Storage Space
You can keep an eye on the health of your Storage Space by opening the Storage Space window as in Step 1, or by going to 'Control Panel > System and Security > Storage Spaces'. You can make sure the Storage Space is working, change its settings and also view the individual drives to ensure none of them has failed.

Learn how to...

Get longer battery life
Increase your device's battery life

WORKS WITH
Windows 8
Windows 8 Pro
Windows RT

Windows 8 is perfect for mobile devices such as laptops and tablet PCs, thanks to its touch-friendly interface. There's also a number of great tools that come with Windows 8 that can help to increase the battery life of the device. These tools are easy to set up and configure, and you'll see a big difference in how long your device will last between charges. Long journeys will fly by now that you can confidently use your Windows 8 device without worrying about the battery running out on you.

Adjust brightness
In the Windows Mobility Center, you can quickly change the brightness of your screen. Drag the slider to adjust.

Boost your battery life

1 Check your battery life
There's a number of ways to keep an eye on your battery life. Getting into the habit of checking these will save you from running out of juice at an inopportune moment. The first place is in the Lock screen. You can also bring up the Charms bar simply by flicking the right-hand side of the screen. Finally, you can view it in the Taskbar.

2 Adjust screen brightness
A quick way to prolong the life of your battery is to turn the brightness of the screen down. To do this, bring up the Charms bar and select the 'Settings' charm. Click or touch 'Screen' and a draggable bar appears, where you can quickly adjust the brightness of the screen.

86 | Chapter 1   Windows 8: Expert Tips and Tricks

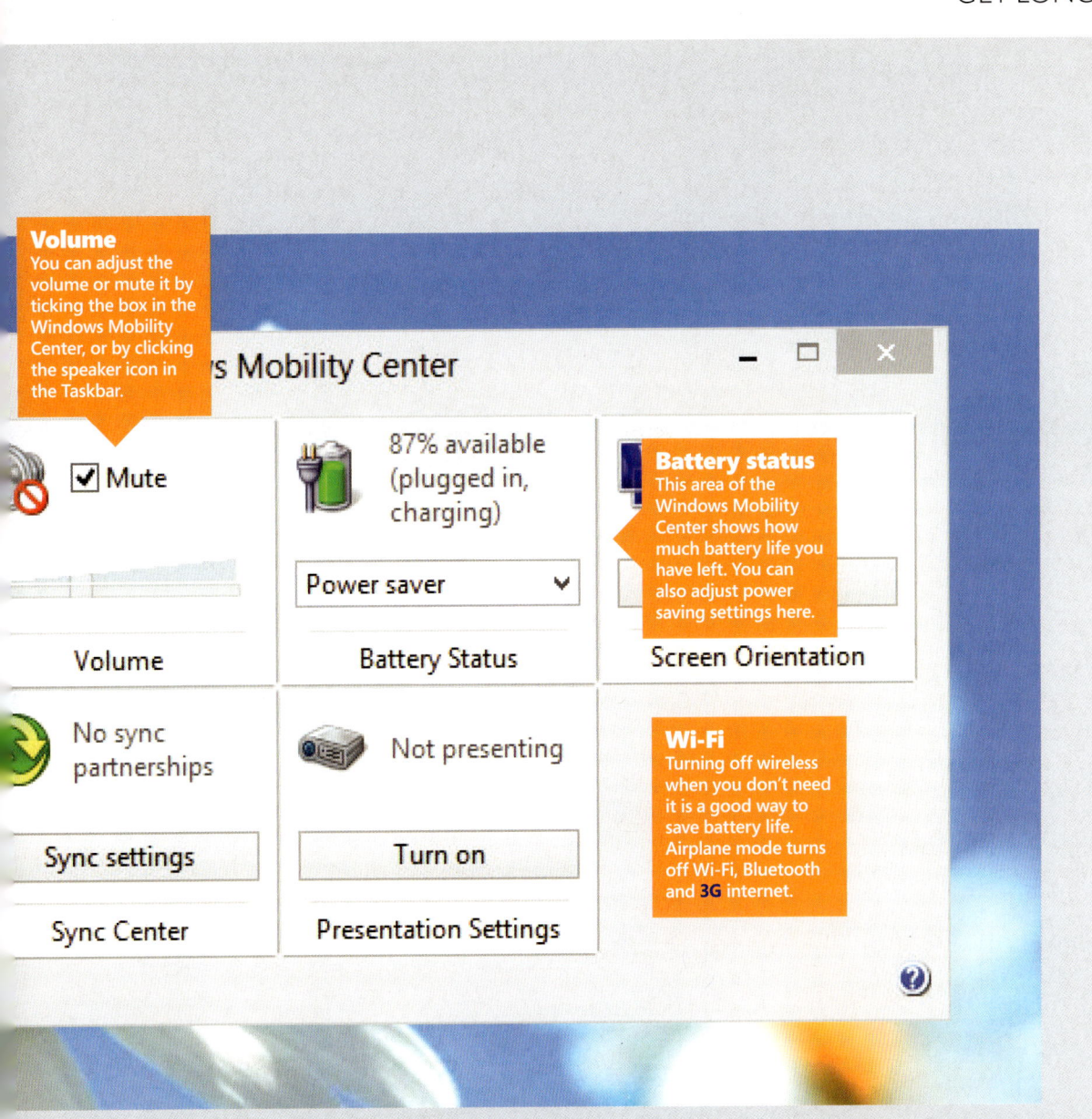

GET LONGER BATTERY LIFE

Volume
You can adjust the volume or mute it by ticking the box in the Windows Mobility Center, or by clicking the speaker icon in the Taskbar.

Battery status
This area of the Windows Mobility Center shows how much battery life you have left. You can also adjust power saving settings here.

Wi-Fi
Turning off wireless when you don't need it is a good way to save battery life. Airplane mode turns off Wi-Fi, Bluetooth and **3G** internet.

Jargon buster!

3G
Stands for the third generation of mobile internet. Normally used by mobile phones to access the internet from almost anywhere in the world, but other devices, such as some ebook readers, also incorporate the technology.

USB
Universal Serial Bus is a connection that enables you to plug devices straight into your computer. Unlike older connections, you do not need to turn off your PC before you plug USB devices in, nor do you need to install any software – Windows should detect and install the device automatically.

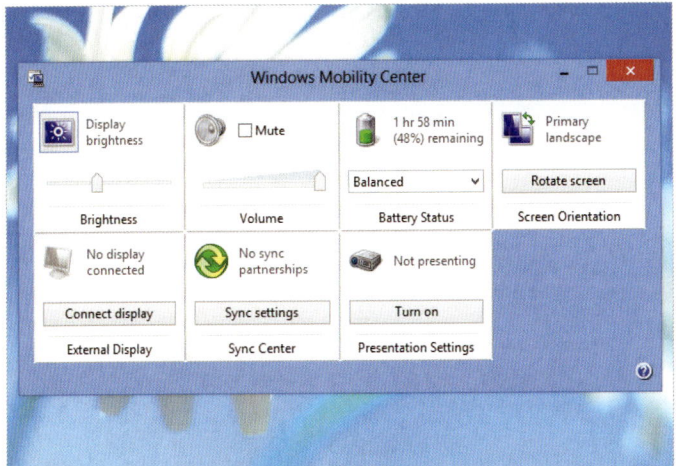

3 Windows Mobility Center
Windows Mobility Center is a great tool for Windows 8 devices. To get to it, type 'Mobility' into the Start screen and select 'Settings'. Click on 'Windows Mobility Center' to open up the program. From here you can change a number of settings to prolong your device's battery life.

4 Mute the volume
It might not be the most obvious thing to do, but you can make a big difference to your battery life if you lower – or, even better, mute – the volume of your mobile device. It means that precious battery power won't be used up on pumping out sounds when you don't need it to.

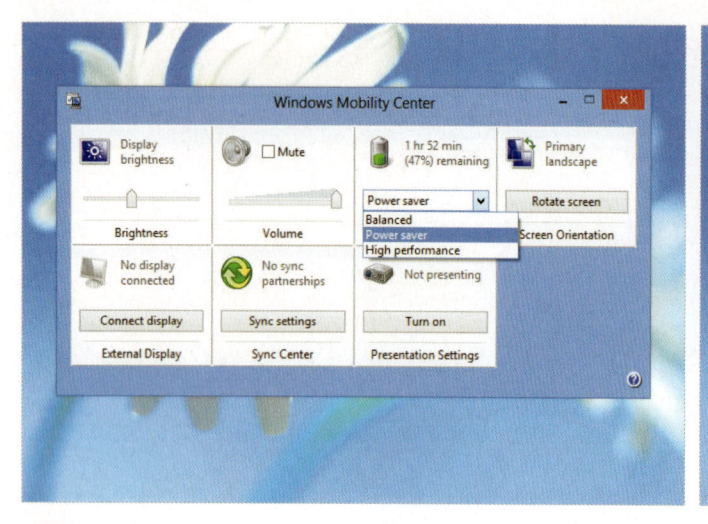

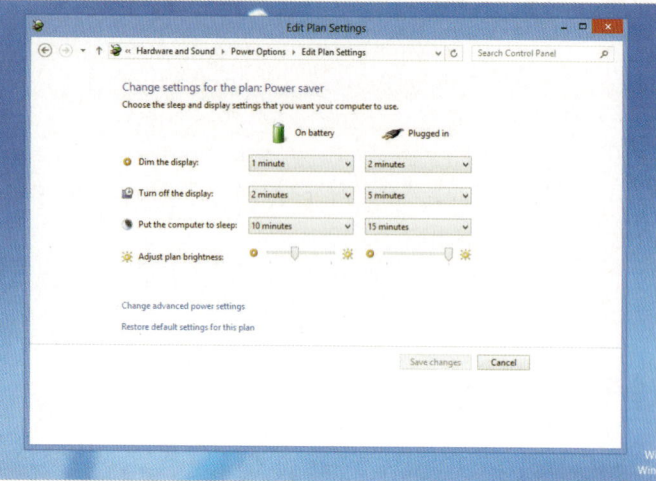

5 Change the power settings

In the Windows Mobility Center you can quickly change the power settings of your device. The default choices are 'Balanced', 'Power saver' and 'High performance'. 'Power saver' tweaks the settings for a longer battery life, but at a slight price when it comes to your device's performance.

6 Advanced power settings

You can tweak the power settings by going to the Start screen and typing in 'power'. Select 'Settings' and then 'Choose a power plan'. Select the power plan you want to edit, then click 'Change plan settings'. You can then change settings, such as how long until the screen dims when not in use.

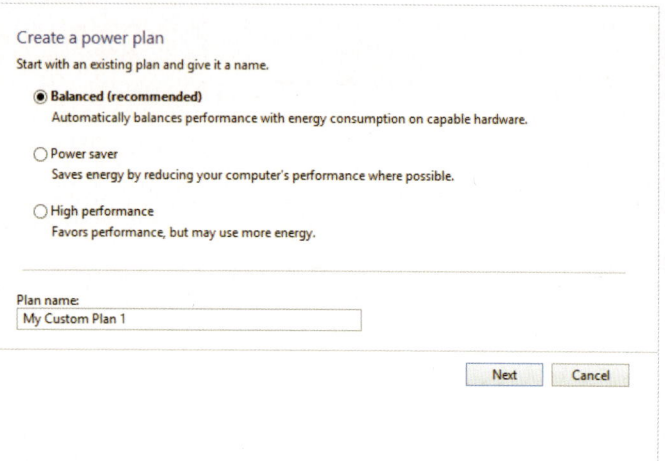

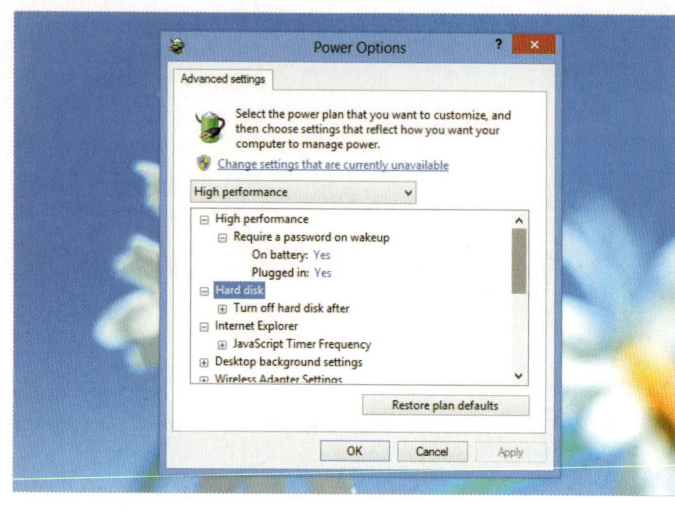

7 Create your own power plan

From the Power Options window you opened in step 6, you can also create a new power plan to suit your needs. Click 'Create a power plan' on the left-hand side of the window, then select which power plan you want to base your new one on. Give it a name, then click 'Next'. Now you can adjust the settings and click 'Create'.

8 More advanced settings

You can access even more advanced power settings if you're confident with using Windows. From the Power Options window, click 'Change plan settings' next to a plan, then select 'Change advanced power settings'. From here you can change settings for when to turn off your hard drive, USB settings and much more.

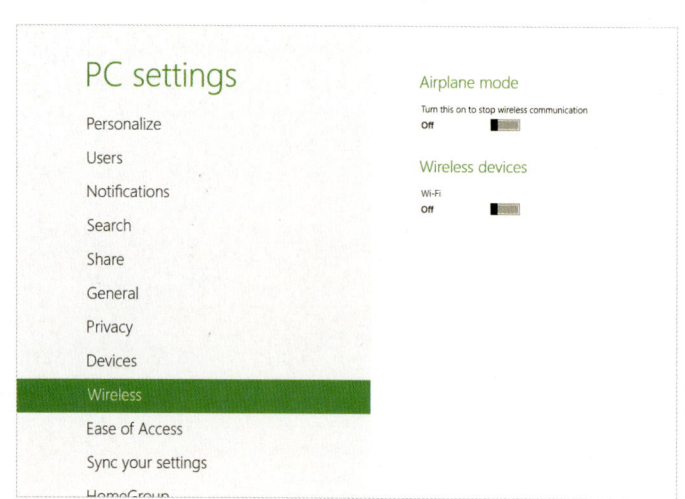

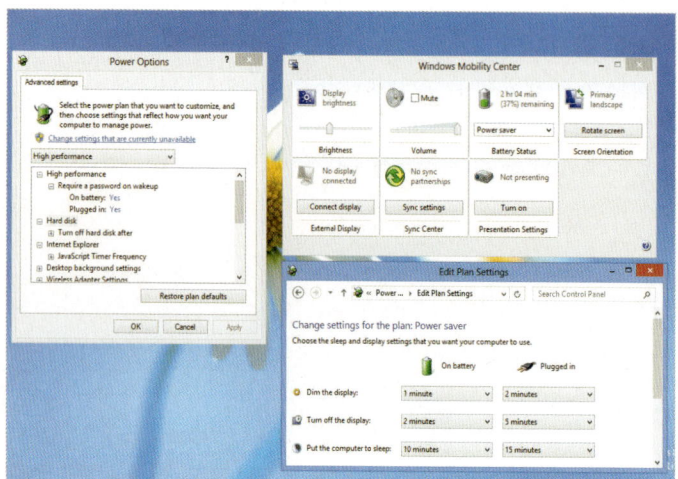

9 Turn off wireless

If you're using your device away from a wireless network, you can turn Wi-Fi off to save your battery power. Bring up the Charms bar in Windows 8 by swiping from the right-hand side of the screen. Now click 'Settings', then 'Change PC settings'. Click 'Wireless' and then change 'Wi-Fi' to 'Off'.

10 Enjoy a better battery life!

Now that you've followed these steps, you should see a noticeable improvement in your battery life. You don't need to do each step to see a benefit, and you should make sure that any changes don't create more problems. A pitch-black screen would boost the battery but will lead to eye strain!

IT'S HERE!

Your favourite magazine is now available on

Google play

Learn how to...

Upgrade to Windows 8 today!
If your current computer is running any version of Windows, you can upgrade it to Windows 8 with the minimum of fuss – we show you how

WORKS WITH
Windows 8
Windows 8 Pro
Windows RT

Thankfully, it's never been easier to upgrade from a previous version of Windows to the latest release, and Microsoft has helpfully made the upgrade process from Windows 7 to Windows 8 as simple as possible. As long as you select the correct option, you can upgrade to Windows 8 without losing any of your Windows settings, personal files and apps that you've installed in Windows 7. The good news is that if you are upgrading from Windows Vista or Windows XP, then the process is also really easy. All you need to do is follow our walkthrough and you'll have Windows 8 up and running in no time at all.

Upgrade to Windows 8

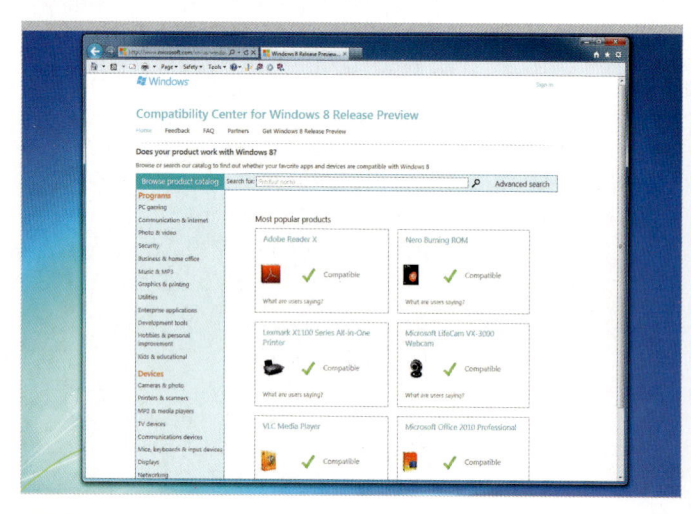

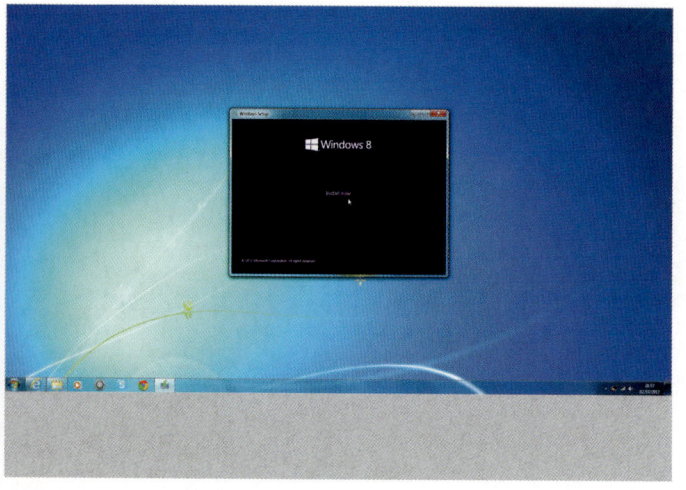

1 Check compatibility
If you're upgrading from Windows 7 and have mostly new hardware and software, compatibility shouldn't be a problem, but we advise visiting www.microsoft.com/en-us/windows/compatibility/en-US/CompatCenter/Home. This site lets you type in your hardware or software and check to make sure you can use it in Windows 8.

2 Insert the disc
Once you are happy to begin the upgrade, insert the Windows 8 installation disc into your computer. If you have purchased and downloaded Windows 8 online, click the 'Install Windows 8' icon. After a few seconds, a window appears. Select 'Install now' to begin the installation process.

90 | Chapter 1 Windows 8: Expert Tips and Tricks

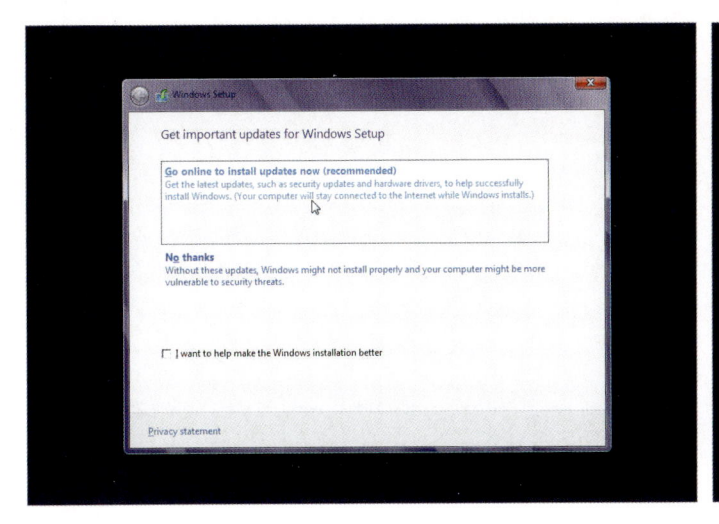

UPGRADE TO WINDOWS 8 TODAY!

3 Install important updates
To ensure the installation goes as smoothly as possible, make sure the installation process updates itself when prompted. This fixes any problems or bugs that Microsoft has found. On the next screen, click 'Go online to install updates now'. If you don't have an internet connection, however, click 'No thanks'.

4 Accept the licence terms
The next step is important, because without agreeing to the licence terms, you will not be able to complete the installation. Depending on what version of Windows 8 you're installing, the licence terms will be different, so it can be worth a quick read. Click 'I accept the licence terms', then 'Next'.

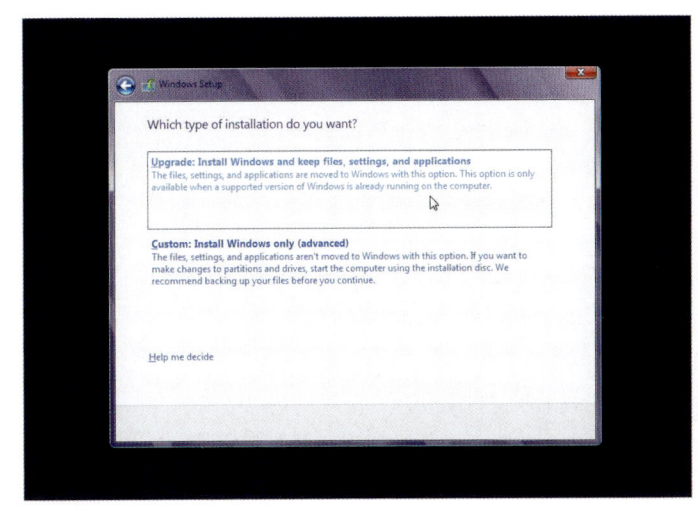

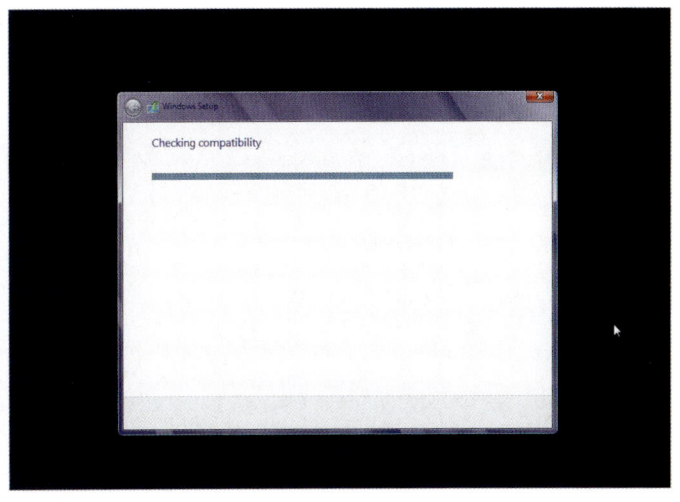

5 Choose to upgrade
In the next step of the installation process, you're asked how you want to install Windows 8. It is vitally important to select 'Upgrade: Install Windows and keep files, settings, and applications'. If you select the other option – 'Install Windows only' – then you run the risk of losing your files and settings.

6 Check compatibility and away you go!
The installation process now checks that the version of Windows 7 you're using is compatible with the version of Windows 8 you're upgrading to. Windows 7 Home Premium, Home Basic and Starter can upgrade to Windows 8, while Windows 7 Ultimate and Professional can upgrade to Windows 8 Pro as well.

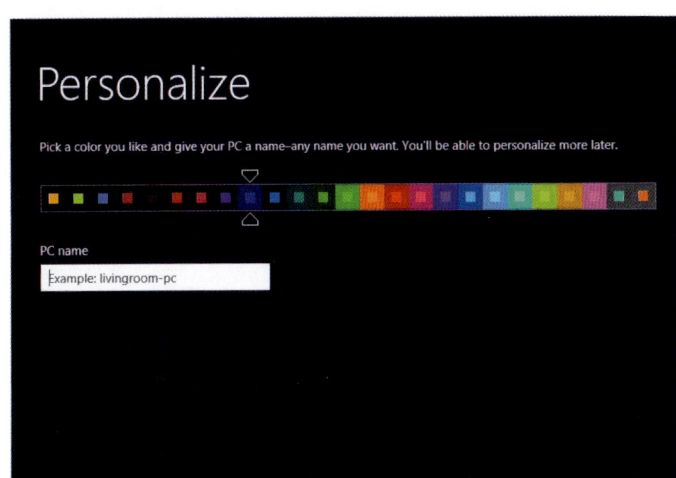

7 Setting up and configuring Windows 8
Assuming all is well, Windows 7 now upgrades itself to Windows 8. During the upgrade process, your computer may restart itself a number of times – but don't worry, because that's normal. Once done, you're asked to configure Windows 8, by setting the colour scheme, for example.

8 Enjoy Windows 8
Congratulations, you have now successfully upgraded your computer from Windows 7 to Windows 8. All your files, folders, programs and settings will still be there, but you get all the great new features of Windows 8 as well. It's the easiest way to get started with Windows 8.

Learn how to...

Use File History to save the day

There's little worse than finding an all-important file has been deleted or become corrupted. Luckily, File History can help salvage any problems

WORKS WITH
Windows 8
Windows 8 Pro
Windows RT

While many of the new features in Windows 8 have had a lot of publicity, some of the best and most useful ones have been introduced with remarkably little fanfare. One such feature is File History, but when used correctly, it can be a real life-saver. Windows 8 takes periodic snapshots of your files as you work on them. If there is any major change, or if the file has encountered a problem that has caused it to become unusable, the File History tool can be used to revert the file to a previous state. Like the best Windows 8 features, File History is powerful, it works well and it's incredibly easy to use.

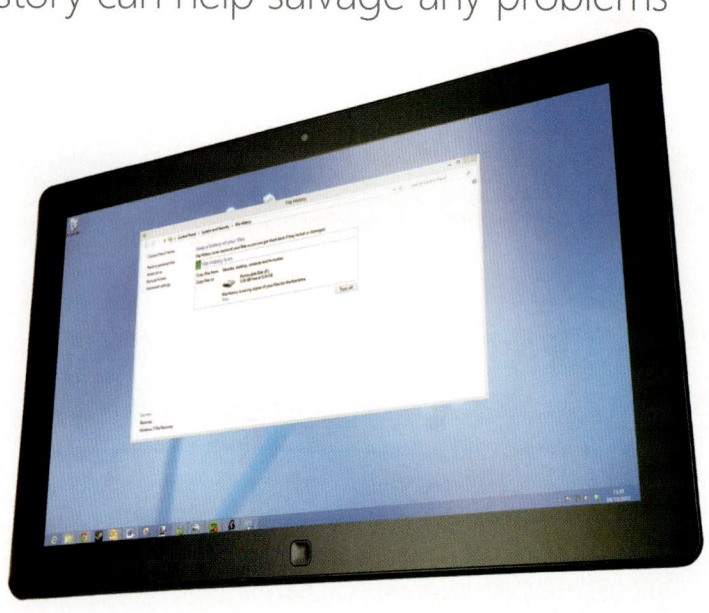

Rescue your files with File History

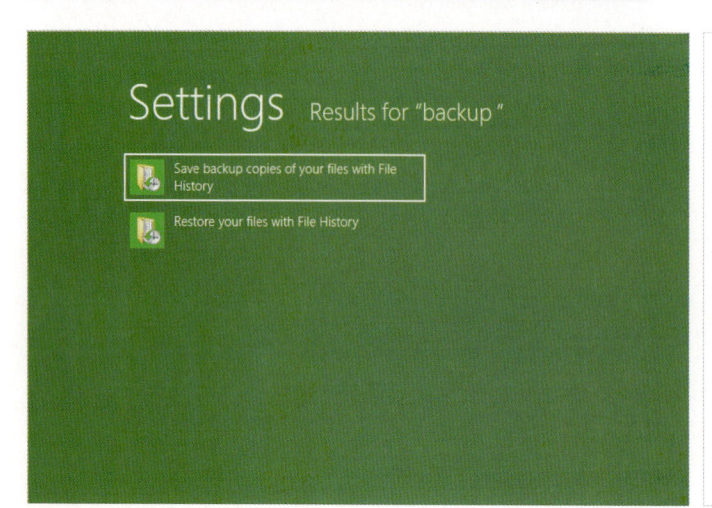

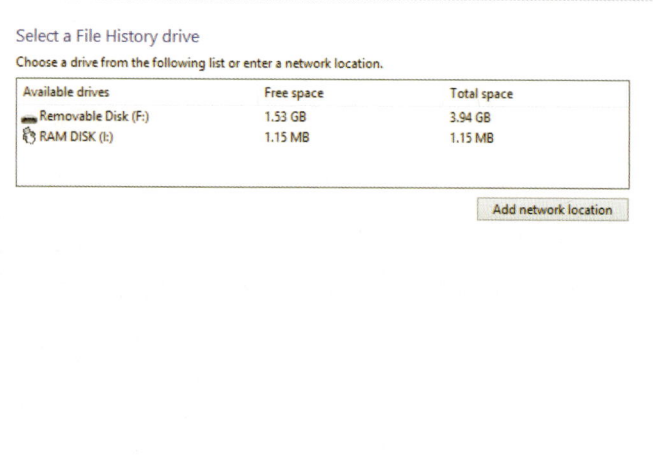

1 Enable File History
By default File History is turned off, so go to the Start screen and type 'backup', then select 'Settings'. Select 'Save backup copies of your files with File History', then select 'Turn on'. If you're asked if you want to recommend the drive you're using to members of your **HomeGroup**, select 'Yes' if on a home network, otherwise click 'No'.

2 Select an external drive
File History can save backups of your files to an external hard drive, or even a **NAS** device. To choose a drive, click 'Select drive' on the left-hand side of the screen. You're then shown a window that lists all the USB drives that are connected to your computer. Select a drive and then click 'OK'.

92 | Chapter 1   Windows 8: Expert Tips and Tricks

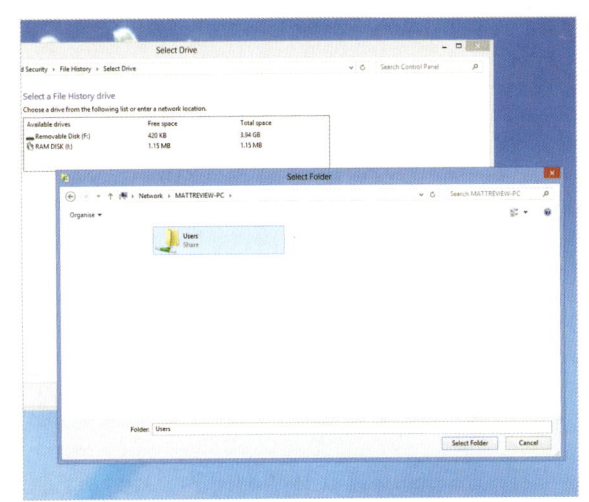

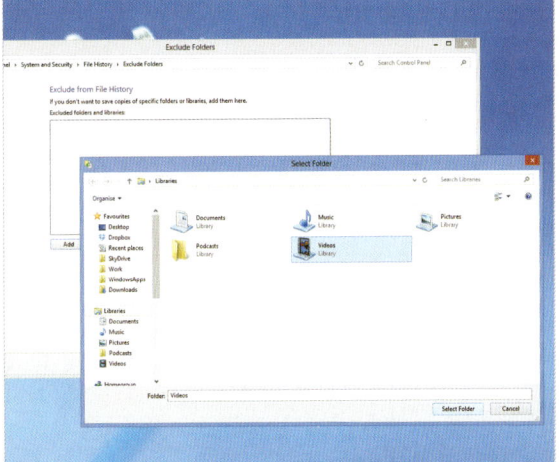

USE FILE HISTORY

Jargon buster!

HomeGroup
The easy way to share files, folders and printers between devices on your home network. By adding PCs and devices running Windows 8 to the same HomeGroup, they can access the files you choose, making home networking extremely easy.

NAS
Network-attached storage – drives that plug straight into your network, via your router, rather than into a PC. The advantage of this is that any PC or device on the network can access the drive and use it as though it were plugged directly into the device.

3 Back up to a network drive
If you have a NAS device, or a USB drive plugged into your router, you can save your File History there. You can even select a folder in another PC on your network. Click 'Select drive', then 'Add network location'. Click where you want to save, then 'Select Folder'.

4 Exclude folders
Backing up all your files and folders can take a lot of time and disk space. Not all of your files need backups, so save time and capacity by leaving out unnecessary folders. From the main screen, select 'Exclude folders', then click 'Add' to add folders you want to be left out.

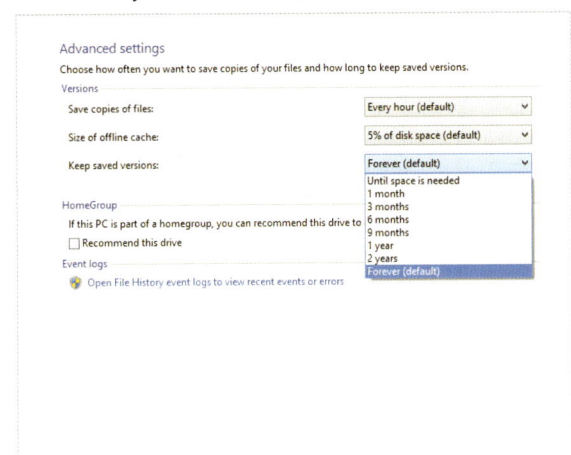

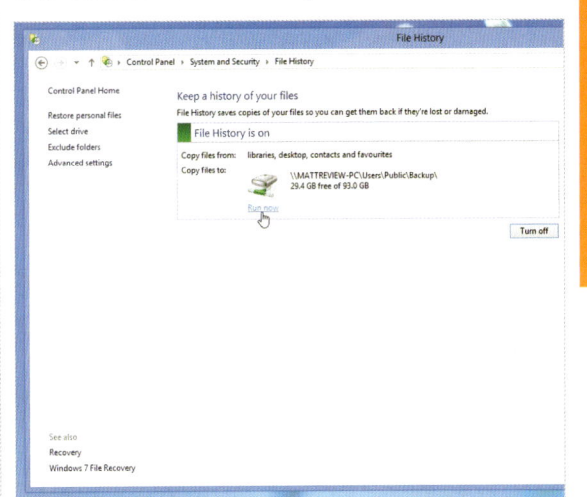

5 Set advanced options
Click 'Advanced settings'. You can set how regularly copies of your files are made, from every 10 minutes to daily, as well as change the size of the offline cache (which limits how much disk space File History takes up), and how long the saved files are kept for.

6 Run File History
When you choose a new drive for File History to use, it begins backing up files automatically. It then periodically backs up files depending on the schedule you set, or every hour if you've left it at its default. You can manually start the process by clicking 'Run now'.

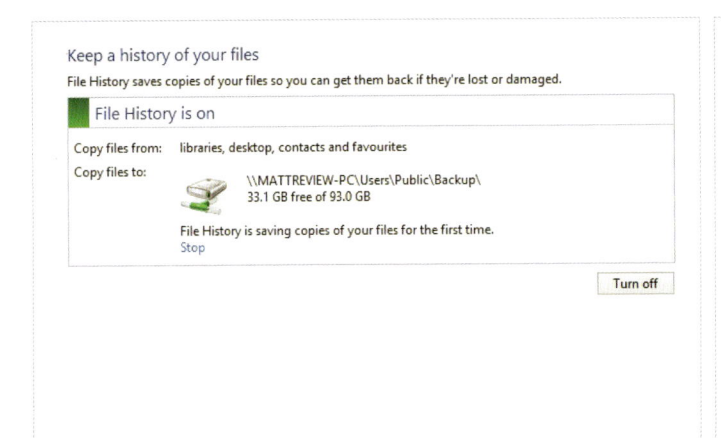

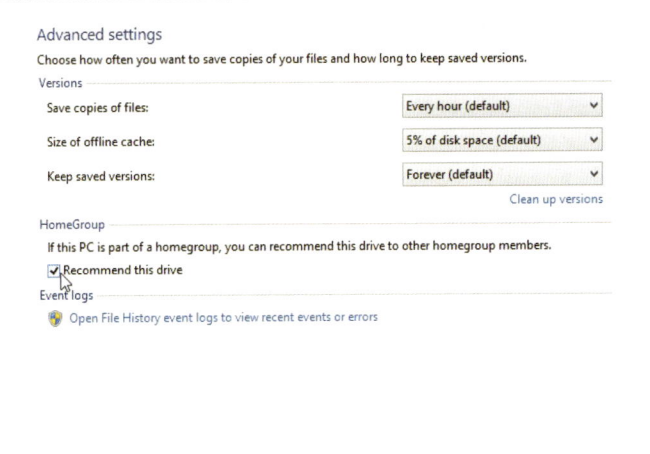

7 Restore previous versions of your files
If disaster strikes, load up File History as in Step 1, and select 'Restore personal files' from the left-hand side of the screen. You can then choose previous versions of the files you have selected for backing up, and restore them to avoid any of the problems or errors that you have encountered.

8 Make sure you're always protected
By following these steps you'll ensure that your important files are always kept safe. If you have a number of Windows 8 devices, make sure that all of them use this great feature. If they are all on the same HomeGroup, you can get them to share the back-up drive by going to 'Advanced settings' and ticking 'Recommend this drive'.

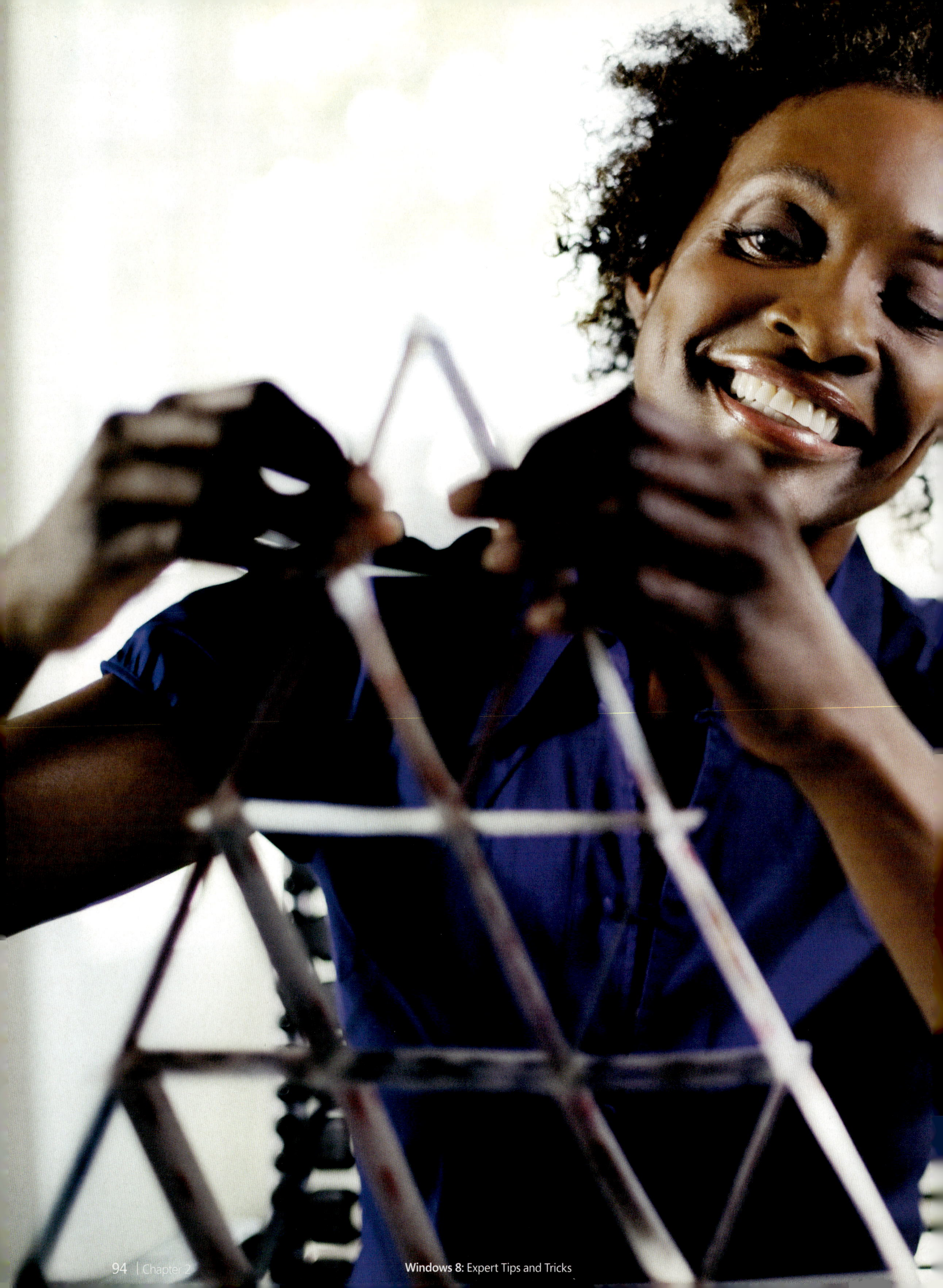

Upgrade

TRY THIS!
Explore the Windows Store
110

Windows 8 is great – but you can make it even better...

Section 5

96	Get more from Windows 8
98	Improving your audio
100	Set default programs
101	Speed up your startup
102	Internet Explorer 10
106	Stay entertained
108	Find your way with Maps
110	Buy amazing apps
112	Schedule maintenance tasks
114	Synchronise settings
116	Set up a HomeGroup
118	10 tips for using SkyDrive

DO THIS NOW...

Get more from Windows 8

There are plenty of ways you can add more functions

Open the unknown

Most of the time you'll have an app on your PC that can open your files, but occasionally you'll come across a file that none of your applications can handle. If that's the case, right-click on the file in Windows Explorer and choose 'Open With...' You'll see a 'Look for an app in the Store' option, which enables Windows 8 to find an app for you. You can also click 'More Options' to see installed programs and apps that may be able to open the file. Quite often, you'll have something that you can at least try to open the file with – it's always worth trying Internet Explorer and Reader because they can open many different types of files.

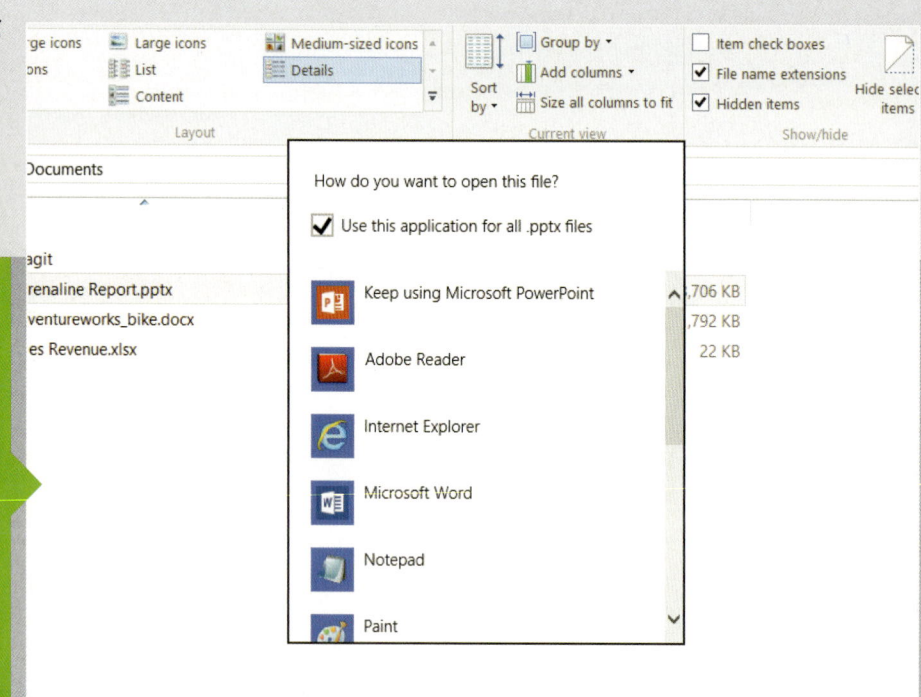

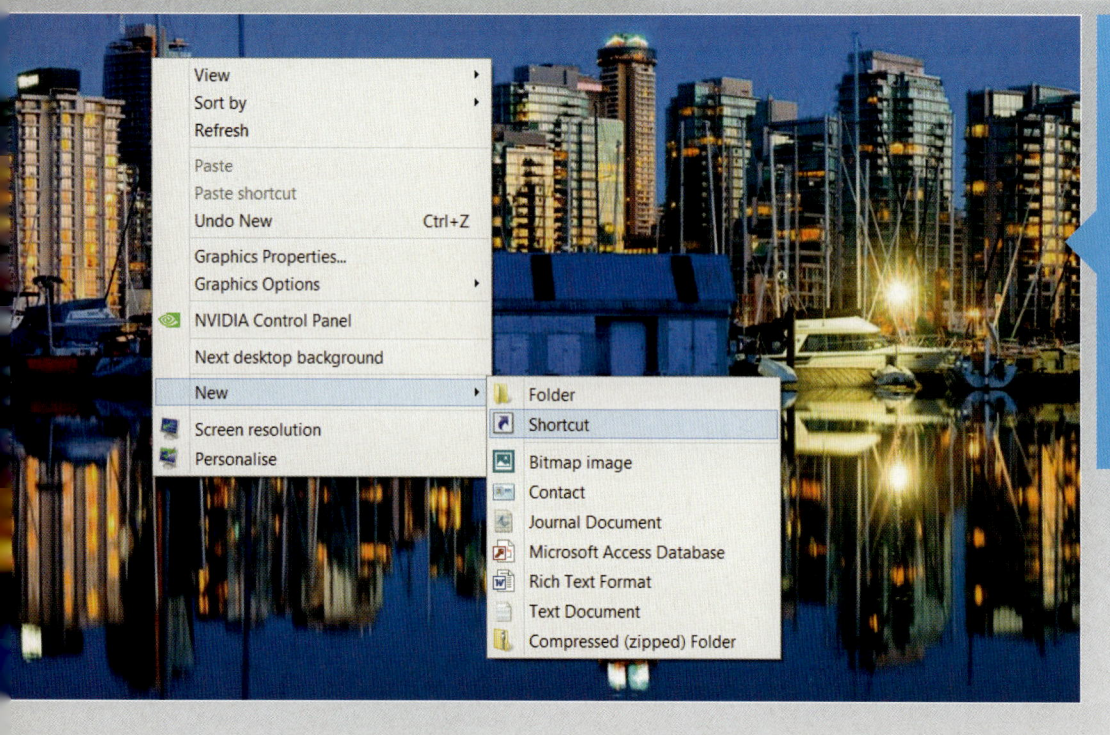

Launch quickly

Windows 8 still supports shortcuts, so you can use a little trick to be able to get to the apps you need from the desktop, which is perfect if, say, you want to shut down your PC with a click. Launch the desktop app, right-click an empty part of the desktop and click 'New > Shortcut'. Browse to the application you'd like to launch and click 'Finish'. You can then launch applications directly from your desktop instead of having to go to the Start screen. If you do want to add a new shortcut to the Start screen, right-click the shortcut, select 'Pin to ' and it should appear on the far right of the Start screen – just drag the tile wherever you like.

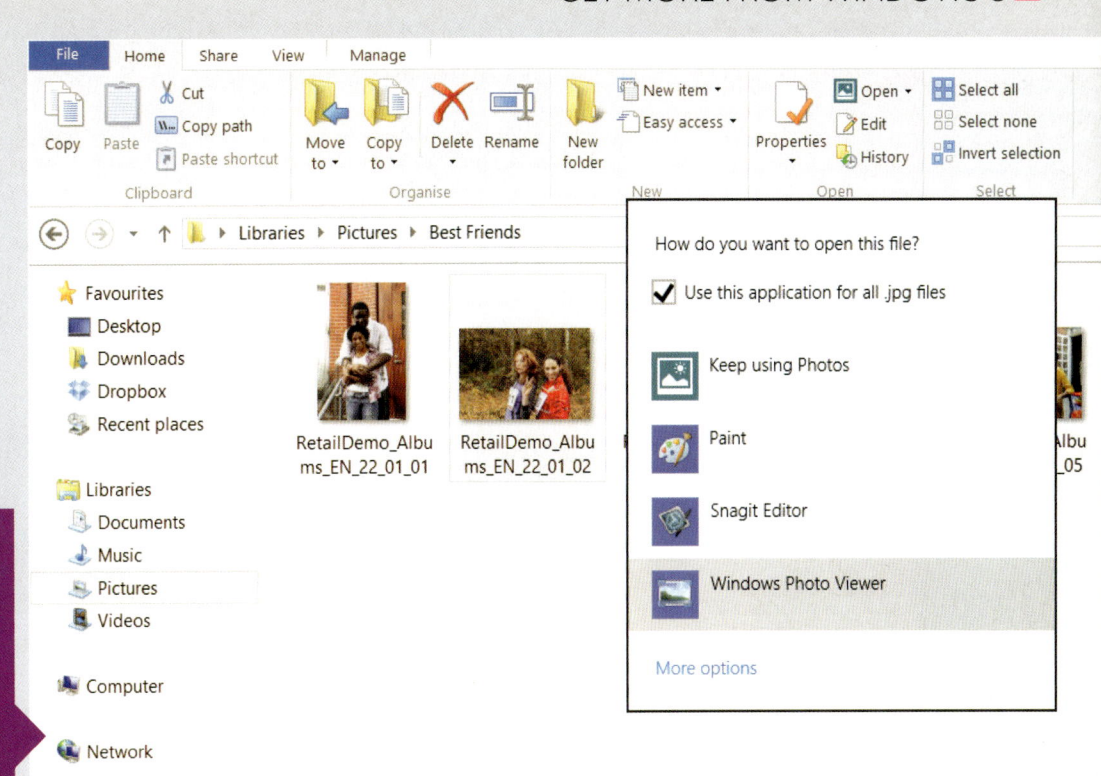

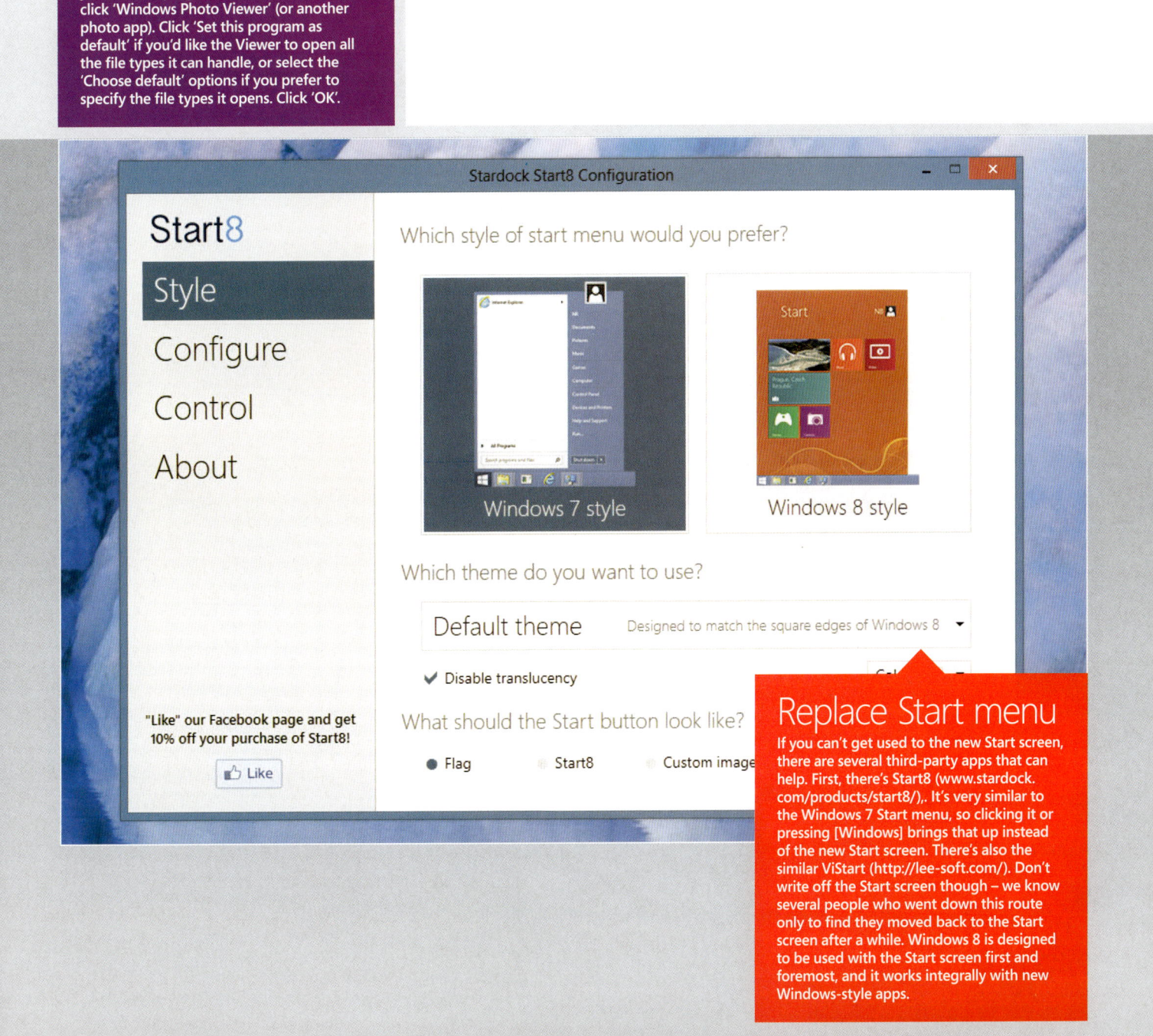

GET MORE FROM WINDOWS 8

Open photos
If you double-click an image file in Windows Explorer, it doesn't open in a Photo Viewer window; instead it switches to the full-screen Photos app. That's fine for viewing single photos but not great if you want to stay in the desktop. To choose where you'd like photos to open, go to 'Control Panel > Programs > Default Program' and select 'Set your default programs'. Scroll down and click 'Windows Photo Viewer' (or another photo app). Click 'Set this program as default' if you'd like the Viewer to open all the file types it can handle, or select the 'Choose default' options if you prefer to specify the file types it opens. Click 'OK'.

Replace Start menu
If you can't get used to the new Start screen, there are several third-party apps that can help. First, there's Start8 (www.stardock.com/products/start8/),. It's very similar to the Windows 7 Start menu, so clicking it or pressing [Windows] brings that up instead of the new Start screen. There's also the similar ViStart (http://lee-soft.com/). Don't write off the Start screen though – we know several people who went down this route only to find they moved back to the Start screen after a while. Windows 8 is designed to be used with the Start screen first and foremost, and it works integrally with new Windows-style apps.

Windows 8: Expert Tips and Tricks

Chapter 2 | 97

25 TOP TIPS FOR...
Improving your audio

Listen very carefully: Windows 8 makes managing audio easier and more comprehensive than ever before

1 Let's start simple: you can access Windows 8's Modern-themed volume control from the Charms bar; move your mouse to the bottom-right, click 'Settings', then look for the volume icon at the bottom of the panel.

2 While you can drag the Modern-themed volume slider up and down to change volume, and see its percentage, there's an option that isn't as obvious – click the volume icon above the slider to mute the sound.

3 Windows 8 supports hardware volume buttons. If you have volume buttons on your tablet, volume keys on your keyboard, or [Fn]+[F-key] combos on your laptop, you'll see a handy overlay on-screen as you adjust.

4 Unfortunately, there's no way to tweak the audio of different Windows 8 apps individually. You have to alter the main volume – which is accessible within apps such as Music.

5 The desktop offers more precision when it comes to the volume levels of running programs. Click the volume icon on the Taskbar, then click 'Mixer' (or type 'volume mixer' at the Start screen) to see sliders corresponding to all of your running programs.

6 You'll notice, in the volume mixer, that there's a line running along the top linking the main volume (on the left) to the highest volume of the others. This is your top level; reduce the main volume and the others go with it, or drag another slider up and you push the main volume up with it.

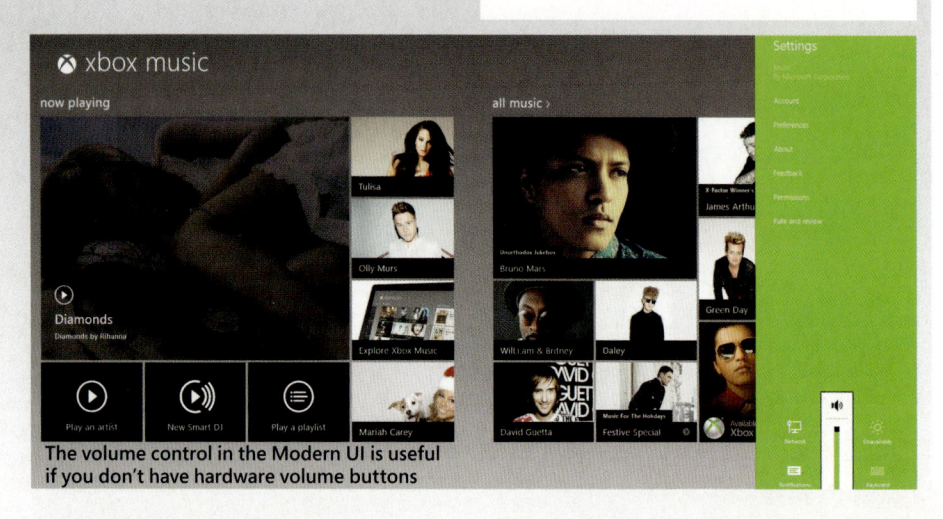

The volume control in the Modern UI is useful if you don't have hardware volume buttons

98 | Chapter 2

Windows 8: Expert Tips and Tricks

IMPROVING YOUR AUDIO

7 The icons at the top of the volume mixer can be useful – click certain icons and they send you to an appropriate settings screen or program.

8 Want to shut up a particular program without muting your whole PC? The speaker icon below each slider is an individual mute for that app, so you can quiet it without needing to adjust its volume level. Click the mute icon on the left to mute the whole system.

9 Right-click the volume icon on the desktop, then click 'Playback devices'. You'll see all the audio outputs your PC has, everything from headphone and speaker sockets to digital audio output and even the audio sent via your HDMI port, if you have one.

10 In the playback devices screen, right-click an audio source and select 'Test' to emit a test tone on each output. If one sounds louder than the other, or can't be heard at all, it may indicate a problem with your speakers or headphones, or a balance issue.

11 To check your audio device's balance, click the device then click 'Properties'. Here you can view all sorts of information about that device, but it's the levels tab we're interested in – click 'Balance', then adjust each slider to hear whether it makes a difference.

12 You can add effects to an audio device to sweeten up its sound. In the device properties screen, go to the 'Enhancements' tab. The list enables you to tweak all sorts of things; some require you to have a mic plugged in. The list depends on your device.

13 On the Volume mixer, click the button above 'System Sounds' to bring up the main Sound panel. Click the drop-down box at the top and select 'No Sounds' to disable system sounds and keep Windows quiet. This doesn't affect any other sound from programs.

14 You can use the Sound panel to determine which sounds play at which times. If you'd like to quiet down the generic notification sound, for instance, find 'Notify' in the list and use the drop-down box to select 'None'.

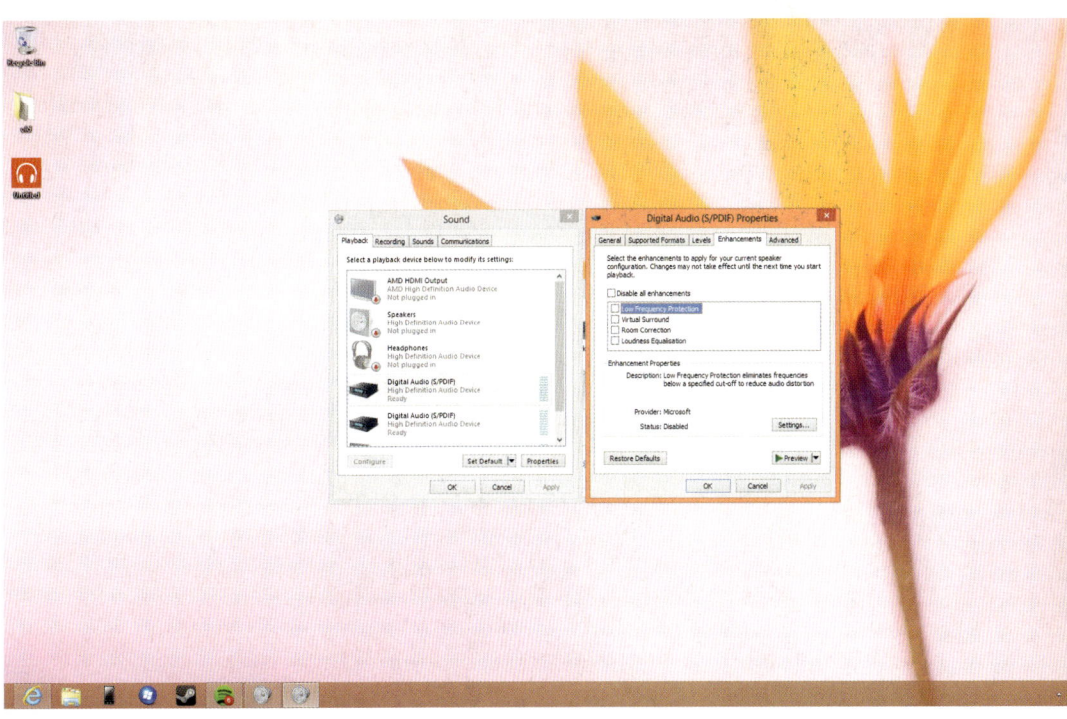

15 You add custom sounds to Windows events, even ones that wouldn't normally have a sound. Click the event you want to customise, click 'Browse', and hunt out a file in .wav format. Use the 'Test' button to check how it sounds.

16 When you've changed a few sounds, you'll notice that the sound scheme box at the top of the Sounds window says '(modified)'. If you're happy with your new sound scheme, click 'Save As…' to save it, or pick the default one again to forget any changes you made.

17 Go to the Communications tab on the sound panel. There's not much to tweak here, but it's a critical spot if you use the Skype app. We're partial to setting all of our other sounds to Mute rather than 80% when receiving a call.

18 If you have a microphone, you can record personal notes and sounds, as you might with a Dictaphone. Go to the Start screen and type 'sound recorder' to find the desktop app; it's easy to use. Record with the button, then save your file when finished.

19 You can also use your mic to control your PC, at least in theory. The practice might not be entirely accurate! Go to the Start menu, type 'speech', and you're sent to the Speech Recognition wizard, which will get you set up.

20 Want Windows 8 to talk to you? Just use the Narrator function. Search for it on the Start screen, or switch it on from the icon at the bottom-left of the login screen. It reads text boxes and whatever you focus on, perfect if you have trouble reading text on screen.

Turn on enhancements to get even more from your sound devices and balance your surround sound speakers

Quick tips

21 Want something to listen to? Try the Xbox Music app, which should be installed on your Start screen by default. If it's not, you can always hunt it out and download it from the Windows Store.

22 Spotify is a fantastic source of music, and you can listen free – up to a certain limit – by downloading its desktop app from www.spotify.com.

23 Want to listen to some spoken word? You could do worse than downloading the Audioboo app from the Windows Store. It has plenty.

24 TunerFree, which is available from the Windows Store, enables you to stream BBC radio stations live, so you can keep up with music, sport and more.

25 If TunerFree doesn't have enough for you, Radyo's massive collection of world radio stations should surely keep your ears satisfied!

Windows 8: Expert Tips and Tricks

Learn how to...

Set default programs in Windows 8

You may find that Windows 8 uses full-screen apps whenever you try to open certain files, but if you want your favourite program to open them up instead, it can be easily done with a little tweak

WORKS WITH
Windows 8
Windows 8 Pro
Windows RT

Windows 8 comes with a host of new apps that are used to open certain types of files. For example, clicking on a photograph opens the Photos app, which displays your photos in an attractive and easy-to-browse way. However, the app is full-screen, which might not be what you want when you're quickly clicking through picture files. Luckily, it's pretty easy to change the default program, so you can use all your favourite software from previous versions of Windows to open your files instead. It takes no time at all, but it can save you a lot of frustration if you're not particularly keen on using full-screen apps. We take you through how to make the change below.

Change the default programs

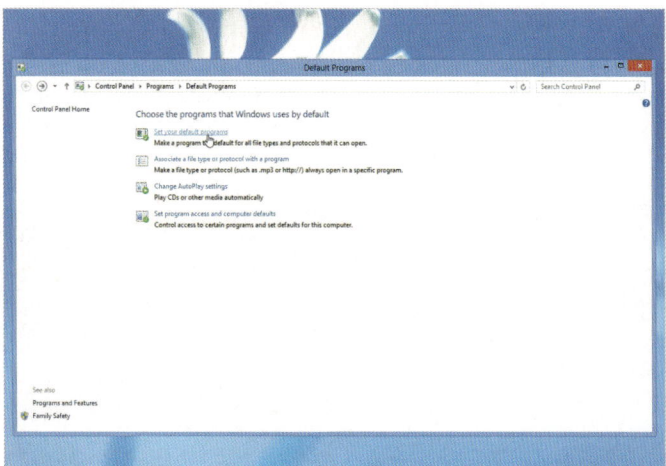

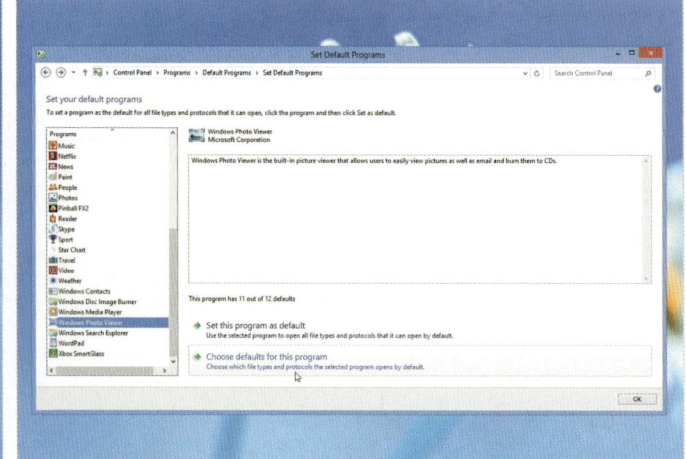

1 Open up Default Programs
To change what programs are used to open files by default, type 'Default' into the Start screen and then select 'Default Programs'. The Default Programs window now opens. Select 'Set Default Programs' and Windows 8 scans your computer for all of your installed programs.

2 Select the program you want
From the list, select the program you want to use to open certain files. For example, if you want Windows Photo Viewer to open photos rather than the Photos app, click 'Windows Photo Viewer' from the left. Choose 'Set this program as default'. If you want more control, select 'Choose defaults for this program'.

Learn how to...

Speed up your startup

If you always find yourself itching to get going as soon as you switch on your PC, you can bypass the login screen to quickly boot into Windows 8

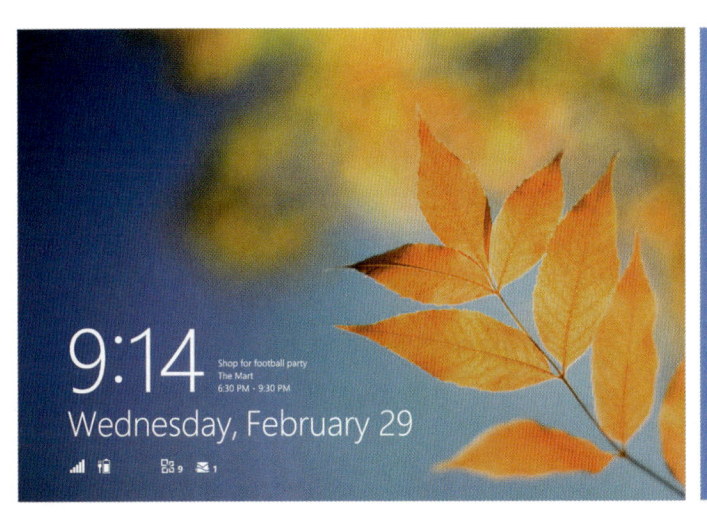

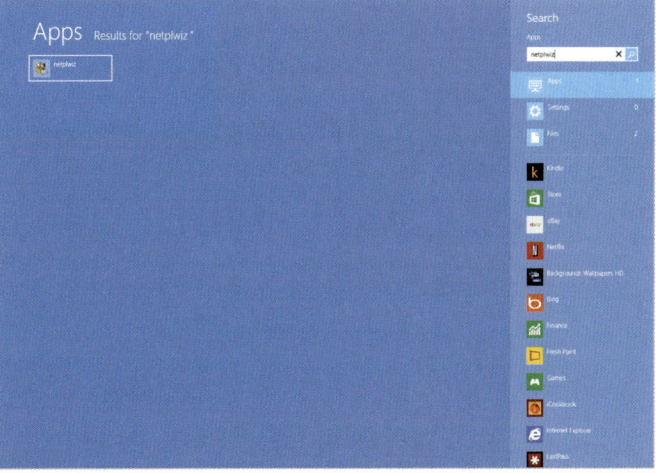

1 What for?
Bypassing the login screen when Windows 8 starts up is a good idea if nobody else accesses your computer. It saves the hassle of clicking the screen and having to type in a password. This means you can get into Windows quicker and start using it. It can't be turned off by default, so here's how to do it.

2 Open User Accounts
Go to the Start screen and begin typing in 'netplwiz'. The search function automatically opens up and the word is typed into the appropriate place. You'll now see the application Netplwiz appear in the left-hand area, so just click or tap on this to open the User Accounts window.

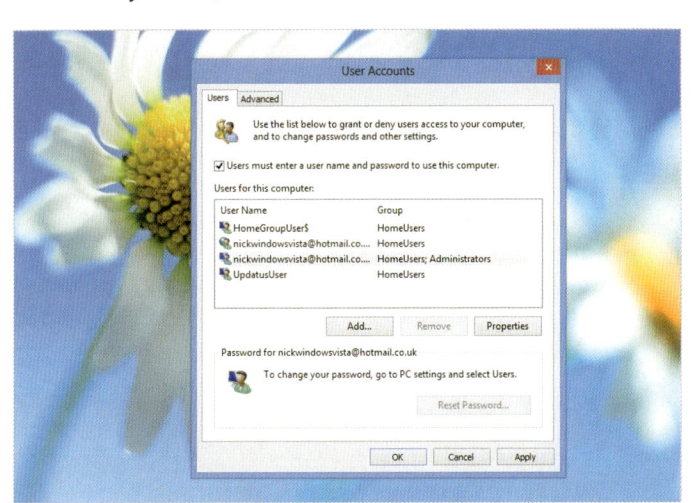

3 Remove restriction
Within the User Accounts window, you'll see a list in the User Name area – select the one that you use to log in with (your email address, with the word 'Administrators' next to it). Then uncheck the tick box above, next to where it says 'Users must enter a user name...' and click on 'OK'.

4 Start it up!
A new window appears asking you to type your original password in twice, then just hit 'OK'. That's it! Now, when you next start up your Windows 8 PC, it will go straight to the Start screen without any prompting from you. If you decide you don't like it, just go through the process again and check the tick box.

10 ways to exploit Internet Explorer 10

Windows 8 comes with a brand new version of Internet Explorer – we show you how to get the most out of it

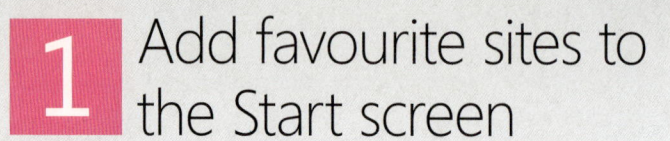

1 Add favourite sites to the Start screen

One of the quickest and easiest ways of getting to your favourite websites is to pin them to the Start screen. When in Internet Explorer's full-screen mode, you'll see a drawing pin icon next to the address bar. Navigate to your favourite website, then click the icon and select 'Pin to Start'. By using this really handy feature, you can create an area on your Start screen where you'll be able to quickly access the websites you visit the most. This is particularly useful when you are using touchscreen tablets, because you won't need to type in any fiddly web addresses using the on-screen keyboard – just a quick tap of the website's tile sends you straight to your favourite part of the internet.

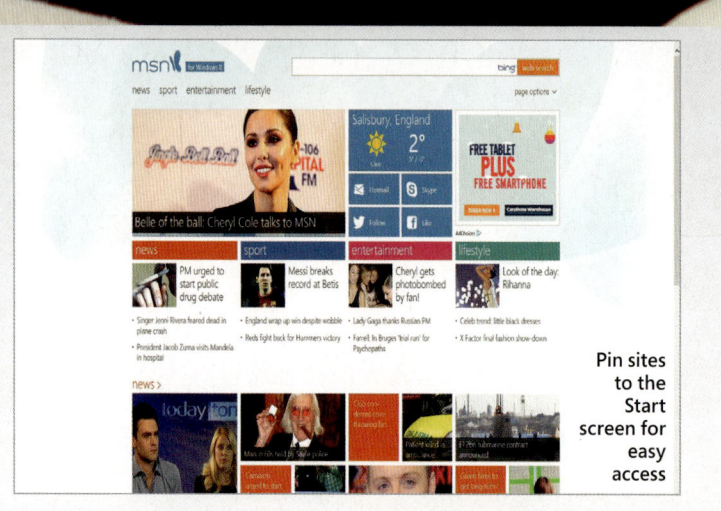

Pin sites to the Start screen for easy access

INTERNET EXPLORER 10 TIPS

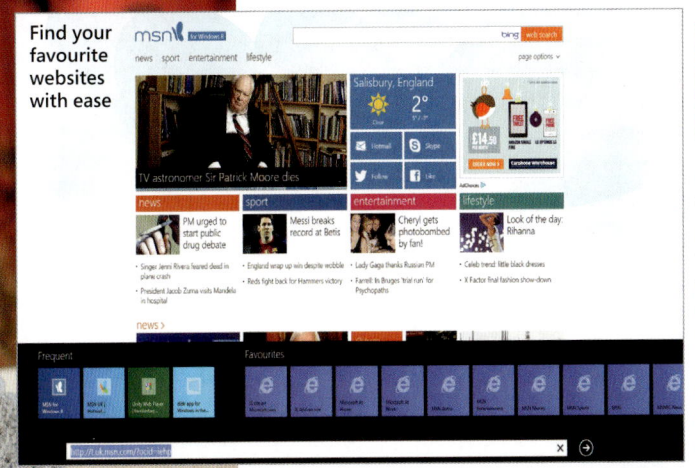

2 View frequently visited websites

Internet Explorer 10 has a clever way of noticing the websites you visit frequently, and assumes that as you go there often, they're probably some of your favourite sites. You can quickly see these, and then click to go there by clicking on the address bar in the full-screen version, or by pressing [Alt]+[D] on the keyboard. In the desktop version, click the 'Star' icon to see a list of your favourite websites. You can add a website to your list of favourite sites easily by either clicking the 'Star' icon in the desktop version and selecting 'Add to favourites' or by pressing the keyboard shortcut [Ctrl]+[D]. Adding sites to your Favourites list makes it easy to quickly go to your favourite websites and web pages in just a few simple clicks.

Find your favourite websites with ease

3 Easily flip through websites

When using the full-screen version of Internet Explorer, you can use the new flip ahead feature, which makes reading a website similar to flicking through a magazine on your Windows 8 device. To turn it on, open Internet Explorer from the Start screen and open the Charms bar by flicking your finger from the right-hand side of the screen. Select 'Internet Options', then set 'Turn on flip ahead' to 'On'. Now when you're browsing websites using the full-screen version of Internet Explorer, you'll see a small box with an arrow on the left-hand side of the screen. Internet Explorer 10 automatically loads the next page if the website when you tap it.

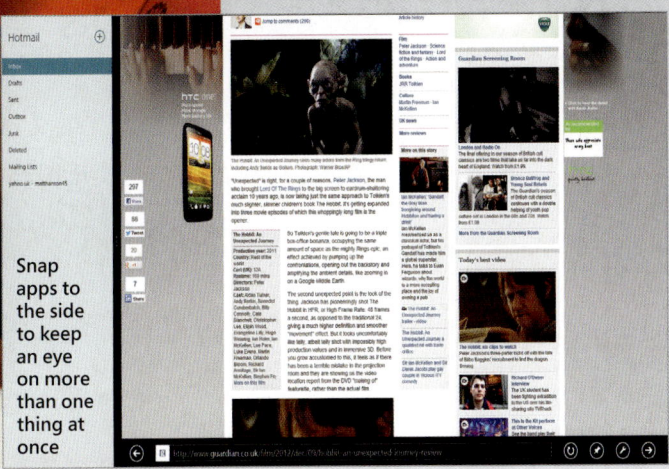

You can flick through pages using the flip ahead feature

4 Snap windows to multitask

When using a touchscreen device, you can easily use another app while browsing the internet, so you can talk to friends on the Messenger app, for example, while seeing what live music is on at a local bar. To snap a window, move your mouse to the top-left corner of the screen, then click on the thumbnail, or swipe from the left side of the screen with your finger to snap the previous app to the side. Once an app has been snapped to the side of the screen, you can easily control it, because the app will be rearranged to fit the small part of the screen. You can click and drag the side of a snapped app to take up more of the screen if you wish.

Snap apps to the side to keep an eye on more than one thing at once

5 Use tabs to navigate around the web

Using tabs while browsing the internet is a really good way of being able to read a number of websites at once. To open a new tab in Internet Explorer 10, right-click or swipe your finger up from the bottom of the screen. You'll see any open tabs, and clicking the '+' sign opens a new tab. Click the '...' button to open an InPrivate browsing session for complete privacy. A useful shortcut for opening a new tab is to press [Ctrl]+[T] on the keyboard. If you're using a mouse, you can open a link on a web page in a new tab by clicking on the link using the middle scroll button of the mouse. You can quickly close a tab by clicking on its title using the middle mouse button as well.

Keep an eye on several sites at once with tabs

Windows 8: Expert Tips and Tricks

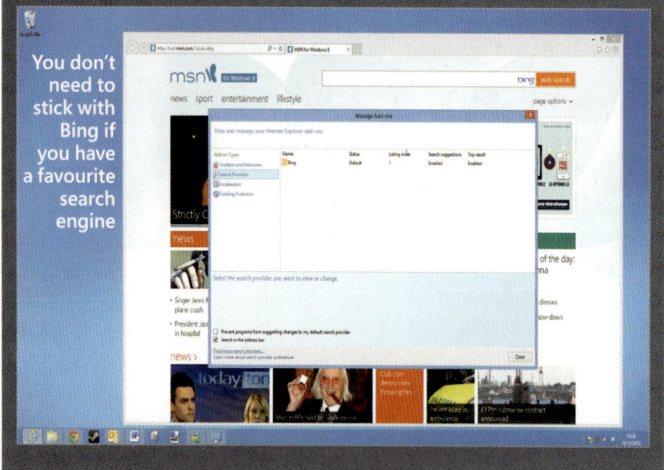

7 Manage add-ons for extra speed

The simplified touch-friendly version of Internet Explorer 10 doesn't allow add-ons, but the desktop version does. Add-ons are good for adding extra functionality to Internet Explorer, and for opening and playing media straight from a website. Open the desktop version of IE 10 and click the 'Settings' icon, then select 'Manage add-ons' to see what add-ons you're using. On the left-hand side of the window you'll see the various types of add-ons there are, such as toolbars and search providers. Clicking each type displays the various add-ons you have installed on the right-hand side of the window. Having too many add-ons can impact on Internet Explorer 10's performance, so disable any that you do not use regularly for a speed boost.

You don't need to stick with Bing if you have a favourite search engine

6 Change the default search provider

By default, Internet Explorer 10 uses Microsoft's Bing search engine to scour the web for what you're looking for. If you want to use a different search provider, open up Internet Explorer in the desktop view of Windows 8 and click the 'gears' icon, which represents Settings. Click 'Manage add-ons > Search Providers', then click 'Find more search providers' to add your favourite search engine. A new web page will open, and from the list click the 'search' link. A list of search providers are displayed. Click the one you want, then click 'Add to Internet Explorer'. In the next window, tick 'Make this my default search provider'.

Keep your add-ons in check to prevent slowdown

8 Stop advertisers seeing you

It's a fact of life that advertising on the internet is becoming more intelligent – and more intrusive. Internet Explorer 10 brings a new feature that helps protect your privacy, called 'Do not track'. It's set on by default, so you can surf safely, but if you want to turn it off, open 'Settings' and go to 'Internet Options' and then 'Advanced'. You can add more advanced protection by opening Internet Explorer on the desktop, clicking the 'Settings' icon, then 'Manage Add-ons'. Click 'Tracking Protection' from the 'Add-on Types' list, then select 'Your Personalised List' and click 'Settings' to add websites and advertisers you want to block.

9 Protect the privacy of your location

Some websites use your location to tailor content depending on where you are. While this feature can be useful – when using mapping websites to find directions from your location, for example, or getting film times from a local cinema – if you don't want to share this information, open the Charms bar, click 'Settings', then 'Internet Options'. Under 'Permissions' you'll see the 'Ask for location' switch. Click the switch to turn it to the 'Off' position. You can also clear any stored location data that websites and apps have accessed while the setting was on by clicking the 'Clear' button that you'll find below the 'Ask for location' switch.

10 See whether the website has an app

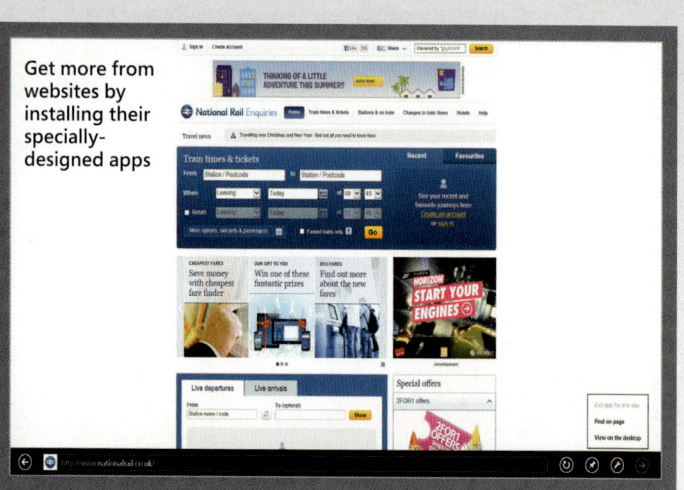

Get more from websites by installing their specially-designed apps

Some websites have specially-designed apps for Windows 8, which give you additional tools and features to help you enjoy the site's content. The advantage of these apps is that they are specially designed to work in Windows 8, so not only do they look great, but they are also laid out to be as easy to navigate on a touchscreen device as possible. Formatting of text and photos, as well as extra interactivity, makes the websites more comfortable to read on small screen devices, such as tablets. Some apps also have Live tiles that keep you informed of any updates to the site. To see whether a website has an app, tap on the address bar while you're on the site, then select 'Page tools'. Click or tap on 'Get an app for this site'.

Is Apple under Tim Cook now a better place?

Can Google ever be toppled in the search market?

tech.
the week in technology

Has Facebook given us all social networking fatigue?

tech. the week in technology
FROM THE MAKERS OF **techradar.**
23rd November 2012 Issue 01

Size matters.
Can Apple make small beautiful?

Why Wii U gets Nintendo back in the game. | How Apple lost its way with Maps. | The chess master beaten by a bug.

The essential new weekly iPad magazine for people who love technology.
Only 69p.

Available on the App Store

FROM THE MAKERS OF **techradar.**

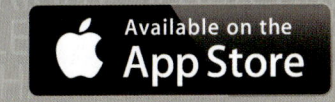

Learn how to...

Stay entertained

Thanks to Windows 8, movies, music and games are now right at your fingertips, turning your device into a marvellous multimedia machine

GAMES

Games galore
The new home of gaming is the Xbox Live Games app, but you can also buy games in the Windows Store. It offers the best of everything, from the latest big-budget releases to simple timewasters, and works whether you're using a touchscreen or a keyboard and mouse.

All about Xbox
The Xbox Windows Games Marketplace and Xbox Games Marketplace are also included in the Xbox Live Games app. This means you can not only buy and download new games to play on your Windows 8 computer from here, you can also get games for your Xbox console.

Gamerscore
The Xbox Live Games app signs into your Xbox Live or Microsoft Account so you can keep track of your Gamerscore from your Windows 8 PC or tablet. What's more, you can boost your Gamerscore by playing on your PC – even with classics such as Minesweeper and Mahjong.

Use your avatar
As part of the Xbox Live integration, you can access your Xbox profile and Achievements list and can create an avatar if you don't already have one. Game saves are no longer limited to one device, and you can save games across the platforms via the internet, too.

STAY ENTERTAINED

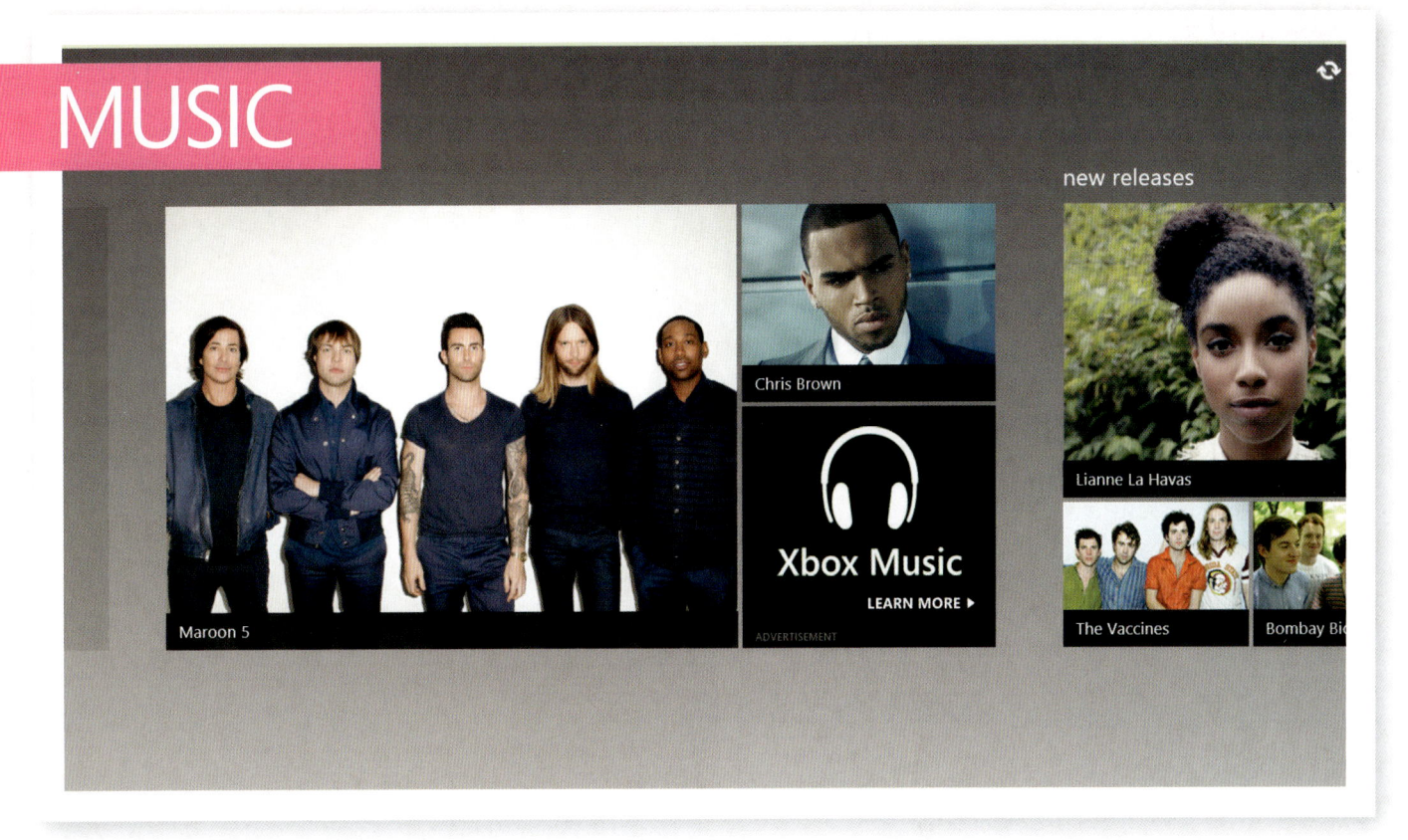

MUSIC

Import your tunes
Windows 8 can import all the music from your old computer. You're not restricted to music in your music library either – you can open a file from anywhere.

Buy music
The Music app includes a Marketplace where you can browse for and buy new songs. Music is downloaded directly to your library.

Stream it
You can also listen to music via the Xbox Music service, which enables you to access tunes on your Windows 8 device as well as Xbox and Windows Phone.

Other tools
The built-in app isn't the only way to access music via your PC – you can also download and stream music from web-based services, such as Spotify.

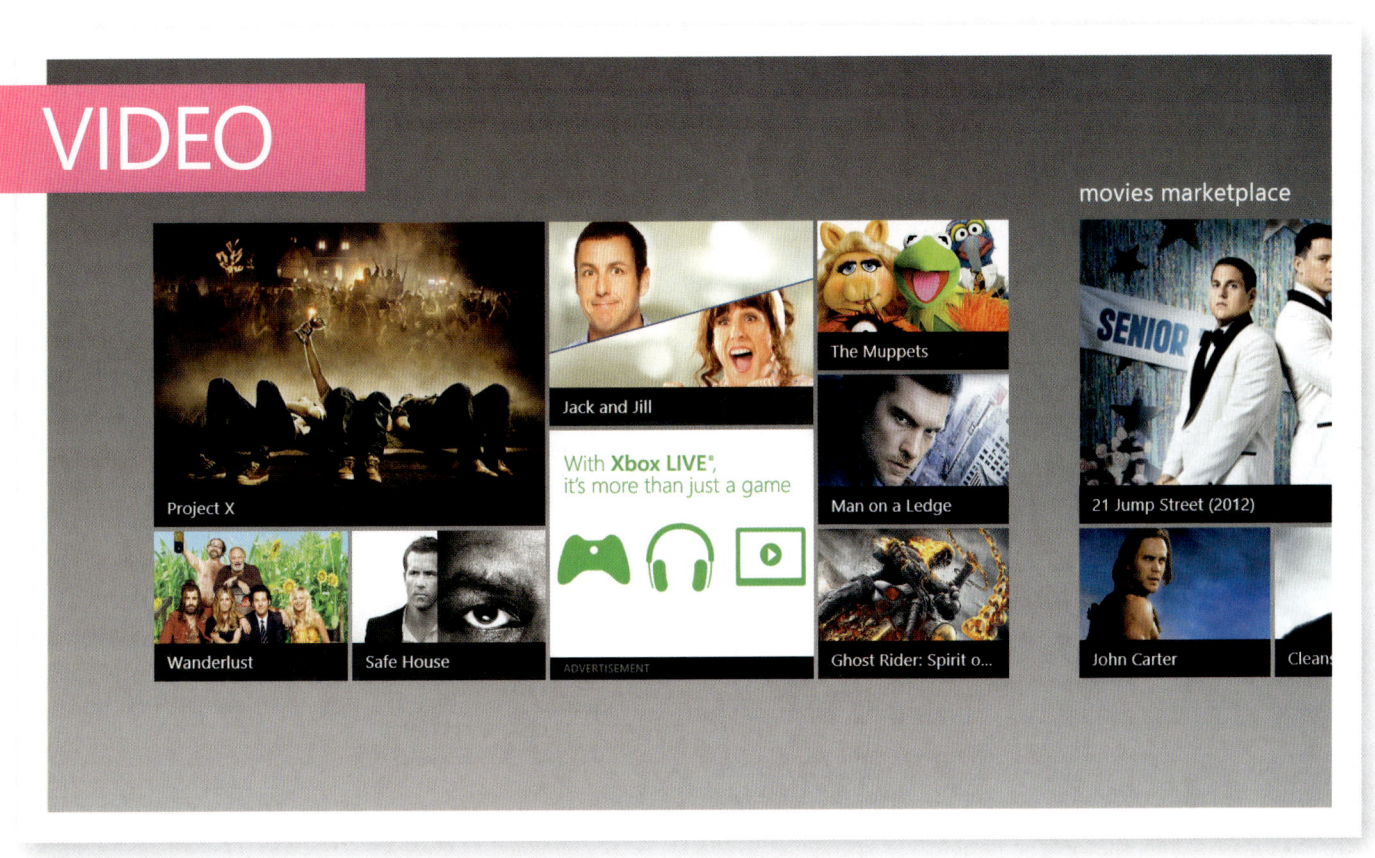

VIDEO

Rent and buy
With the Video app, you can rent or buy films and television shows. Click or tap on an image to see a synopsis, running time and more. Click back to see other options.

Store and view
All your own videos are displayed within the Video app. You can also open a video within the Video app even if it isn't part of your library. Just tap or click and select it.

Play on Xbox
Click the movie you want to watch and you'll see there's the option to 'Play on Xbox'. If you have an Xbox hooked up to your TV, you can send the video directly to it.

Video on other apps
Other video providers, such as Dailymotion, have already released apps for Windows 8, so you can easily keep up to date with the very latest videos uploaded worldwide.

Learn how to...

Find your way with Maps

It's easy to get to grips with the Maps app in Windows 8 so that you can get directions wherever you want to go, and keep an eye on the traffic

WORKS WITH
Windows 8
Windows 8 Pro
Windows RT

The Maps app is one of the most powerful of the default apps in Windows 8. It's easy to navigate around with a keyboard and mouse but it comes into its own with a Windows 8 touchscreen device, where you can pinch-to-zoom into maps and use standard Windows 8 gestures to swipe in from the bottom and right-hand side to see more options and share map information respectively. You can also check out the traffic near your location, get and navigate through step-by-step directions, and zoom into landmarks using the Aerial view. By the time you have finished this tutorial, you'll be so proficient with Maps on Windows 8 that you'll probably use it instead of looking up maps in your web browser – though with Windows 8, the choice is yours, of course.

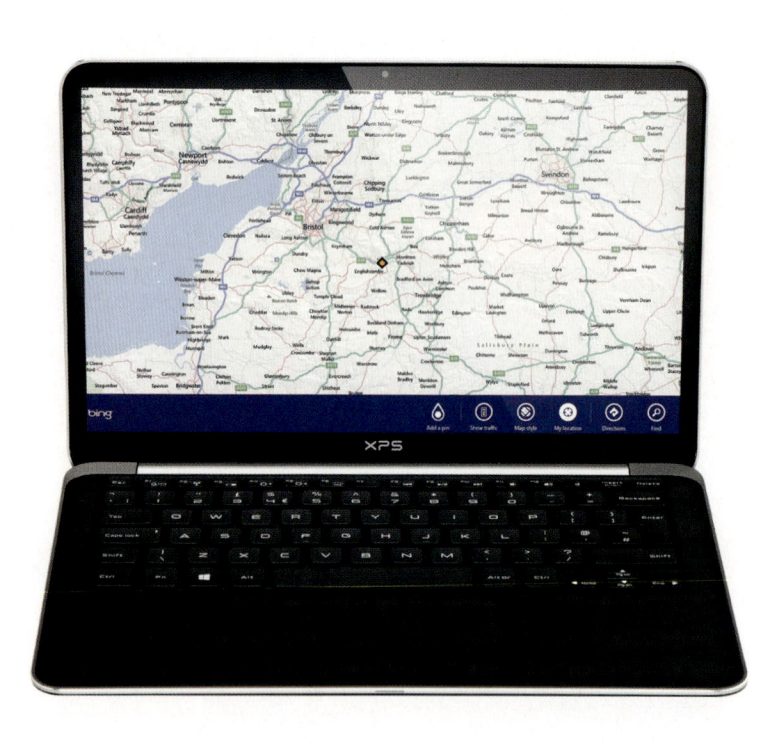

Maps in Windows 8

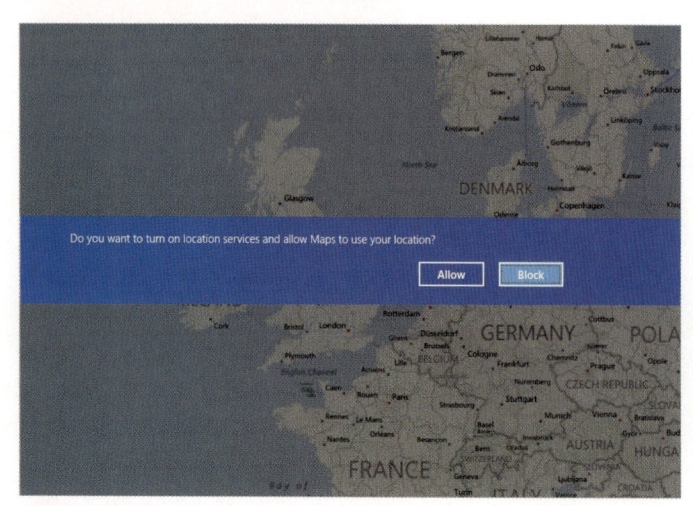

1. Allow the use of your location
When Windows 8 apps start up, they check what permissions they have. If they don't have the permission they need to use certain aspects of your PC, such as your location, or the webcam, the app asks for it. So when Maps asks if it can use your location, answer yes, otherwise you can't get directions from your current location.

2. Search for a place
You can search for anywhere using the standard Search charm in Windows 8; swipe in from the right using a finger or mouse, tap or click 'Search', then start typing the place you want to find. Hit [Return] or click or tap the looking glass search icon. This can be a place, but it can also be local info, such as the name of a shop.

108 | Chapter 2 — Windows 8: Expert Tips and Tricks

FIND YOUR WAY WITH MAPS

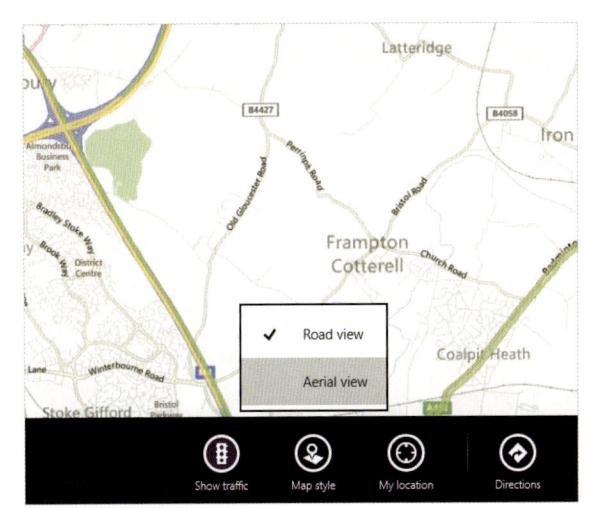

Top tip

Make it big
Zoom in and out of maps using the + and - controls that appear on the left of the Maps screen – but it's easier to use touch if your device has that capability.

3 Check the traffic
Right-click on the map to bring up the App bar. You can click to see the traffic flow (green > amber > red) on major roads, as well as switch between the type of mapping, and zoom in on your current location (this is why your computer needs to know where you are).

4 Get directions
You can also switch between the Road view and Aerial view. We've also clicked to get directions from the App bar, so we see this pop-up. Type the locations you want to navigate between; your current location is there by default, but you can change it to whatever you want.

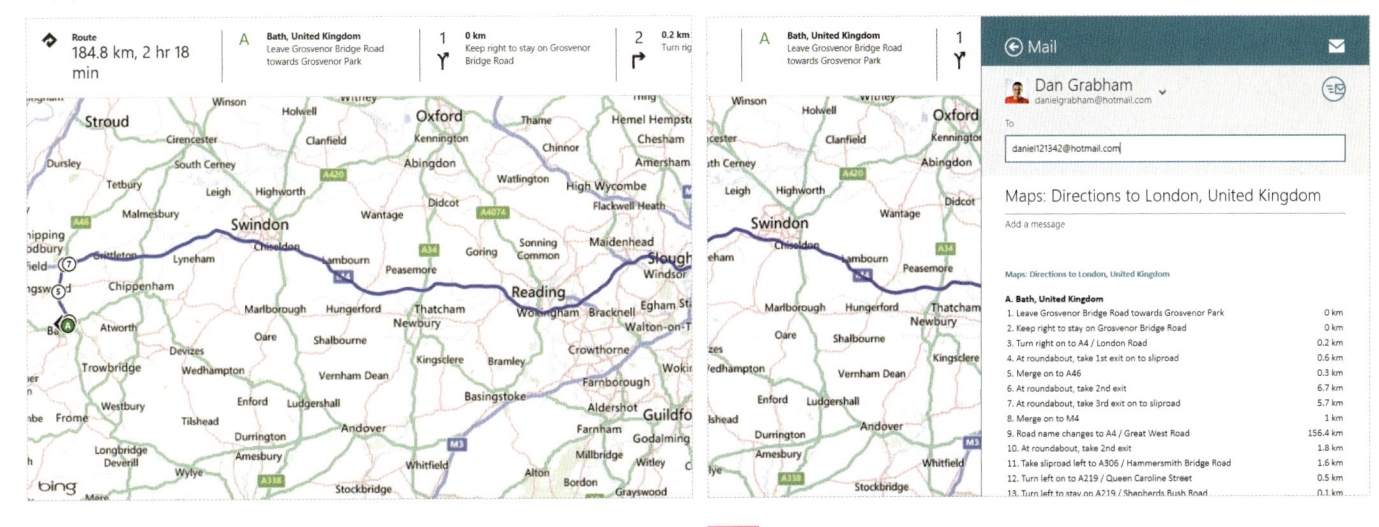

5 Navigate through directions
Now you're given your directions. As you see, there is full direction information at the top of the screen, and you can swipe across to see more of this. Each step is numbered, and these are shown on the map along with the route (in blue) – zooming into the route would reveal more of the numbered steps.

6 Share maps and directions
This is a great example of where the Share charm comes in useful; swipe in from the right and click 'Share'. You then see the apps you can share with. These include the Mail app, so we've clicked that. You get a screen like this, with the directions, and a map below, in the body of an email. Enter an address, then click 'Send'.

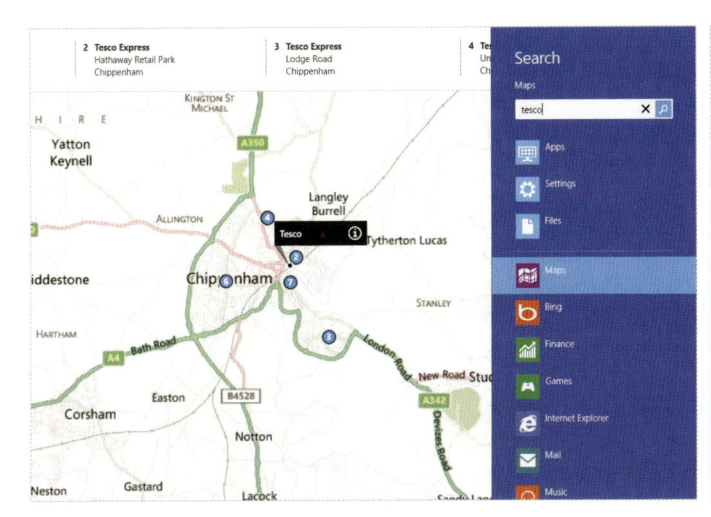

7 Get local
The Maps app is also a great way to look up local information. We've searched for Tesco to show how the app uses information with several results. We can click on any of these numbered circles to get the black information icon up – tapping or clicking this gives you another screen with address and contact information.

8 All mapped out
Finally, we want to draw your attention to the detailed aerial photography in the Maps app – it works really well with zooming in using a touchscreen, if you have one. It's great to look at landmarks and other familiar places from above, whether they're physical features or man-made, like this example.

Windows 8: Expert Tips and Tricks   Chapter 2 | 109

Learn how to...

Buy amazing apps in the Windows Store

Get more from Windows 8 by installing new apps for the Start screen

WORKS WITH
Windows 8
Windows 8 Pro
Windows RT

Windows 8 isn't just a great operating system because of its powerful new features; it's also brilliant because of the Windows Store. This new app store is the best way to get apps for your PC, and it includes plenty of new Windows 8-style apps in addition to more traditional desktop apps. Some are paid-for, while plenty of others don't cost a bean. The Store is also where you get updates for existing apps; the Windows Store app live tile tells you if updates are available (a number appears on the tile on the Start screen), while you're informed of any updates in the top-right when you open the app. You can search for any app using the Windows 8 Search charm; open the Windows Store, then swipe in from the right of the screen, tap or click 'Search' and start typing.

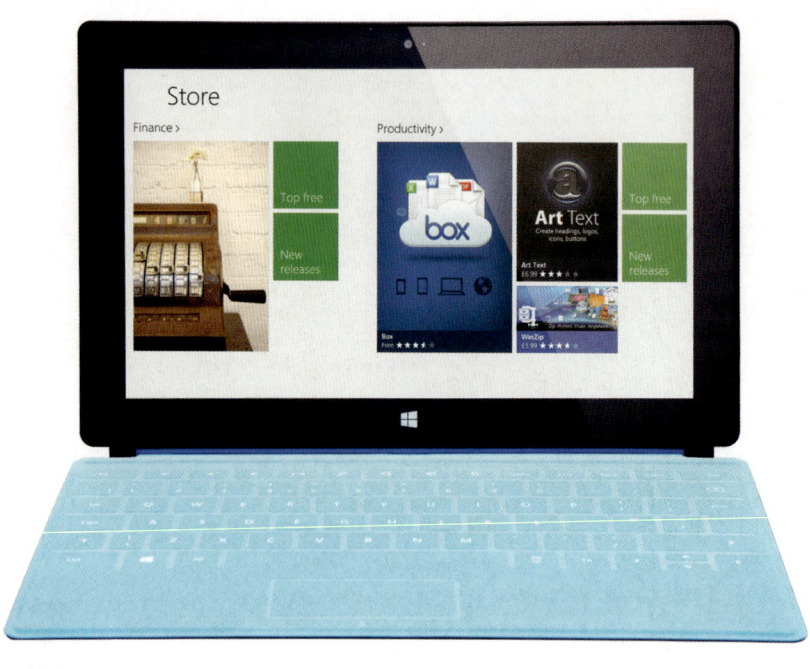

Browse through the Windows Store

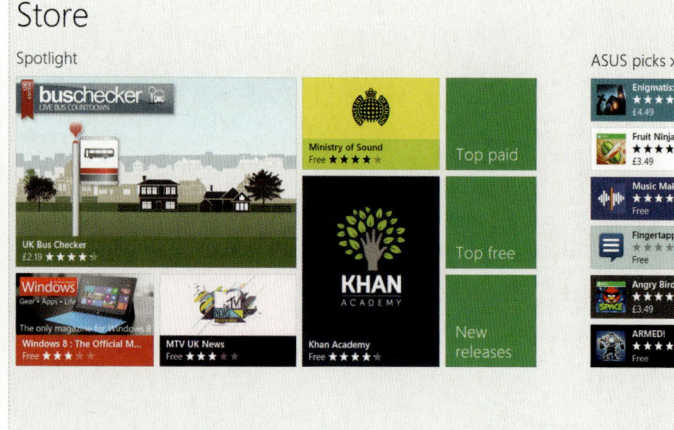

1 Start the Store
Open the Windows Store from your Windows 8 Start screen. The Store automatically pulls in data if you're connected to the internet – unfortunately, you do need to be connected to see what's on offer in the store. If you're not online, a message appears warning you to try again when you're connected to the internet.

2 Under the Spotlight
Spotlight is the entrance to the Windows Store and shows you the very latest and greatest apps, as well as enabling you to access other areas of the Windows Store. Just out of view in the top-right of the above screen, there's a message to say we have app updates waiting – click that text to be taken to the update install screen.

110 | Chapter 2 — Windows 8: Expert Tips and Tricks

BUY AMAZING APPS

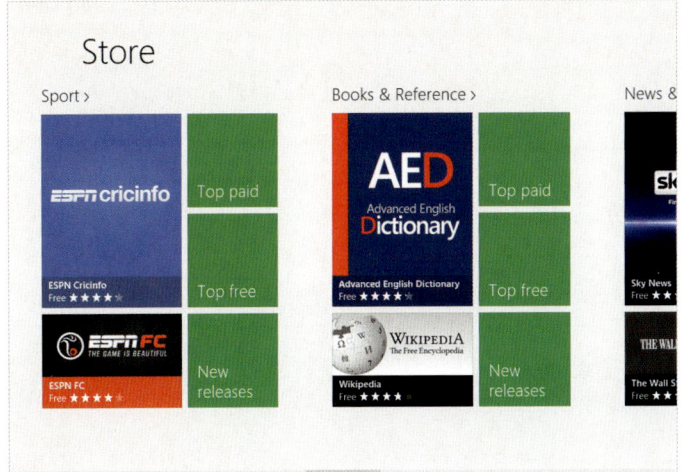

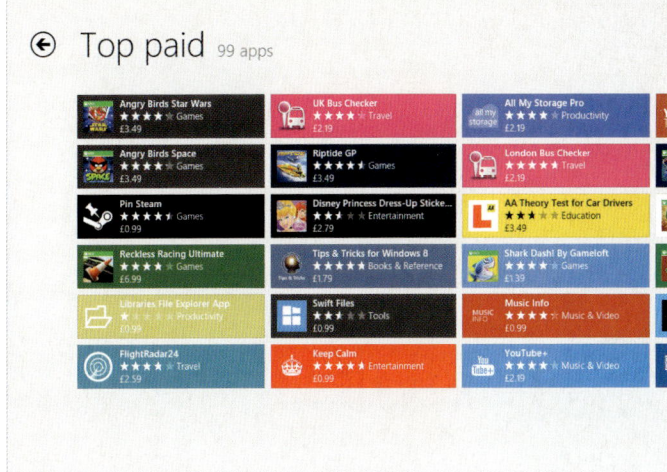

3 Scroll for more
The Windows Store is separated into categories, which you can see by scrolling along from the Spotlight screen. If you've bought a new Windows 8 PC, there's a section from the seller of that PC. Thereafter you'll see sections on Games, Social apps, News and Weather, Sports and more. Click through to explore each section.

4 Top paid and free
From Spotlight, you can also browse to three key screens. The first two are the most downloaded paid-for and free apps – as you can see, Angry Birds Star Wars is the most popular paid-for app at the time of writing. Clicking on any app tile takes you to a screen that tells you more about that app.

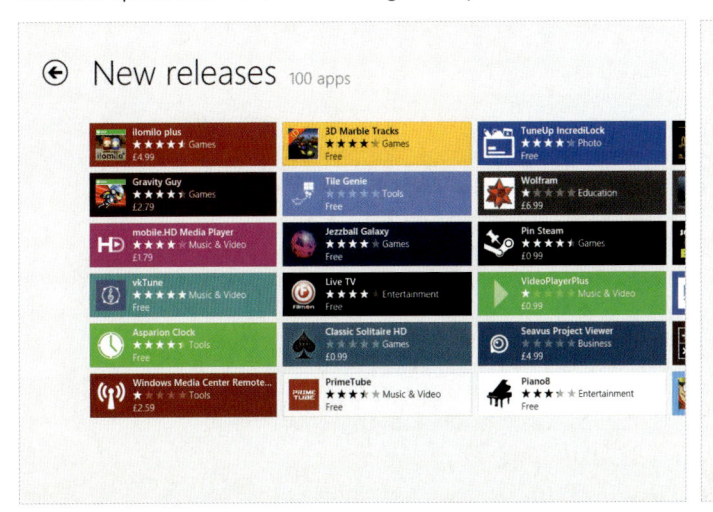

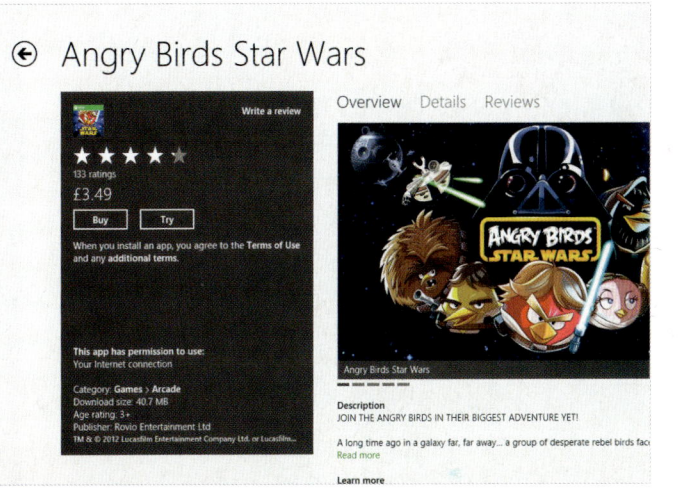

5 In with the new
The third key screen you can access from Spotlight takes you to this, the New releases screen. As with any screen in the Windows Store, you can tap or click the arrow in the top-left to get back to the previous screen. You'll notice all the apps also have star ratings – you can leave your own ratings in the screen about individual apps.

6 The app screen
When you click on any app in the Windows Store, you'll see this screen – you can click or tap to look through images of the app, scroll down to see more details (if it's a game, it takes you through the back story), the star rating and, most importantly, the buttons to install the app if it's free, or to buy the app if it's paid-for.

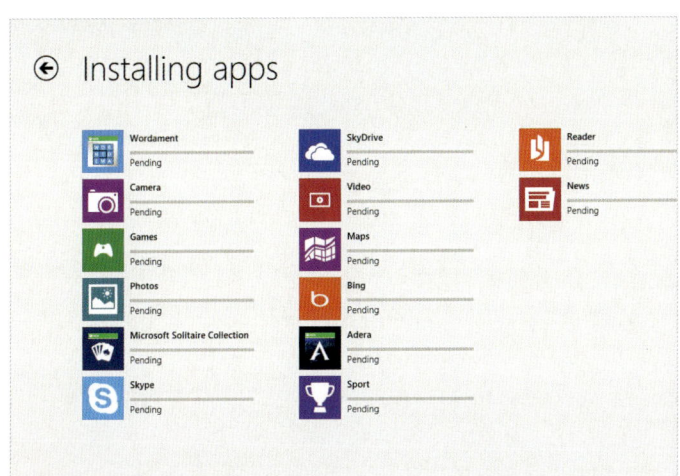

7 Installing apps
Many paid-for apps have a 'Try' button so you can download the app with limited functions, then upgrade later. When you install an app or updates, you see a screen like this, showing the progress of your app installations. We set a big update installing – it's unlikely you'd have this many apps installing at the same time on your PC.

8 Happy apping!
When you've installed an app from the Windows Store, it's added to your Start screen – as you can see, we've installed Angry Birds Star Wars here. You can then drag to re-order the tiles on your Start screen as you wish. And that's it – you've learned all there is to know about installing apps from the Windows Store.

Learn how to...

Schedule maintenance tasks

Running certain tasks can be essential for keeping Windows 8 in tip-top condition. They're not always easy to remember to run, but you can schedule them to run automatically to save you the bother

WORKS WITH
Windows 8
Windows 8 Pro
Windows RT

There's a lot of useful maintenance tools in Windows 8 that can keep your PC running fresh and fast. For example, regularly running Disk Cleanup can stop your hard disk getting clogged up. Rather than remembering to run it periodically, you can set it to run automatically on a certain day at a certain time. This can be a one-off event or a recurring one. It means once set up, you don't need to worry about it again, because Windows 8 does the hard work. It's useful for running complicated events that take up a lot of processing power when you're not using your Windows 8 device. You can also use it to run programs when you start Windows 8 – for example, getting Outlook to open and download your emails as soon as your PC turns on.

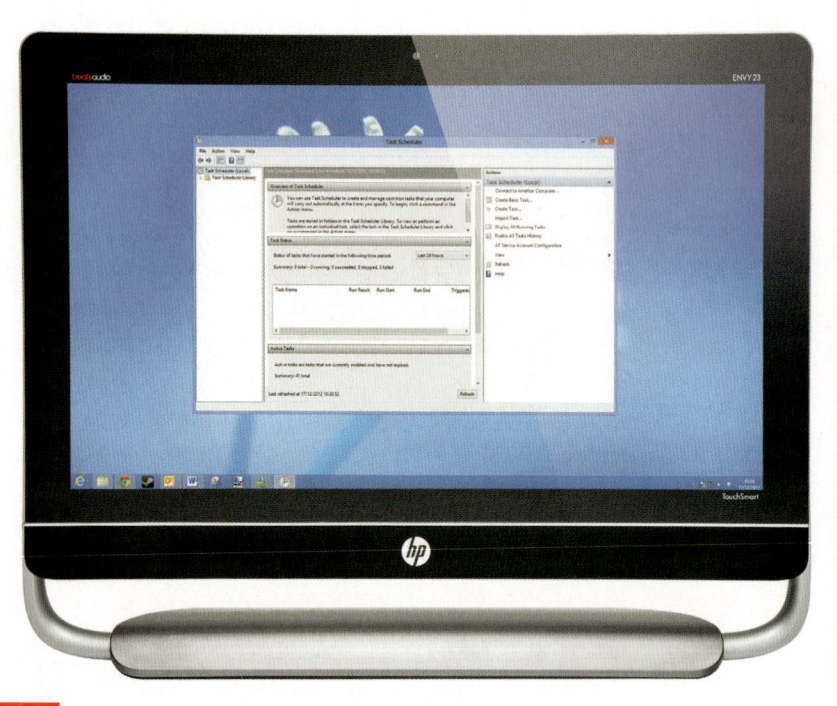

Schedule tasks for your PC's health

1 Trial-run the tasks you want
Because Windows 8 will be running these tasks automatically, it's a good idea to run them manually first, to ensure that they do what you need and to make sure no errors or unintended side-effects are created in the running of the task. Once you're happy that the task performed correctly, you can begin scheduling it.

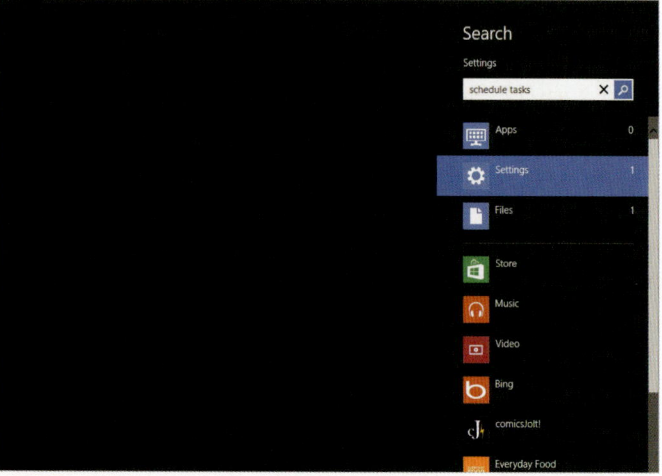

2 Run Task Scheduler
First, press the [Windows] key to return to the Start screen, then type in 'Schedule task' to begin searching for the Windows 8 task scheduler tool. Click on 'Settings' to view the results of your search, and then click 'Schedule tasks' to open up the useful Task Scheduler window.

112 | Chapter 2   Windows 8: Expert Tips and Tricks

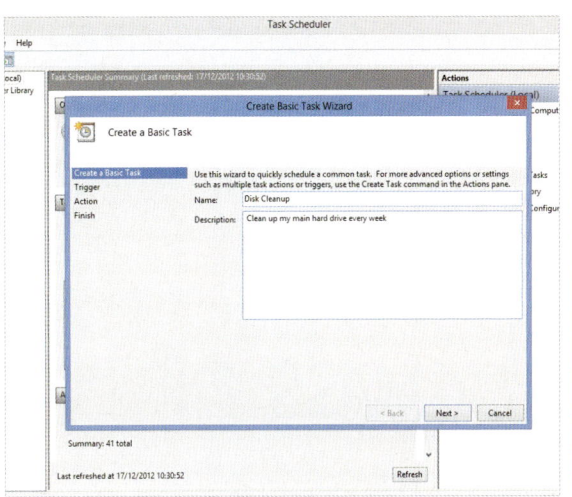

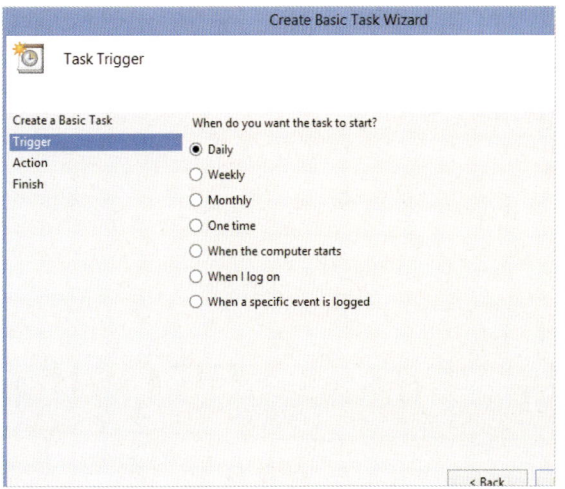

SCHEDULE MAINTENANCE TASKS

Jargon buster!

.exe
For most programs, the main file that launches the program has a .exe file extension. These are powerful files, so always make sure you only run or modify .exe files that you're absolutely certain about.

Trigger
When scheduling a task, the term trigger refers to the time, date or action that launches – or triggers – the task. This can be as simple or as complicated as you like, though for more advanced triggers, you'll need to know how to use scripts and advanced Windows codes.

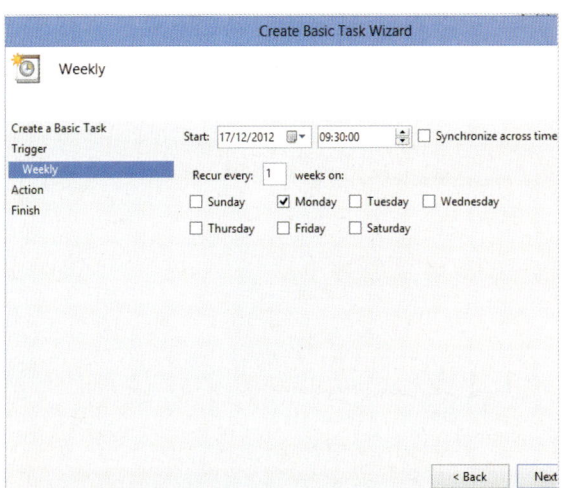

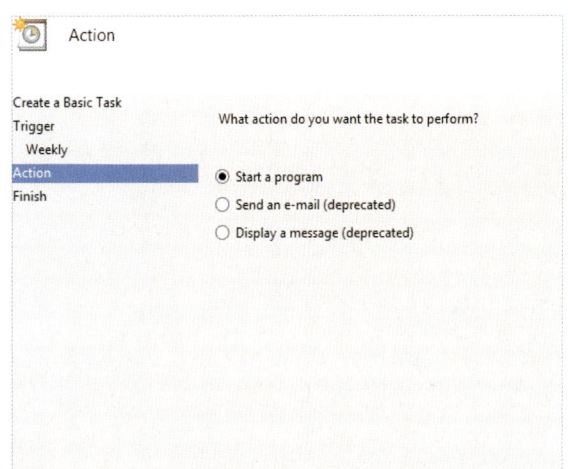

3 Create a basic task
Creating a task to run automatically is pretty straightforward. Click the link that says 'Create Basic Task' to begin. In the new window, give the task a memorable name and, if you like, a description. This will help you keep track of the tasks you create. Then click 'Next'.

4 Set how often the task runs
Now you need to select when the task will trigger. This could be every day, week or month, or if it runs just once. You can also choose whether the task runs when the computer starts, when you log on or if a specific event – such as the creation of a new file - happens.

5 Set the specifics
Click 'Next' and you can set more detailed specifics. Depending on what you chose in step 4, you can set the precise time, day and frequency, or what event is used as the trigger. If you chose to run the task when the PC turns on, or you log on, you skip this step.

6 Select the action
In the next window, choose to start a program, send an email or display a message. The first is the most useful, and if you select it and click 'Next', you can select the correct program by clicking 'Browse', then going to where the program is installed and selecting its .exe file.

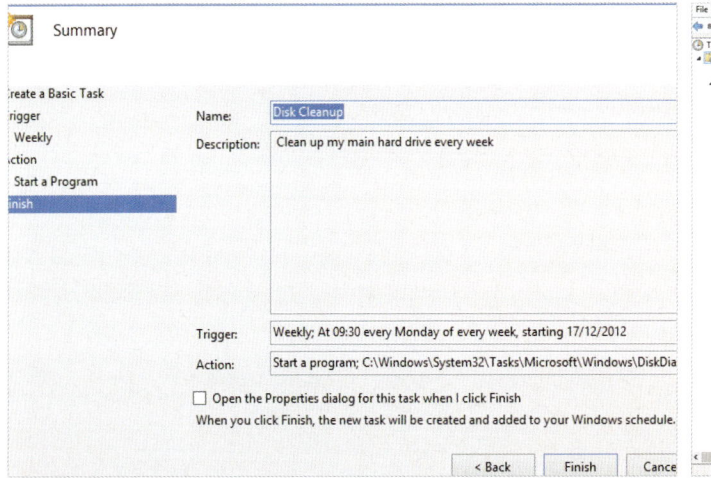

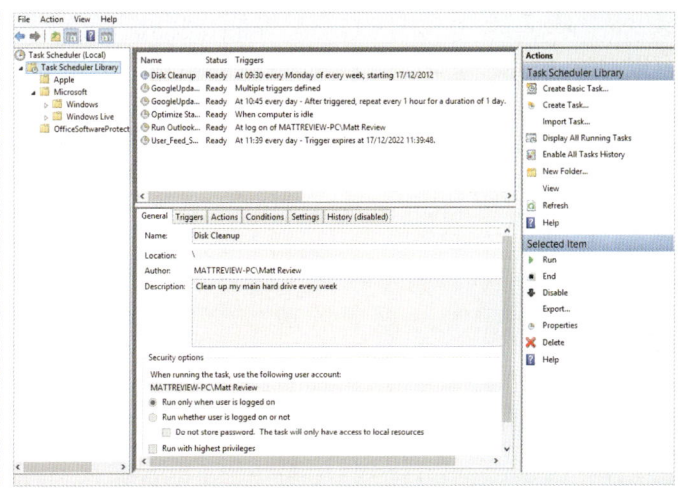

7 Review and finish
After clicking 'Next', you're taken to a final window, which gives you an overview of the task you've just created. Take time to review the selections you've made to ensure that the task will perform as you want it to. If you're happy, click 'Finish', otherwise click 'Back' to change the settings.

8 View and modify tasks
You've created your first automatic task. At any time you can review and update your tasks by opening Task Scheduler and clicking 'Task Scheduler Library'. You'll see a list of tasks, some created by you, others created by programs or Windows 8. Clicking on a task enables you to change any of the settings you want.

Chapter 2 | 113

Learn how to...

Synchronise settings across all your Windows 8 devices

Now you can get a unified experience regardless of the device you use

WORKS WITH
Windows 8
Windows 8 Pro
Windows RT

Getting Windows 8 to look and work the way you want is an important part of getting to grips with the new operating system. Choosing your Lock screen, method of inputting a password, as well as personalising your Start screen and remembering your favourite websites and passwords, makes you feel right at home with your new Windows 8 device. And the cool thing about Windows 8 is that if you have several devices all running the new operating system, you can synchronise them so that your personalisation options, Internet Explorer 10 history, favourite websites, app settings and passwords are used on every device you use. This means, no matter what device you're on, your Windows 8 experience is the same.

Synchronise your Windows 8 devices

1 Open up settings
To begin syncing your Windows 8 devices, you need to access Windows 8's settings. To do this, open the Charms bar by either dragging your finger from the right-hand side of the screen to the left, or by hovering your mouse cursor on the top or bottom right-hand side. Select 'Settings > Change PC Settings'.

2 Use a Microsoft account
Your Windows 8 preferences and settings are synchronised via your Microsoft account. If your Windows 8 account is just a standard local account, you need to change it to a Microsoft account to take advantage of the synchronisation features. Select 'Users' on the left-hand side of the screen, then 'Switch to Microsoft account'.

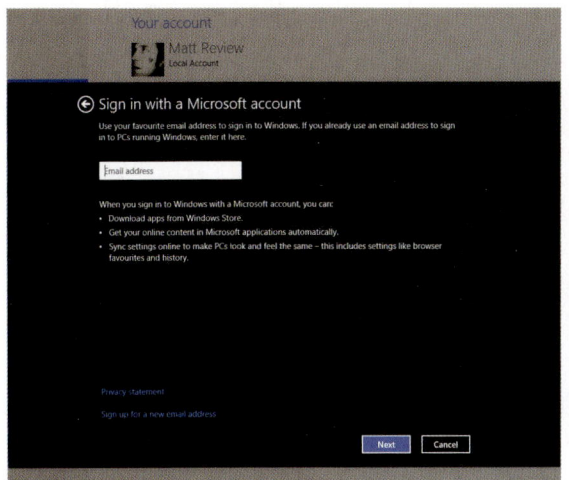

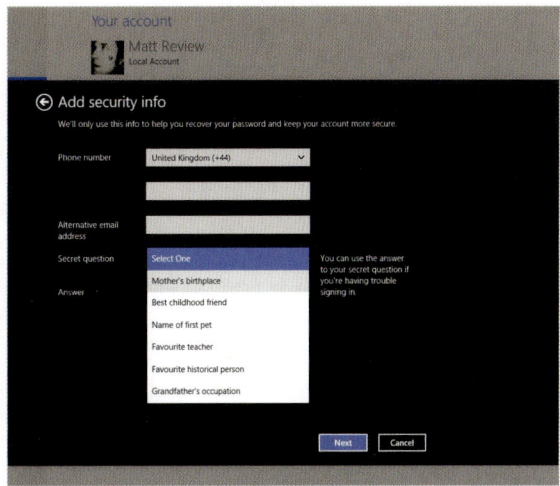

SYNCHRONISE SETTINGS

3 Log in or create a Microsoft account
If you already have a Microsoft account, log in to it by first entering the password of your local account. Next enter the email address of your Microsoft account. If you don't have one, click 'Sign up for a new email address' and follow the instructions. Then click 'Next'.

4 Additional security info
Enter the password for your Microsoft account, and Windows 8 loads it up. Then you're asked to add security information, such as an alternative email address and secret question. This gives the synchronised settings more security, and helps if you forget your login details.

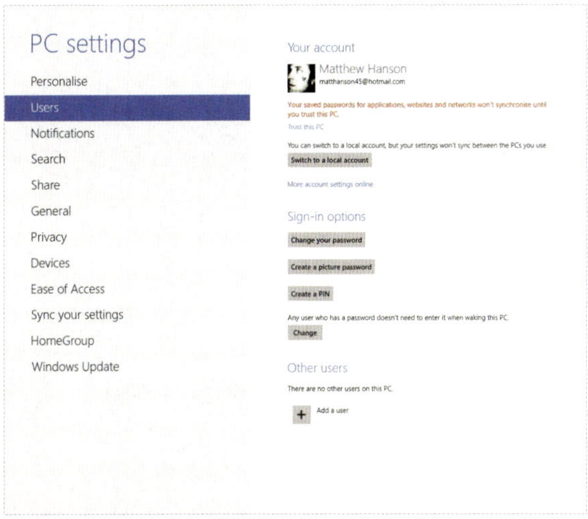

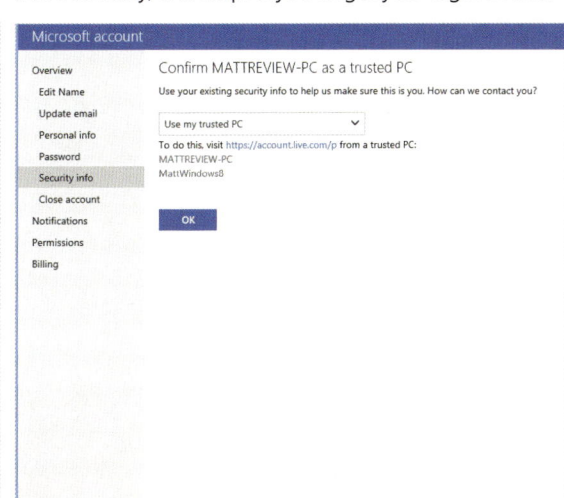

5 Trust your PC
Once logged in, you need to 'trust' your PC to synchronise settings and passwords. Every PC you trust can share your settings. Only trust your own PCs, not other people's, and certainly not shared public PCs. Go to 'Settings' as in step 1, click 'Users', then 'Trust this PC'.

6 Confirm your choice
Log in to your Microsoft account on the web page you're taken to. You're then asked to confirm your PC as trusted. The name of the PC is displayed, along with other Windows 8 devices you've assigned to your account. Click 'OK', review your PCs, then click 'OK' again.

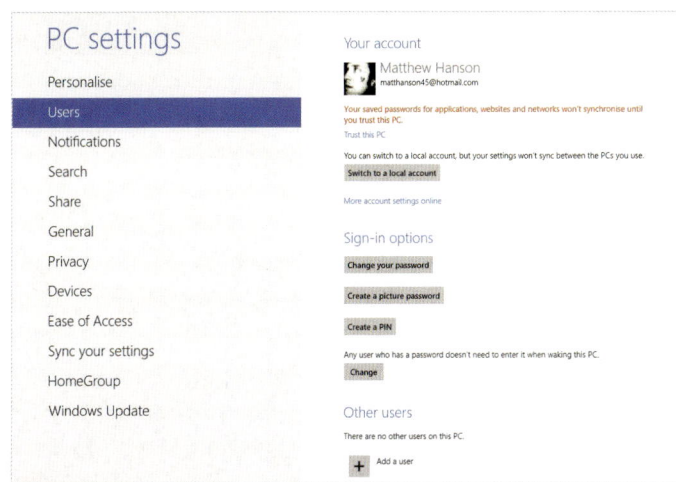

7 Log on to your other devices
You can now log on to your other Windows 8 devices using your Microsoft account. Then you need to go into 'Settings' as in step 1 and trust the device you're on, as in step 5. You'll then see that your personalisation options, as well as your settings and internet favourites, are present on both devices.

8 Windows 8 your way – on every device
You've now successfully synced your devices and you'll notice you get a uniform experience for Windows 8. It makes getting to grips with the operating system even easier, and you don't have to spend time tweaking settings and adding your favourite websites when you get a new device.

Jargon buster!

Charms bar
The Charms bar is a new addition to Windows 8 that gives you quick access to some of the most important tools, no matter where you are in the operating system. Simply flick your finger in from the right-hand side of the screen, or hover your mouse pointer at the top-right or bottom-right side of the screen to bring it up.

Personalisation options
You can give Windows 8 the personal touch by changing the desktop background, windows colours and sound schemes, Start screen colour and pattern, and even the Lock screen to suit your tastes. Most of these settings can then be synced between devices.

Windows 8: Expert Tips and Tricks   Chapter 2 | 115

Learn how to...

Share files in Windows 8

Thanks to Windows 8, you're not limited to using one computer – you can share your files between any device that uses the operating system

WORKS WITH
Windows 8
Windows 8 Pro
Windows RT

Sharing files and folders has never been easier than it is with Windows 8. By setting up your Windows 8 devices correctly, you'll be able to access your files on one computer by using another. So if you have a movie file on your Windows 8 all-in-one PC upstairs, you can easily watch it on your Windows 8 tablet downstairs. Not only is it a fantastic way to enjoy your media and use Windows 8's technology to its full potential, but it's also incredibly easy to do. It doesn't have to be media you share either. You could be working on a document or photo on one computer, share it with another and carry on working from there. There are huge possibilities to this technology, and we're going to show you how to make the most out of it.

Share in Windows 8

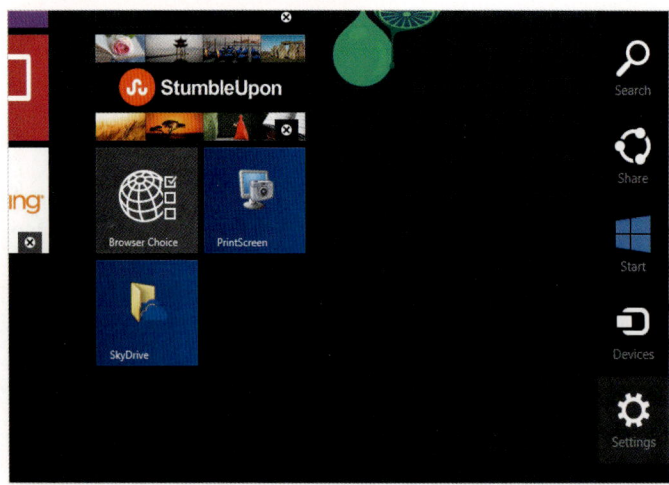

1 Introducing HomeGroups
HomeGroups were first introduced in Windows 7, and have proved very popular with people looking for an easy way to share files between their different computers. To set up a HomeGroup, open up the Charms bar and select the 'Settings' charm, then select 'Change PC settings'.

2 Create a HomeGroup
In the Settings screen, select 'HomeGroup', then click 'Create' to set up your own HomeGroup. Windows 8 now creates a brand new HomeGroup for you to customise the way you want. It may take a few minutes to get everything sorted, however, so just sit tight while Windows 8 gets to work.

SHARE FILES IN WINDOWS 8

Jargon buster!

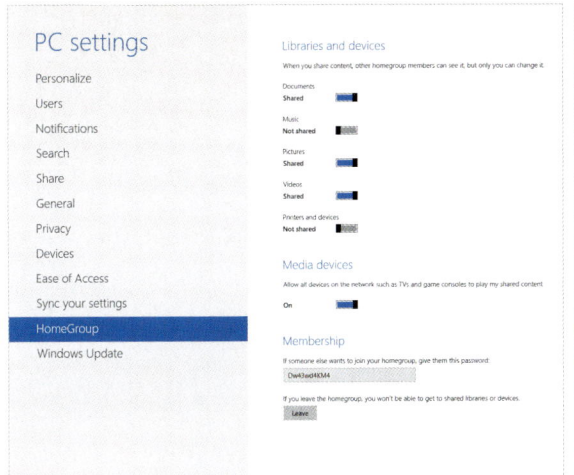

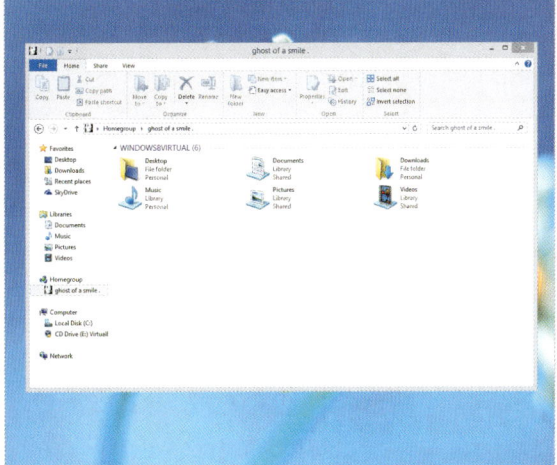

HomeGroup
Enables you to connect two or more computers running Windows 7 or 8 on your home network to automatically start sharing your media and document libraries, as well as printers, with other people in your home.

Tablet
Full touchscreen devices between 7 and 10 inches with no physical keyboard.

3 Add a PC to your HomeGroup
Make a note of the password under 'Membership'. You need to enter that password in any Windows 8 device you want to add to your HomeGroup. On your other PC, go to the 'Settings' charm, click 'Change PC settings', then 'HomeGroup' and enter the password.

4 View your HomeGroup
You can view the files and folders you share in your HomeGroup as if they were folders on your PC. On the desktop, click the 'Libraries' icon on the Taskbar and click on 'HomeGroup' on the left. Click the user name of the other computer to see what it is sharing.

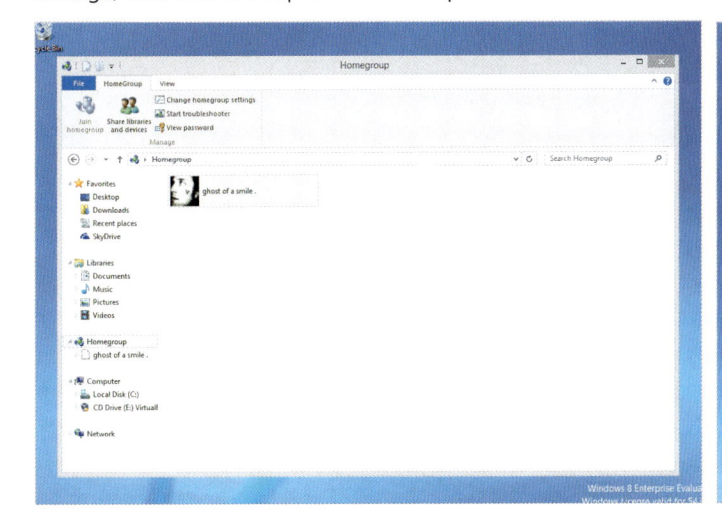

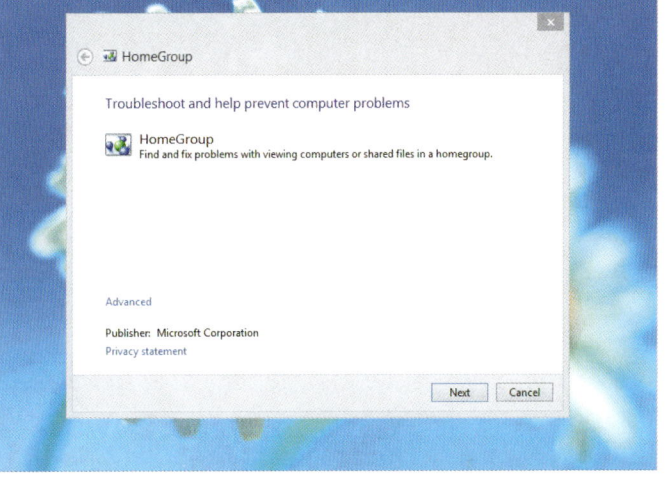

5 Change the HomeGroup settings
Click on the 'HomeGroup' icon in the left-hand side of the window again and you'll see that Windows Explorer now offers a selection of new options in its ribbon bar. Click 'Change HomeGroup settings' to change what you share with the HomeGroup, view the password and more.

6 Troubleshoot problems
If you have any problems with HomeGroups, Windows 8 can help you identify and fix them with the HomeGroup troubleshooter. To launch it either click on 'HomeGroup' in Windows Explorer and select 'Start troubleshooter', or type 'HomeGroup' into the Start Screen and select 'Find and fix problems with HomeGroup'.

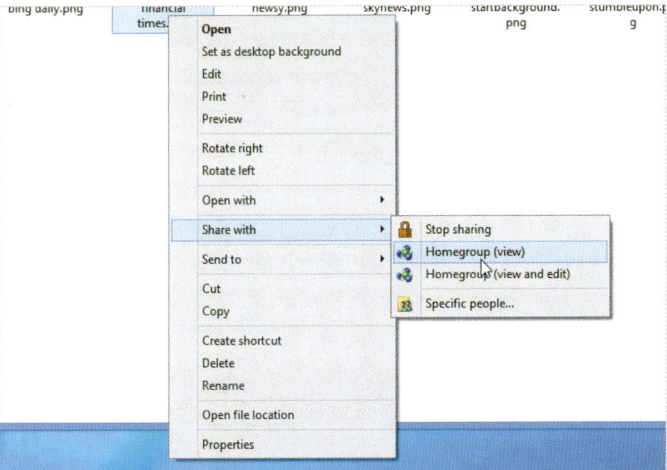

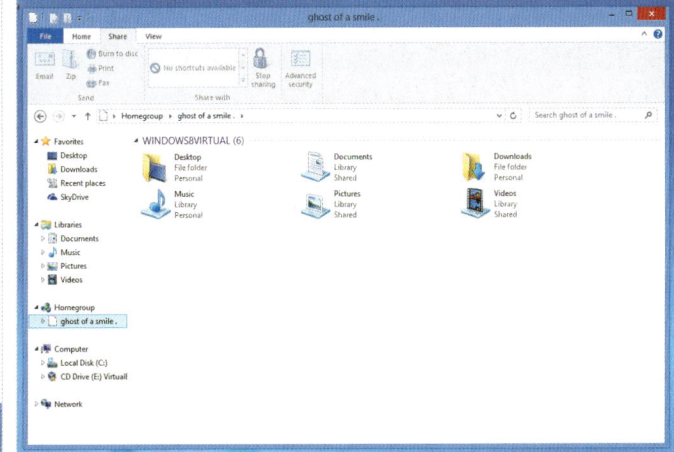

7 Quickly share files and folders
While you can set which folders Windows 8 shares in the HomeGroup, or drop files and folders into your Shared folders, you can also share individual files. Right-click on a file or folder and select 'Share with > HomeGroup (view)' or 'HomeGroup (view and edit)'. The latter lets other people edit files, so be careful what you select.

8 Make the most out of sharing your files!
Now you've set up a HomeGroup and added your devices to it, you can enjoy your shared media from any of the devices you like, browse another PC's photos, edit a document on a number of tablets and so much more. Have a play and you'll find some excellent uses for sharing in Windows 8.

10 tips for using SkyDrive

SkyDrive is a great way to store your important files in the cloud, but it can do so much more...

1 Automate your SkyDrive

You may have never heard of If This Then That (www.ifttt.com) before, but it's a brilliant service that enables you to automate everyday things that you do online, making your life easier and freeing up a little more of your time to do more interesting stuff. A handy plug-in for If This Then That is available for SkyDrive, which means that you can do some really smart things, such as adding photographs to your SkyDrive account every time you are tagged in a picture on Facebook; or getting all your files on Dropbox to sync with SkyDrive, so they're added automatically when placed in your Dropbox folder. Just sign up to the service, search for 'SkyDrive recipes' and start using them.

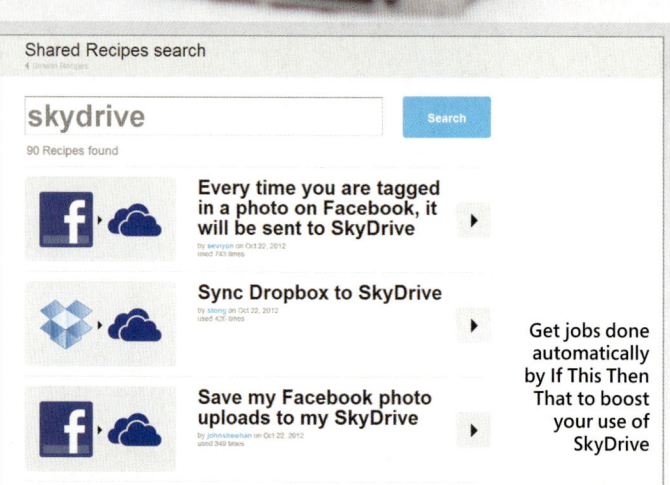

Get jobs done automatically by If This Then That to boost your use of SkyDrive

SKYDRIVE TIPS

2 Use the SkyDrive app to save in style

Store your files in style by downloading the SkyDrive app

SkyDrive.com is certainly a fine way to browse all your files online, but with the advent of Windows 8, there's now an alternative way of doing it, which is far more beautiful and intuitive. By downloading the SkyDrive app for Windows 8 from the Windows Store, you can instantly access your SkyDrive account right from your desktop, without having to go to the SkyDrive website first. It makes finding your files much easier because the layout uses the entirety of your screen real estate, with everything laid out clearly in front of you. You can add new folders, download files to your computer and much more, just as you can through the website, but now you can do it with added panache.

3 Use any other app with SkyDrive

SkyDrive links to other apps on your PC to make using it even easier

Because SkyDrive is such an integral part of the Windows 8 operating system, you may notice that you can access it no matter where you are or what you're doing on your computer. For example, if you're in an app that enables you to save images, SkyDrive appears in the list of possible places where you can save your file. Or, if you're looking at photos in the Photo app, you automatically see all the photos on your SkyDrive account. Just look for the SkyDrive logo whenever you're in an app, and you can quickly and easily make use of the features that are relevant to that particular app.

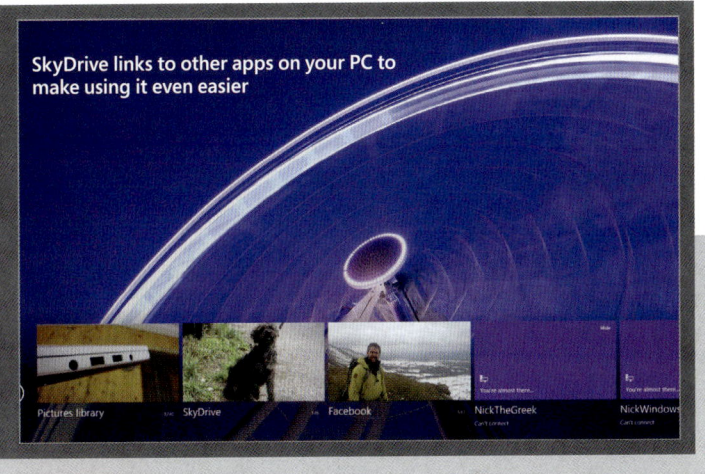

4 Get SkyDrive for your desktop

The desktop app can be treated just like any other folder on your computer

If you prefer to use the old-style desktop over the new-style Start screen, the desktop app might be a better choice for you than the SkyDrive app from the Windows Store. To get it, go to www.skydrive.com, log in and select 'Get SkyDrive applications' in the lower left-hand menu. Choose 'Windows desktop' from the menu and hit 'Download now'. Once installed, you're able to sync files from SkyDrive to your desktop and vice versa, so both places are in sync whenever you add or remove files. The real beauty of the desktop app is that you can treat it just like an ordinary folder, so files can be dragged and dropped to it, making it really easy to manage.

5 Integrate SkyDrive with your Libraries

Link SkyDrive to your Libraries for even more computing convenience

People say that cloud file storage is the way forward and SkyDrive enables you to test the water. You can set up SkyDrive on your PC to act as though it were a part of your normal drive, by including its file locations within your Libraries (places where you store documents, pictures, music and video). For example, including SkyDrive in the Libraries means that when you open your regular Documents folder, you can see the contents of the Documents folder from SkyDrive. To do this, right-click the Documents folder with the Libraries, choose 'Add', and browse to the Documents folder on SkyDrive and select 'Include folder'. Select it in the list and hit 'Set save location'. Do the same for the remaining folders.

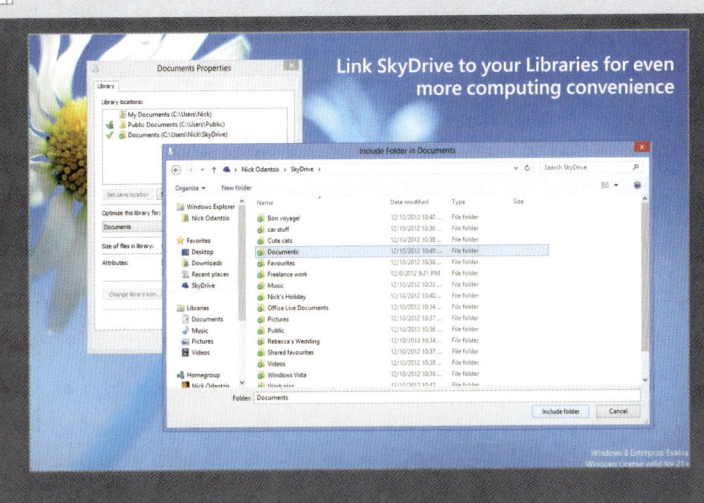

7 Get more even more storage space

By default, SkyDrive comes with 7GB of storage space for all the files you upload to it (and this space, of course, doesn't cost you a penny). You could create a number of different Outlook logins so you get several SkyDrive accounts and add to your storage that way, but it would really defeat the object of having all your files together under one roof. So the better option is to choose a plan that offers you a bigger allowance of file storage. Go to 'Manage storage' in the options menu (the little cog in the top bar) and select 'Get more storage'. You'll see a range of plans available for more space, starting from £6 per year for an extra 20GB, going up to £32 per year for a whopping extra 100GB of storage.

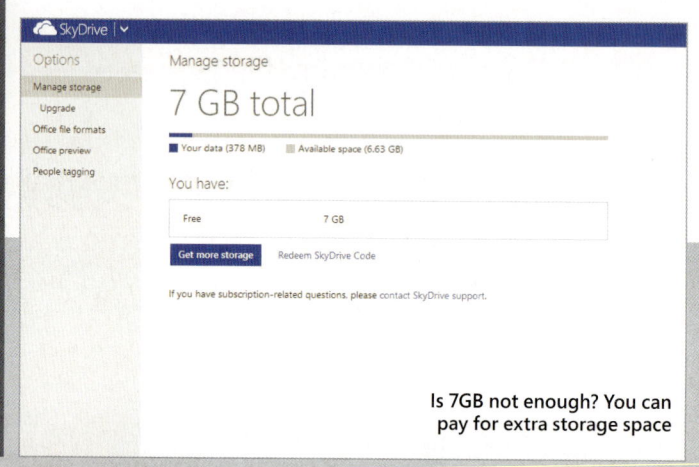

It's easy to work with others, thanks to SkyDrive's Office Web Apps

6 Collaborate on documents

SkyDrive comes with an online productivity suite called Office Web Apps, much like the Microsoft Office that you're already used to. It includes Word, PowerPoint, Excel and OneNote, and all documents can be created and edited right within SkyDrive. The real magic of this online way of working is that these files can be shared with other people, who can then look at them and work on those files from their own PC while you do exactly the same thing. This means changes can be made while the other person can see what's happening, and there is only one version to work on – so there's no confusion to be had.

Is 7GB not enough? You can pay for extra storage space

8 Access all your files from anywhere

Go to SkyDrive.com and sign in – in the left-hand menu you'll see a heading called 'PCs' and under this you'll see any computer from which you've signed into SkyDrive. SkyDrive remembers them all and, provided that PC is turned on, you can access the files on it. Only those who have access to your Microsoft account can do this, for obvious security reasons, and you'll need to use a special security code, which is sent to your mobile (or emailed to you), so that you can sign into that PC. Once you've done that, you'll be able to browse your hard drive as though you were on it. Once you're done, don't forget to hit 'Disconnect PC from SkyDrive' in the top bar.

9 Get organised and stay in control

While it's easy to just chuck everything into one pot within SkyDrive and forget about basic house-keeping rules, this is a bad way of working, and soon enough you'll begin to find it very difficult to locate the particular file you're looking for among the mass of documents and photos you've stored online. So, it pays to be a little more organised in your approach – put the right sort of files in the right folders to begin with (such as pictures in the Picture folder, and so on), and then create folders within them to keep items categorised. You can either do this via www.skydrive.com, or right from the desktop app.

10 Start recycling your files

If something happens to get lost in your SkyDrive folder, or you accidentally delete a file or folder that you actually wanted to keep, there's no need to panic. Chances are, it's ended up right in the handy Recycle Bin provided by SkyDrive. It works just like the one that sits on your computer desktop. Just click on 'Recycle Bin' in the lower left-hand menu (underneath your storage allowance), select the file you want to retrieve, and hit 'Restore' in the top bar to put it back where it came from. Alternatively, if you have a file saved on SkyDrive that you know you're never going to need again, choose 'Delete' instead to permanently get rid of it and reclaim some valuable storage space.

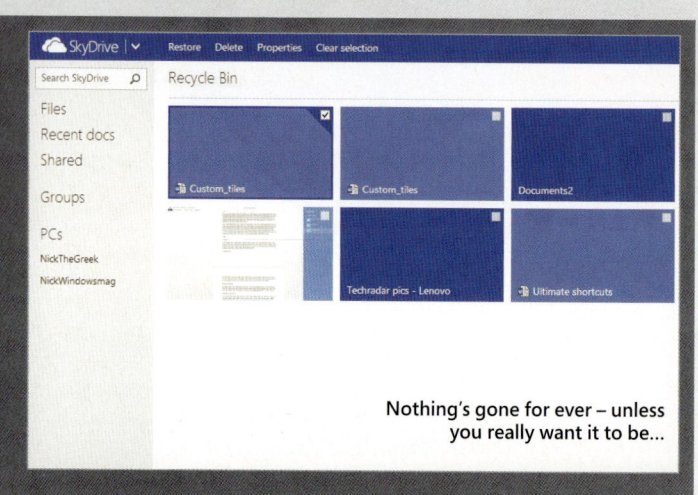

Nothing's gone for ever – unless you really want it to be…

ALL THE ROCK YOU'LL EVER NEED IN ONE APP

This Day In
★CLASSIC★ ROCK

Search 'This Day In Classic Rock' in the App Store

★ 2,000+ DAILY ENTRIES – 366 DAYS ★
★ 300+ INTERACTIVE QUIZ QUESTIONS ★
★ 250+ TRIVIA FACTS ★
★ 75,000 WORDS ON 50 CLASSIC ALBUMS ★
★ FREE RINGTONE & WALLPAPER ★
★ LOADS OF ROCK IMAGES & LINKS ★
★ LISTED TRACKS PLAYABLE FROM THE APP ★
AND MUCH MORE!

Available on the App Store

for iPhone, iPad and iPod Touch
See the video here
www.tinyurl.com/classicrockapp

DAY BY DAY ROCK FACTS FOR ONLY £1.99

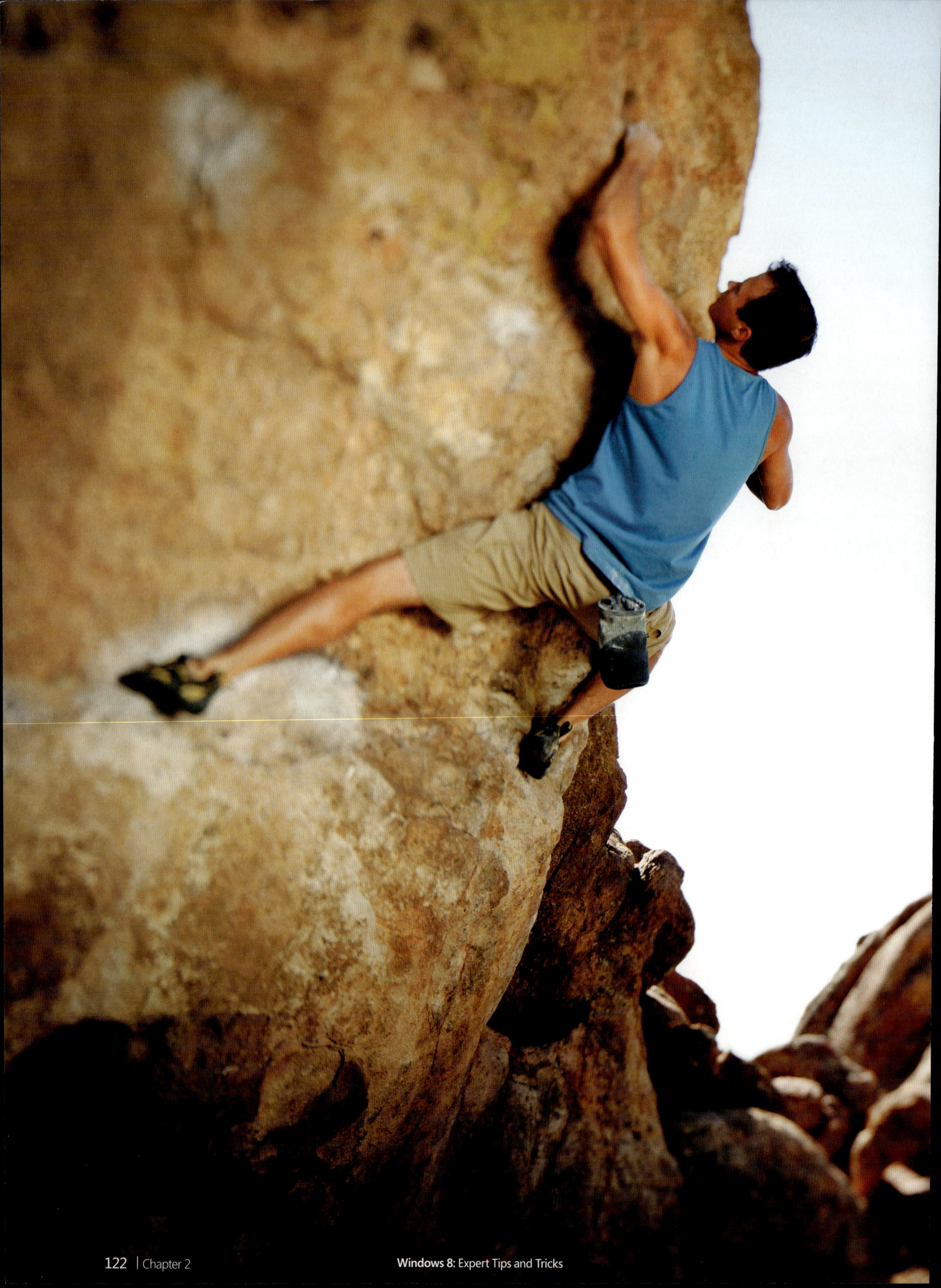

Security & safety

TRY THIS!
Set a picture password
130

Protect your identity, your data, your kids and your computer

Section 6

124 Stay safe with Windows 8
126 Improving internet security
128 Look after your kids
130 Uncrackable passwords

DO THIS NOW...

Stay safe with Windows 8

With Windows 8, it's easier than ever to keep control

Choose what info apps can use

By default, Windows 8 apps can use your name, location and account picture, but you can restrict them. Go to the Settings charm (or press [Windows]+[I]) and choose 'Change PC Settings'. Select 'Privacy' and click buttons to disable any details you'd rather not share. There's no reason why you should worry about giving this information to apps, but if you are concerned, this gives you peace of mind. Apps also send information back to Microsoft and app developers about the web content used within them – you can turn this off here should you wish, too.

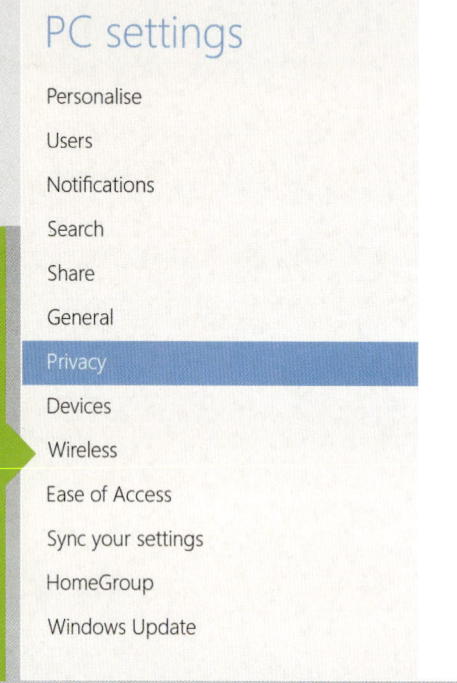

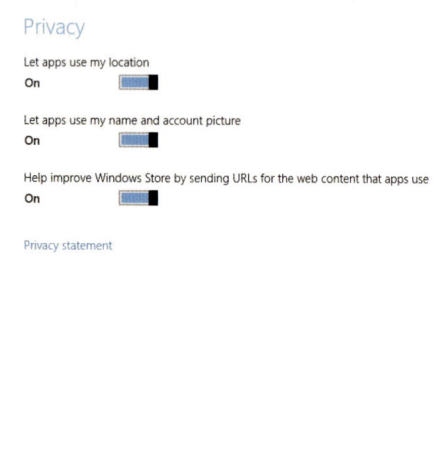

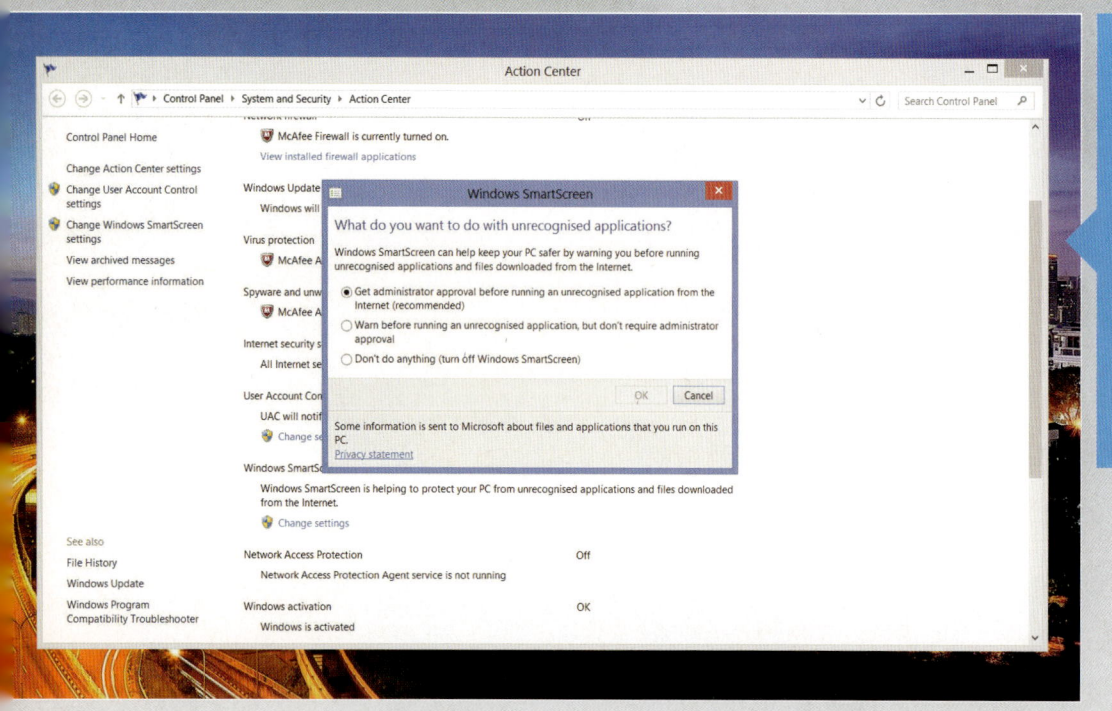

Install any apps

Most mobile platforms recommend you only install apps from approved sources, and Windows 8 only allows you to install trusted apps from the Windows store. But most of us want to install more than just Windows Store apps – web downloads, for example – and for that you need to tell your PC it's OK (if you're an administrator, right-click an app and choose 'Run as administrator'). Press [Windows]+[W] for the Settings search (or use the Search charm and select 'Settings'). Type 'smart' and go to 'Change SmartScreen settings'. Choose 'Change Windows SmartScreen settings' and choose to get a warning or turn off the approval.

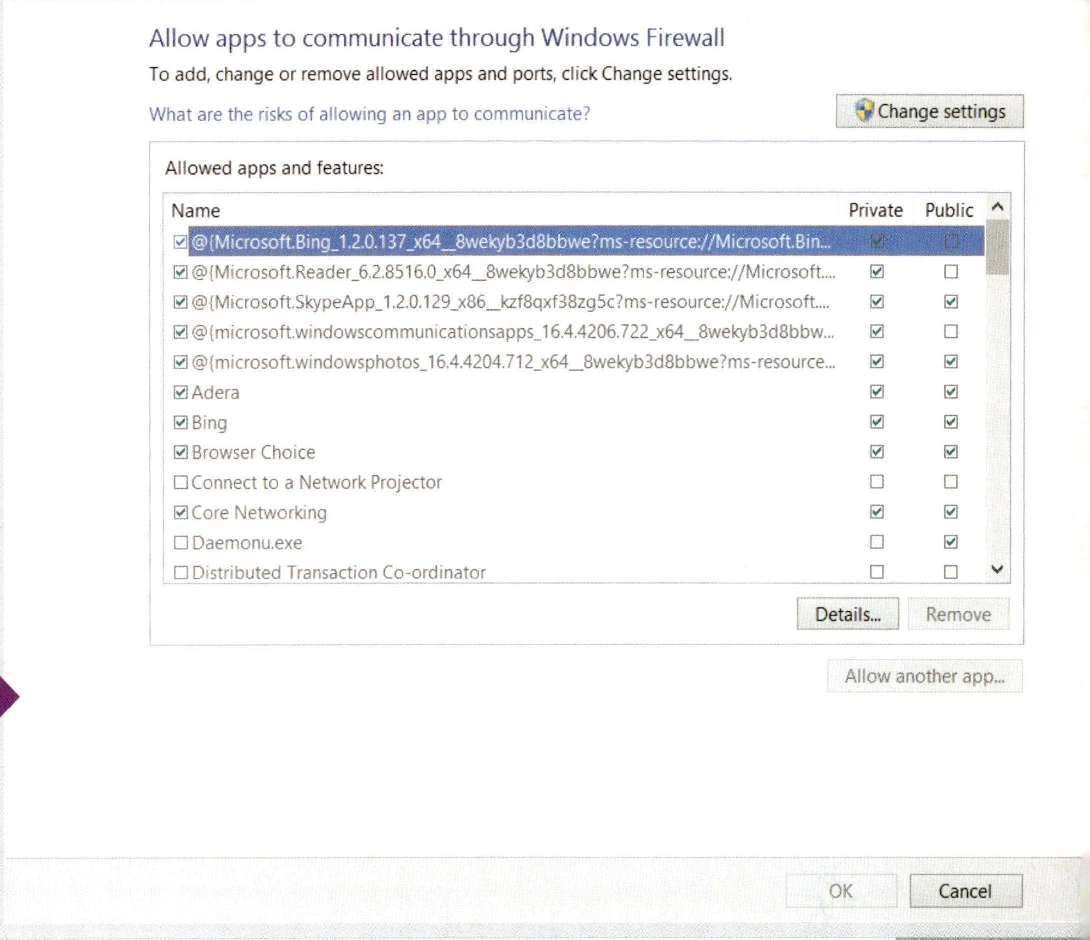

STAY SAFE WITH WINDOWS 8

Manage the firewall

The Windows Firewall with Advanced Security is more advanced than ever and it checks with you whenever an app requests access through it – but you can manually set up access for apps, too. Press [Windows]+[W] and search for 'Windows Firewall', then click or tap 'Allow an app or feature through Windows Firewall'. You can choose which apps have private and public access, though you need administrator rights. Click 'Change settings' to get access to the checkbox list. This part of the Control Panel also enables you to amend any rules associated with your firewall settings, and create, import and export different security policies.

Sort out sync

One very useful Windows 8 feature is its ability to synchronise your settings with other devices through your Microsoft account. So if you set up a phone or another Windows 8 PC with the same account, it synchronises your contacts, email details and so on. This is very convenient but there may be times when it's not a good idea. If several people use a device, you'd ideally have different accounts – but this might not always be the case. Control everything that Windows might sync by going to the Settings charm, then tapping 'Change PC Settings'. Go to 'Sync Your Settings' to disable anything you'd rather not sync.

Windows 8: Expert Tips and Tricks

25 TOP TIPS FOR...
Improving security

The web is a dark, scary place. Make sure you're prepared for it properly with these handy hints

1 Windows 8 is dedicated to protecting your passwords. The Windows Credential Manager does the hard work, looking after web passwords and any local network passwords you have. Type 'credential' at the Start screen.

2 The Credential Manager looks after your passwords if you save them when logging in. It's worth periodically backing up logins, in case Windows is reset. Click 'Back Up Credentials' and point it to a safe location to do this.

3 Think carefully about the passwords you use. If they're easy to guess, or based on dictionary words, you risk someone with the right tools breaking in. We like to create passwords from a string of random words – for example, greenwellingtonmonkeyfighting is super secure and easy to remember.

4 You can also generate dictionary-proof passwords. These aren't easy to remember but they are rock-solid. Try the PCTools generator at www.pctools.com/guides/password/ to create something automatically.

5 There's another password generator if you don't trust a web service. Search the Windows Store for 'Random Password Generator'. Install it, then drag the slider to determine the length of your password, and hit 'Generate'.

6 The real key to password management, particularly if using complex passwords, is online storage. LastPass is the field leader, and it has a Windows 8 app to help you keep your logins in check. Find out more on page 130.

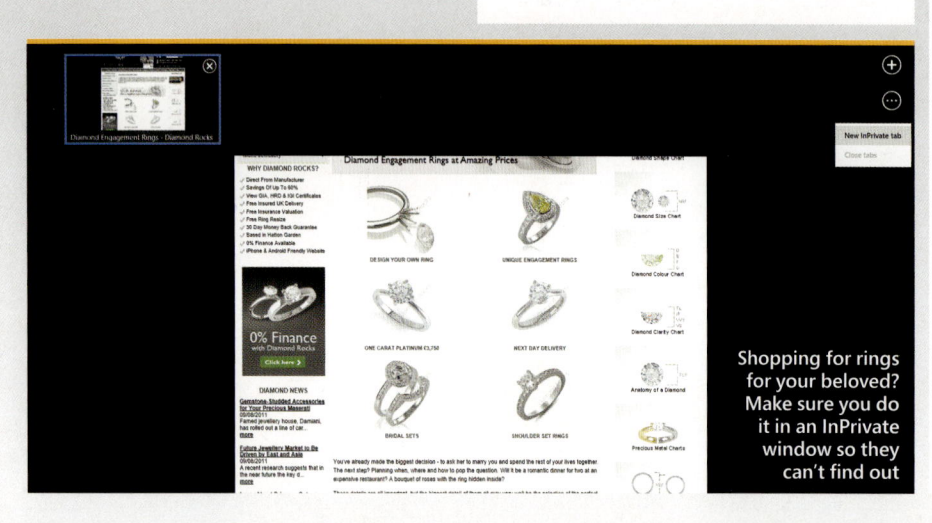

IMPROVING SECURITY

7 Using the LastPass Modern browser isn't as convenient as your choice of desktop browser, though. Use LastPass' plugins (from https://lastpass.com/misc_download.php), which hook into every desktop browser.

8 Security is also about covering your tracks; if someone gets on to your PC, you don't want them to see what you've been up to. In Modern Internet Explorer, right-click to get the Tab menu and click the ellipsis (...) icon to start a new InPrivate tab.

9 InPrivate tabs (or Incognito tabs in Chrome, and Private Browsing in Firefox) run in a protected environment. You can use them to buy gifts for others without leaving a trace in your history.

10 It's worth periodically clearing your history and cookies. This means sites forget who you are, but it also stops intruders seeing what you've visited, and confuses advertisers. Open Modern IE, press [Windows]+[I], go to 'Settings > Internet Options', then click the button at the top to clean up.

11 Many sites let you connect securely, so the data you send can't be intercepted. The method varies from site to site, but you can try changing the 'http' at the start of a web address to 'https' instead. It works in many cases.

12 The most private way of browsing is through a virtual private network, or VPN. It means even your ISP can't see what you're doing; your traffic is encrypted from one end to the other. Try Hotspot Shield (www.hotspotshield.com) – it's free, supported by ads.

13 Install Hotspot Shield (avoiding the toolbar during installation) and run it to get secured. If you set it to 'Always turn on' mode when you first run, your laptop is protected whenever you're on an untrusted network.

14 Make sure the site you're using is the real thing. On a desktop browser, look in the address bar for a token that verifies its identity; on Chrome there's a lock icon on the left, on Firefox there's a green bar on the left, and on IE there's a small lock on the right.

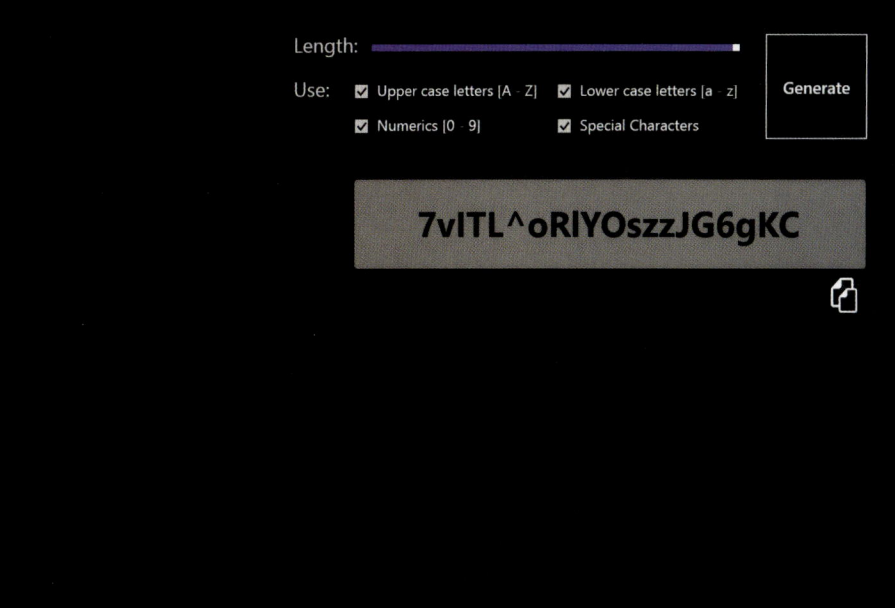

15 If you do stumble on to an unsafe website – or one that's been reported as trying to steal your personal information – you should see a big red warning page. Don't ignore this. And don't rely on it; if it's a new threat, the warning might not appear.

16 Sometimes a legitimate site might be misreported as compromised. Whichever browser you use, there'll be an 'advanced' or 'more information' link on the warning page; report the page as being mistakenly flagged here.

17 If you suspect a site, check the address bar. Make sure it's a properly formed web address of the format you might expect from the site you're visiting. If it's not, copy the address and send it to www.phishtank.com, which catalogues such things.

18 Pay attention to your email. You might get something purporting to be from your bank, which is in fact a phishing attack, trying to trick you into giving up personal details. Look out for spurious addresses, bad grammar, and links that take you to odd addresses.

19 Your children's safety is important. Use parental controls (page 128), or a picture password on your main account (page 130), so they can't misbehave. Untrusted users should never be able to log in to your account.

20 Make sure you have safe search switched on in your search engine to protect your kids from accidentally stumbling on lewd images. To do it in Bing, click the cog at the top-right of the screen and set SafeSearch to 'strict'.

You can generate a nice random password through Windows 8 apps. You'll never remember it, but that's pretty secure

Quick tips

21 Antivirus is very important. Windows comes with some built-in protection to help you out – just type 'defender' at the Start screen to find it.

22 Windows Defender should run scans automatically, but you can run a quick scan on demand (if you're worried) by clicking the 'Scan now' button.

23 A full scan (click the 'full' radio button, and then 'Scan now') takes rather a long time to complete, but covers everything on your computer.

24 You can use the Update tab to quickly refresh Defender's cache of known viruses and threats, so it's ready for anything you might throw at it.

25 You might like to try a stronger solution than Windows Defender. AVG offers a complete free antivirus tool from http://free.avg.com. Give it a try!

Windows 8: Expert Tips and Tricks

Learn how to...

Set up Family Safety

Keep your younger family members safe when they're online, even if you don't have time to watch them every second of the day

WORKS WITH
Windows 8
Windows 8 Pro
Windows RT

Protecting your children is of utmost importance when it comes to computing. Your laptop or tablet is always connected to the internet, completely portable, and a potential portal to some rather unpleasant things. But not everyone needs to be subject to the same restrictions. You might want to keep your junior away from Facebook and stop them using the computer after 8pm, for instance, but allow your teenager a little more leeway. And, of course, you want unfettered access for yourself. Windows 8 makes all of this easy to achieve. First, make sure your own user account is password-protected. If you log in with a Microsoft account, this isn't an issue, but if you use a local account, you need to lock it down.

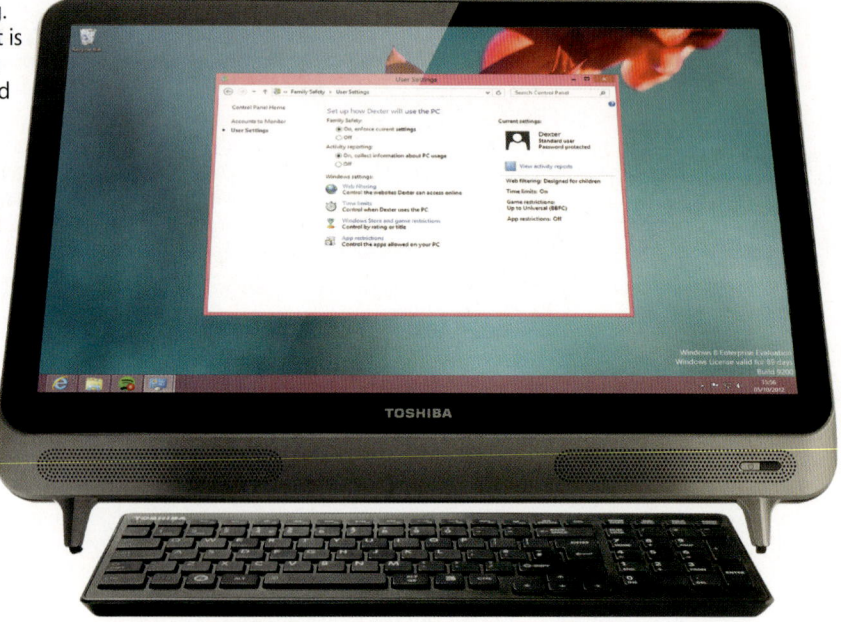

Create a locked-down account

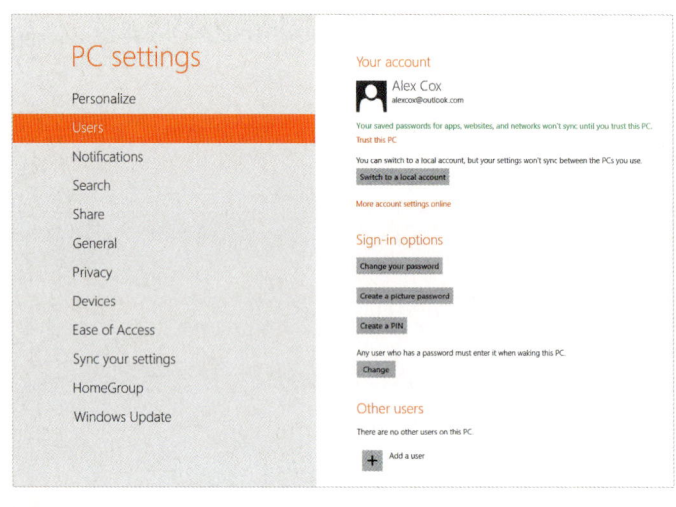

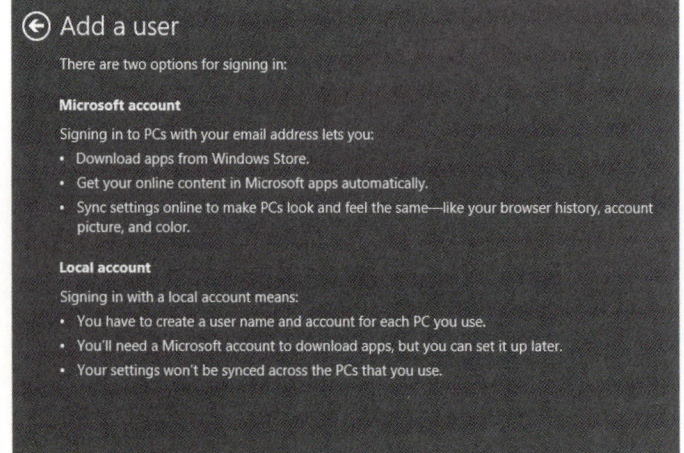

1 Add users
Before starting with Family Safety, we need to make sure your computer is properly set up. If you're sharing a single user account between your family, it's time to divide and use one account each. Bring up the Charms bar on the Start screen, choose 'Settings > Change PC Settings', and finally the 'Users' menu.

2 Choose rights
Here you can create a new user account with standard rights – that is, restricted access, which has no potential to harm your computer. Scroll down to the bottom of the page and select the plus sign next to 'Add a User'. Because we're creating restricted, local accounts, choose 'Sign in without a Microsoft account'.

SET UP FAMILY SAFETY

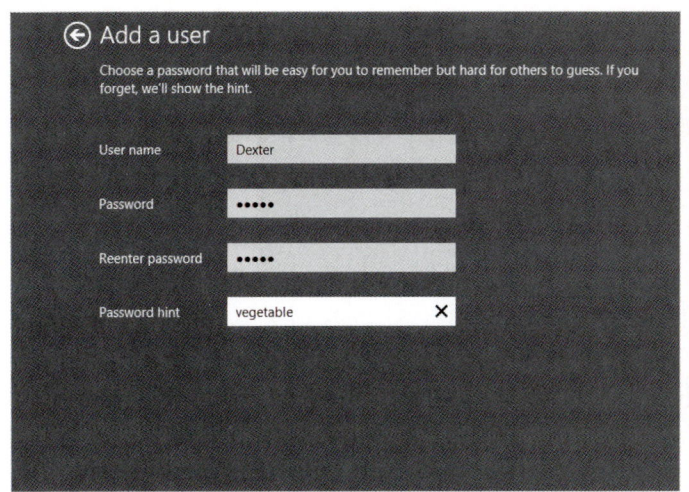

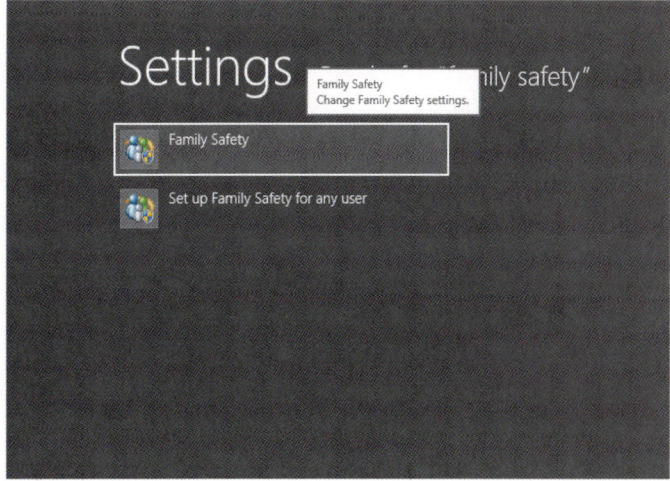

3 Name and password
Select 'Local Account'. Put in the name of the user in the top box, then decide whether you want the account to be password-protected; even with children, it's a good idea, so they can't log into each other's accounts. Just make sure you know the password in case anything goes wrong with the account in the future.

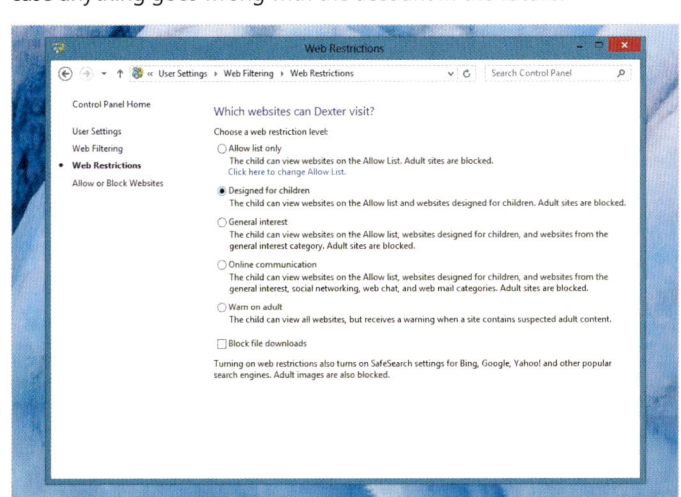

4 Find Family Safety
Tick the box next to 'Is this a child's account?', then click 'Finish'. Your new user is created; repeat as appropriate for each member of your family. Press [Windows] to get back to the Start screen, then type 'family safety', choose 'Settings', and select 'Family Safety' to be taken to the desktop-based control panel.

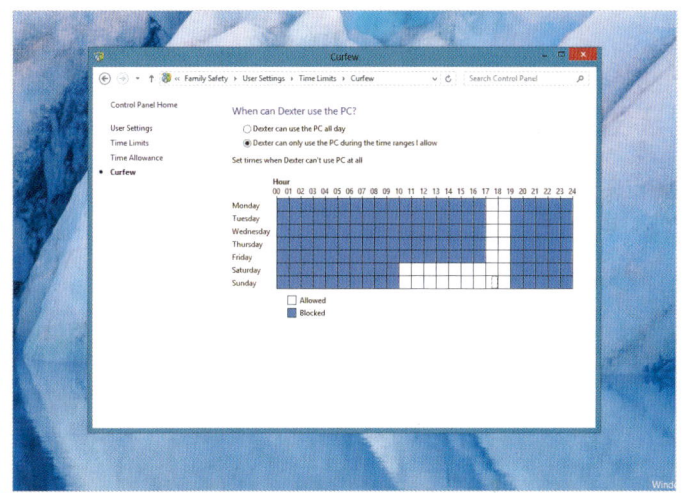

5 Lock the web
To restrict web access, choose an account name, tap 'Web filtering', then 'Set web filtering level'. There's a number of choices: 'Designed for Children' should be fine for young kids, and 'Online Communication' for older children. If you're especially cautious, choose 'Allow List Only' and click the link to set allowed sites.

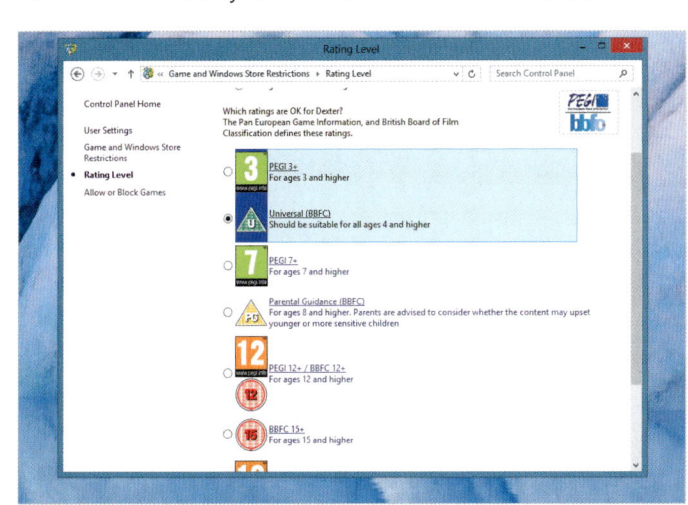

6 Set the clock
Select 'User settings' to go back to the main menu for this user, then 'Time Limits'. You can set a time allowance (say an hour per day) with the top link; bear in mind that you can override this if more time is required for homework or similar. Setting a curfew restricts the hours your child can access the PC.

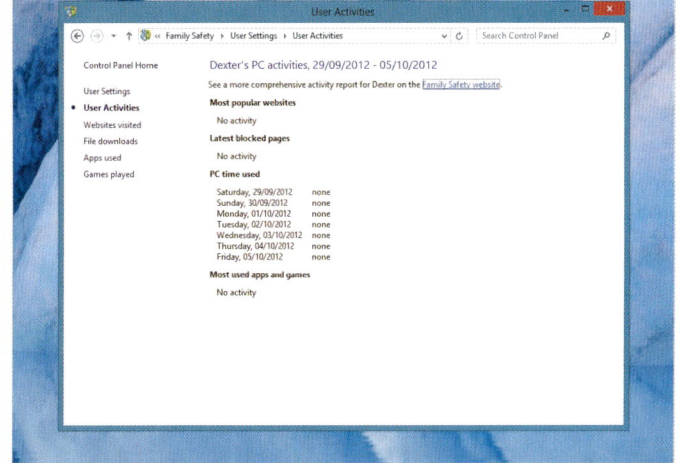

7 Define age limits
Go back to 'User settings'. The bottom two links can be used to set what that user can and cannot download from the Windows Store, and what ages are deemed appropriate in terms of games and age-rated apps. The local accounts we have created don't have access to the Windows Store anyway.

8 Watch the logs
Perhaps the most devious part of the Family Safety centre is on the right of the user settings screen. Select 'View activity reports' to see exactly what that user has been up to, from blocked sites they've tried to visit to the amount of time used. If there's something there that shouldn't be, it's time for a little chat...

Learn how to...

Make Windows tough to crack
Increase your password strength

WORKS WITH
Windows 8
Windows 8 Pro
Windows RT

How often do you use a password? For most of us, it's likely that entering a secure password is a daily occurrence. But it might not be as secure as you think. Clearly, none of us wants to be at risk of anyone being able to get into our computer and access our files or steal sensitive data, so it's crucial that your password is as strong as it can be. Microsoft has stayed ahead of the game when it comes to security, and Windows 8 comes with a handy feature called Picture Password, which enables you to draw your own password – once we've shown you how to set it up, there's no guessing it. We'll also cover a great app called LastPass, which creates unique ultra-secure passwords for all your online accounts using one password, so read on to stay protected.

Gesture steps
When creating your picture password, draw your *gesture* on the screen three times and repeat it again to ensure you entered it correctly.

Beef up your security

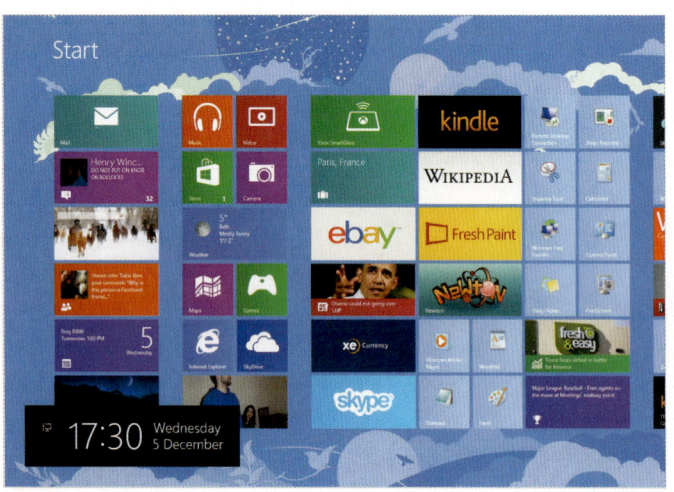

1 Open settings
You log in to your PC every day, but you certainly don't want anyone to be able to access your personal account – even if it's just a partner or your kids. So create a picture password, which will save you having to type an uncrackable password every time. Just start your PC, open the Charms bar and select the 'Settings' option.

2 Picture perfect
Select 'Change PC settings' and then choose 'Users' from the left-hand menu. Underneath the 'Sign-in' option, select 'Create a picture password' and input your current password (if you have one). First things first – choose a picture that you like from the area on your PC where you store them.

MAKE WINDOWS TOUGH TO CRACK

Good draw
You draw your gestures in the area where your picture is located. It can be a combination of circles, taps and straight lines.

Unique picture
By using a picture that is personal to you, you're more likely to remember the sequence of the password you need to enter each time.

Jargon buster!

Browser
This is what you use to access the internet and look at websites. There is a variety of browsers available, including Internet Explorer, Firefox and Chrome.

Gesture
Much like in real life, a gesture is a physical action that you perform to manipulate the Windows 8 environment – for instance, swiping right to access the Charms bar.

3 Get drawing
Once you have located a suitable picture, select 'Use this picture' and then you can start building your picture password. Doing this is a three step process – choose a part of the picture and draw three things. It can be a circle, a simple tap (of your mouse or screen) or a line, or any combination of them all.

4 Confirm your password
You need to confirm your password to ensure you entered it correctly, then hit 'Finish' and your picture password is complete – your PC is far more secure than with a conventional password. If you have multiple Windows 8 devices, click 'Trust this PC' from the 'User account' menu to sync the picture password with other devices.

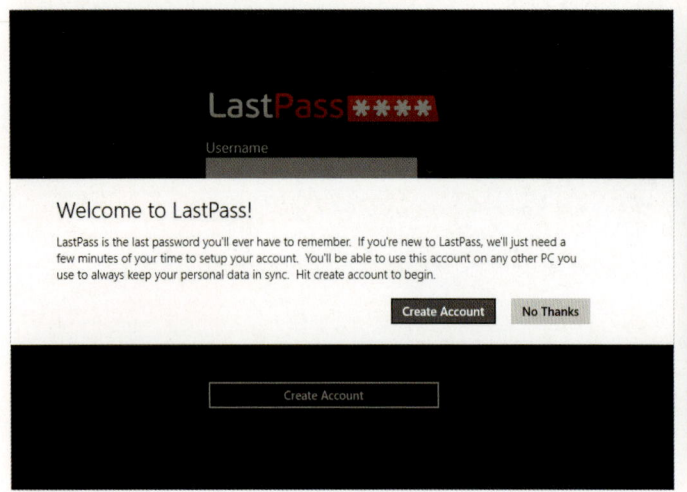

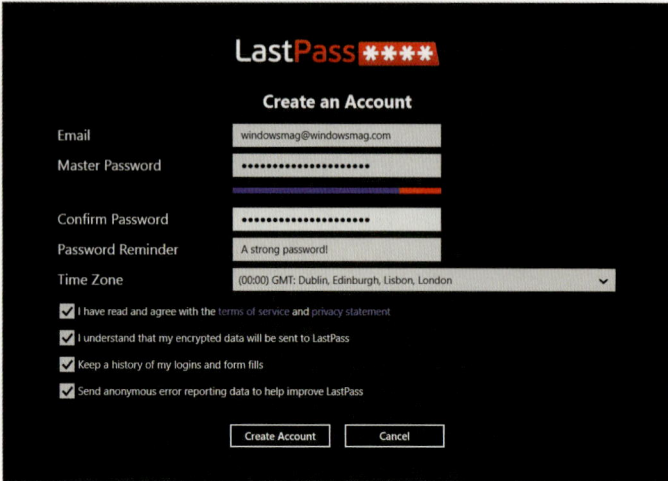

5 Online accounts
Now you should improve the way you log in to favourite sites. Using LastPass, life is much easier because you don't have to log in to all your favourites sites each time you start your PC – LastPass does the hard work for you. Download and install LastPass from the Windows Store, choose 'Create account' and enter your details.

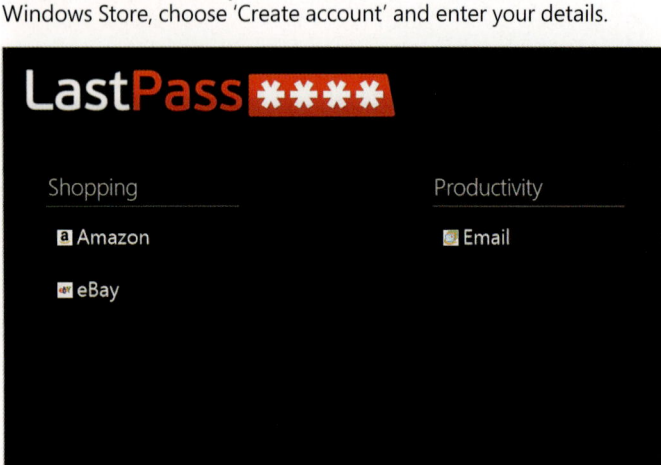

6 Your master
The Master Password is the password you need to input every time you log in to LastPass. Make it as strong as possible by using a mixture of upper and lower case letters and numbers, making it at least eight characters long. The meter below the text box indicates how strong your master password is – it needs to turn purple.

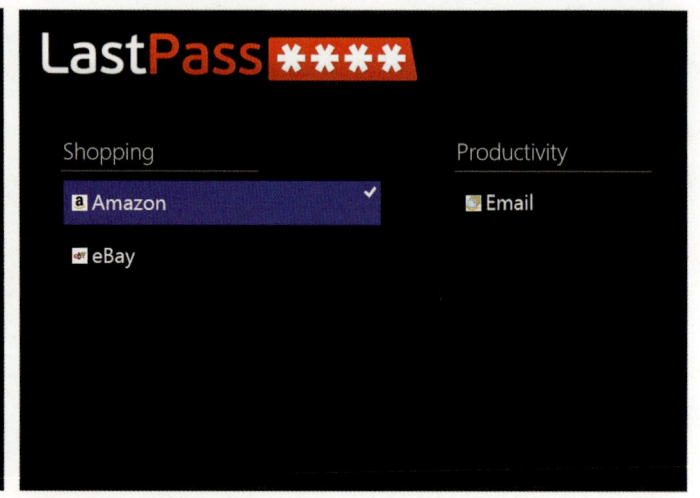

7 Add sites
Once you've logged in to LastPass, the first screen you see is blank, which is disconcerting, but fear not – this is your blank canvas with which to create your own LastPass vault. Right-click your mouse (or swipe from above) to access the menu and choose 'Add Site' to add your favourite password-protected online accounts to LastPass.

8 Fill in the blanks
Enter the details of the site you'd like to add, with the password you normally use for that account. You can add the site to a group (such as shopping) to organise your sites better. At the bottom there are checkboxes if you'd like to be auto-logged into the site or make the site a favourite. Hit the tick on the right to finish.

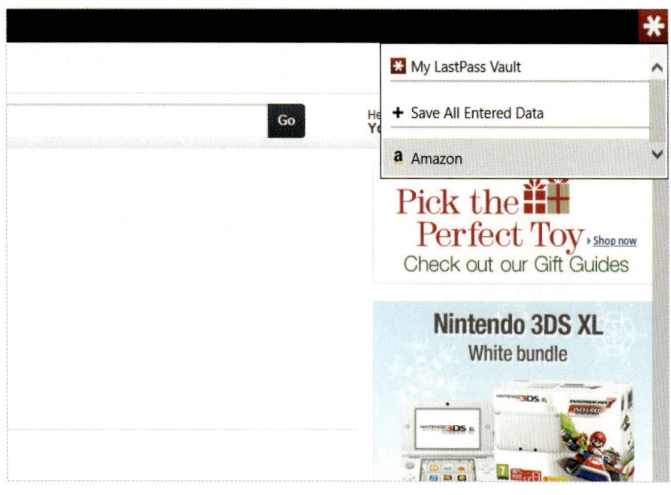

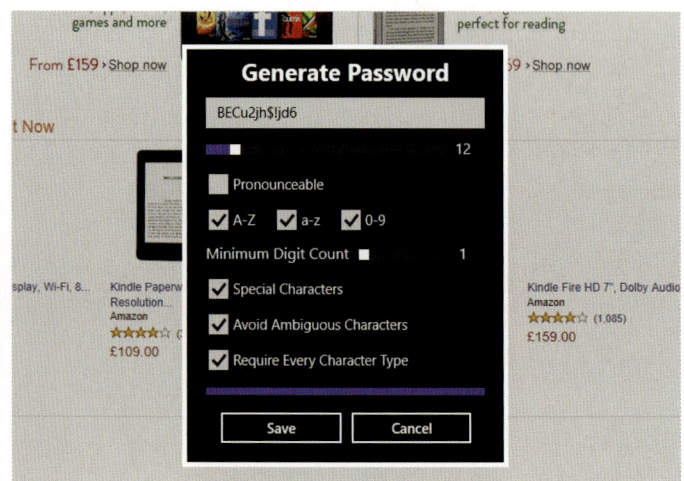

9 Log in quickly
Now, whenever you want to use one of your favourite online accounts, simply check the tick box on the account and hit 'Browser'. You're taken to the account, and if you've selected to auto-login, you don't need to do anything else. If not, click the 'LastPass' menu and choose the name of the login you need.

10 Safe and sound
You've made passwords a lot safer – and easier to remember. If you'd like to increase the safety of your LastPass accounts, go to the browser for any account, right-click (or swipe from the bottom) and select 'Generate password'. LastPass creates a unique super-strong password for that account. Click 'Save' and that's it.

FIND THE BEST PC GAMES

THE GREATEST PC Games OF ALL TIME

FROM THE MAKERS OF **PC GAMER**

THE BEST 100 PC GAMES EVER

RANKING THE PC'S BEST GAMES

148 GAMES INSIDE!

WHO IS NUMBER ONE?
Discover the PC game you MUST play…

- HOW TO GET OLD GAMES WORKING
- FIND CLASSIC GAMES FOR ANY PC
- GAME-MAKING SECRETS SPILLED

ON SALE NOW!

"Twenty dwarves are torn limb from limb"
THE PC'S BEST INDIE GAME GOES TO HELL

GET OLD GAMES WORKING

GATEWAYS TO GAMING The PC's greatest games explained

RPG | SHOOTER | ADVENTURE | STRATEGY

FLIP FOR MORE

PC CLASSICS YOU CAN PLAY RIGHT NOW

Future MEDIA WITH PASSION

Buy your copy **in store** or on **Newsstand** for **iPad**, **iPhone** and **iPod touch** — Available on the App Store

FROM THE MAKERS OF **PC GAMER** MAGAZINE

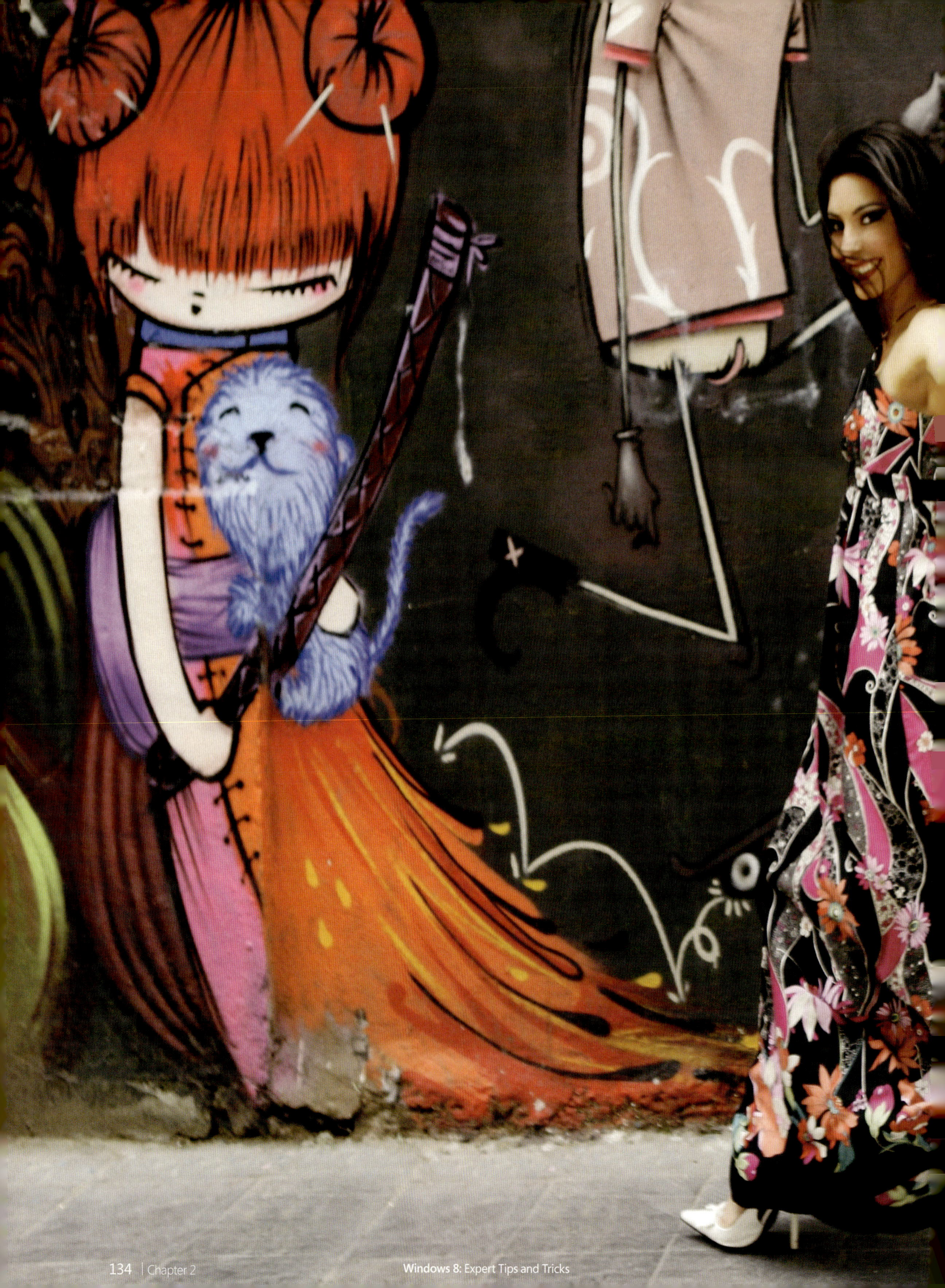

Get creative

TRY THIS!
Get more done daily
140

Unleash your imaginative side with a host of creative tips and tricks

Section 7

136	Do more with Windows 8
138	Getting more creative
140	Be more productive
142	Try the Photo app
146	Make a note of anything!
147	Get Microsoft Office for free!

DO THIS NOW...

Do more with Windows 8

You've got the basics, now it's time to be inspired

Get old files back

Windows 8 can keep a history of files you've worked on, so if you need to get an older version of a project back, you can. File History can regularly and automatically back up your libraries, desktop, contacts and favourites to a second drive, even if it's an external USB flash drive – just connect it, and choose 'Configure this drive for backup using File History'. To start File History off, go to 'Control Panel > System and Security > File History'. Click 'Exclude Folders' to define what you're saving, 'Advanced Settings' to choose the frequency, 'Change Drive' to choose the destination, and 'Turn On' to enable the feature with your settings.

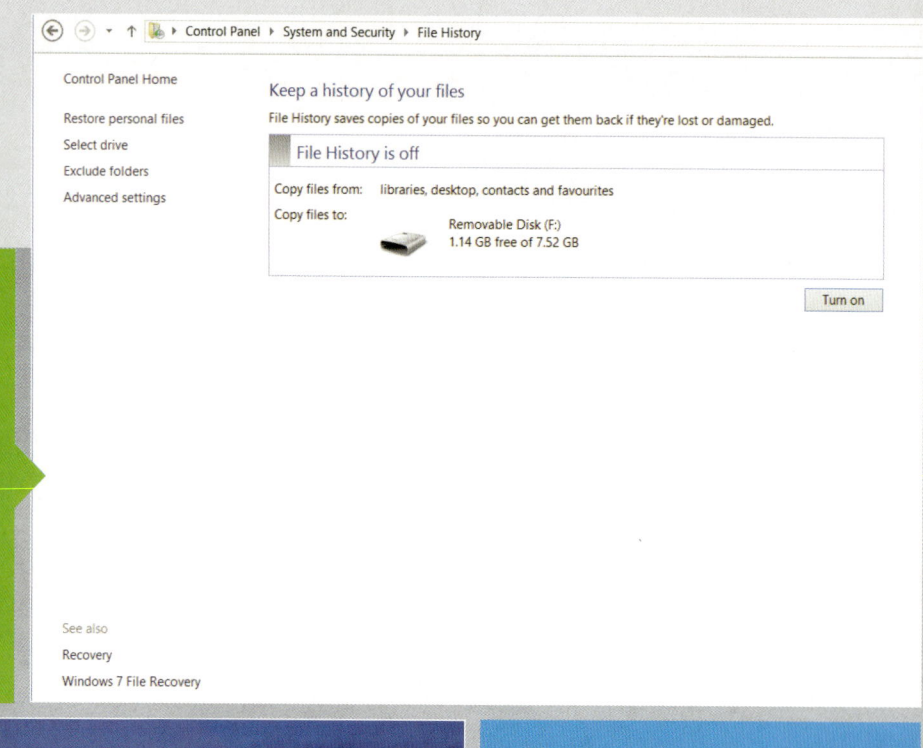

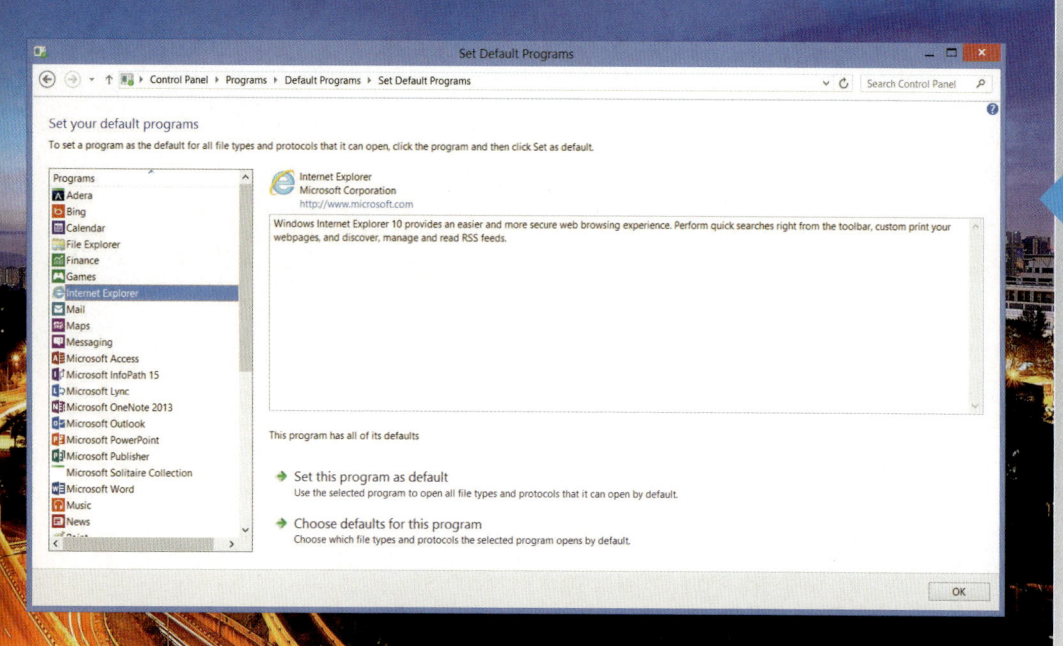

Change your default programs

If you want to ensure that a program opens all the different files it can, there's a Control Panel applet that enables you to select the default programs for each file type, and for commands such as what happens when you click email links. Go to 'Control Panel > Programs > Default Programs' and click 'Set your default programs'. Click an application then 'Set this program as default' if you'd like it to open all the file types it can handle, or 'Choose default options' to specify which file types it should open. Click 'OK'.

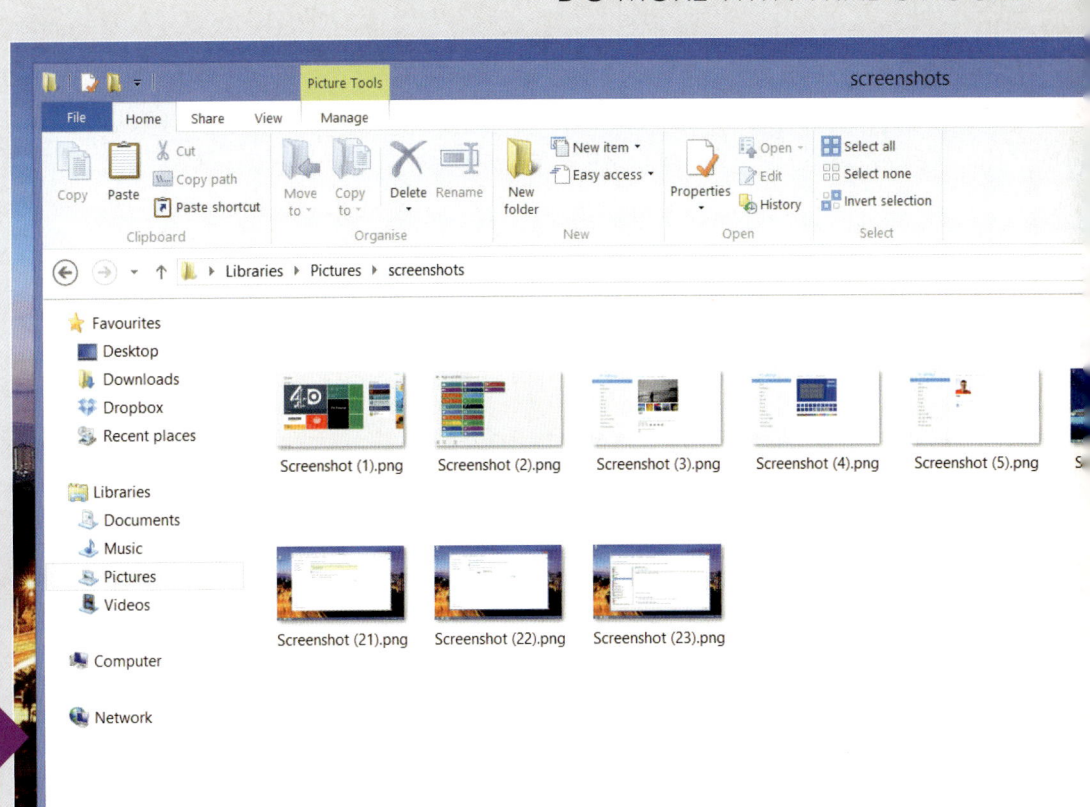

DO MORE WITH WINDOWS 8

Save screenshots

The [Print Screen] ([PrtSrc]) button isn't used much, but it's given new meaning by teaming it with the [Windows] key. [PrtSrc] can still be used to copy an image of a page to the clipboard, which can then be pasted into an application such as Paint, Photoshop Elements or even Word. But by pressing [PrtSrc] at the same time as [Windows] in Windows 8, the screenshot is saved in a Screenshots folder in your Pictures library with the name Screenshot.png (and then Screenshot(1).png, Screenshot(2).png and so on). If you need more complex screenshots of open windows and so on, try the Snipping Tool, also included with Windows 8.

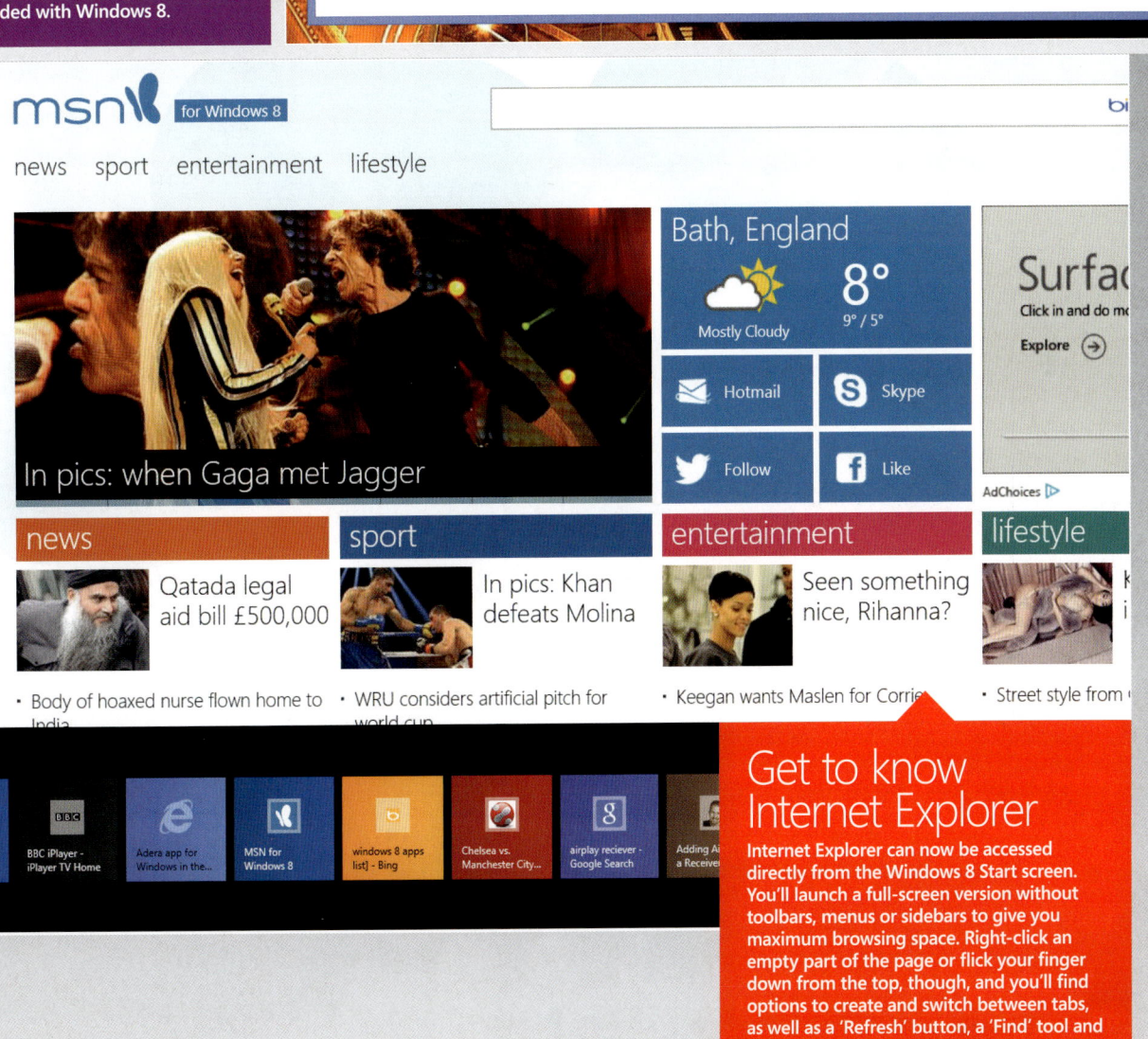

Get to know Internet Explorer

Internet Explorer can now be accessed directly from the Windows 8 Start screen. You'll launch a full-screen version without toolbars, menus or sidebars to give you maximum browsing space. Right-click an empty part of the page or flick your finger down from the top, though, and you'll find options to create and switch between tabs, as well as a 'Refresh' button, a 'Find' tool and the ability to pin an internet shortcut to the Start page. Click the spanner and select 'View on the desktop' to switch across to the full desktop version of Internet Explorer.

Windows 8: Expert Tips and Tricks

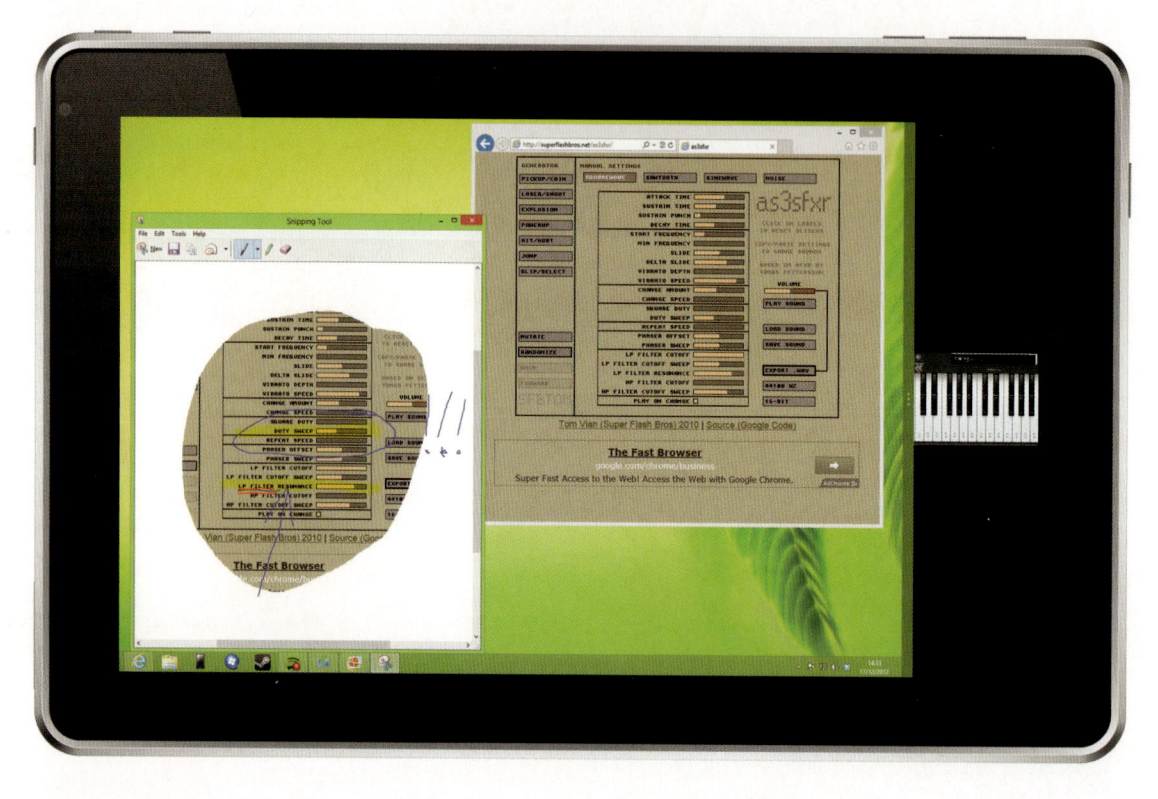

25 TOP TIPS FOR...
Getting more creative

From pretty pictures to glorious sounds, you can do a lot more with Windows 8

1 Are you an old-school Windows user? You're probably familiar with Paint. It might look as though it's disappeared from Windows 8 but it hasn't. Go to the Start screen, press [Windows]+[Q], and search for 'paint'.

2 There's a good reason that Paint has been tucked under the rug a little – Microsoft has a new artistic app that supports multi-touch, fancy brushes and more. It's called Fresh Paint and it's available from the Windows Store.

3 Fresh Paint is very nice, but it's more artistic than practical. You can use it to make a pretty picture, but not to edit one. If you want to tweak your snaps, you need Microsoft's Photo Gallery, available from http://windows.microsoft.com/en-GB/windows-live/photo-gallery-get-started.

4 Photo Gallery can make dull snaps colourful and bright by adjusting the exposure. Open a suspect photo, go to the 'Edit' menu, then click the fine-tune button on the ribbon; use the sliders to tweak it until you're happy.

5 Photo Gallery can also stitch photos together into panoramas. Your results may vary – particularly if you've been snapping in inconsistent light, or including moving elements – but you'll find the option in the 'Create' menu.

6 If you want super-deep control over photo and image editing, you need a third-party tool. The GIMP (www.gimp.org) is well regarded and free, with power akin to Photoshop, but in a less professional package.

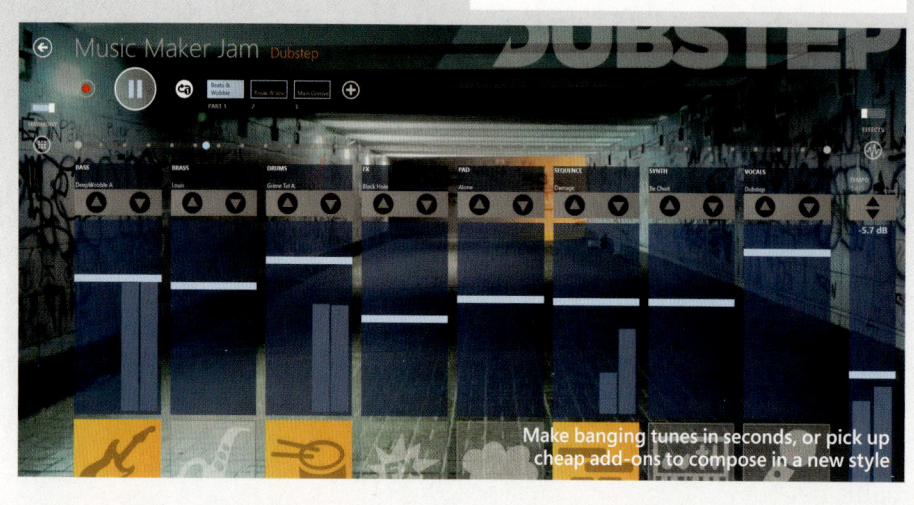

Make banging tunes in seconds, or pick up cheap add-ons to compose in a new style

GETTING MORE CREATIVE

7 Done something pretty with Windows? Want to show it off? Windows 8 features a much improved screenshot tool. Press [Windows]+[Print Screen] at the same time, and you'll find the shot in the Screenshots folder in Pictures.

8 You can still use the old screenshot method (press [Print Screen] on its own) to send the current screen to the clipboard. If you're on the desktop, you can also use [Alt]+[Print Screen] to capture only the current active window without any of the other desktop elements around it.

9 For an even more specific way of capturing your screen, use the Snipping Tool. Type 'snip' on the Start screen to find it. You can cut free-form shapes, rectangles and windows from your desktop; use the down arrow next to the 'New' button to select which type you'd like, then click 'New'.

10 One you've taken a snip with the Snipping Tool, you can save it or email it, or you could embellish it first. There's a number of pens in different colours, and a highlighter tool.

11 Time for some audio creativity. There are plenty of apps in the Windows Store that enable you to muck about with music – the cool Music Maker Jam is free and will turn you into a copy-and-paste dubstep master. You might not make a chart topper, but it's certainly fun.

12 Windows 8's touchscreen affinity means it's perfect for simulating instruments. They don't have the same impact if you use a keyboard and mouse, but we recommend Accordion8 and Organ8, free from the Windows Store.

13 Dig around in the Store for Metronome+ if you want a decent tick to keep in tempo when making proper music, or give Retro Stepper a try for an old-school sounding drum machine.

14 If you fancy making some nifty new Windows sounds, head to the desktop, fire up your web browser, and go to www.superflashbros.net/as3sfxr/ – drag the sliders or use the randomiser to make a sound, then export as WAV.

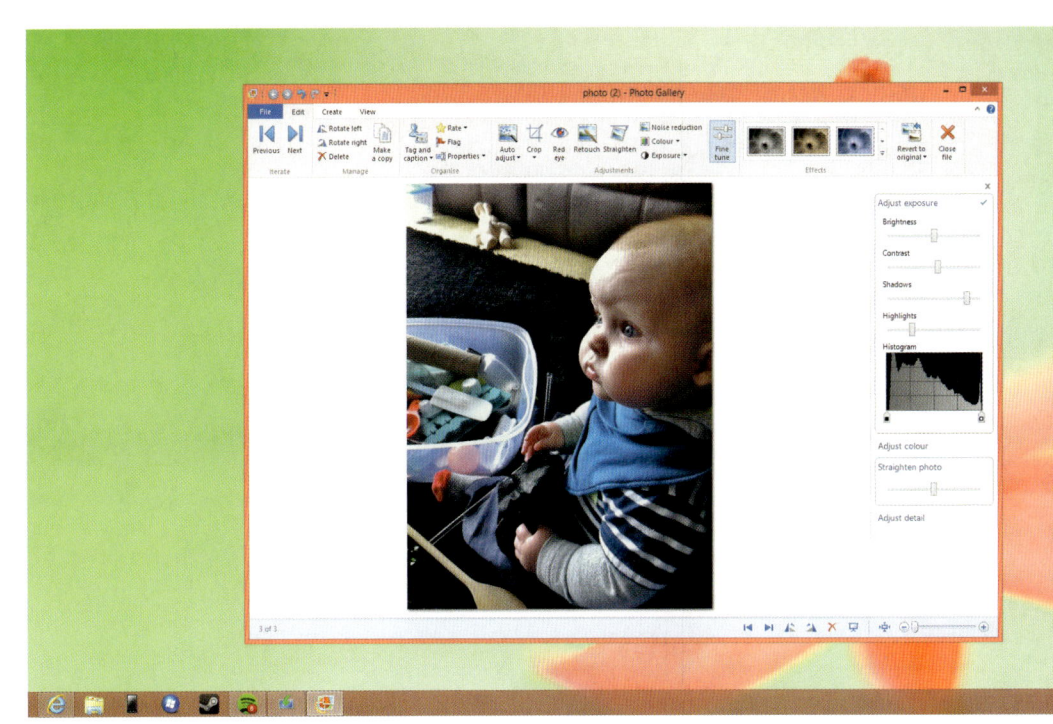

15 Got a microphone? Want to record, say, a podcast? Windows Sound Recorder can do it – sort of – but you get much better results, and you can edit the podcast as well, if you download Audacity for free from http://audacity.sourceforge.net.

16 Bear in mind that Audacity saves, by default, in its own AUP project format. This is perfect if you want to go back and edit your recording, but not if you want to share it. Make sure that you export your file rather than save it.

17 Annoyingly, Audacity doesn't export as MP3 without a tweak, as it can't legally be distributed with the MP3 encoder. You have to download that separately. There's a full guide on the Audacity site at http://bit.ly/LzsaJz.

18 MP3 files are small, but they can be made smaller; if recording a speech podcast, for example, use the 'Options' button on the 'Save' dialog to lower the bit rate – you don't need a high bit rate for speech, and the file size will be significantly reduced.

19 There are lots of providers who can make your podcast available to the world – we like www.libsyn.com – but for small-scale distribution, you can't beat SkyDrive. Upload your podcast, log in via www.skydrive.com, right-click the file and select 'Share'.

20 You don't just have to share creations via email. Click the link on the left adorned with Facebook, Twitter and LinkedIn logos, and use 'Add Services' to ensure SkyDrive is connected. Then point friends to your share with ease.

You can tweak any old snap to get the absolute best out of it using Photo Gallery's handy sliders

Quick tips

21 Check out what others have done. If you're in to art – particularly in a manga style – DeviantArt (www.deviantart.com) is a great place to start looking.

22 Musicians often preview early mixes and tacks they've made on www.soundcloud.com. It's free to listen, and you can upload your own creations, too.

23 You've probably heard of YouTube, but cast your eye over www.vimeo.com – it's a great source of incredibly high quality video content.

24 Creative types who want to get an idea off the ground are increasingly turning to www.kickstarter.com. Find something you like, and you can chip in towards it.

25 Why stop at art or music? There are plenty of people out there making free games for you to enjoy. We always like to check out www.tigsource.com for the latest and greatest. ■

Learn how to...

Be more productive in your day-to-day tasks

Boost your productivity with these downloads from the Windows Store

WORKS WITH
Windows 8
Windows 8 Pro
Windows RT

A lot of apps in the Windows Store have a fee attached to them, but we've trawled the shelves to save you the bother, and these are the best free Windows 8 productivity apps you could find. They all work using the Windows 8 Start screen rather than the desktop, but many of them have equivalents you can use on the desktop, too. One of the key apps we look at here is SkyDrive – cloud storage that you can access from any of your PCs or phones – but it's also worth checking out Box. It's a similar free Windows 8-style app that offers up to 5GB of storage for you to share across devices. Cloud storage is now definitely a must if you want to be as productive as possible – the best thing about it is that you'll never be without a file again.

Top free productivity apps for Windows 8

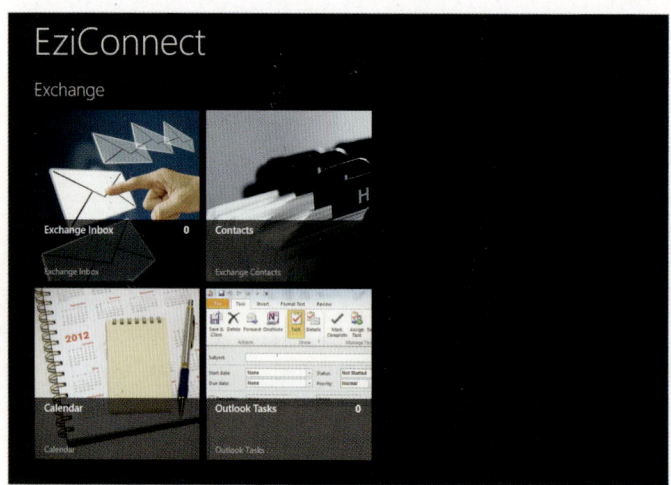

1 EziConnect
As no desktop apps are available on Windows RT, there's no Microsoft Office Outlook, so EziConnect bridges the gap and enables you to connect to Microsoft Exchange accounts, so you can view tasks, mail and calendar appointments. It's most useful for tasks, because you can still use Mail and Calendar with Exchange.

2 OneNote
Microsoft's note-taking app saves information to the cloud, so you can access it on any Windows device. OneNote's boon is its flexibility, so you can type, draw, swipe or take pictures to input information. Notes can be accessed via OneNote apps for other devices, including Windows Phone, iPhone, iPad and Android.

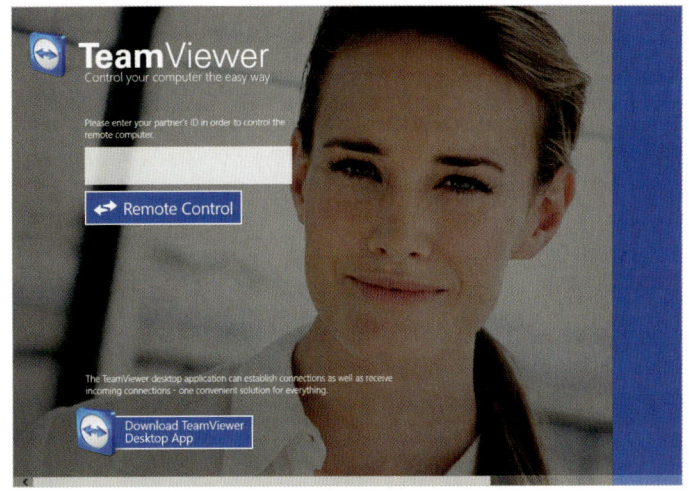

BE MORE PRODUCTIVE

3 TeamViewer
Remote control software that enables you to take control of another PC and hold online meetings over a secure connection. Free for personal use, there are desktop and Windows 8-style apps. The viewer-only TeamViewer Touch (for outgoing remote sessions) is a Windows 8-style app and supports all three versions of Windows 8.

4 Evernote
Evernote enables you to keep a record of just about anything, from the photo you snapped of the new T-shirt you want, to notes you took in last week's meeting. These notes, web page links and records (apps are available for various browsers, so you can link to pages) can be as ordered or chaotic as you like. Invaluable!

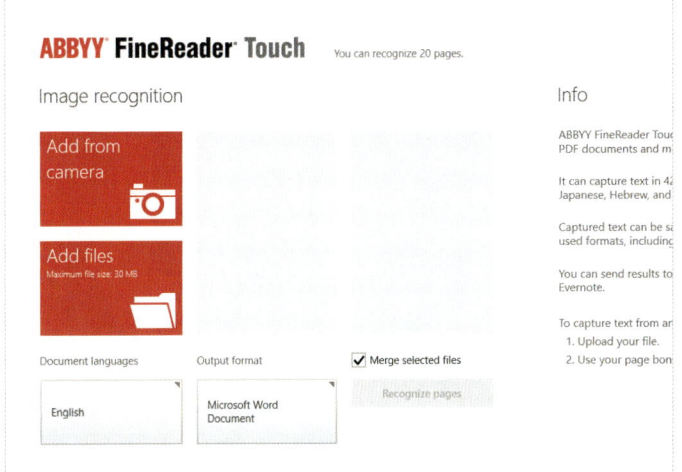

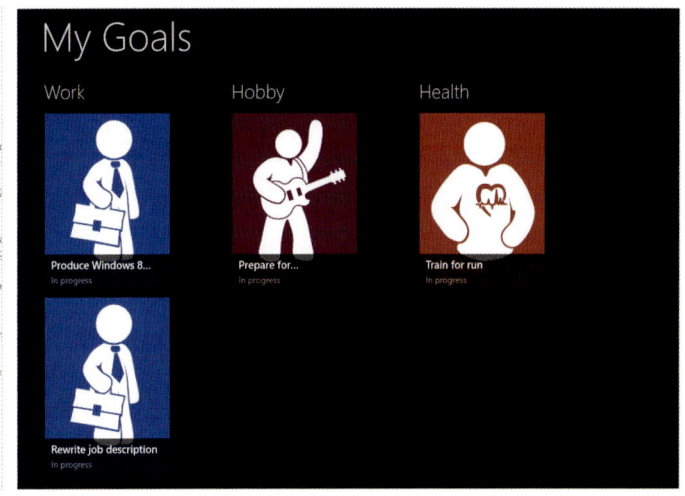

5 FineReader Touch
Ever come across a scanned image of a document that you wish you had as a text document? Now you can – FineReader Touch is a Windows 8-style app that uses Abbyy's OCR (optical character recognition) experience to turn documents into usable formats. They can be outputted in various ways, including as PDFs and Word docs.

6 Goals
Whatever you want to achieve in life, Goals can help. Whether it's training for a run, aiming for a promotion at work or just making sure you go to get the supermarket shopping, Goals enables you to set categorised tasks you need to aim for and attach a time and date to them. You can then chalk off the tasks as they're achieved.

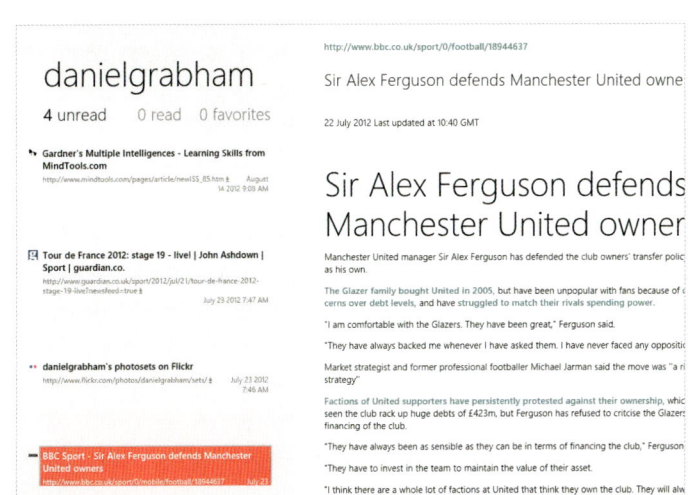

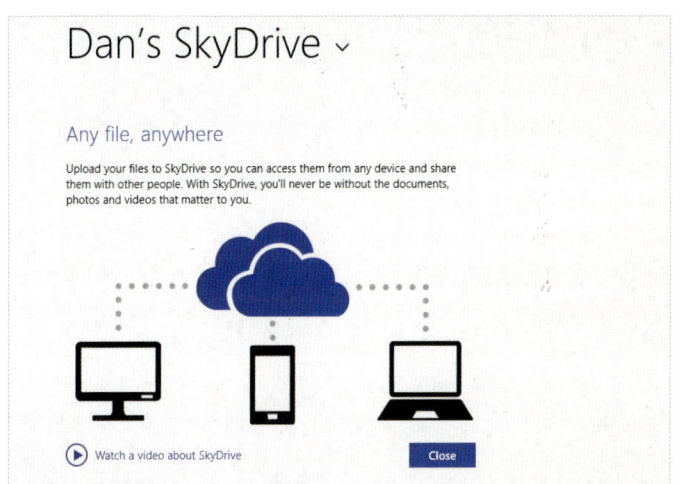

7 Latermark
Pocket (www.getpocket.com) is a service that uses browser plug-ins to save web pages and more to a cloud-based account. These are usually pages you want to read later (indeed, Pocket used to be called Read It Later). Latermark is a Windows 8-style client for Pocket that enables you to browse your saved pages.

8 SkyDrive
Before we finish, there's something powerful you need to know about. SkyDrive is Microsoft's cloud storage service and it comes with a free 7GB of data, so you can save files to it. That way, they're available on any PC you use – just install the free SkyDrive software there, too. Read more about SkyDrive on page 116.

Learn how to...

Organise your photographs
Always keep your snaps at hand

WORKS WITH
Windows 8
Windows 8 Pro
Windows RT

Everywhere we go, we take a camera with us. Whether it's a fancy SLR or a 4-megapixel phone, there's usually a snapping device within reach. We're recording our lives, one picture at a time. And soon, that expanding cache of photos becomes difficult to manage. Enter the Windows 8 Photos app, which takes the design ethos of the Modern UI and applies it to a cause to which it is well suited. Using Photos is like flicking through a real photo album. But can you re-jig a real photo album automatically if you want to see more pictures? Can you fill it with photos from Facebook and Flickr? No. So jump on board – you'll be pleased with the results.

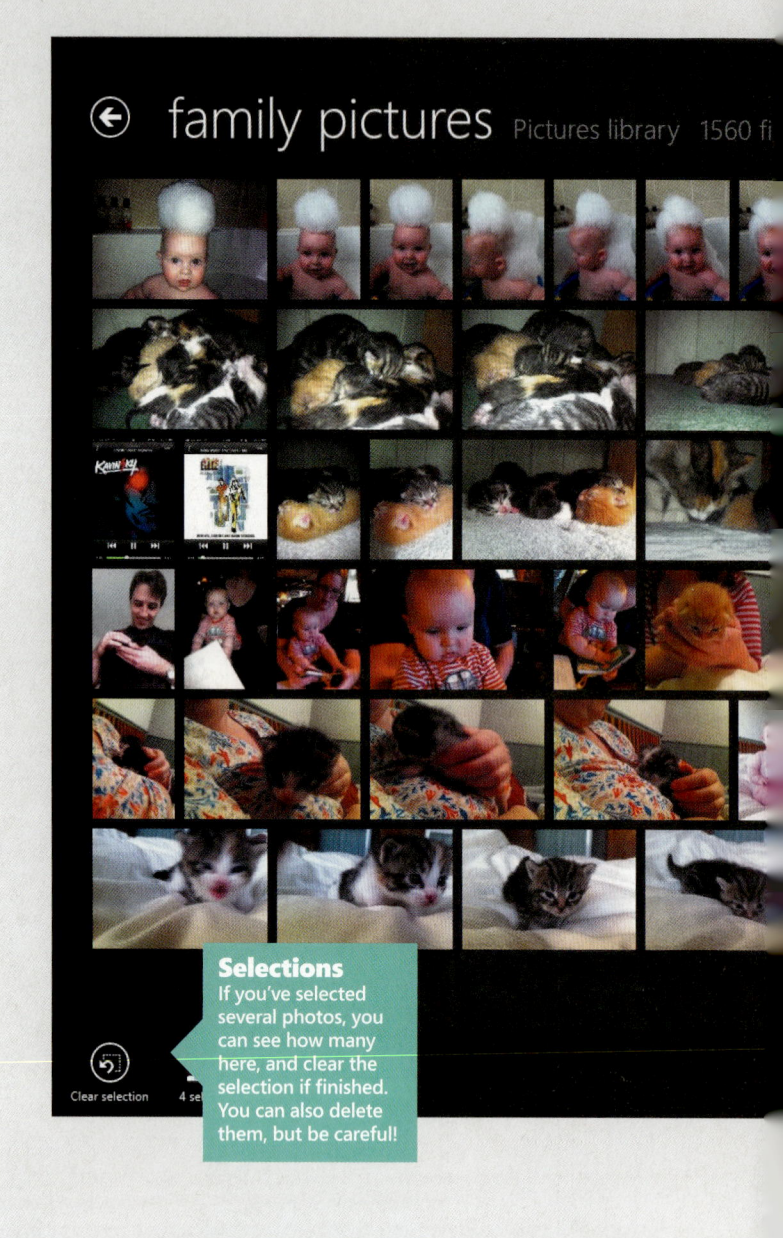

Selections
If you've selected several photos, you can see how many here, and clear the selection if finished. You can also delete them, but be careful!

Make the most of photos

1 Find the app
The Photos app should be sitting on your homescreen – it has a blue background. We've dragged it into its own column here for ease of identification. Your app might have had its Live tile activated, particularly if you've added images to your Pictures folder, so look out for a tile with personal images on if you can't find it.

2 Your first run
If you haven't yet added any pictures, Photos probably looks a bit bare. There's a nice picture of a big wheel in the background, but not much else. Prove to yourself that it's working by taking a screenshot – press [Windows] + [Printscreen] together, or hold the [Windows] button and press the volume rocker if you're on a tablet.

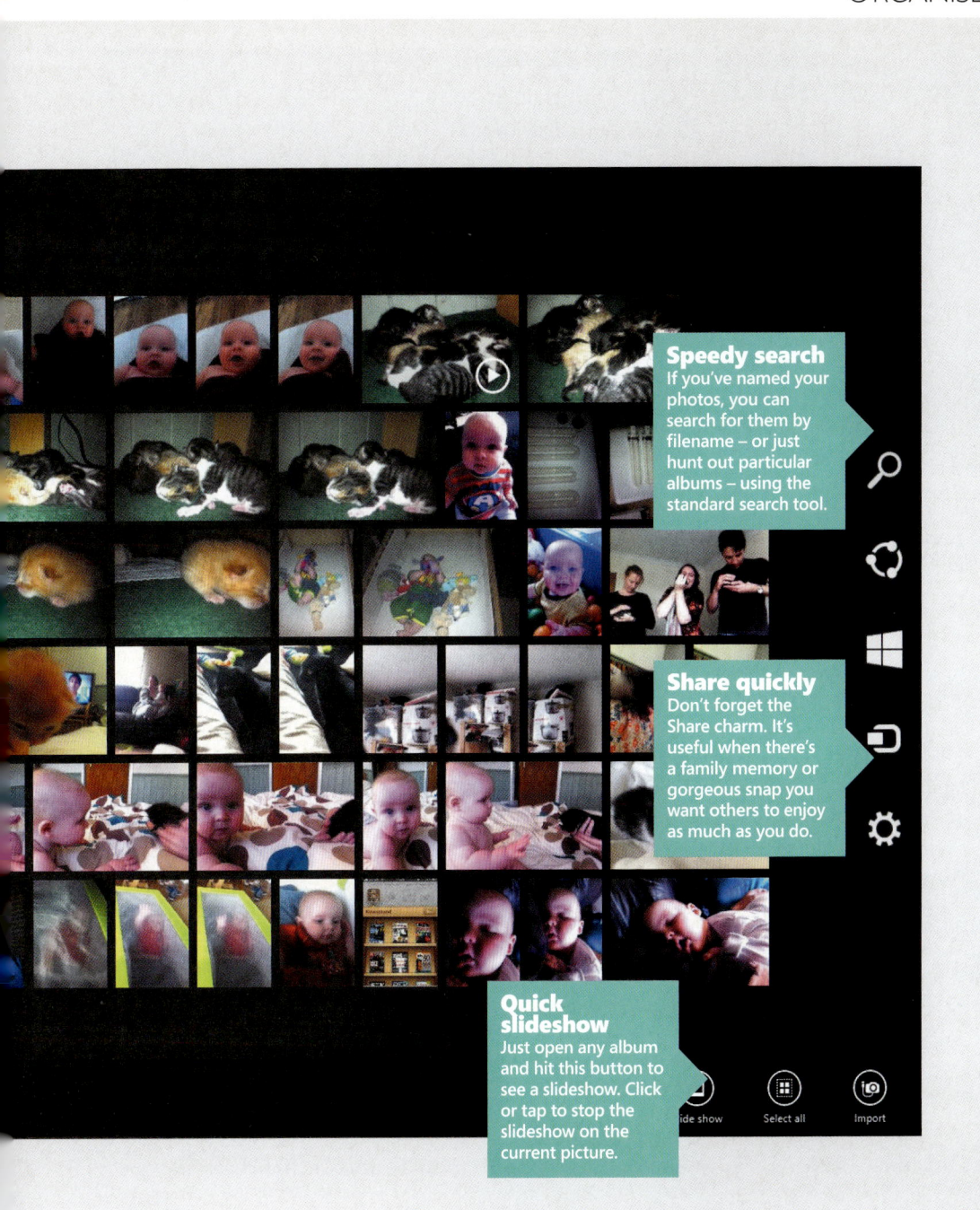

ORGANISE YOUR PHOTOGRAPHS

Speedy search
If you've named your photos, you can search for them by filename – or just hunt out particular albums – using the standard search tool.

Share quickly
Don't forget the Share charm. It's useful when there's a family memory or gorgeous snap you want others to enjoy as much as you do.

Quick slideshow
Just open any album and hit this button to see a slideshow. Click or tap to stop the slideshow on the current picture.

Instant import
Insert a device containing photos, and this tool lets you copy your selection directly to your Pictures library. It's quick and very easy.

Jargon buster!

Library
Libraries are a single view of your files, even when those files are stored in different locations. There are four – Documents, Music, Pictures and Videos.

SLR
Single lens reflex – a camera that enables you to see what you're photographing through its viewfinder and has an interchangeable lens, giving you more control over your photography.

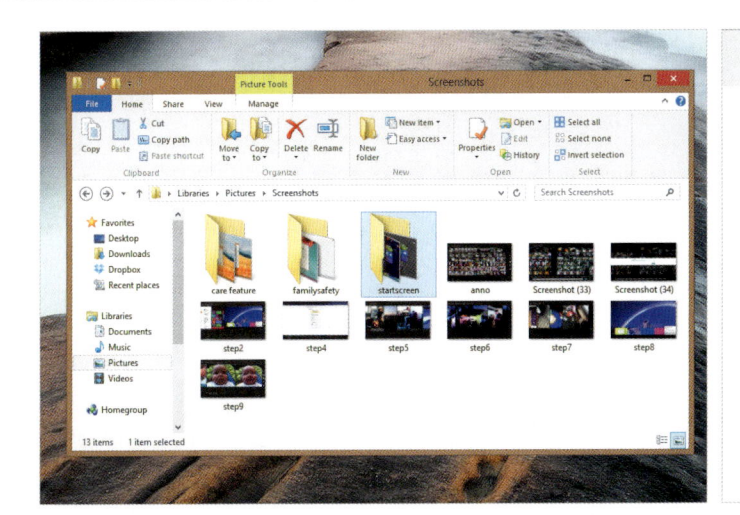

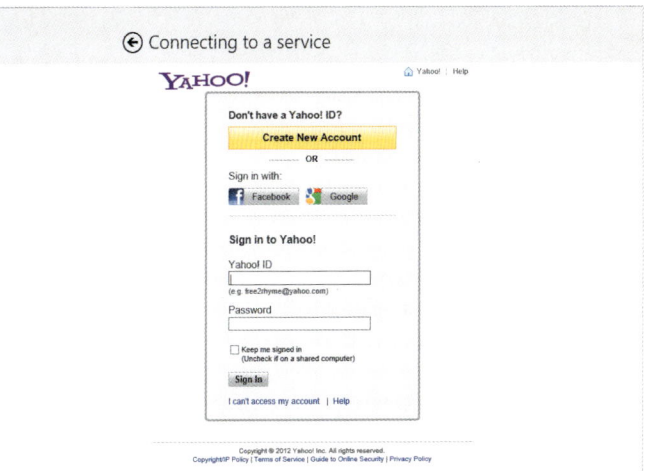

3 Find your photos
By default, screenshots are saved to a folder in your Pictures library. You can open the desktop and have a poke around if you'd like to see it for yourself. You should see that the screenshots you've taken have been added to the Pictures library section of the Photos app. Copy more pictures to that folder, and they should follow suit.

4 Connect to a service
If you want to use Facebook or Flickr with the Photos app, you need to hook up the appropriate accounts. It's easy to do, if you've not already linked your account in another app. Select the link at the bottom of the screen that points to the section you're interested in adding, tap 'Connect' and log in with your usual details.

Windows 8: Expert Tips and Tricks   Chapter 2 | 143

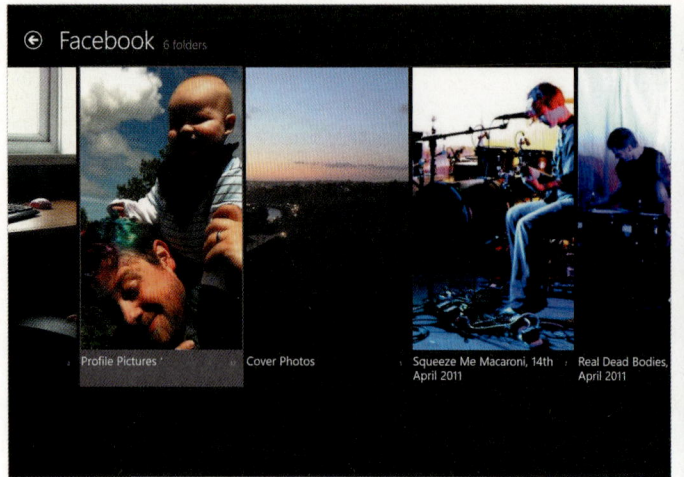

5 Browse snaps
Link your Facebook account – or stick some folders of photos within your Pictures library – then tap the appropriate link to see all the albums you've uploaded. If there is a lot of albums, pinch the screen to zoom out or hunt for the tiny minus sign at the bottom-right corner of the screen. Tap an album to bring up its contents.

6 Resize to see
The Photos app automatically arranges the photos to fit. By default you're shown a line of photos, and clicking one brings it full screen – click again, then click the arrow at the top-right to go back. Zoom in and you get a single photo full screen, with arrows either side to browse; zoom out to see as many as possible.

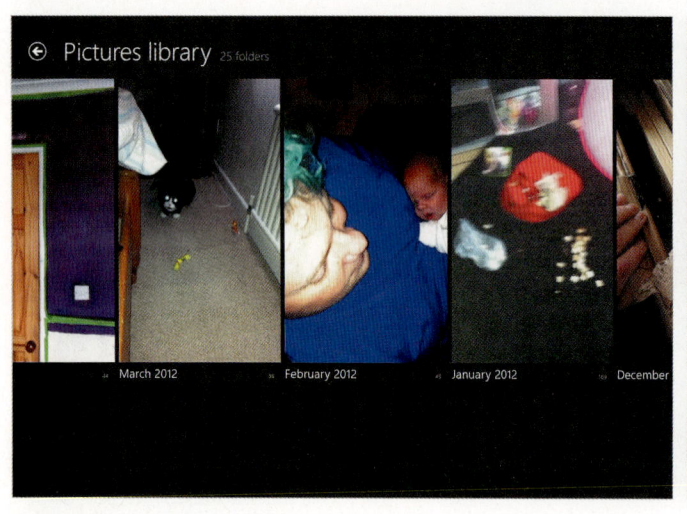

7 See a slideshow
Right-click or swipe up from the bottom of the screen as you're viewing an album, and tap the appropriate button to view a slideshow of its pictures. Go back a screen to the album overview, and the same action leads you to a different sort order; rather than viewing by folder, you can view your pictures by date.

8 Import automatically
Right-click or swipe up on the first screen of Photos, and you see the Import option. If you have a camera or smartphone plugged in, you can automatically import its contents to your Pictures library by clicking 'Select All' on the screen that follows, choosing a folder name at the bottom of the screen, then clicking 'Import'.

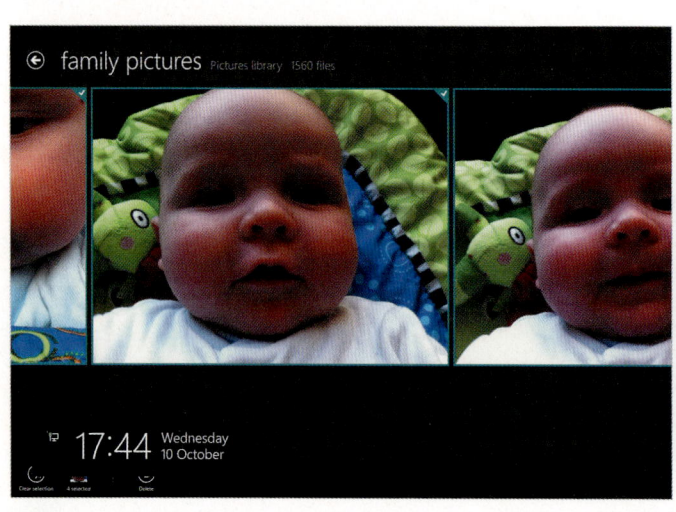

9 Share a few
Open up one of your folders, and select a number of photos you like by right-clicking (or hold-tapping) them each in turn. Bring up the Charms bar (mouse into a right-hand corner, or swipe in from the left) then select 'Share' to easily send a number of snaps directly to a friend using the Mail app.

10 Don't forget SkyDrive
Any images you put in your SkyDrive folder can be viewed in the Photos app, no matter what machine you're using. You can also use the Share charm to create a web-viewable gallery of your pictures, which is perfect if you want to show people your snaps without clogging up their inboxes with huge images.

Discover Britain's biggest and best photo magazine...

ON SALE NOW

Don't miss the latest issue of Digital Camera

EXCITING FREE GIFTS! Every issue comes with a range of free gifts, including a packed video disc, fold-out guide to key camera skills, special supplements and more!

Visit our website at www.digitalcameraworld.com
and join our friendly online communities

Facebook
www.facebook.com/
Digitalcameraworld

Twitter
@DCamMag

Flickr
www.flickr.com/groups/
digitalcameraworld/

Learn how to...

Make a note of anything!

Take the hassle out of trying to remember everything in life – get your Windows 8 device to memorise it all for you with the OneNote app

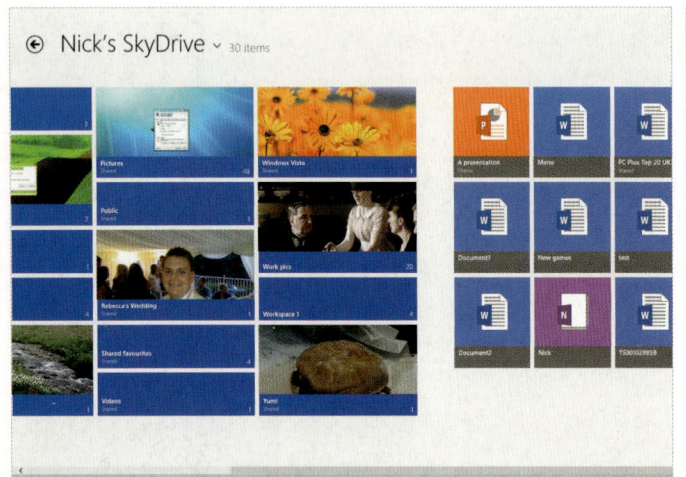

1 Get your notes anywhere
Once you create a note in the Windows 8 OneNote app, it's saved to the cloud so you can access it from anywhere. If you're on another PC, open your SkyDrive account and the file is ready to open. You can get apps for a variety of mobile devices, too (such as iPhone or Windows Phone) so you can check notes from any device.

2 Search instantly
You can search notebooks in Windows 8 by using the search function that's available from anywhere. Find search from the Charm bar and type what you're looking for, or use the shortcut [Windows key]+[Q]. Enter your search terms and press [Enter] to bring up potential results and choose the correct one from the menu.

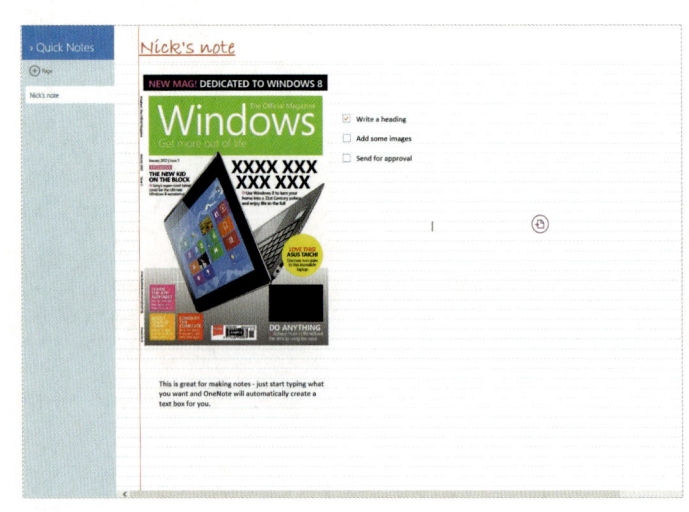

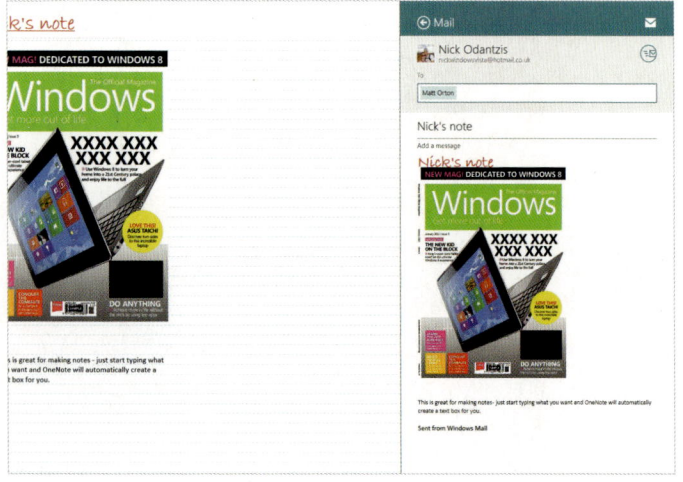

3 Add a list
Once you've created a note, you can supplement it with a handy to-do list, with checkboxes that you can tick once you've completed them. To do this, start typing some text, hit the circular box that appears and choose 'Tag > To do' from the circular menu. Then just check the tick box once you've completed that task.

4 Share notes
When you've finished with a note, you can share it with friends so they can see what you've been up to. Use the Share charm from the Charms bar (or use [Windows key]+[H]), select the Mail program and type the name of the person you want to send it to. You'll notice that your note is embedded within the email.

Learn how to...

Get Microsoft Office for free!

You don't need to pay lots of cash to get Word, Excel and PowerPoint – they're available for free and you can use them wherever you are

At present, the basic version of Microsoft Office 2010 – Home and Student, that is – costs £99.99, and for that you get Word, Excel, PowerPoint and OneNote. But what if we were to let you in on a little secret? You can get all the above for absolutely nothing! It's not a scam – Microsoft has made all the above available through its online cloud service at www.outlook.com, and OneNote is also available as a free standalone app to download via the Windows Store. So what's the catch? Well, Office Web Apps, as it's called, is a 'light' version of Microsoft Office, featuring only the basic capabilities of the powerful productivity suite, but provided you're not a power user – maybe you just need to write a simple document or create a quick spreadsheet without the bells and whistles – it's perfect. Oh, and once again, in case you didn't quite catch it – it's free.

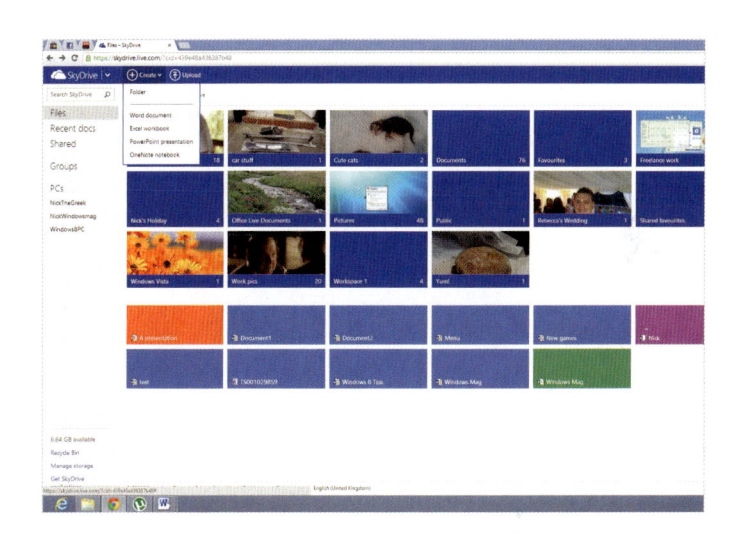

1 Get started with Office Web Apps
Sign into www.outlook.com with your Windows ID (or create one where it says 'Sign up now'). Then click or tap the down-facing arrow next to where it says Outlook.com in the top-left and choose 'SkyDrive'. This is where you can upload documents, photos, videos and more, and you can also start using Office Web Apps from here.

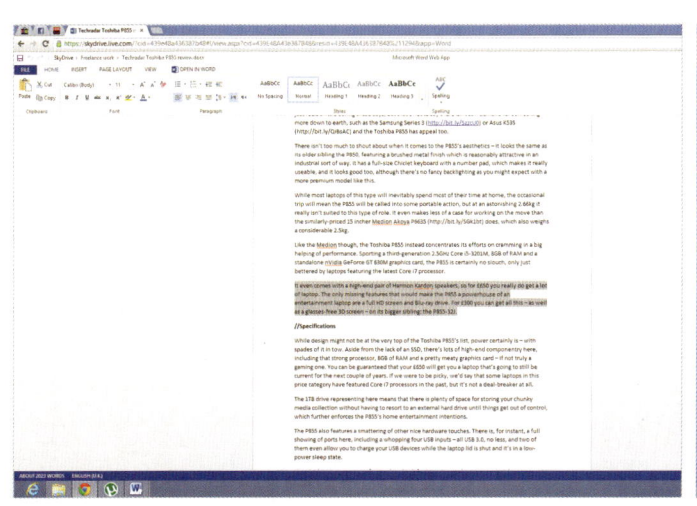

2 Your first document
Hit 'Create', choose the type of document you want to make and give it a name. You then go to a new screen within your browser window, enabling you to work on your document. The beauty of this browser-based version of Office is that no matter which PC you're on, you always have access to it, provided you can get online.

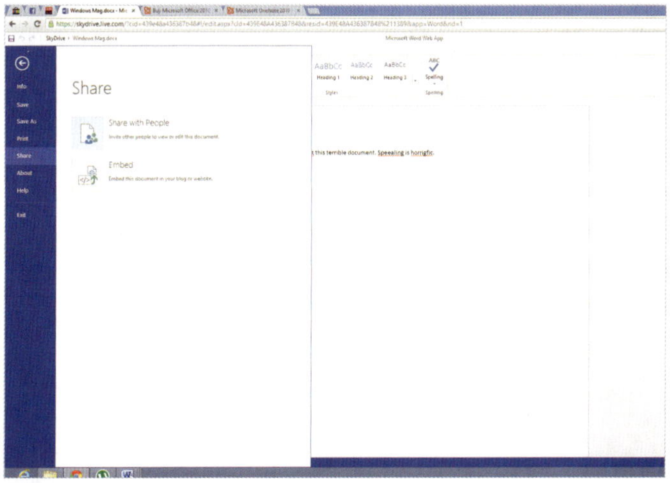

3 Share the workload
Another neat thing about Office Web Apps is that whenever you're working on a document, you can share it with other people so they can view it in their own Office Web Apps account and you can even allow them to edit the same document while you're working on it. Give it a go and you'll see just how capable Office Web Apps is.

Windows 8: Expert Tips and Tricks

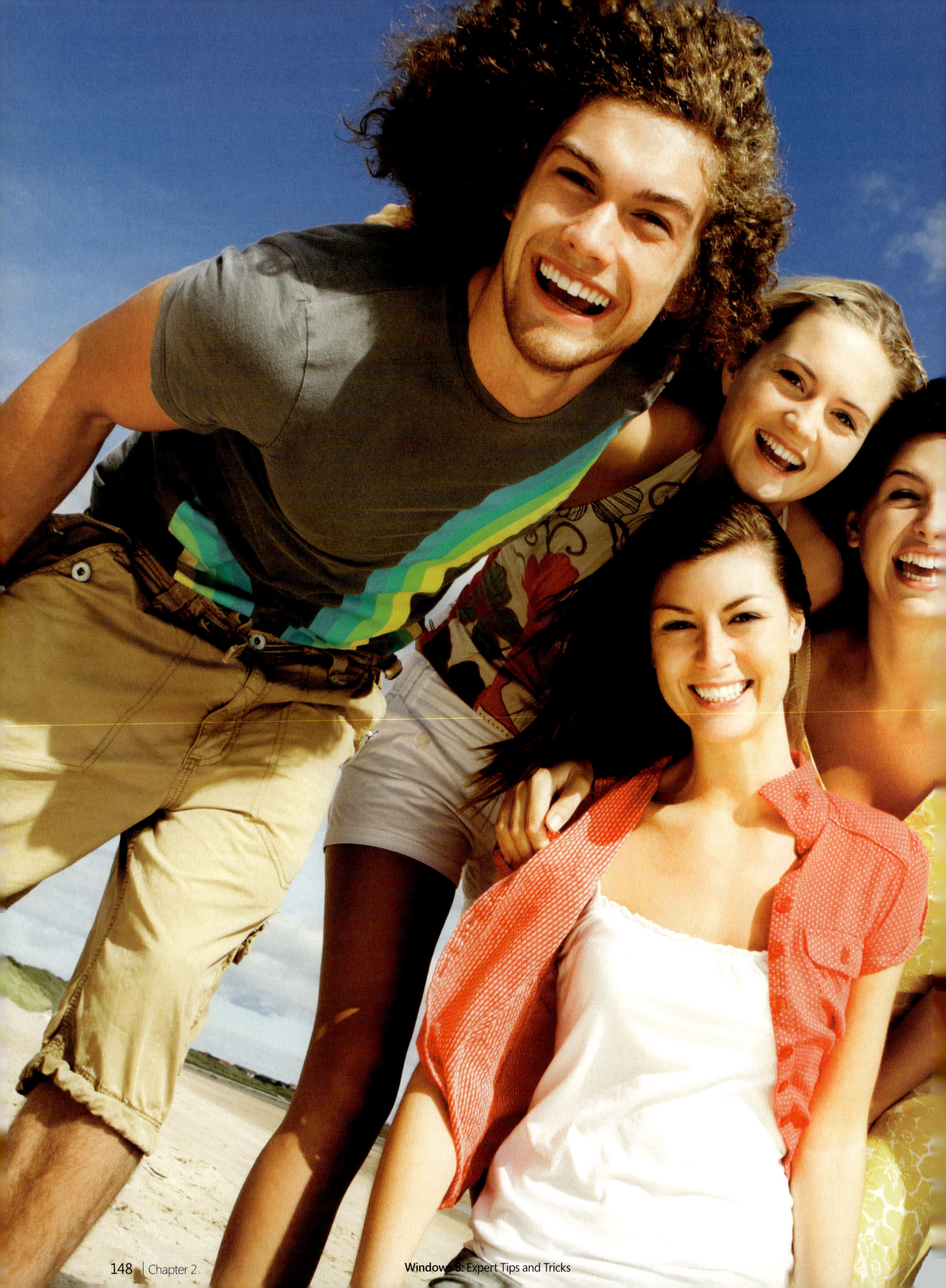

TRY THIS!
Explore the People app
154

Enhanced social life

Discover how to stay in touch with friends old and new

Section 8

150 Get more from social networks
152 Improving social horizons
154 Keep in contact with People
158 Do more with Mail
160 Social networking

DO THIS NOW...

Get more from social networking

Windows 8 brings a whole new level to social networks

Manage notifications

Notifications are little pop-up messages that you get on Windows 8 when you receive an instant message or new email – all apps can use them, but you can decide which apps display notifications. Use the 'Notifications' option in Settings (go to the Settings charm or press [Windows]+[I] and choose 'Change PC Settings' at the bottom). You'll see this screen, which enables you to disable app notifications, remove them from the Lock screen, or stop sounds from being played. Handily, you can also stop notifications appearing from particular apps, so if you don't want notifications when you have a new email in Mail, stop it happening here.

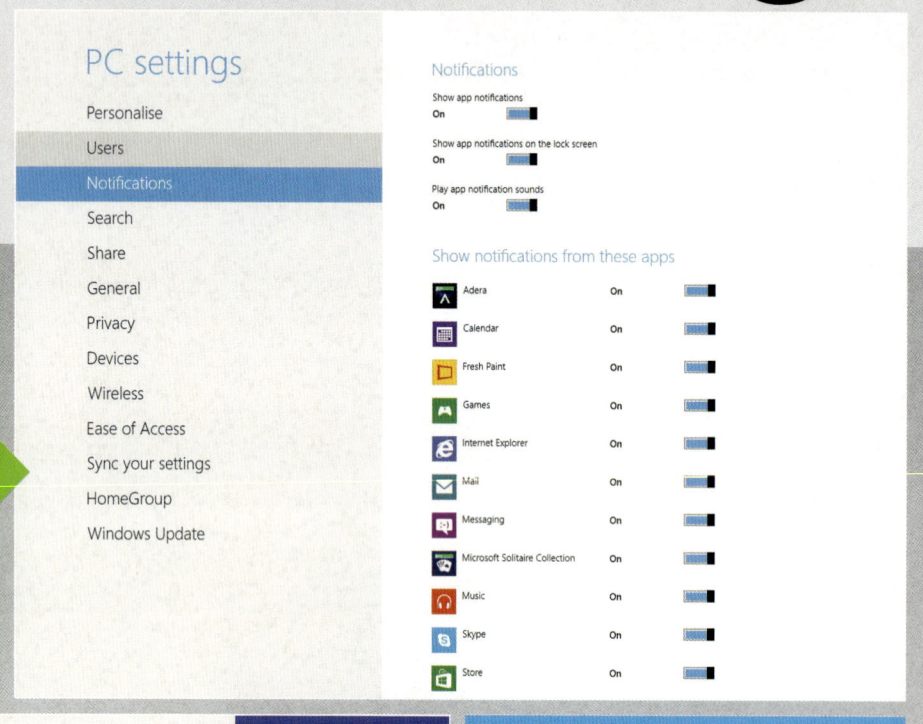

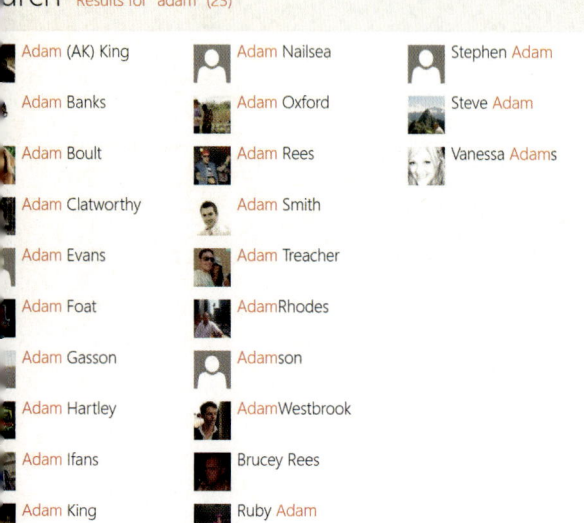

Search for people

The integrated search within Windows 8 makes it extremely easy to find people. In the People app, you just need to start typing and you can quickly find the person you were thinking of. It works when you're using the Skype app, too, which you can download for free from the Windows Store. Once you've found the person you're looking for, simply click on their name and you're taken to their contact page, which enables you to send them an instant message, if they are set up for that, an email, or a message on Facebook, provided they are on your friends list. You can also check out their latest social posts here.

GET MORE FROM SOCIAL NETWORKING

Change your sharing settings

In PC Settings, you can change the settings the Share charm uses, too – you can decide whether to show the most frequently-used apps at the top, or choose which apps are enabled for sharing. This is useful if you have two apps you can send an email or a tweet from – perhaps you only want to have one in your list. Apps enable themselves for sharing by default, so it's good to have this control. All sharing-enabled apps are displayed here; we only have four on this PC, but it's likely that you'll see many more in this list if you've installed a bunch of apps on your PC.

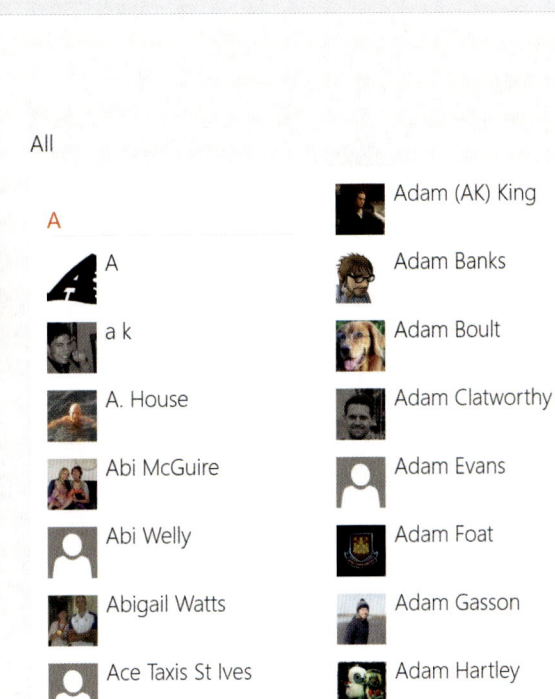

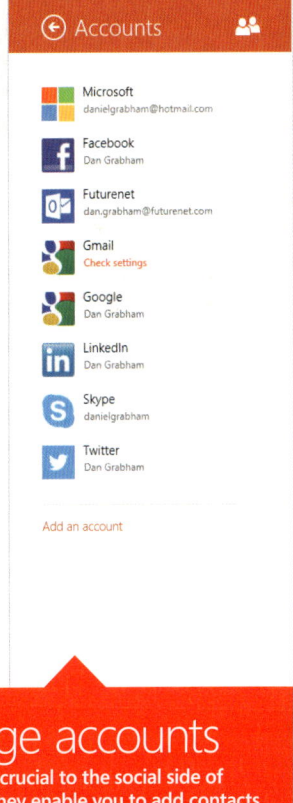

Manage accounts

Accounts are crucial to the social side of Windows 8; they enable you to add contacts, share and email. Windows 8 supports many accounts by default, including mail, calendar and contacts from Microsoft and Google, as well as social accounts for contacts from Twitter, Skype and LinkedIn. Windows 8 pulls in data from all these accounts to different apps – so it influences the contacts you have, the social updates you get and the emails you see. You can also add other types of email, notably Microsoft Exchange work email. The best way to check which accounts are enabled is to go to the People app, bring up the Settings charm and select 'Accounts'.

Windows 8: Expert Tips and Tricks

Chapter 2 | 151

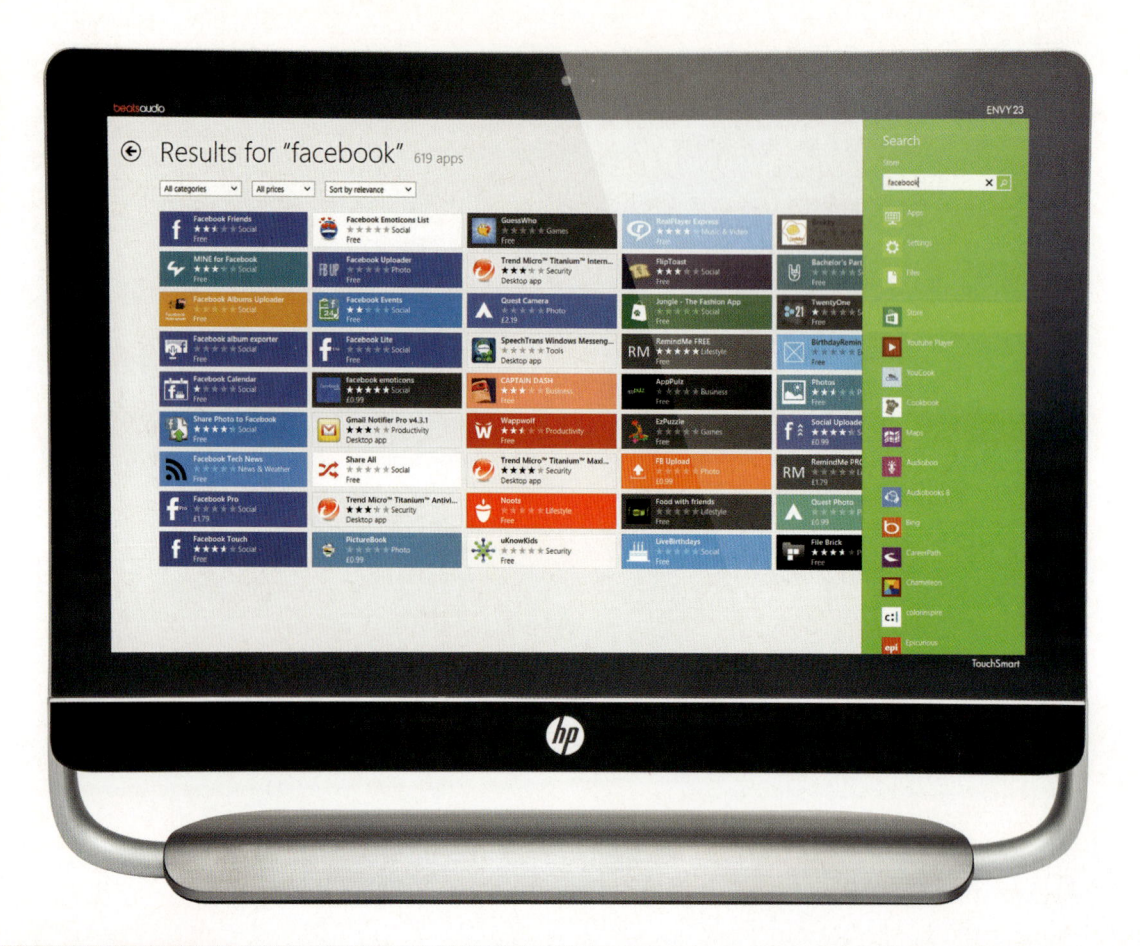

25 TOP TIPS FOR...
Improving social horizons

Make new connections and get better acquainted with this collection of super-friendly tips

1 You've heard of Facebook. You must have heard of Facebook. Although there's no official Facebook app for Windows 8 as yet, there is a heap of compatible apps in the Windows Store. We recommend 'Facebook Touch'.

2 You can, of course, just use Facebook within your browser, but if you're using it on the desktop, hit [F11] for the complete experience – this makes your window fill the screen completely. Press [F11] again to switch back.

3 Facebook chat can be a bit overwhelming – particularly given the number of people you only-sort-of know that it connects you to. But if you like using it, you could download the IM+ app from the Windows Store, which brings it to the Modern interface.

4 You can hook up a host of other chat clients to IM+, including Windows Live Messenger and Google Talk. We find that it's better than the built-in Messenger app, and possibly even better than the Skype app. It's free, so you can decide for yourself.

5 Chat notifications are useful but you may want to turn them off: hit [Windows]+[I], go to 'Change PC Settings', open the 'Notification' panel, and flick the switch for apps you want to silence.

6 How about Twitter? There's a number of Twitter apps on the Windows Store, but they're not perfect; although there's no official app yet, Twitter has imposed limits on the number of users unofficial apps can support. Try MetroTwit – it seems to work fine.

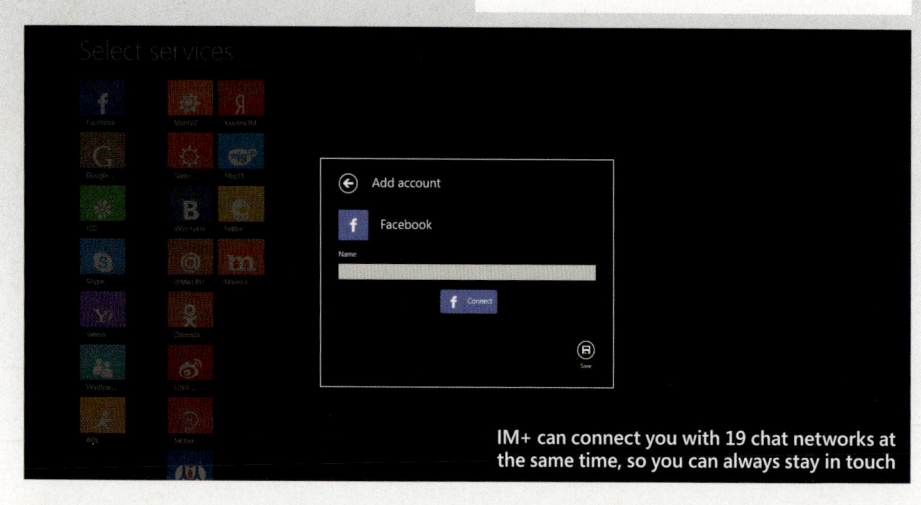

IM+ can connect you with 19 chat networks at the same time, so you can always stay in touch

IMPROVING SOCIAL HORIZONS

7 The best way to use Twitter and Facebook is on the desktop; pick up Tweetdeck from www.tweetdeck.com and sign your accounts up to it – you can keep in touch with both streams at once, schedule posts, and much more.

8 If you're not at your home PC you might think the Tweetdeck experience is lost, but it isn't. Sign up for the web service, and you can access all the same accounts via tweetdeck.com. Or find Hootsuite online; essentially the same service but with a different look.

9 Using the web directly isn't the only way to stay in touch on an unfamiliar PC. Pop Miranda Portable on a USB stick (http://portableapps.com/apps/internet/miranda_portable), run it once to set it up, and you can run it from any machine you plug that stick in to.

10 If you're chatting on Skype with a headset, make sure the correct microphone is selected. Go to the desktop, right-click the volume icon on the Taskbar, go to 'Recording Devices', then right-click the mic you want to use and select 'Set as Default Communication Device'.

11 There's another way to pick which mic to use in Skype, but it's not obvious. Run Skype, press [Windows]+[I] to bring up the settings pane, then select 'Options' to find the settings for all of your plugged in devices.

12 Use the 'Communications' tab of the Sound panel to set what happens to the rest of your volume when Skype fires up. It's convenient to have other volume muted when a call comes in.

13 Although the Skype app is neat, you get more control with the desktop version. Head to www.skype.com, click 'Downloads', and scroll to find it. Install, and it appears it on the Taskbar.

14 Desktop Skype does get in the way if you're not using it. That massive Taskbar icon is a little conspicuous for an app that works best in the background. You can relegate it to its proper place by opening Skype, going to 'Tools > Options', and unchecking the appropriate box in 'Advanced Settings'.

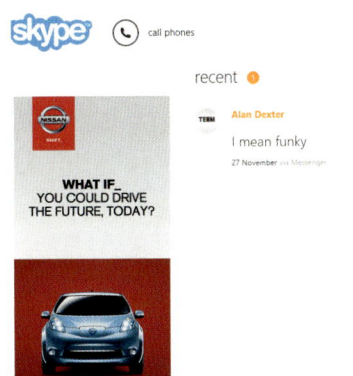

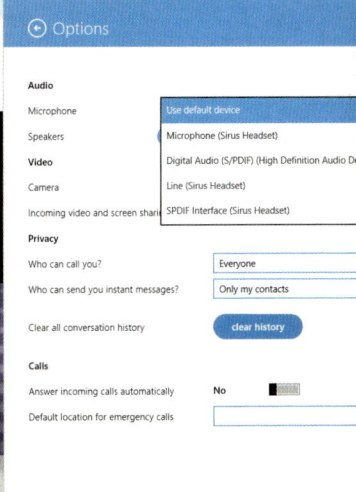

15 There's another benefit of Skype desktop: 'Click to Call'. Make sure the option is ticked when you install it, and it puts a hook into your web browser, which means you can call any phone number on a web page directly. You need Skype credit to do this.

16 If you install Skype for the desktop, it tries to change your homepage to Bing. You might want this, but chances are you don't, so ensure you untick the appropriate box during installation.

17 Want to video chat online to a few people at once? Try Google. Open up Gmail to see your usual chat contacts list in a box on the bottom-left, click a contact you're interested in, then click the 'Invite to hangout' option. You can invite up to nine people to a hangout.

18 You can do much more than video chat with Google Hangouts. You can watch YouTube videos together, for example, or live streams. Whatever you want to do with it, you need to install a plug-in, but the process is automatic when you start your first hangout.

19 Need slightly more people than a Google Hangout? Want to be able to record your chat for posterity, too? Don't want to use Google? Oovoo offers free 12-way video chat, and you can save your meetings to YouTube as well. Check it out at www.oovoo.com.

20 Want to use your webcam for more than just socialising? If you have a working camera, you should see the Camera app pop up on your Start screen. You can use it to capture videos, or to take still pictures as well.

Make sure you're using the correct microphone in Skype. If you're not, you might not be able to make yourself heard

Quick tips

21 Fancy chatting with like-minded individuals, or just seeing what the heart of the internet has to say? We highly recommend a trip to www.reddit.com.

22 Reddit's community is user-created and user-moderated. If you like something you see, click the up arrow to give it your approval.

23 Register for a Reddit account and you can post your own submissions; if others upvote your posts, you receive positive karma, improving your reputation.

24 If you're viewing Reddit in a web browser that isn't Internet Explorer, then we recommend the Reddit Enhancement Suite from www.redditenhancementsuite.com. It really improves the experience.

25 You can also enjoy Reddit from within the Modern Windows 8 interface. There are a few clients; Reddit to Go is our favourite. It's free from the Windows Store.

Learn how to...

Keep in contact

The People app is Windows 8's contact and social centre, and is the perfect way to stay in touch

WORKS WITH
Windows 8
Windows 8 Pro
Windows RT

The People app is one of the key elements of Windows 8 – it's the central hub of social activity, an all-encompassing address book. It draws together a traditional contacts book, address books from your email accounts, and contacts from your social networks. Details are combined, so you have a single, aggregated contact card for each person you know. To start with, the People app doesn't have any contacts, but if you connected your Microsoft Account – or any other email or social accounts – when you first started Windows 8, the People app begins to drag this data in. So don't be surprised to find the app already populated with data about your friends and acquaintances. And, as we'll explain in this tutorial, it's really easy to add more accounts.

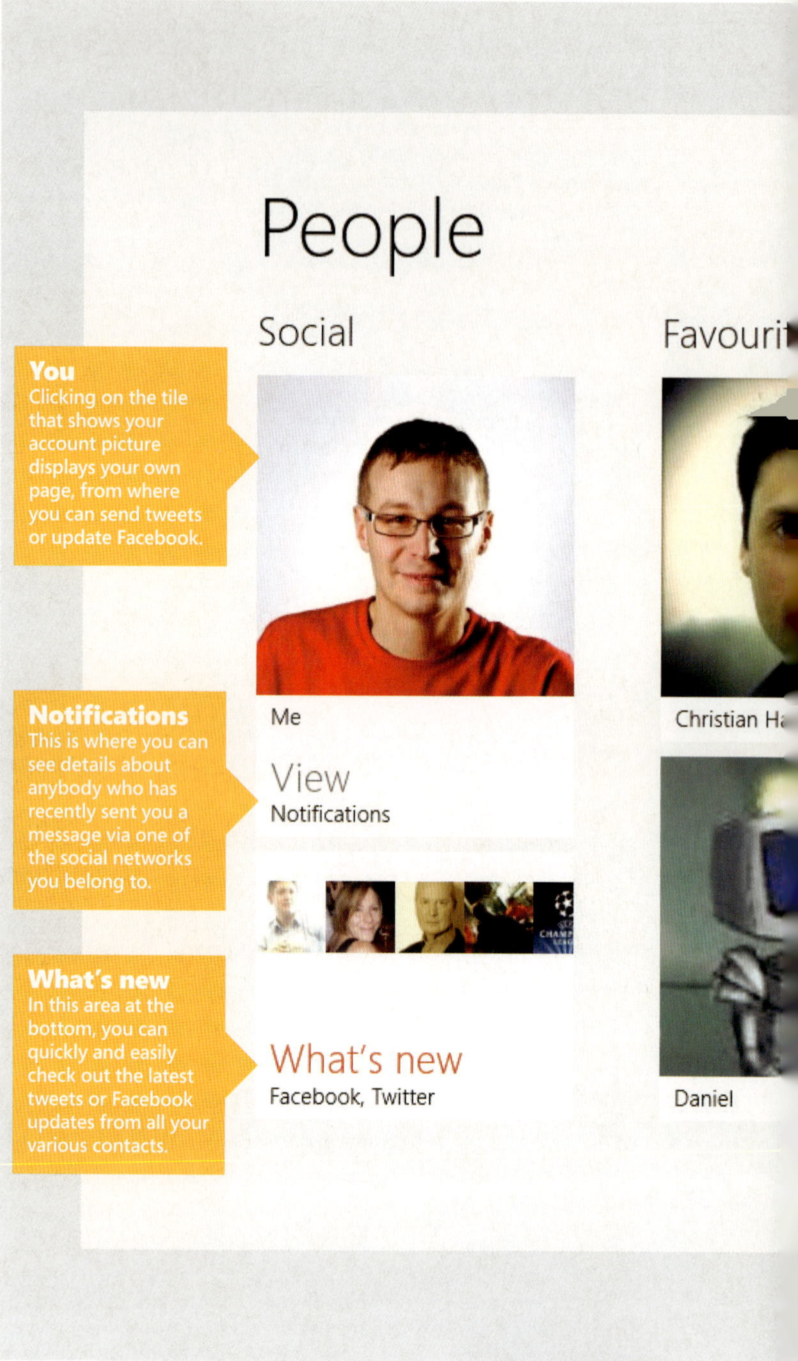

Perfect your People skills

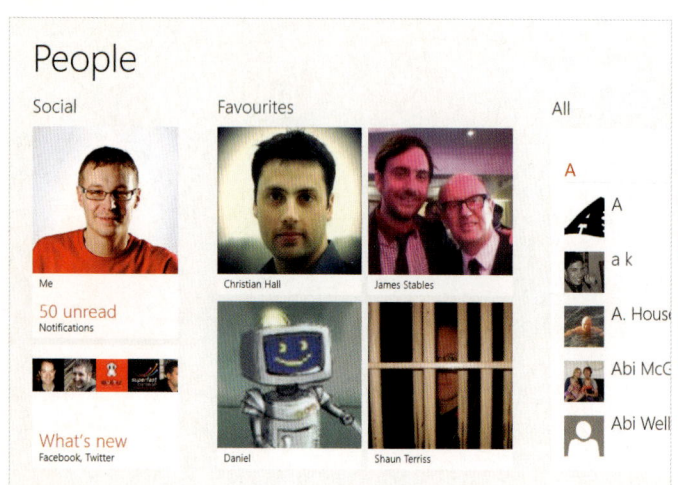

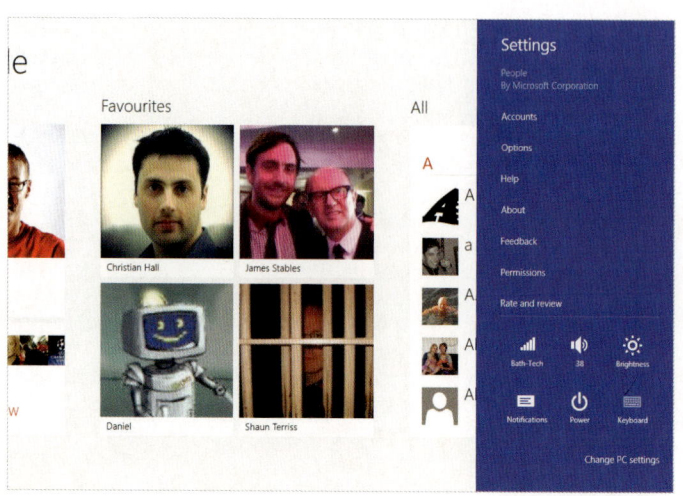

You
Clicking on the tile that shows your account picture displays your own page, from where you can send tweets or update Facebook.

Notifications
This is where you can see details about anybody who has recently sent you a message via one of the social networks you belong to.

What's new
In this area at the bottom, you can quickly and easily check out the latest tweets or Facebook updates from all your various contacts.

1 Your People
Open the app and you see three elements: your own social activity; your favourite contacts; and the start of your A to Z of contacts. Swipe right or use your mouse and the bar on the bottom to move right. You can tap or click anything – tapping an individual (including your own picture) takes you to their contact page.

2 Add your accounts
If you've connected your Microsoft Account to Windows 8, contacts stored there are imported. But you can add other accounts, too, including Facebook, Twitter and email, such as a Microsoft Exchange work account. Swipe or move to the right to get to the Settings charm, click it, then click 'Accounts'. Click 'Add an account'.

KEEP IN CONTACT

Jargon buster!

App bar
If you swipe up from the bottom of the screen or right-click in a Windows 8-style app, you see more options – this is called the App bar.

Charm
Move your mouse to the right-hand side of the screen or swipe in using your finger and you'll see the Windows 8 Charms – you can use these to perform key tasks such as Search and Share.

Connected accounts
Windows 8 can use information from email and social accounts that you already own – such as Facebook, Twitter and LinkedIn – in apps such as Calendar and People.

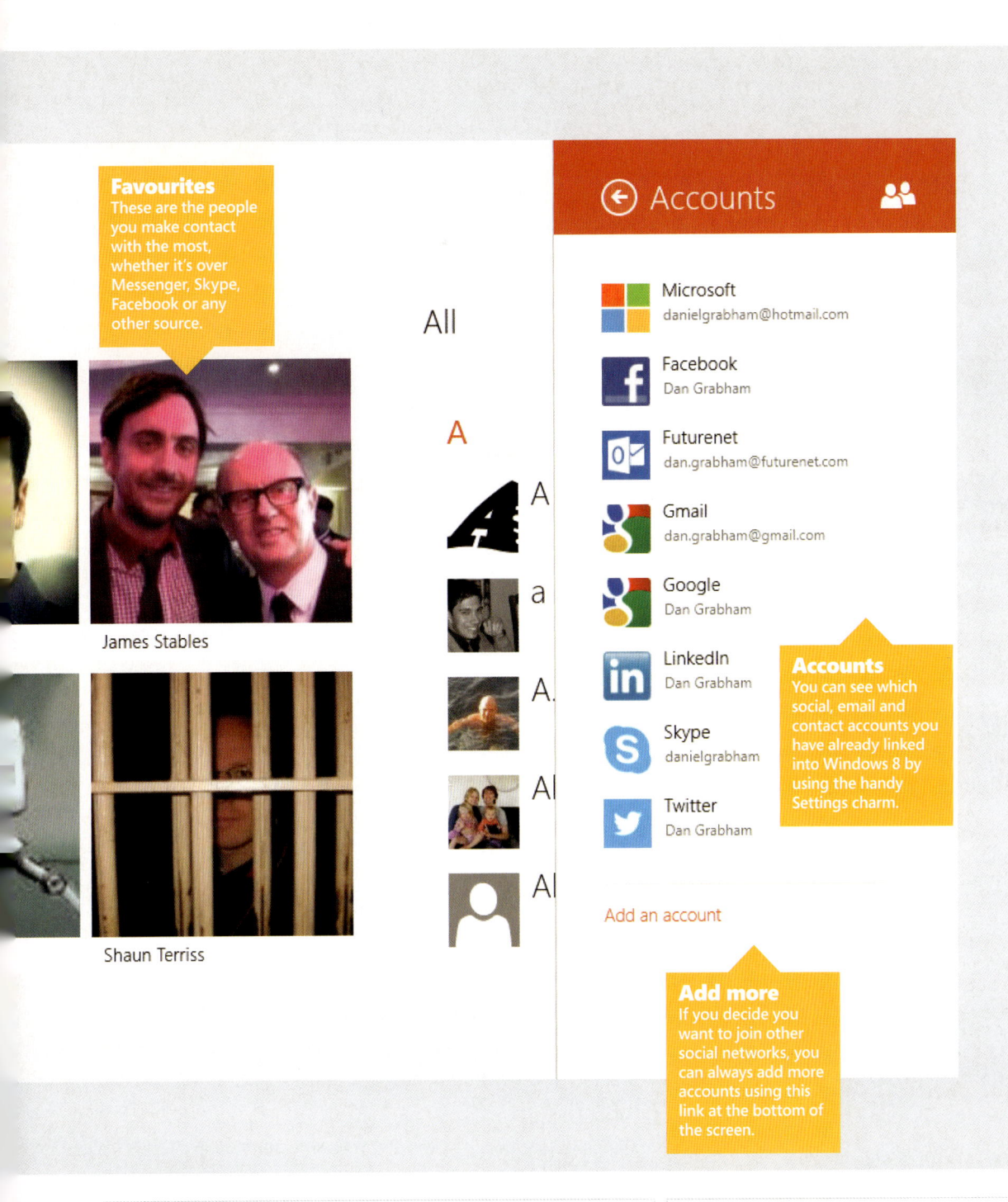

Favourites
These are the people you make contact with the most, whether it's over Messenger, Skype, Facebook or any other source.

James Stables

Shaun Terriss

Accounts
You can see which social, email and contact accounts you have already linked into Windows 8 by using the handy Settings charm.

Add more
If you decide you want to join other social networks, you can always add more accounts using this link at the bottom of the screen.

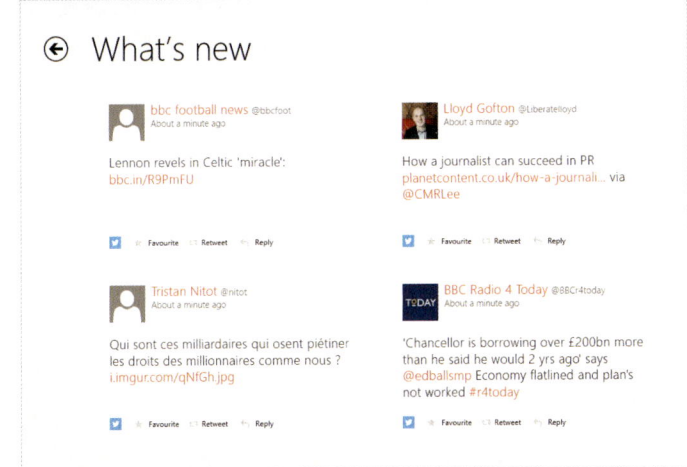

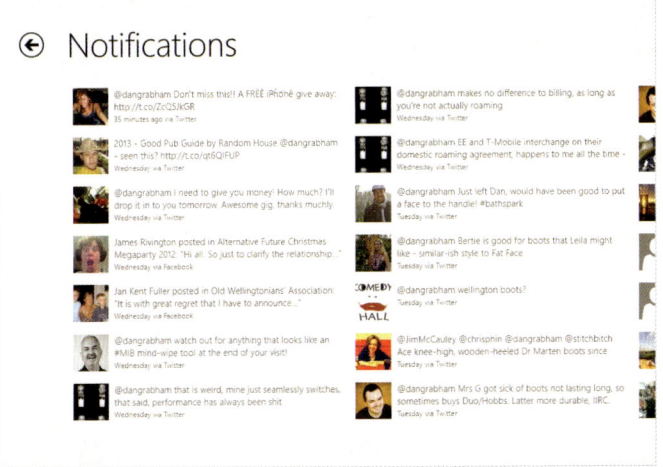

3 Check what's new
Click or tap 'What's new'. You're taken to a page like this, detailing the latest social activity on the social networks that you've connected to Windows 8. If you're on Twitter, this is generally the latest tweets, because Twitter gets updated more regularly than other apps. You can Favourite, Retweet or Reply to tweets from here.

4 See your Notifications
Again from the first screen, click 'Notifications'. This shows the latest replies to you on social networks and enables you to get a quick overview of what's happening in your world and what needs replying to. As always, use the top-left arrow to go back. You can connect Facebook, Twitter and LinkedIn accounts to Windows 8.

Windows 8: Expert Tips and Tricks | Chapter 2 | 155

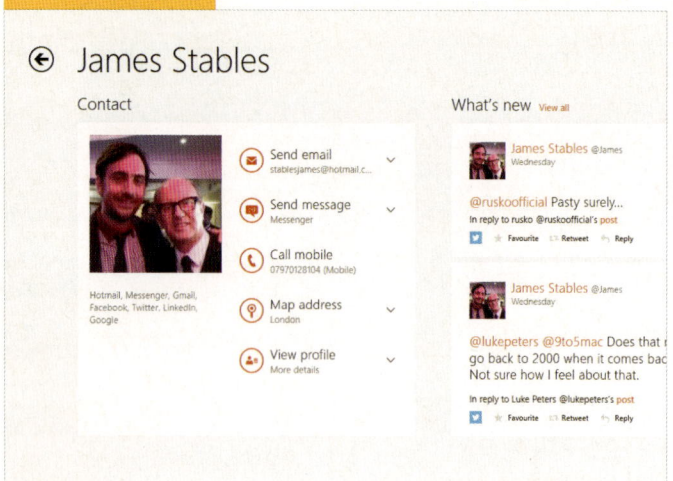

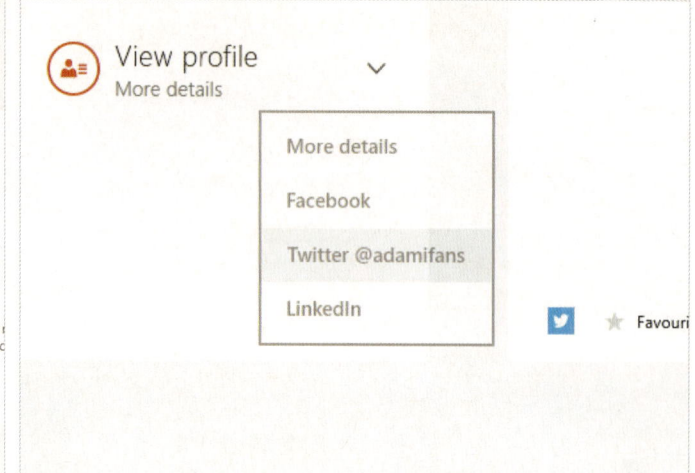

5 See a contact's page
As we said previously, clicking or tapping on any person takes you to a page about that contact. Here's one – you can see a 'What's new' area for the individual. Once again, this person is on Twitter, so it's latest tweets you see, but clicking 'View all' at the top of this block reveals more varied updates from various networks.

6 Contact your friends
Each contact's page also shows you a full list of the ways you can contact them. Simply click or tap the down arrow on each of these to view more details, such as accessing that person's Facebook contact if they're one of your Facebook friends. You can also send them an instant message or email directly from here.

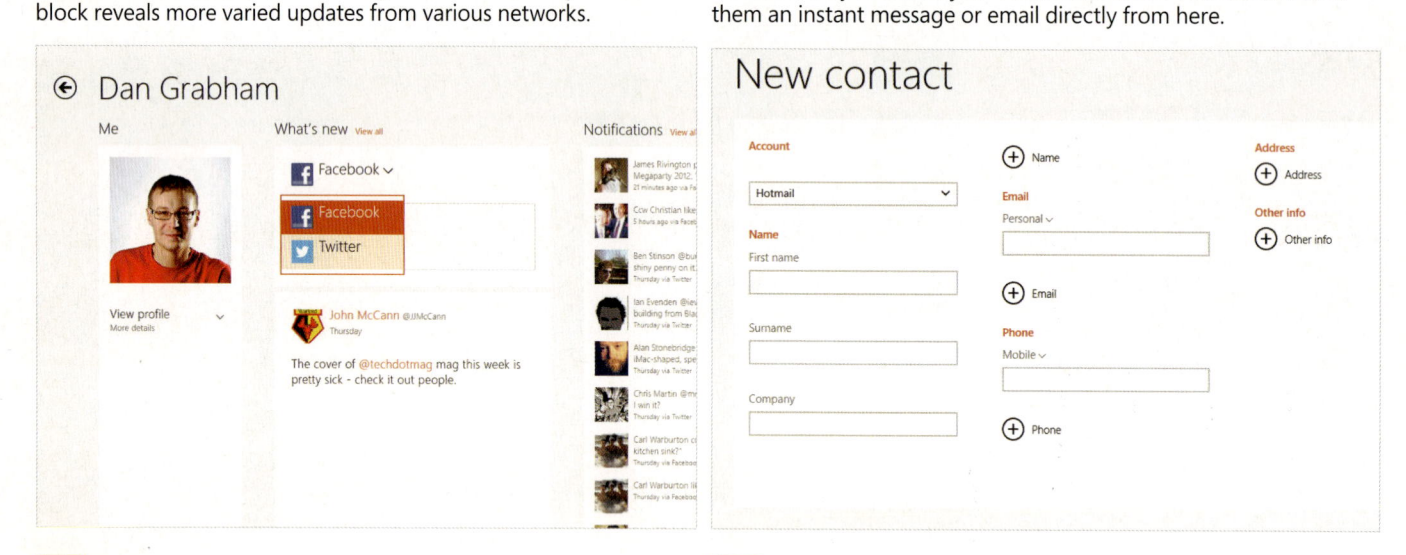

7 Your page
If you click your own account picture on the front page, you'll see this – it's a variation on the contact page that enables you to make a social post (click the drop-down for more networks), see your latest social posts and see your latest Notifications and Pictures. You can click to view more detail in any section – take a look around!

8 Add a new contact
With any Windows 8-style app, swiping up from the bottom (or right-clicking) brings up the **App bar**, with more options. We've clicked the '+' icon on the App bar to add a new contact. Fill in the details and click 'Save'. You can add whatever information you want, notably which **connected account** you want the data saved in.

9 Check out photos
Scrolling right on any person's page also takes you to that contact's latest photos from their various social networks (including mobile uploads from Facebook) and Microsoft SkyDrive. You can see your own photos on your own page, too. You can also click the various image folders to see the photos in more detail.

10 Play with People
That's the end of our whistle-stop tour of the People app. The key thing is to have a play with it. Everyone's People app is different – ours is filled with Twitter activity more than anything else, but you may find that Facebook is more prevalent in yours. It's an app that's designed to fit around you and the contacts you have.

Discover where you come from today...

It's always nice to have something to look back on, especially in terms of family heritage. *Your Family Tree* offers helpful, practical advice, written by experts, on all areas of family history research.

Download once... read offline forever!
Single digital issues and money-saving subscription deals are available.

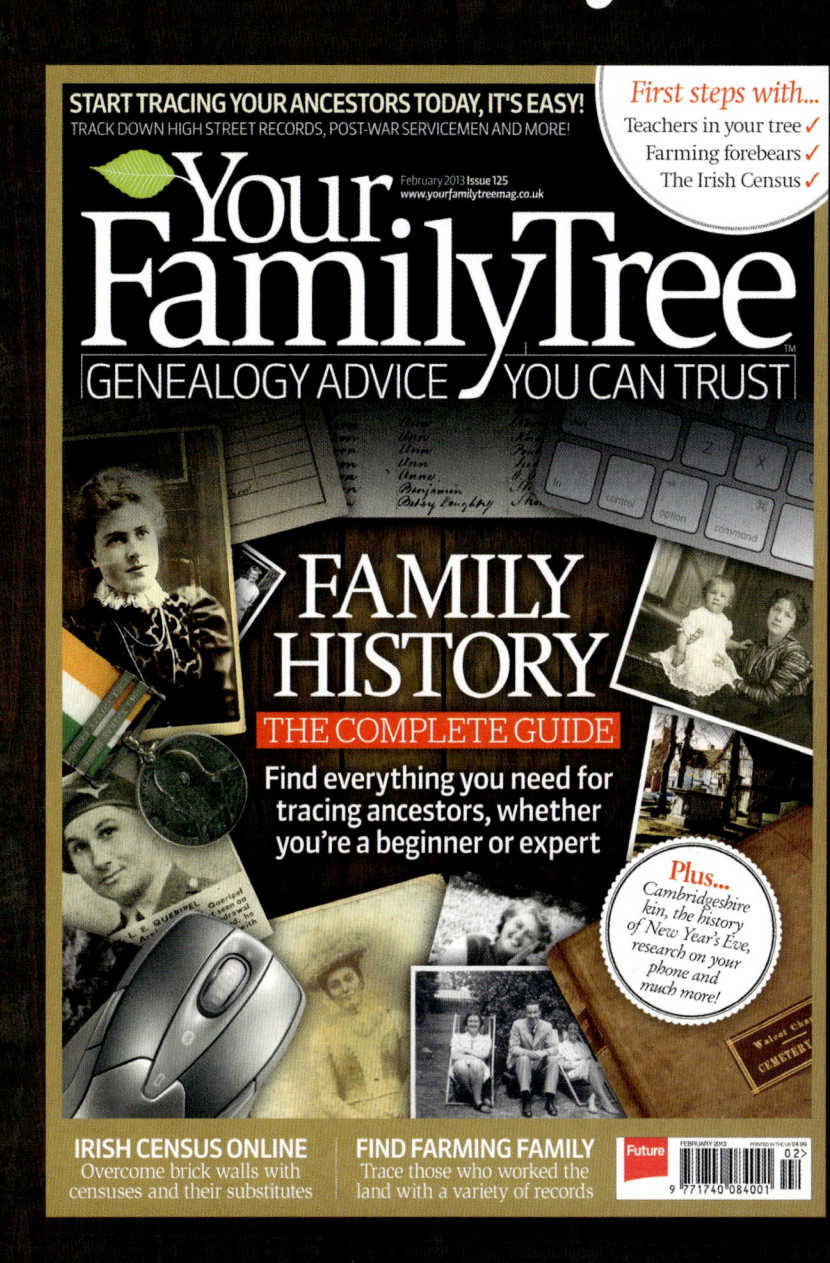

NO. 1 FOR GENEALOGY... LET OUR EXPERTS ANSWER YOUR PROBLEMS!

Available on the App Store · zinio · nook by Barnes & Noble

www.myfavouritemagazines.co.uk/genealogy

Learn how to...

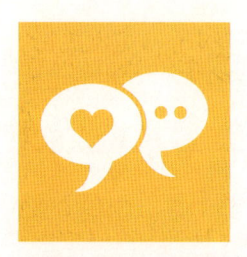

Make more of your email

Everyone has a webmail address but a desktop client gives you a much richer experience, as the free Mail app shows

WORKS WITH
Windows 8
Windows 8 Pro
Windows RT

The Mail application can really help you organise your life in one place on your computer. With a standard webmail account, such as Hotmail, you're stuck with having to sign in and out and are left with only the most basic email features. With the Mail app, however, you can add and see multiple email accounts such as Hotmail, Gmail and Yahoo! Mail. You can even see your email, calendars and contacts when you don't have an internet connection. If you love the style of Gmail's conversation grouping, then you can get that in Mail, too. If you use your email a lot for sending photographs, Mail is also ideal; you can send a high-resolution photo to contacts without filling up their inboxes, because it links to SkyDrive.

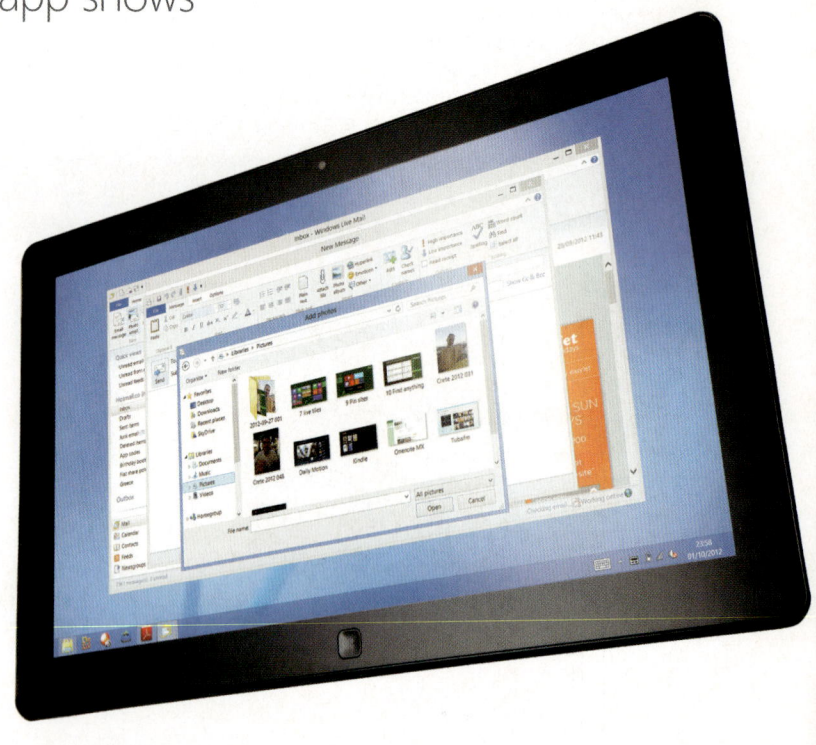

Get mail on your desktop

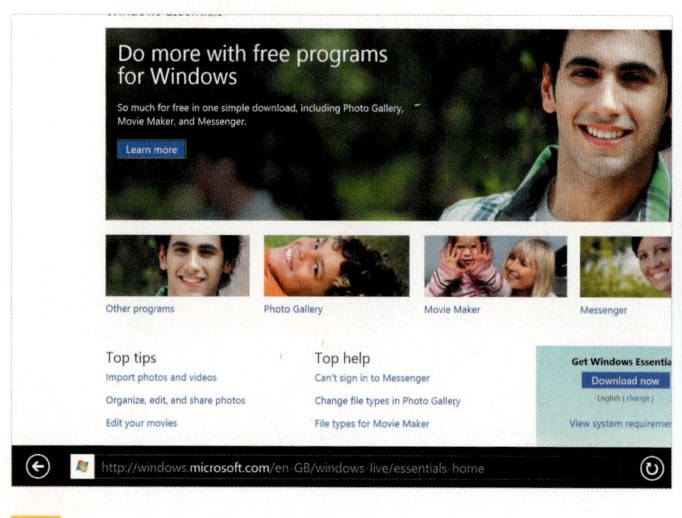

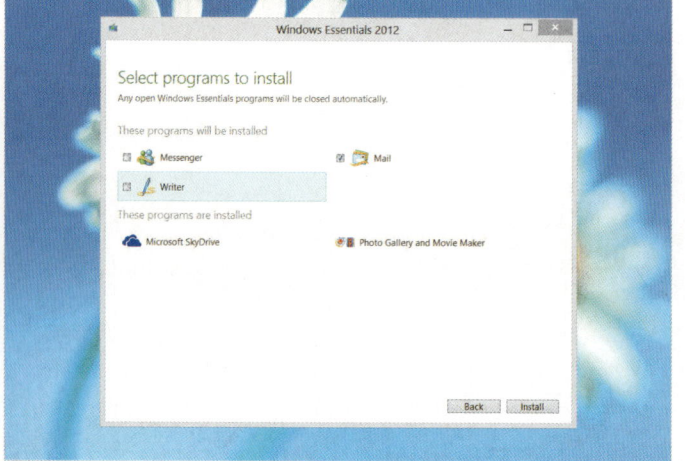

1 Download latest version
Mail is available from (http://windows.microsoft.com/en-GB/windows-live/essentials-home). Choose 'Download now' from the website and click on the downloaded installer to begin setup. Save the installer to your hard drive, then once you've found it, run it to get things started.

2 Add account
The download is the complete Windows Essentials setup manager and you can install many applications through it, such as Messenger, Writer and others, but we're just going to select 'Mail'. So, click 'Install', then your PC needs to restart. When up and running, you add an email account by following the initial wizard.

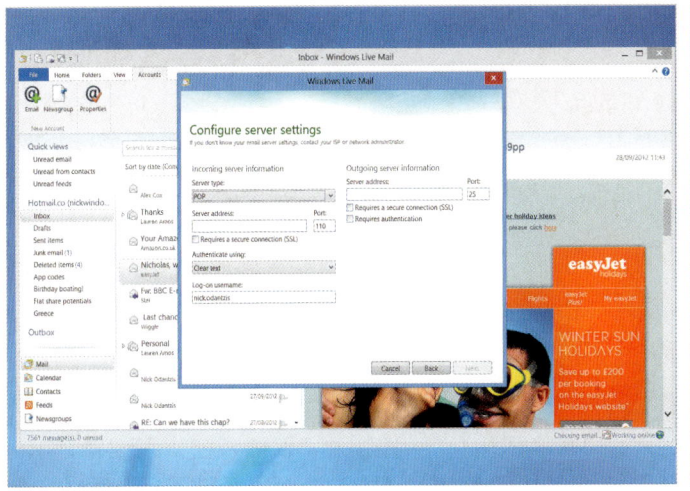

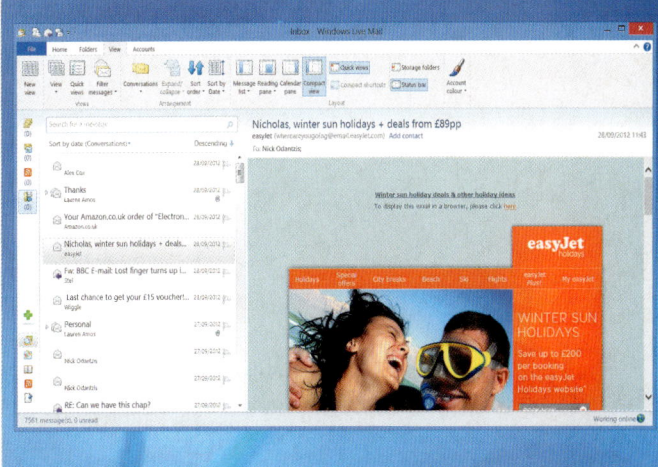

MAKE MORE OF YOUR EMAIL

3 Mail servers
Mail supports three types of email servers. You don't need to understand the finer details, thankfully; you just need to find out which one your email service uses for both incoming and outgoing emails, for example: pop.gmail.com (for incoming) and smtp.gmail.com (for outgoing). The simplest way is by using Bing.

4 Change view
When you're up and running you'll see a variety of options shown on the Ribbon. If you go to the 'View' tab, you can select a particular view for your email – you don't have to stick to the default. Choose the one you prefer. 'Compact View' gives the most minimalist appearance, which is ideal for smaller screens.

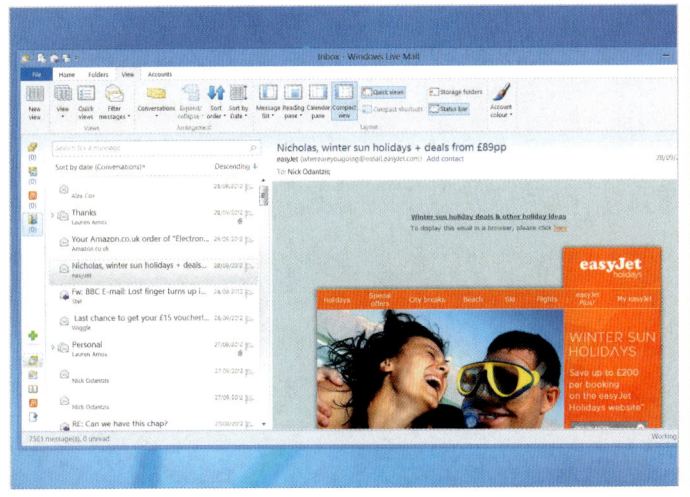

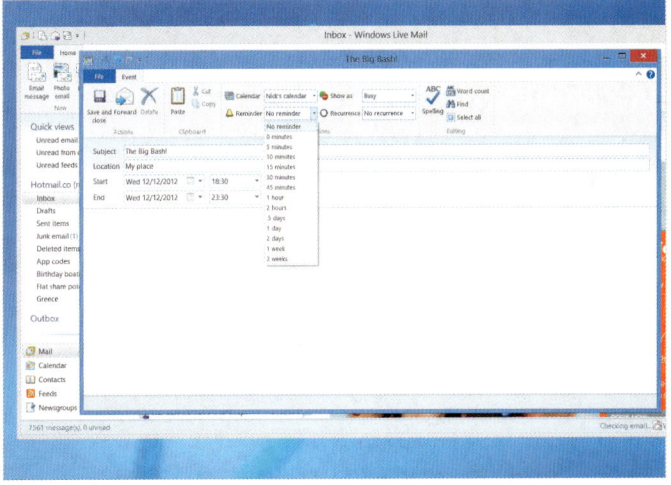

5 Send a photo email
By using your free SkyDrive account, you can send large photos to friends without overloading their inboxes. Choose 'Home > Photo email', then in the new window, add photos from your PC and enter recipients and a subject line. Thumbnails of the photos appear in the message body, where you can also add album details.

6 Create an event
There are two ways. First, look under the 'Items' menu on the Home tab. Choose 'Event' from the drop-down list and add the details, choose 'Forward' and enter email addresses. Or you can create an event from an email, useful if you are discussing an event with friends. Select the relevant email then choose 'Add to'.

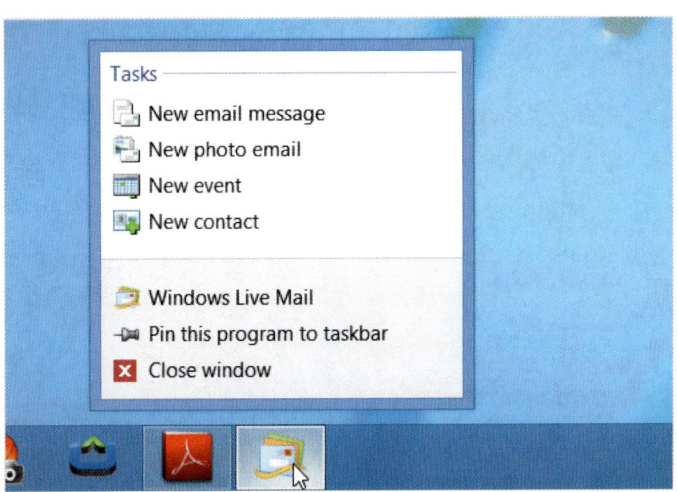

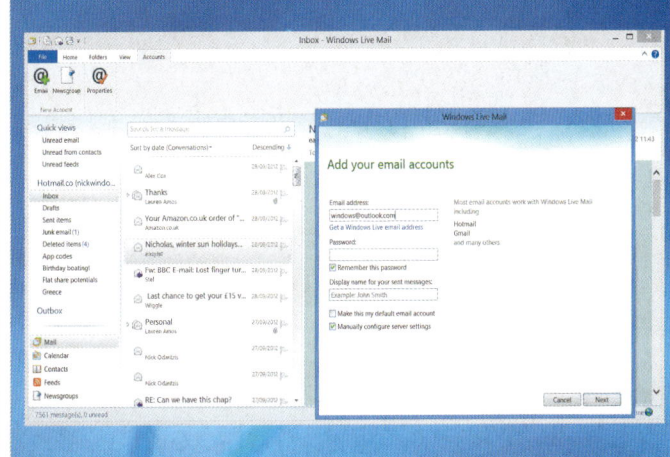

7 Quick Launch options
When using Mail, you can use the Quick Launch options for your major tasks, such as sending emails, sending a photo email or adding a new event or contact to your email account. Simply right-click on the 'Mail' icon in the Taskbar and choose the option you want from the menu under the 'Tasks' heading.

8 Add another account
Mail enables you to add more accounts. Go to 'Accounts > Email' to begin adding another email account. Enter the email address and password, and tick 'Manually configure server settings' to add the correct incoming and outgoing mail servers for that account. Click 'Finish' and you're done.

Learn how to...

Socialise with social networking

There are some amazing Windows 8 apps for Facebook, Twitter and more available from the Windows Store, enabling you to keep up to date with everything that's going on in your whirl of social networks

WORKS WITH
Windows 8
Windows 8 Pro
Windows RT

Windows 8 comes with the People app, which shows you updates from friends and enables you to post to Facebook and Twitter (see page 152 for details). It imports your contacts from services such as Facebook, Twitter, LinkedIn, Skype and other email accounts you link up. But we're used to using apps on our phones for social networks and instant messaging, so why should Windows 8 be any different? Luckily, there are plenty of apps available, and we've collected together eight of our favourites right here. Now you can always keep an eye on what's happening, make Skype calls, send instant messages, tweet or post things to Facebook using Windows 8 Start screen apps. Many also feature Live tiles, so you can see what's going on from the Start screen itself.

Top free social apps for Windows 8

1 MetroTwit
There's no official Twitter client for Windows 8, but there are several good Twitter-capable clients. MetroTwit is great when running full-screen, although you can only see two columns at once, such as your timeline and @replies. There's a clear bar for writing new tweets in, while previews of web links open in a nice large pane.

2 Skype
Although there's a Messaging app in Windows 8, the Skype app merges Skype and Messenger (and your Skype and Microsoft account). You can see recent calls and chats made on multiple Skype devices, your favourite contacts and people you've talked to recently – or you can see your full address book as tiles.

SOCIALISE WITH SOCIAL NETWORKING

3 FlipToast
This app enables you to see updates from Facebook, Twitter, LinkedIn and Instagram. You see the most recent updates, photos, notifications, messages, birthdays and your first 20 or so friends. Click or tap a pane to get a longer list of each. To see updates from just one service, pinch to zoom out and you get tiles to pick from.

4 IM+
Whatever IM service you use, the likelihood is it's covered by IM+, including Google, Jabber, ICQ, Messenger, AOL, Facebook, Skype and Yahoo, plus international ones like RenRen and Yandex. There are plenty of handy options, from blocking people you don't know to getting email alerts for messages you miss when offline.

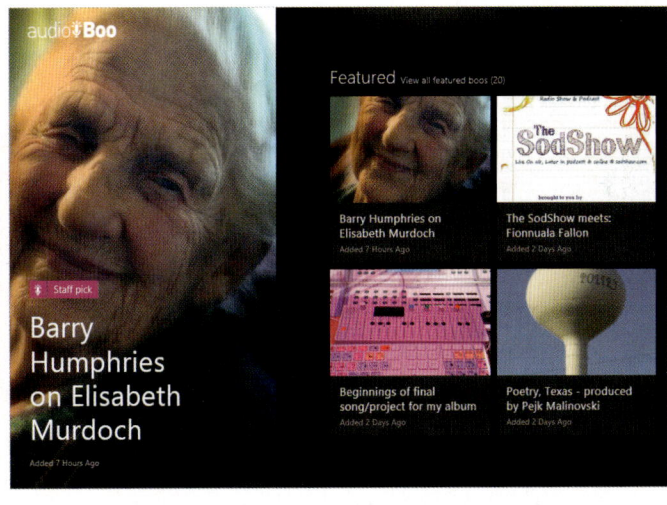

5 Rowi
Rowi doesn't have a Live tile and its black and green interface only fits one column of tweets and one of photos, leaving lots of space for seeing one tweet in a large font, with its replies. So it's not the most comprehensive Twitter experience available (especially with the fixed ad at the top) but it's fine if you're not a big Twitter user.

6 AudioBoo
An app for browsing and listening to audio clips (or boos) from around the world. You can listen to the latest featured and trending boos, or browse channels from the BBC, Sky News, Absolute Radio and more. Using the app in snapped view means that you can listen to boos while carrying out other tasks.

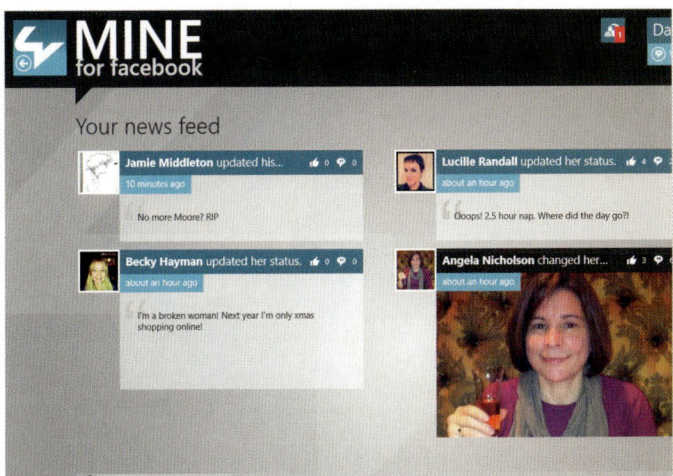

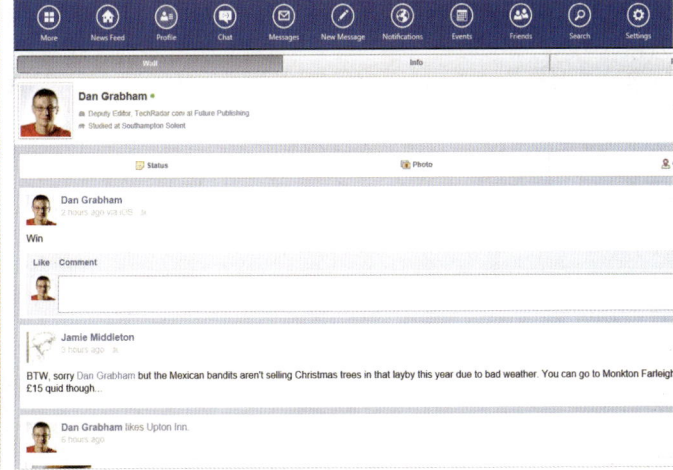

7 MINE for Facebook
One of the best Facebook clients we've seen for Windows 8 – it enables you to see your Facebook feed the way you want. You can just view it in standard mode and see your timeline, post updates, comment and like posts, or customise all your feeds until they exactly match what you want to see when you log in to Facebook.

8 Facebook Touch
If you're used to the Facebook experience on your mobile phone, this app is worth looking at. Facebook Touch essentially takes the mobile Facebook site and puts a Windows 8-style interface on top, so it's easier to control than ever. And, as you'd expect, it works brilliantly with a touchscreen interface.

DON'T JUST SIT THERE.
MAKE YOUR FORTUNE.

The ultimate guide to building your own personal enterprise

START A SMALL BUSINESS

▶ Turn a tiny idea into a **big** success!

Do it right
Find out everything you need to know to start a legal, protected business

Set it up
Configure all the kit you'll need yourself – with no IT department

Make money with your PC!

- ✓ Master eBay selling
- ✓ Start an online shop – fast
- ✓ Build an app and get it on the Apple app store

They did it!
From coffee shops to communal camping – the start-ups that made a mint

OUT NOW!

CBN28 2012 £9.99
Printed in the UK
ISBN 1-858704-84-7

future
MEDIA WITH PASSION

9 781858 704845